DICCIONARIO
POR TEMAS
Inglés - Español   Español - Inglés

José Merino
Ex-profesor del Instituto Británico de
Madrid y de la Escuela Oficial de Idiomas

Con la colaboración de
Ana Merino

DICCIONARIO POR TEMAS

Inglés ~ Español   Español ~ Inglés

1990

MADRID

SEGUNDA EDICION CORREGIDA Y AMPLIADA

© JOSE MERINO
Madrid (España)

© EDITORIAL PARANINFO, S.A.
C/ Magallanes, 25 - 28015 Madrid
Teléfono 446 33 50 Fax 445 62 18

Diseño de cubierta:
© Dacuñha & Creativos

Reservados los derechos para todos los países. Ninguna
parte de esta publicación, incluido el diseño de la cubierta,
puede ser reproducida, almacenada o transmitida de ninguna
forma, ni por ningún medio, sea éste electrónico, químico,
mecánico, electro-óptico, grabación, fotocopia o cualquier
otro, sin la previa autorización escrita por parte de la Editorial

Impreso en España
Printed in Spain

ISBN: 84-283-1765-8

Depósito legal: M. 24.674.—1990

 Magallanes, 25 - 28015 - MADRID   (06313/40/62)

Artes Gráficas BENZAL, S.A., Virtudes, 7 - 28010 MADRID

PRESENTACIÓN

Este es un libro de consulta en el que se recogen 100 vocabularios inglés-español y viceversa, con cerca de 10.000 palabras.

Los textos de estudio de años atrás se apoyaban básicamente en el vocabulario para aprender el inglés y dejaban relegados a un segundo término el estudio y la práctica de las estructuras del idioma. Por el contrario, los textos modernos dan más importancia al estudio de las estructuras y no consideran tan necesario el vocabulario. En el primer caso, el estudiante aprendía muchas palabras y no sabía cómo emplearlas; en el segundo, el alumno aprende las estructuras, pero no con gran riqueza de vocabulario.

Este libro viene a suplir la necesidad de tener a mano una selección de palabras de uso diario para enriquecer el vocabulario del estudiante, según los distintos aspectos de la vida diaria.

Estimamos que el vocabulario de un idioma debe adquirirse de la siguiente manera:

a) Un núcleo de palabras estructurales: verbos auxiliares, preposiciones, pronombres, conjunciones, etc.

b) Una serie de sustantivos, adjetivos, verbos, adverbios, de empleo muy extendido, para dar expansión al núcleo estructural.

c) Un gran número de palabras de gran utilidad en la vida diaria para dar mayor amplitud al idioma, a partir de lo dicho en b).

d) Un grupo de vocablos específicos para la vida profesional y técnica: médicos, ingenieros, etc.

Este libro pretende suplir la necesidad señalada en c), amén de adentrarse en el campo del punto d) desde un panorama puramente práctico.

La pronunciación de las palabras se ilustra mediante los símbolos de la Asociación Fonética Internacional.

Se incluyen también normas fonéticas de pronunciación española para los lectores o estudiantes de habla inglesa familiarizados con nuestra lengua.

EL AUTOR

CLAVE PARA LA INTERPRETACIÓN DE LA TRANSCRIPCIÓN FONÉTICA

N.º	SÍMBOLO	DESCRIPCIÓN	EJEMPLO
		VOCALES	
1	i:	«i» muy larga	MEAT, SEE
2	i	«i» muy corta. Lengua retrasada	HILL, IT
3	e	«e» como en «ver»	PEN, BED
4	æ	Entre «a» y «e»	HAT, BACK
5	ɑ:	«a» larga y profunda	CAR, PARK
6	o	«o» corta	HOT, DOLL
7	o:	«o» larga	PORT, TALL
8	u	«u» corta	BOOK, PUSH
9	u:	«u» larga	SHOE, FOOD
10	ʌ	«a» rápida	CUT, COME
11	ə:	«e» larga. Dientes muy poco separados	SIR, HER
12	ə	igual que el 11, pero muy corto	A, ABOUT, BETTER

DIPTONGOS

1	ei	combinación de e + i	LAKE, EIGHT
2	ou	combinación de o + u	OLD, NO
3	ai	combinación de a + i	LIKE, EYE
4	au	combinación de a + u	COW, HOW
5	eə	combinación de e + ə	AIR, HARE
6	oi	combinación de o + i	COIN, BOY
7	iə	combinación de i + ə	BEER, DEAR
8	uə	combinación de u + ə	POOR, SURE

CONSONANTES

1	p	«p» con una corriente de aire simultánea	PEN, CUP
2	t	«t» con una corriente de aire simultánea	TAKE, EIGHT
3	k	«k» con una corriente de aire simultánea	COME, TAKE
4	b	«b» como en «comba», no como en «cuba»	BOY, ROB
5	d	«d» como en «donde», no como en «dedo»	DAY, ADD
6	g	«g» como en «lengua», no como en «lago»	GO, EGG
7	f	«f» como en «fino»	FINE, LIFE
8	v	«v», no «b»	VERY, LIVE
9	θ	«z» como en «lápiz»	THINK, MONTH
10	ð	«d» como en «codo», vibrando las cuerdas vocales; no como en «donde»	THEY, BATHE

11	s	«s» como en «hasta», no como en «mismo»	SEA, GOOSE
12	z	«s» como en «mismo», vibrando las cuerdas vocales; no como en «hasta»	ZOO, PLEASE
13	ʃ	«s» con labios abocinados	SHE, ASH
14	ʒ	igual que el n.º 13, pero vibrando las cuerdas vocales	MEASURE, PLEASURE
15	tʃ	«ch» como en «chaqueta»	CHILD, REACH
16	dʒ	«n+y», como en «con yeso»	JUST, PAGE
17	m	«m» como en «mano»	MAN, COME
18	n	«n» como en «nada»	NO, ON
19	ŋ	«n» como en «ángulo»	THING, SONG
20	l	«l» como en «los»	LOOK, COOL
21	r	«r» con la punta de la lengua dirigida al paladar	RIGHT, RED
22	h	«h» aspirada; no es una jota	HOUSE, HIM
23	w	«w» como en «huevo»	WELL, WALL
24	j	«i» como en «hielo»	YES, YOU

KEY TO SPANISH PRONUNCIATION

SPANISH LETTER(S)	APPROXIMATE PRONUNCIATION	EXAMPLES
a	*a* as in *father*, but shorter.	pan, sal.
b	*b* as in *ruby*.	lobo *(fricative, between two vowels)*, ambos *(plosive, preceded by «m»)*.
c + a	*k* as in *sky*,	casa, cama.
c + o	*k* as in *sky*,	cosa, como.
c + u	*k* as in *sky*,	cubo, cuna.
c + e	*th* as in *think*, not as in *this*.	cena, cerca.
c + i	*th* as in *think*, not as in *this*.	cine, cinco.
c + const.	*k* as in *sky*,	creo, actor.
ch	*ch* as in *chin*, not as in *echo*.	chico, techo.
d	*d* as in *day*.	cada *(fricative, between two vowels)*, conde *(plosive, preceded by «n»)*.
e	*e* as in *ten*.	este, Pepe.
f	*f* as in *fine*.	foto, feo.
g + a	*g* as in *gun*.	pagar *(fricative, between two vowels)*, manga *(plosive, preceded by «n»)*.

g + o	g as in gone	lago (fricative, between two vowels), hongo (plosive, preceded by «n»).
g + u	g as in good.	agua (fricative, between two vowels), ángulo (plosive, preceded by «n»).
gue	g as in get.	guerra. (The «u» is silent.)
gui	g as in guilty.	guitarra. (The «u» is silent.)
güe	g + oo + e.	Argüelles. (The «u» is pronounced.)
g + e	ch as in loch (Scottish).	general, gente.
g + i	ch as in loch (Scottish).	página, gitano.
g + const.	g as in grey, glide.	grito, globo.
h	always silent: as in hour, not as in hat.	hora, ahora.
i	ee as in see, but shorter; not as in bit.	listo, pipa.
j	ch as in loch (Scottish).	jamón, jefe.
k	k as in sky,	kilo, kilómetro.
l	l as in let, not as in tell.	león, ala, tal.
ll	l + y as in call you.	llave, lluvia.
m	m as in man.	mano, mono.
n	n as in nine.	no, con.
ñ	n + y as in canyon.	cañón, moño.
o	o as in lot, not as in go.	toro, oso.
p	p as in Spain,	pan, pipa.
que	k as in sky,	queso. (The «u» is silent.)
qui	k as in sky,	equipo. (The «u» is silent.)
r	trilled	rico (initial), amar (final).
const. + r	trilled	traje, gris.
r + const.	trilled	largo, carne.
r	r as in very.	oro, tiro, caro (between two vowels).
rr	trilled.	guerra, perro.
s	s as in so.	solo, oso, tres
t	t as in stall,	todo, hotel.

u	*oo* as in *food*, but shorter; not as in *good*.	cubo, tú.
v	*b* as in *ruby*.	vino, avenida (*Exactly like «b»*).
w	*b* as in *ruby*.	Wenceslao, «water» (*Exactly like «b»*).
x	*x* as in *box*.	exacto, Félix.
y	*y* as in *yes* (initial) *y* as in *day, boy* (final).	yeso, yo. hay, ley, voy.
z	*th* as in *think*, not as in *this*.	zapato, pez.

NOTES ON SPANISH ACCENTUATION

a) *All syllables with an accent mark written above them are to be pronounced with special emphasis, e.g.,*

   Andrés, Martín, batería, lápiz, cinturón, clínica, síntomas, vértigo, día, eléctrico, andén, árbol, triángulo, política, policía.

b) *Words with no written accent are to be pronounced as follows:*
   1. *Words ending in a vowel: the emphasis is on the penultimate syllable, e.g.,*

      vaca, calle, carta, alto, sello, ganado, colmena, primavera, verano, diciembre, España, Inglaterra, pescado, armario, desierto.

   2. *Words ending in a consonant (except «s» or «n»): the emphasis is on the last syllable, e.g.,*

      ajedrez, papel, amar, comer, venir *(all verbs)*, electricidad, conductor, caracol, tapiz, central, umbral, español, albañil, material, lunar.

   3. *Words ending in «s» or «n»: the emphasis is on the penultimate syllable, e.g.,*

      abejas, cajas, andan, zapatos, ponen, enfermedades, instrumentos, comieron, armarios, fueron, diccionarios, libros, vacaciones, medidas, violines.

NOTAS SOBRE EL MANEJO DE LA OBRA

a) Dos puntos (:) detrás de una vocal indican que ésta es larga. Las vocales que no tienen puntos detrás son cortas.
b) Un diptongo tiene tanta duración como una vocal larga.
c) Se emplea la forma débil (tə) delante de los verbos que comienzan por consonante. Delante de los verbos que empiezan por vocal o por sonido (w), se usa la forma fuerte (tu).
d) La intensidad va marcada por un acento delante de la sílaba acentuada: (ˈægrikʌltʃə).
e) Las combinaciones *pl, bl, tl, dl, kl, gl, sl, zl*, se han escrito con la vocal (ə) cuando concurren tres consonantes, con el objeto de evitar un grupo de sonidos que pueden parecer difícil al estudiante.
f) No se han marcado los acentos secundarios.
g) En la transcripción fonética las palabras aparecen unidas, salvo en aquellos casos en que la unión de varias consonantes sea motivo de confusión.
h) El símbolo (j) se usa en sílaba acentuada. En sílaba no acentuada se cambia por (i) en la combinación (jə) = (iə).
i) (sus.) = sustantivo; (adj.) = adjetivo; (adv.) = adverbio.
j) (GB) De uso en Gran Bretaña; (USA) De uso en Estados Unidos.
k) Un asterisco (*) significa que hay un tema con ese mismo título.
l) En cada tema las palabras van clasificadas en orden alfabético.
m) La partícula *to* característica del infinitivo, aparece detrás de cada verbo.
n) Los números que van entre paréntesis detrás de cada título indican el orden que tiene en su idioma respectivo.

ÍNDICES

PRIMERA PARTE

INGLÉS - ESPAÑOL

(Los números entre paréntesis en la parte española corresponden al orden que tienen en dicho apartado)

	CONTENTS ENGLISH	CONTENIDO ESPAÑOL
1	AGE (eidʒ)	LA EDAD (33)
2	AGRICULTURE ('ægrikʌltʃə)	AGRICULTURA (3)
3	AIRCRAFT, AN (ən'eəkrɑːft)	UN AVIÓN (11)
4	AIRCRAFT, TYPES OF ('taipsəv'eəkrɑːft)	TIPOS DE AERONAVES (1)
5	AIRPORT, AN (ən'eəpoːt)	UN AEROPUERTO (2)
	ALLOYS (See METALS, 61)	
	AMPHIBIANS (See REPTILES, 77)	
6	ANIMAL, AN (ən'æniməl)	UN ANIMAL (5)
	ANIMALS, DOMESTIC (See MAMMALS, 58)	
	ANIMALS, WILD (See MAMMALS, 58)	
	ANNELIDS (See INSECTS, 51)	
	ARACHNIDS (See INSECTS, 51)	
7	ARCHITECTURE ('ɑːkitektʃə)	ARQUITECTURA (9)
8	ARITHMETIC AND MATHEMATICS (ə'riθmətikənmæθə'mætiks)	ARITMÉTICA Y MATEMÁTICAS (7)
9	BANKING ('bæŋkiŋ)	LA BANCA (12)
10	BARBER'S, AT THE (ətðə'bɑːbəz)	EN LA BARBERÍA (13)
11	BATHROOM, A (ə'bɑːθrum)	UN CUARTO DE BAÑO (30)
12	BICYCLE, A (ə'baisikl)	UNA BICICLETA (16)

ENGLISH		ESPAÑOL

13	BIRDS (bə:dz)		PÁJAROS (75)
14	BONES AND MUSCLES		HUESOS Y
	('bounzən'mʌsəlz)		MÚSCULOS (51)
	BUILDING, A (See A HOUSE, 47)		
15	BUSINESS AND TRADE		LOS NEGOCIOS
	('biznisən'treid)		Y EL COMERCIO (71)
16	CAR, A (ə'kɑ:)		UN COCHE (22)
17	CARDS (kɑ:dz)		NAIPES (70)
	CEREALS (See FRUITS, 36)		
18	CHEMISTRY ('kemistri)		QUÍMICA (85)
19	CHESS (tʃes)		AJEDREZ (4)
20	CINEMA AND THE THEATRE, THE		EL CINE
	(ðə'sinəməənðə'θiətə)		Y EL TEATRO (20)
21	CLOCKS AND WATCHES		
	('kloksən'wotʃiz)		RELOJES (87)
22	CLOTHING ('klouðiŋ)		VESTIMENTA (98)
23	COLOURS ('kʌləz)		COLORES (24)
24	COOKERY ('kukəri)		ARTE CULINARIO (10)
25	COSMETICS (koz'metiks)		COSMÉTICOS (27)
26	DOCTOR AND THE		EL MÉDICO
	HOSPITAL, THE		Y EL HOSPITAL (32)
	(ðə'doktərənðə'hospitl)		
	DOMESTIC ANIMALS		
	(See MAMMALS, 58)		
	DRESSMAKER, THE		
	(See THE TAILOR, 86)		
27	DRINKS (driŋks)		BEBIDAS (15)
28	ELECTRICITY (elik'trisiti)		ELECTRICIDAD (34)
29	FAMILY, THE (ðə'fæmili)		LA FAMILIA (37)
30	FARM, A (ə'fɑ:m)		UNA GRANJA (46)
	FESTIVITIES (See HOLIDAYS, 45)		
31	FISH AND MOLLUSCS		PECES Y
	('fiʃən'moləsks)		MOLUSCOS (76)
32	FISHING ('fiʃiŋ)		LA PESCA (79)
	FLOWERS (See TREES, 94)		
33	FOOTBALL ('futbo:l)		EL FÚTBOL (42)
34	FOOTWEAR ('futweə)		CALZADO (18)
35	FRUIT (fru:t)		FRUTA (40)
36	FRUITS, VEGETABLES, CEREALS		FRUTOS, HORTALIZAS,
	('fru:ts, 'vedʒətəbəlz,'siəriəlz)		LEGUMBRES Y
			CEREALES (41)
37	FURNITURE ('fə:nitʃə)		MOBILIARIO (67)
	GAMES (See SPORTS, 84)		

ENGLISH		ESPAÑOL

38	GARAGE, AT THE (ətðə'gæraː3)	EN EL GARAJE (43)
39	GARDEN, A (ə'gaːdən)	UN JARDÍN (56)
40	GEOGRAPHY (dʒi'ɔgrəfi)	GEOGRAFÍA (44)
41	GEOMETRY (dʒi'ɔmətri)	GEOMETRÍA (45)
42	HAIRDRESSER'S, AT THE LADIES' (ətðə'leidiz'heədresəz)	EN LA PELUQUERÍA DE SEÑORAS (77)
43	HEAD-DRESS ('heddres)	PRENDAS DE CABEZA (82)
44	HISTORY ('histəri)	HISTORIA (49)
45	HOLIDAYS AND FESTIVITIES ('holidizənfəs'tivitiz)	FIESTAS Y FESTIVIDADES (38)
	HOME (See LIFE AT HOME, 55)	
	HOSPITAL (See THE DOCTOR, 26)	
46	HOTEL, A (əhou'tel)	UN HOTEL (50)
47	HOUSE, A (ə'haus)	UNA CASA (19)
48	HOUSE-BUILDING ('hausbildiŋ)	CONSTRUCCIÓN DE UN EDIFICIO (25)
49	HUMAN BODY, THE (ðə'hjuːmən'bodi)	EL CUERPO HUMANO (29)
50	ILLNESSES ('ilnisiz)	ENFERMEDADES (35)
51	INSECTS, ARACHNIDS AND ANNELIDS ('insekts, ə'ræknidz ən 'ænəlidz)	INSECTOS, ARÁCNIDOS Y ANÉLIDOS (54)
	INSTRUMENTS (See TOOLS, 89; See MUSICAL INSTRUMENTS, 65)	
52	JEWELLERY ('dʒuːəlri)	JOYERÍA (57)
53	KITCHEN, A (ə'kitʃən)	UNA COCINA (23)
54	LAW, THE (ðə'loː)	LA LEY (58)
55	LIFE AT HOME ('laifət'houm)	LA VIDA EN EL HOGAR (100)
56	LIFE AT SCHOOL ('laifət'skuːl)	LA VIDA EN LA ESCUELA (99)
57	LITERATURE ('litərətʃə)	LITERATURA (59)
58	MAMMALS ('mæməlz)	MAMÍFEROS (60)
	DOMESTIC ANIMALS (də'mestik'æniməlz)	ANIMALES DOMÉSTICOS (60)
	WILD ANIMALS ('waild'æniməlz)	ANIMALES SALVAJES (60)
	MATHEMATICS (See ARITHMETIC, 8)	
	MEASURES (See WEIGHTS, 98)	

ENGLISH		ESPAÑOL
59	MECHANICS (mə'kæniks)	MECÁNICA **(62)**
60	METALLURGY (mə'tælədʒi)	METALURGIA **(64)**
61	METALS, MINERALS AND ALLOYS ('metəlz, 'minərəlz ənd 'æloiz)	METALES, MINERALES Y ALEACIONES **(63)**
62	METEOROLOGY (mi:tiə'rolədʒi) MINERALS (See METALS, 61)	METEOROLOGÍA **(65)**
63	MINING ('mainiŋ) MOLLUSCS (See FISH, 31) MUSCLES (See BONES, 14)	MINERÍA **(66)**
64	MUSIC ('mju:zik)	MÚSICA **(69)**
65	MUSICAL INSTRUMENTS ('mju:zikl'instrəmənts)	INSTRUMENTOS MUSICALES **(55)**
66	NAMES (neimz) MEN'S NAMES ('menz'neimz)	NOMBRES **(72)** NOMBRES MASCULINOS **(72)**
	WOMEN'S NAMES ('wiminz'neimz)	NOMBRES FEMENINOS **(72)**
67	OCCUPATIONS (ɔkju:'peiʃənz)	PROFESIONES **(83)**
68	OFFICE, AN (ən'ofis)	UNA OFICINA **(74)**
69	PAINTING AND SCULPTURE ('peintiŋən'skʌlptʃə)	PINTURA Y ESCULTURA **(81)**
70	PERSON, A (ə'pə:sən)	UNA PERSONA **(78)**
71	PERSONAL BELONGINGS ('pə:sənəlbi'loŋgiŋz)	OBJETOS PERSONALES **(73)**
72	PHOTOGRAPHY (fə'togrəfi) PLANTS (See TREES, 94)	LA FOTOGRAFÍA **(39)**
73	POST, THE (ðə'poust)	EL CORREO **(26)**
74	PRINTING ('printiŋ) RADIO (See TELEVISION, 87)	LA IMPRENTA **(52)**
75	RAILWAY STATION, A (ə'reilwei'steiʃən)	UNA ESTACIÓN DE FERROCARRIL **(36)**
76	RELIGION (ri'lidʒən)	RELIGIÓN **(86)**
77	REPTILES AND AMPHIBIANS ('reptailzəndæm'fibiənz)	REPTILES Y ANFIBIOS **(88)**
78	RESTAURANT, AT THE (ətðə'restərənt) SCHOOL (See LIFE AT SCHOOL, 56) SCULPTURE (See PAINTING, 63)	EN EL RESTAURANTE **(89)**
79	SEA-PORT, A (ə'si:po:t)	UN PUERTO DE MAR **(84)**

ENGLISH		ESPAÑOL
80	SEASIDE, AT THE (ətðə,'si:said)	EN LA COSTA **(28)**
81	SHIP, A (ə'ʃip)	UN BARCO **(14)**
82	SHIPS, TYPES OF ('taipsəv'ʃips)	TIPOS DE BUQUES **(17)**
83	SHOPS (ʃops)	TIENDAS **(93)**
84	SPORTS AND GAMES ('spo:tsən'geimz)	DEPORTES Y JUEGOS **(31)**
85	TABLEWARE ('teibəlweə)	VAJILLA **(97)**
86	TAILOR AND THE DRESSMAKER, THE (ðə'teiləəndə'dresmeikə)	EL SASTRE Y LA MODISTA **(90)**
87	TELEVISION AND RADIO ('televiʒənən'reidjou)	TELEVISIÓN Y RADIO **(91)**
	THEATRE, THE (See THE CINEMA, 20)	
88	TIME (taim)	EL TIEMPO **(92)**
89	TOOLS AND INSTRUMENTS ('tu:lzənd'instrəmənts)	HERRAMIENTAS E INSTRUMENTOS **(48)**
90	TOURISM AND TRAVELLING ('tuərizmən'trævəliŋ)	TURISMO Y VIAJES **(96)**
91	TOWN, A (ə'taun)	UNA CIUDAD **(21)**
	TRADE (See BUSINESS, 15)	
92	TRAFFIC ('træfik)	EL TRÁFICO **(94)**
93	TRANSPORTATION (trænspo:'teiʃən)	EL TRANSPORTE **(95)**
	TRAVELLING (See TOURISM, 90)	
94	TREES, PLANTS AND FLOWERS ('tri:z, 'plɑ:nts ən 'flauəz)	ÁRBOLES, PLANTAS Y FLORES **(6)**
95	TYPEWRITER, A (ə'taipraitə)	UNA MÁQUINA DE ESCRIBIR **(61)**
	UNIVERSE, THE (See THE WORLD, 100)	
	VEGETABLES (See FRUITS, 36)	
96	WARFARE ('wo:feə)	LA GUERRA **(47)**
	WATCHES (See CLOCKS, 21)	
97	WEAPONS ('wepənz)	ARMAS **(8)**
98	WEIGHTS AND MEASURES ('weitsən'meʒəz)	PESOS Y MEDIDAS **(80)**
	WILD ANIMALS (See MAMMALS, 58)	
99	WOOD INDUSTRY ('wud'indəstri)	INDUSTRIA DE LA MADERA **(53)**
100	WORLD AND THE UNIVERSE, THE (ðə'wə:ldəndə'ju:nivə:s)	EL MUNDO Y EL UNIVERSO **(68)**

SEGUNDA PARTE

ESPAÑOL - INGLÉS

(Los números entre paréntesis en la parte inglesa corresponden al orden que tienen en dicho apartado)

	ESPAÑOL	ENGLISH
1	AERONAVES, TIPOS DE	TYPES OF AIRCRAFT (4)
2	AEROPUERTO UN	AN AIRPORT (5)
3	AGRICULTURA	AGRICULTURE (2)
4	AJEDREZ	CHESS (19)
	ALEACIONES (Véase METALES, 63)	
	ANÉLIDOS (Véase INSECTOS, 54)	
	ANFIBIOS (Véase REPTILES, 88)	
5	ANIMAL, UN	AN ANIMAL (6)
	ANIMALES DOMÉSTICOS (Véase MAMÍFEROS, 60)	
	ANIMALES SALVAJES (Véase MAMÍFEROS, 60)	
6	ÁRBOLES, PLANTAS Y FLORES	TREES, PLANTS AND FLOWERS (94)
7	ARITMÉTICA Y MATEMÁTICAS	ARITHMETIC AND MATHEMATICS (8)
8	ARMAS	WEAPONS (97)
9	ARQUITECTURA	ARCHITECTURE (7)
10	ARTE CULINARIO	COOKERY (24)
	AVES (Véase PÁJAROS, 75)	
11	AVIÓN, UN	AN AIRCRAFT (3)
12	BANCA, LA	BANKING (9)
	BAÑO, CUARTO DE (Véase CUARTO DE BAÑO, 30)	

ESPAÑOL		ENGLISH
13	BARBERÍA, EN LA	AT THE BARBER'S (10)
14	BARCO, UN	A SHIP (81)
	BARCOS, TIPOS DE (Véase BUQUES, TIPOS DE, 17)	
15	BEBIDAS	DRINKS (27)
16	BICICLETA, UNA	A BICYCLE (12)
	BUQUE, UN (Véase UN BARCO, 14)	
17	BUQUES, TIPOS DE	TYPES OF SHIPS (82)
18	CALZADO	FOOTWEAR (34)
	CARTAS, JUEGO DE (Véase NAIPES, 70)	
19	CASA, UNA	A HOUSE (47)
	CEREALES (Véase FRUTOS, 41)	
20	CINE Y EL TEATRO, EL	THE CINEMA AND THE THEATRE (20)
21	CIUDAD, UNA	A TOWN (91)
22	COCHE, UN	A CAR (16)
	COCINA (Véase ARTE CULINARIO, 10)	
23	COCINA, UNA	A KITCHEN (53)
24	COLORES	COLOURS (23)
	COMERCIO, EL (Véase LOS NEGOCIOS, 71)	
25	CONSTRUCCIÓN DE UN EDIFICIO	HOUSE-BUILDING (48)
26	CORREO, EL	THE POST (73)
27	COSMÉTICOS	COSMETICS (25)
28	COSTA, EN LA	AT THE SEASIDE (80)
29	CUERPO HUMANO, EL	THE HUMAN BODY (49)
30	CUARTO DE BAÑO, UN	A BATHROOM (11)
31	DEPORTES Y JUEGOS	SPORTS AND GAMES (84)
32	DOCTOR Y EL HOSPITAL, EL	THE DOCTOR AND THE HOSPITAL (26)
33	EDAD, LA	AGE (1)
	EDIFICIO (Véase UNA CASA, 19)	
	EDIFICIO, CONSTRUCCIÓN DE UN	

ESPAÑOL		ENGLISH
	(Véase CONSTRUCCIÓN DE UN EDIFICIO, 25)	
34	ELECTRICIDAD	ELECTRICITY (28)
35	ENFERMEDADES	ILLNESSES (50)
	ESCUELA, LA (Véase LA VIDA EN LA ESCUELA, 99)	
	ESCULTURA (Véase PINTURA, 81)	
36	ESTACIÓN DE FERROCARRIL, UNA	A RAILWAY STATION (75)
37	FAMILIA, LA	THE FAMILY (29)
	FERROCARRIL (Véase UNA ESTACIÓN DE FERROCARRIL, 36)	
	FESTIVIDADES (Véase FIESTAS, 38)	
38	FIESTAS Y FESTIVIDADES	HOLIDAYS AND FESTIVITIES (45)
	FLORES (Véase ÁRBOLES, 6)	
39	FOTOGRAFÍA, LA	PHOTOGRAPHY (72)
40	FRUTA	FRUIT (35)
41	FRUTOS, HORTALIZAS, LEGUMBRES Y CEREALES	FRUITS, VEGETABLES AND CEREALS (36)
42	FÚTBOL	FOOTBALL (33)
43	GARAJE, EN EL	AT THE GARAGE (38)
44	GEOGRAFÍA	GEOGRAPHY (40)
45	GEOMETRÍA	GEOMETRY (41)
46	GRANJA, UNA	A FARM (30)
47	GUERRA, LA	WARFARE (96)
48	HERRAMIENTAS E INSTRUMENTOS	TOOLS AND INSTRUMENTS (89)
49	HISTORIA	HISTORY (44)
	HOGAR (Véase LA VIDA EN EL HOGAR, 100)	
	HORTALIZAS (Véase FRUTOS, 41)	
	HOSPITAL, EL (Véase EL DOCTOR, 32)	
50	HOTEL, UN	A HOTEL (46)
51	HUESOS Y MÚSCULOS	BONES AND MUSCLES (14)
52	LA IMPRENTA	PRINTING (74)

ESPAÑOL		ENGLISH
53	INDUSTRIA DE LA MADERA	WOOD INDUSTRY **(99)**
54	INSECTOS, ARÁCNIDOS Y ANÉLIDOS	INSECTS, ARACHNIDS AND ANNELIDS **(51)**
	INSTRUMENTOS (Véase HERRAMIENTAS, 48)	
55	INSTRUMENTOS MUSICALES	MUSICAL INSTRUMENTS **(65)**
56	JARDÍN, UN	A GARDEN **(39)**
57	JOYERÍA	JEWELLERY **(52)**
	JUEGOS (Véase DEPORTES, 31)	
	LEGUMBRES (Véase FRUTOS, 41)	
58	LEY, LA	THE LAW **(54)**
59	LITERATURA	LITERATURE **(57)**
	MADERA (Véase INDUSTRIA DE LA MADERA, 53)	
60	MAMÍFEROS	MAMMALS **(58)**
	ANIMALES DOMÉSTICOS	DOMESTIC ANIMALS **(58)**
	ANIMALES SALVAJES	WILD ANIMALS **(58)**
61	MÁQUINA DE ESCRIBIR, UNA	A TYPEWRITER **(95)**
	MAR, UN PUERTO DE (Véase UN PUERTO DE MAR, 84)	
	MATEMÁTICAS (Véase ARITMÉTICA, 7)	
62	MECÁNICA	MECHANICS **(59)**
	MEDIDAS (Véase PESOS, 98)	
63	METALES, MINERALES Y ALEACIONES	METALS, MINERALS AND ALLOYS **(61)**
64	METALURGIA	METALLURGY **(60)**
65	METEOROLOGÍA	METEOROLOGY **(62)**
	MINERALES (Véase METALES, 63)	
66	MINERÍA	MINING **(63)**
67	MOBILIARIO	FURNITURE **(37)**
	MODISTA, LA (Véase EL SASTRE, 90)	
	MOLUSCOS (Véase PECES, 76)	

ESPAÑOL		ENGLISH
	MUEBLES (Véase MOBILIARIO, 67)	
68	MUNDO Y EL UNIVERSO, EL	THE WORLD AND THE UNIVERSE (100)
	MÚSCULOS (Véase HUESOS, 51)	
69	MÚSICA	MUSIC (64)
70	NAIPES	CARDS (17)
71	NEGOCIOS Y EL COMERCIO, LOS	BUSINESS AND TRADE (15)
72	NOMBRES	NAMES (66)
	NOMBRES MASCULINOS	MEN'S NAMES (66)
	NOMBRES FEMENINOS	WOMEN'S NAMES (66)
73	OBJETOS PERSONALES	PERSONAL BELONGINGS (71)
74	OFICINA, UNA	AN OFFICE (68)
75	PÁJAROS	BIRDS (13)
76	PECES Y MOLUSCOS	FISH AND MOLLUSCS (31)
77	PELUQUERÍA DE SEÑORAS, EN LA	AT THE LADIES' HAIRDRESSER'S (42)
78	PERSONA, UNA	A PERSON (70)
79	PESCA, LA	FISHING (32)
80	PESOS Y MEDIDAS	WEIGHTS AND MEASURES (98)
81	PINTURA Y ESCULTURA	PAINTING AND SCULPTURE (69)
	PLANTAS (Véase ÁRBOLES, 6)	
	PLAYA, EN LA (Véase EN LA COSTA, 28)	
82	PRENDAS DE CABEZA	HEAD-DRESS (43)
83	PROFESIONES	OCCUPATIONS (67)
84	PUERTO DE MAR, UN	A SEA-PORT (79)
85	QUÍMICA	CHEMISTRY (18)
	RADIO (Véase TELEVISIÓN, 91)	
86	RELIGIÓN	RELIGION (76)
87	RELOJES	CLOCKS AND WATCHES (21)
88	REPTILES Y ANFIBIOS	REPTILES AND AMPHIBIANS (77)
89	RESTAURANTE, EN EL	AT THE RESTAURANT (78)

ESPAÑOL		ENGLISH
	ROPA (Véase VESTIMENTA, 98)	
90	SASTRE Y LA MODISTA, EL	THE TAILOR AND THE DRESSMAKER (86)
	SOMBREROS (Véase PRENDAS DE CABEZA, 82)	
	TEATRO, EL (Véase EL CINE, 20)	
91	TELEVISIÓN Y RADIO	TELEVISION AND RADIO (87)
92	TIEMPO, EL	TIME (88)
93	TIENDAS	SHOPS (83)
94	TRÁFICO	TRAFFIC (92)
95	TRANSPORTE, EL	TRANSPORTATION (93)
96	TURISMO Y VIAJES	TOURISM AND TRAVELLING (90)
	UNIVERSO (Véase EL MUNDO, 68)	
97	VAJILLA	TABLEWARE (85)
98	VESTIMENTA	CLOTHING (22)
	VIAJES (Véase TURISMO, 96)	
99	VIDA EN LA ESCUELA, LA	LIFE AT SCHOOL (56)
100	VIDA EN EL HOGAR, LA	LIFE AT HOME (55)
	ZAPATOS (Véase CALZADO, 18)	

PRIMERA PARTE
INGLÉS - ESPAÑOL

1

AGE	LA EDAD (33)
ENGLISH	ESPAÑOL

Adolescence (ædə'lesəns) adolescencia
adolescent (ædə'lesənt) adolescente
adult ('ædʌlt) adulto
age of discretion
    ('eidʒəvdis'kreʃən) uso de razón

Baby ('beibi) bebé
birth (bə:θ) nacimiento
birthday ('bə:θdei) cumpleaños
boy (boi) muchacho

Centenarian (sentə'neəriən) centenario
child (tʃaild) niño, niña
child in arms ('tʃaildin'a:mz) niño de pecho
childhood ('tʃaildhud) niñez

Death (deθ) muerte
dotage ('doutidʒ) chochez
dotard ('doutəd) viejo chocho
dote, to (tə'dout) chochear

Elderly ('eldəli) entrado en años

Girl (gə:l) muchacha
grow old, to (tə'grou'ould) envejecer
grow up, to (tə'grou'ʌp) crecer

Infancy ('infənsi) infancia
infant ('infənt) infante

Lad (læd) muchacho
lady ('leidi) señora
  old lady ('ould'leidi) anciana
  young lady ('jʌŋ'leidi) señorita
lass (læs) muchacha
life (laif) vida
lifetime ('laiftaim) (el tiempo de) la vida
longevity (lon'dʒeviti) longevidad

Man (mæn) hombre
  old man ('ould'mæn) anciano

AGE — LA EDAD

   young man ('jʌŋ'mæn)
manhood ('mænhud)
minor ('mainə)

Old (ould)
old age ('ould'eidʒ)
old people ('ould'pi:pl)

Senile ('si:nail)
sexagenarian
       (seksədʒi'neəriən)

Teenager ('ti:neidʒə)

todler ('todlə)

Woman ('wumən)
  old woman ('ould'wumən)
  young woman ('jʌŋ'wumən)
womanhood ('wumənhud)

Young (jʌŋ)
young people ('jʌŋ'pi:pl)
youngster ('jʌŋstə)
youth (ju:θ)

joven (sus.)
madurez (de un hombre)
menor

viejo
vejez
los ancianos

senil

sexagenario

persona que tiene entre los 13 y 19 años
niño que comienza a andar

mujer
anciana
señorita
madurez (de una mujer)

joven (adj.)
los jóvenes
jovencito
juventud

2

AGRICULTURE — AGRICULTURA (3)

ENGLISH	ESPAÑOL

Agricultural (ægri'kʌltʃərəl)

Barn (bɑ:n)
binder ('baində)

Cattle ('kætl)
chaff (tʃæf)
cereals* ('siəriəlz)
crop (krop)
  rotation of crops
     (rə'teiʃənəv'krops)

agrícola

granero
agavilladora

ganado
paja
cereales
cosecha

rotación de cultivos

AGRICULTURE — AGRICULTURA

cultivate, to (tə'kʌltiveit) — cultivar
cultivation (kʌlti'veiʃən) — cultivo
cultivator ('kʌltiveitə) — cultivador, máquina cultivadora

Dung (dʌŋ) — estiércol

Ear (iə) — espiga

Farm* (fɑ:m) — granja
fertilizer ('fə:tilaizə) — fertilizante
field (fi:ld) — campo
  stubble-field ('stʌbəlfi:ld) — rastrojera
  wheat-field ('wi:tfi:ld) — trigal
fodder ('fodə) — forraje
forest ('forist) — monte alto, bosque
forestry ('foristri) — silvicultura
fruits* (fru:ts) — frutos
furrow ('fʌrou) — surco

Grain (grein) — grano
grass (grɑ:s) — hierba
graze, to (tə'greiz) — pacer
ground (graund) — terreno
grove (grouv) — arboleda
  oak-grove ('oukgrouv) — robledal
  olive-grove ('olivgrouv) — olivar
  pine-grove ('paingrouv) — pinar
grow, to (tə'grou) — crecer, cultivar
grub, to (tə'grʌb) — desyerbar
grubber ('grʌbə) — máquina desyerbadora

Harrow ('hærou) — grada
harrow, to (tə'hærou) — gradar
harvest ('hɑ:vist) — recolección
harvester ('hɑ:vistə) — máquina cosechadora
hay (hei) — heno

Irrigation (iri'geiʃən) — riego

Kitchen garden ('kitʃən'gɑ:dən) — huerta

Land (lænd) — tierra
  arable land ('ærəbəl'lænd) — tierra de labranza
  barren land ('bærən'lænd) — tierra estéril
  fertile land ('fə:tail'lænd) — tierra fértil
  irrigated land ('irigeitid'lænd) — tierra de regadío
  unwatered land (ʌn'wo:təd'lænd) — tierra de secano
livestock ('laivstok) — ganado

Manure (mə'njuə) — abono

AGRICULTURE — AGRICULTURA

meadow ('medou)	prado
mow, to (tə'mou)	segar
mower ('mouə)	máquina segadora
Orchard ('o:tʃəd)	huerto
Pastures ('pɑ:stʃəz)	pastos
pick up, to (tə'pik'ʌp)	recoger
plant* (plɑ:nt)	planta
plant, to (tə'plɑ:nt)	plantar
plough, to (tə'plau)	arar
plough (plau)	arado
ploughman ('plaumən)	labrador
ploughshare ('plauʃeə)	reja del arado
Reap, to (tə'ri:p)	segar
reaper ('ri:pə)	segador, máquina segadora
reaping ('ri:piŋ)	siega
reaping-machine	
('ri:piŋməʃi:n)	máquina segadora
ripe (raip)	maduro
root (ru:t)	raíz
Seed (si:d)	semilla
seedtime ('si:dtaim)	tiempo de siembra
seed-plot ('si:dplot)	semillero
sheaf (ʃi:f)	gavilla
sheaves (ʃi:vz)	gavillas
soil (soil)	suelo
sow, to (tə'sou)	sembrar
sower ('souə)	sembrador
straw (stro:)	paja
stubble ('stʌbl)	rastrojo
Thresh, to (tə'θreʃ)	trillar
thresher ('θreʃə)	máquina trilladora
threshing ('θreʃiŋ)	trilla
tillage implements	
('tilidʒ'impliments)	aperos de labranza
tractor ('træktə)	tractor
tree* (tri:)	árbol
Vineyard ('vinjəd)	viña
Water, to (tu'wo:tə)	regar
winnow, to (tu'winou)	aventar
wood (wud)	bosque
brushwood ('brʌʃwud)	monte bajo

3

AIRCRAFT, AN   UN AVION (11)

ENGLISH	ESPAÑOL
Ailerons ('eilərənz)	alerones
altimeter ('æltimi:tə)	altímetro
automatic pilot (o:tə'mætik'pailət)	piloto automático
Cockpit ('kokpit)	carlinga
compass ('kʌmpəs)	brújula
control cabin (kən'troulkæbin)	cabina de pilotaje
control stick (kən'troulstik)	palanca de mando
joy-stick ('dʒoistik)	palanca de mando
Elevator ('eləveitə)	timón de profundidad
engine ('endʒin)	motor
jet-engine ('dʒetendʒin)	motor de reacción
Fin (fin)	aleta vertical de cola
flaps (flæps)	«flaps»
flight deck ('flaitdek)	cabina de pilotaje
fuel tank ('fju:əltæŋk)	depósito de combustible
fuselage ('fju:zəlɑ:ʒ)	fuselaje
Landing gear ('lændiŋgiə)	tren de aterrizaje
leading edge ('li:diŋ'edʒ)	borde de ataque
Navigation light (nævi'geiʃənlait)	luz de situación
nose-wheel ('nouzwi:l)	rueda de morro
Passenger cabin ('pæsəndʒəkæbin)	cabina del pasaje
propeller (prə'pelə)	hélice
Rudder ('rʌdə)	timón de dirección
Speed indicator ('spi:dindikeitə)	indicador de velocidad
Tail (teil)	cola
tail unit ('teilju:nit)	conjunto de cola
trailling edge ('treiliŋ'edʒ)	borde de salida
Undercarriage ('ʌndəkæridʒ) tricycle undercarriage	tren de aterrizaje

AIRCRAFT, AN   **34**   UN AVION

        ('traisikl'ʌndəkæridʒ)   tren de aterrizaje triciclo
undercarriage bay
        ('ʌndəkæridʒ'bei)   alojamiento del tren de aterrizaje

Vertical stabilizer
        ('və:tikəl'steibilaizə)   estabilizador vertical

Wheel   (wi:l)   rueda
wings   (wiŋz)   alas
wing span   ('wiŋspæn)   envergadura

4

AIRCRAFT, TYPES OF   TIPOS DE AERONAVES (1)

      ENGLISH   ESPAÑOL

Aeroplane   ('eərəplein)   aeroplano
aircraft   ('eəkrɑ:ft)   avión
air-liner   ('eəlainə)   avión de pasajeros
airplane   ('eəplein)   aeroplano
airship   ('eəʃip)   dirigible

Balloon   (bə'lu:n)   globo
biplane   ('baiplein)   biplano
bomber   ('bomə)   avión de bombardeo
  dive bomber   ('daivbomə)   avión de bombardeo en picado
  fighter bomber   ('faitəbomə)   caza-bombardero
  heavy bomber   ('hevi'bomə)   avión pesado de bombardeo
  light bomber   ('lait'bomə)   avión ligero de bombardeo

Fighter   ('faitə)   avión de caza
flying-boat   ('flaiiŋ'bout)   hidroavión

Glider   ('glaidə)   planeador

Helicopter   ('helikoptə)   helicóptero

Jet   (dʒet)   reactor

AIRCRAFT, TYPES OF — TIPOS DE AERONAVES

Monoplane ('monəplein) — monoplano
  high-wing monoplane
      ('haiwiŋ'monəplein) — monoplano de ala alta
  low-wing monoplane
      ('louwiŋ'monəplein) — monoplano de ala baja
  mid-wing monoplane
      ('midwiŋ'monəplein) — monoplano de ala media

Plane (plein) — avión, aeroplano
  cargo plane ('kɑ:gouplein) — avión de transporte
  four-engined plane
      ('fo:endʒind'plein) — cuatrimotor
  jet-plane ('dʒetplein) — avión de reacción
  light plane ('lait'plein) — avioneta
  long-range plane
      ('loŋreindʒ'plein) — avión de gran radio de acción
  multi-engined plane
      ('mʌltiendʒind'plein) — avión polimotor
  pilotless plane
      ('pailətlis'plein) — avión sin piloto
  seaplane ('si:plein) — hidroavión de flotadores
  single-engined plane
      ('siŋgl'endʒind'plein) — avión monomotor
  single-seater plane
      ('siŋgəlsi:tə'plein) — avión monoplaza
  three-engined plane
      ('θri:endʒind'plein) — avión trimotor
  training-plane ('treiniŋplein) — avión escuela
  transport plane
      ('trɑ:nspo:tplein) — avión de transporte
  twin-engined plane
      ('twin'endʒind'plein) — avión bimotor
  twin-jet plane
      ('twindʒet'plein) — avión birreactor
  two-seater plane
      ('tu:si:tə'plein) — avión biplaza

Rocket ('rokit) — cohete

Spaceship ('speisʃip) — nave espacial
skyrocket ('skairokit) — cohete

Triplane ('traiplein) — triplano

5

AIRPORT, AN   UN AEROPUERTO (2)

ENGLISH	ESPAÑOL
Aircraft* ('eəkrɑ:ft)	avión
civil aircraft ('sivil'eəkrɑ:ft)	avión civil
aircrew ('eəkru:)	tripulación
air-hostess ('eəhoustis)	azafata
air-liner ('eəlainə)	avión de pasajeros
airlines ('eəlainz)	líneas aéreas
airline ticket ('eəlain'tikit)	billete de avión
airman ('eəmən)	aviador
airport tower ('eəpo:t'tauə)	torre del aeropuerto
air-route ('eəru:t)	ruta aérea
air-ticket ('eətikit)	billete de avión
air transport ('eətrɑ:nspo:t)	transporte aéreo
airways ('eəweiz)	líneas aéreas
apron ('eiprən)	pista de estacionamiento
arrival (ə'raivəl)	llegada
Boarding-card ('bo:diŋkɑ:d)	tarjeta de embarque
boarding-pass ('bo:diŋpɑ:s)	tarjeta de embarque
booking-office ('bukiŋofis)	oficina de billetes
Cabin staff ('kæbinstɑ:f)	personal al servicio de los pasajeros
carrier ('kæriə)	compañía aérea
check-in time ('tʃek'in'taim)	hora de presentación de los pasajeros
civil aviation ('sivileivi'eiʃən)	aviación civil
concourse ('koŋko:s)	vestíbulo
control tower (kən'troultauə)	torre de control
Customs, the (ðə'kʌstəmz)	la Aduana
Customs-house ('kʌstəmzhaus)	oficina de Aduanas
Departure (di'pɑ:tʃə)	partida
Fare (feə)	precio del viaje
full fare ('ful'feə)	billete entero
half fare ('hɑ:f'feə)	medio billete

| AIRPORT, AN | UN AEROPUERTO |

first class ('fə:st'klɑ:s)
first-class compartment
('fə:stklɑ:skəm'pɑ:tmənt)
flight (flait)
  domestic flight
(də'mestik'flait)
  international flight
(intə'næʃənəl'flait)
  regular flight ('regjulə'flait)
fly, to (tə'flai)
flying engineer
('flaiiŋindʒiniə)
forward entrance
('fo:wəd'entrəns)
Gallery ('gæləri)
gangway ('gæŋwei)

ground staff ('graundstɑ:f)
Hangar ('hæŋgə)
Inter-continental airport
('intəkonti'nentəl'eəpo:t)
Land, to (tə'lænd)
landing ('lændiŋ)
  forced landing
('fo:st'lændiŋ)
long-range services
('loŋreindʒ'sə:visiz)
loudspeaker ('laud'spi:kə)
lounge (laundʒ)
luggage ('lʌgidʒ)
  excess luggage
(ik'ses'lʌgidʒ)
Meteorological information
(mi:tiərə'lodʒikəlinfə'meiʃən)
meteorological station
(mi:tiərə'lodʒikəl'steiʃən)
Navigator ('nævigeitə)
Passenger ('pæsəndʒə)
passenger list ('pæsəndʒəlist)
passenger manifest
('pæsəndʒə"mænifəst)
petrol lorry ('petrəllori)
pilot ('pailət)

primera clase

departamento de primera clase
vuelo

vuelo nacional

vuelo internacional
vuelo regular
volar

mecánico de vuelo

entrada delantera (del avión)

corredor
escalerillas (para subir al avión)
personal de tierra
hangar

aeropuerto intercontinental
aterrizar
aterrizaje

aterrizaje forzoso

servicios de larga distancia
altavoz
sala de espera
equipaje

exceso de equipaje

información meteorológica

estación meteorológica

navegante

pasajero
lista de pasajeros

lista de pasajeros
camión cisterna
piloto

AIRPORT, AN — UN AEROPUERTO

Radar ('reidə) — radar
rear entrance ('riə'entrəns) — entrada posterior (del avión)
refreshment-room (ri'freʃmənt rum) — cafetería
reservation — reserva
  cancel a reservation, to (tə'kænsələrezə'veiʃən) — cancelar una reserva
  defer a reservation, to (tədi'fə:rərezə'veiʃən) — aplazar una reserva
  seat reservation ('si:trezəveiʃən) — reserva de plaza
runway ('rʌnwei) — pista
runway lights ('rʌnweilaits) — luces de pista

Short-range services ('ʃo:treindʒ'sə:visiz) — servicios de corta distancia
steward ('stju:əd) — camarero
stewardess ('stju:ədis) — azafata

Take-off ('teikof) — despegue
take off, to (tə'teik'of) — despegar
taxi, to (tə'tæksi) — rodar (un avión) por la pista
taxi-way ('tæksiwei) — pista de rodadura
terminal ('tə:minəl) — terminal
ticket ('tikit) — billete
time-table ('taimteibl) — horario
tourist class ('tuəristklɑ:s) — clase turista
tourist-class compartment ('tuəristklɑ:skəm'pɑ:tmənt) — departamento de clase turista
tourist ticket ('tuərist tikit) — billete de clase turista
trip (trip) — viaje
  air trip ('eətrip) — viaje aéreo
  return trip (ri'tə:ntrip) — viaje de vuelta

Visibility (vizi'biliti) — visibilidad
  poor visibility ('puəvizi'biliti) — mala visibilidad

Waiting-room ('weitiŋrum) — sala de espera
wind sock ('windsok) — manga que indica la dirección del viento

wireless operator ('waiəlis'opəreitə) — radio telegrafista

ALLOYS — (See METALS, 61)

AMPHIBIANS — (See REPTILES, 77)

6

ANIMAL, AN   UN ANIMAL (5)

ENGLISH	ESPAÑOL
Back (bæk)	lomo
beak (bi:k)	pico curvo
bill (bil)	pico
Claw (klo:)	garra
crest (krest)	cresta
crest of a turkey ('krestəve'tə:ki)	moco de pavo
Down (daun)	plumón
Eyes (aiz)	ojos
Fang (fæŋ)	colmillo
feather ('feðə)	pluma
fin (fin)	aleta
fur (fə:)	piel (con pelo)
Gills (gilz)	agallas
gizzard ('gizəd)	molleja
Head (hed)	cabeza
hide (haid)	pellejo
hoof (hu:f)	pezuña
horse hair ('ho:sheə)	crin
horseshoe ('ho:sʃu:)	herradura
horn (ho:n)	cuerno
Leg (leg)	pata
Mane (mein)	crines, melena
mouth (mauθ)	boca
muzzle ('mʌzl)	hocico
Neck (nek)	cuello
nostrils ('nostrilz)	ollares
Paw (po:)	garra, zarpa
Scales (skeilz)	escamas
skin (skin)	pellejo
snout (snaut)	morro

ANIMAL, AN		UN ANIMAL

spur   (spə:) — espolón
Tail   (teil) — cola, rabo
trunk   (trʌŋk) — trompa
tusk   (tʌsk) — colmillo (de elefante, morsa, jabalí)
Udder   ('ʌdə) — ubre
Web-footed   ('web'futid) — palmípedo
wing   (wiŋ) — ala

ANIMALS, DOMESTIC   (See MAMMALS, 58)

ANIMALS, WILD   (See MAMMALS, 58)

ANNELIDS   (See INSECTS, 51)

ARACHNIDS   (See INSECTS, 51)

7

ARCHITECTURE   ARQUITECTU (9)

ENGLISH   ESPAÑOL

Aisle   (ail) — nave lateral
amphitheatre   ('æmfiθiətə) — anfiteatro
apse   (æps) — ábside
aqueduct   ('ækwidʌkt) — acueducto
arch   (ɑ:tʃ) — arco
  flat arch   ('flæt'ɑ:tʃ) — arco adintelado
  gothic arch   ('goθik'ɑ:tʃ) — arco gótico
  horseshoe arch
           ('ho:sʃu:'ɑ:tʃ) — arco de herradura
  ogee arch   ('oudʒi:'ɑ:tʃ) — arco conopial
  round arch   ('raund'ɑ:tʃ) — arco apuntado
  semicircular arch
           ('semi'sə:kjulə'ɑ:tʃ) — arco de medio punto
  stilted arch   ('stiltid'ɑ:tʃ) — arco peraltado

ARCHITECTURE	ARQUITECTURA

triumphal arch (trai'ʌmfəl'ɑːtʃ) — arco triunfal
architect ('ɑːkitekt) — arquitecto
architectural (ɑːki'tektʃərəl) — arquitectónico
architrave ('ɑːkitreiv) — arquitrabe
archway ('ɑːtʃwei) — arcada
atlantes (at'læntiːz) — atlantes

Base (beis) — basa
basilica (bə'zilikə) — basílica
belfry ('belfri) — campanario
bridge (bridʒ) — puente
build, to (tə'bild) — edificar
building ('bildiŋ) — edificio
buttress ('bʌtris) — contrafuerte
 flying buttress ('flaiiŋ'bʌtris) — arbotante

Capital ('kæpitl) — capitel
 Romanesque capital (roumə'nesk'kæpitl) — capitel románico
caryatid (kæri'ætid) — cariátide
castle ('kɑːsl) — castillo
cathedral (kə'θiːdrəl) — catedral
 Gothic cathedral ('goθikkə'θiːdrəl) — catedral gótica
 Romanesque cathedral (roumə'neskkə'θiːdrəl) — catedral románica
church (tʃəːtʃ) — iglesia
 basilican church (bə'zilikən'tʃəːtʃ) — basílica
 collegiate church (kə'liːdʒiit'tʃəːtʃ) — colegiata
 Romanesque church (roumə'nesk'tʃəːtʃ) — iglesia románica
circus ('səːkəs) — circo
cloister ('kloistə) — claustro
column ('koləm) — columna
 Corinthian column (kə'rinθiən'koləm) — columna corintia
 Doric column ('dorik'koləm) — columna dórica
 Ionic column (ai'onik'koləm) — columna jónica
cupola ('kopjulə) — cúpula
cornice ('koːnis) — cornisa
courtyard ('koːtjɑːd) — patio

Dome (doum) — cúpula
 Byzantine dome (bi'zæntain'doum) — cúpula bizantina

ARCHITECTURE — ARQUITECTURA

English	Español
Entablature (in'tæblətʃə)	entablamento
extrados (eks'treidos)	trasdós
Façade (fə'sɑ:d)	frontispicio
frieze (fri:z)	friso
Gargoyle ('gɑ:goil)	gárgola
House* (haus)	casa
Intrados (in'treidos)	intradós
Keystone ('ki:stoun)	clave (de un arco)
Mansion ('mænʃən)	mansión
mausoleum (mo:sə'liəm)	mausoleo
minaret ('minəret)	minarete
monastery ('monəstəri)	monasterio
monument ('monjumənt)	monumento
prehistoric monument (pri:his'torik'monjumənt)	monumento prehistórico
mosque (mosk)	mezquita
Obelisk ('obilisk)	obelisco
Palace ('pæləs)	palacio
pantheon ('pænθiən)	panteón
pilaster (pi'læstə)	pilastra
portico ('po:tikou)	pórtico
public baths ('pʌblik'bɑ:θs)	baños públicos
pyramid ('pirəmid)	pirámide
Restore, to (təris'to:)	restaurar
rise (raiz)	flecha (de un arco)
rose-window ('rouz'windou)	rosetón
Scotia ('skouʃə)	escocia
shaft (ʃɑ:ft)	fuste
span (spæn)	luz (de un arco)
spire ('spaiə)	aguja (de una torre)
springer ('spriŋgə)	imposta
stadium ('steidjəm)	estadio
steeple ('sti:pl)	aguja (de una torre)
style (stail)	estilo
Baroque style (bə'rouk'stail)	estilo barroco
Byzantine style (bi'zæntain'stail)	estilo bizantino
Gothic style ('goθik'stail)	estilo gótico
Perpendicular style (pə:pən'dikjulə'stail)	estilo perpendicular
Romanesque style (roumə'nesk'stail)	estilo románico

| ARCHITECTURE | ARQUITECTURA |

Temple ('tempəl) templo
  Egyptian temple
        (i'dʒipʃən'tempəl) templo egipcio
  Greek temple ('gri:k'tempəl) templo griego
theatre* ('θiətə) teatro
torus ('to:rəs) toro (de una columna)
tower ('tauə) torre
transept ('trænsept) crucero
tympanum ('timpənəm) tímpano

Vault (vo:lt) bóveda
  barrel-vault ('bærəl'vo:lt) bóveda de cañón
  ribbed vault ('ribd'vo:lt) bóveda de nervios
volutes (və'lju:ts) volutas
voussoirs ('vuswɑ:z) dovelas

Wall (wo:l) muralla, muro, pared
  stone wall ('stoun'wo:l) muro de piedra

8

ARITHMETIC AND MATHEMATICS

ARITMETICA Y MATEMATICAS (7)

ENGLISH   ESPAÑOL

Add, to (tu'æd) sumar
addition (ə'diʃən) suma
arithmetical progression
     (æriθ'metikəlprə'greʃən) progresión aritmética

Bring down, to (tə'briŋ'daun) bajar (un número)

Calculate, to (tə'kælkjuleit) calcular
carry, to (tə'kæri) llevarse (un número)
carry over ('kæri'ouvə) suma anterior
check, to (tə'tʃek) comprobar
count, to (tə'kaunt) contar

Decimal ('desiməl) decimal
denominator (di'nomineitə) denominador
difference ('difərəns) diferencia
divide, to (tədi'vaid) dividir

ARITHMETIC

dividend ('dividənd)	dividendo
divider (di'vaidə)	divisor
divisible (di'vizibl)	divisible
non divisible ('nondi'vizibl)	indivisible
division (di'viʒən)	división
double ('dʌbl)	doble
Equal ('i:kwəl)	igual
equation (i'kweiʃən)	ecuación
exact (ig'zækt)	exacto
Factor ('fæktə)	factor
figure ('figə)	cifra
fraction ('frækʃən)	quebrado
Half (hɑ:f)	mitad
hundreds ('hʌndridz)	centenas
hundreds of millions ('hʌndridzəv'miliənz)	centenas de millón
hundreds of thousands ('hʌndridzəv'θauzəndz)	centenas de mil
Indefinite (in'definit)	indefinido
infinitesimal calculus (infini'tesiməl'kælkjuləs)	cálculo infinitesimal
Logarithm ('logəriðəm)	logaritmo
Mathematical (mæθə'mætikl)	matemático (adj.)
mathematician (mæθəmə'tiʃən)	matemático (sus.)
mathematics (mæθə'mætiks)	matemáticas
millions ('miliənz)	unidades de millón
multiplicand (mʌltipli'kænd)	multiplicando
multiplication (mʌltipli'keiʃən)	multiplicación
multiplication table (mʌltipli'keiʃənteibl)	tabla de multiplicar
multiplier ('mʌltiplaiə)	multiplicador
multiply, to (tə'mʌltiplai)	multiplicar
Number ('nʌmbə)	número
cardinal number ('kɑ:dinəl'nʌmbə)	número cardinal
even number ('i:vən'nʌmbə)	número par
integral number ('intigrəl'nʌmbə)	número entero
mixed number ('mikst'nʌmbə)	número mixto
odd number ('od'nʌmbə)	número impar
ordinal number ('o:dinəl'nʌmbə)	número ordinal

| ARITHMETIC | ARITMÉTICA |

prime number
        ('praim'nʌmbə)
numeral ('nju:mərəl)
  Arabic numerals
        ('ærəbik'nju:mərəlz)
  Roman numerals
        ('roumən'nju:mərəlz)
numerator ('nju:məreitə)

Operation (opə'reiʃən)
  the four elementary
    operations
      (ðəfo:eli'mentəriopə'reiʃənz)

Plus (plʌs)
point (point)
product ('prodʌkt)
proportion (prə'po:ʃən)

Quadruple ('kwodrupl)
quantity ('kwontiti)
a quarter (ə'kwo:tə)
quintuple ('kwintjupl)
quotient ('kwouʃənt)

Remainder (ri'meində)
result (ri'zʌlt)
right (rait)
  the rule of three
        (ðə'ru:ləv'θri:)

Sign (sain)
  addition sign (ə'diʃənsain)
  arithmetical sign
        (æriθ'metikəl'sain)
  division sign (di'viʒənsain)
  equal sign ('i:kwəlsain)
  minus sign ('mainəssain)
  multiplication sign
        (mʌltipli'keiʃənsain)
  plus sign ('plʌssain)
  subtraction sign
        (səb'trækʃənsain)
solution (sə'lu:ʃən)
solve, to (tə'solv)
subtract, to (təsəb'trækt)
subtraction (səb'trækʃən)
sum (sʌm)

Tens ('tenz)

número primo
número, guarismo

números árabes

números romanos
numerador

operación

las cuatro reglas

más
coma (para decimales)
producto
proporción

cuádruple
cantidad
una cuarta parte
quíntuple
cociente

resto
resultado
correcto

la regla de tres

signo
signo de la suma

signo aritmético
signo de la división
signo de igualdad
signo de la resta

signo de la multiplicación
signo de la suma

signo de la resta
solución
resolver
restar
resta
suma, problema

decenas

ARITHMETIC — ARITMÉTICA

tens of millions ('tenzəv'miliənz)	decenas de millón
tens of thousands ('tenzəv'θauzəndz)	decenas de mil
a third (ə'θə:d)	un tercio
thousands ('θauzəndz)	unidades de mil
total ('toutl)	total
triple ('tripl)	triple
Unit ('ju:nit)	unidad
Wrong (roŋ)	equivocado

9

BANKING — LA BANCA (12)

ENGLISH	ESPAÑOL
Account (ə'kaunt)	cuenta
current account ('kʌrəntə'kaunt)	cuenta corriente
open an account, to (tu'oupənənə'kaunt)	abrir una cuenta
Bank (bæŋk)	banco
savings-bank ('seiviŋzbæŋk)	caja de ahorros
bank-clerk ('bæŋklɑ:k)	empleado de banca
bank-manager ('bæŋkmænədʒə)	gerente de banco
bank-note ('bæŋknout)	billete de banco
bankrupt ('bæŋkrʌpt)	bancarrota
bearer ('beərə)	portador
bill of exchange ('biləviks'tʃeindʒ)	letra de cambio
bond (bond)	bono, obligación
borrower ('borouə)	prestatario
Cheque (tʃek)	cheque
cash a cheque, to (tə'kæʃə'tʃek)	cobrar un cheque
cross a cheque, to (tə'krosə'tʃek)	cruzar un cheque

endorse a cheque, to (tuin'do:sə'tʃek)	endosar un cheque
cheque-book ('tʃekbuk)	talonario
coin (koin)	moneda (pieza)
credit ('kredit)	crédito
creditor ('kreditə)	acreedor
currency ('kʌrənsi)	moneda (circulante en un país)
metallic currency (mə'tælik'kʌrənsi)	dinero en moneda
Debt (det)	deuda
debtor ('detə)	deudor
dividend ('dividənd)	dividendo
drawee (dro:'i:)	librado
drawer ('dro:ə)	librador
Endorse, to (tuin'do:s)	endosar
endorsement (in'do:smənt)	endoso
Fund (fʌnd)	fondo
Guaranty ('gærənti)	garantía
Insolvency (in'solvənsi)	insolvencia
interest ('intərəst)	interés
invest, to (tuin'vest)	invertir
invesment (in'vestmənt)	inversión
Lend, to (tə'lend)	prestar
lender ('lendə)	prestamista
loan (loun)	préstamo
Money ('mʌni)	dinero
paper money ('peipəmʌni)	papel moneda
mortgage ('mo:gidʒ)	hipoteca
Pay, to (tə'pei)	pagar
payee (pei'i:)	persona a quien debe pagarse
payer ('peiə)	pagador
payment ('peimənt)	pago
profit ('profit)	beneficio
net profit ('net'profit)	beneficio neto
Save, to (tə'seiv)	ahorrar
share (ʃeə)	acción
solvency ('solvənsi)	solvencia
stockbroker ('stokbroukə)	corredor de Bolsa
Stock Exchange ('stokikstʃeindʒ)	Bolsa de Comercio
stockholder ('stokhouldə)	accionista
Teller ('telə)	cajero

10

BARBER'S, AT THE   EN LA BARBERIA (13)

ENGLISH	ESPAÑOL
Beard (biəd)	barba
brilliantine (briliən'ti:n)	brillantina
Chin (tʃin)	barbilla
cologne (kə'loun)	colonia
comb (koum)	peine
comb, to (tə'koum)	peinar
cut, to (tə'kʌt)	cortar
Hair (heə)	pelo
hair-brush ('heəbrʌʃ)	cepillo para el pelo
hair-clippers ('heəklipəz)	maquinilla para cortar el pelo
hair-cream ('heəkri:m)	fijador
hair-cut ('heəkʌt)	corte de pelo
hairdresser ('heədresə)	peluquero
hair-oil ('heəroil)	brillantina
hair-restorer ('heəristo:rə)	crecepelo
hair-scissors ('heəsizəz)	tijeras de peluquero
hair-tonic ('heətonik)	tónico para el cabello
Lather, to (tə'la:ðə)	enjabonar (para afeitar)
lotion ('louʃən)	loción
after-shave lotion ('a:ftəʃeiv'louʃən)	loción para después del afeitado
pre-shave lotion ('pri:ʃeiv'louʃən)	loción para antes del afeitado
Mirror ('mirə)	espejo
hand mirror ('hændmirə)	espejo de mano
moustache (məs'ta:ʃ)	bigote
Neck (nek)	cuello
Parting ('pa:tiŋ)	raya del pelo
Razor ('reizə)	máquina o navaja de afeitar
razor-blade ('reizəbleid)	hoja de afeitar
cut-throat razor ('kʌtθrout'reizə)	navaja barbera
Safety razor ('seiftireizə)	maquinilla de afeitar

| BARBER'S, AT THE | EN LA BARBERÍA |

Scent sprayer   ('sentspreiə)   atomizador de colonia o perfume
shampoo   (ʃæm'pu:)   champú
  dry shampoo   ('draiʃæm'pu:)   champú en seco
  oil shampoo   ('oilʃæm'pu:)   champú al aceite
shave   (ʃeiv)   afeitado
shave, to   (tə'ʃeiv)   afeitar
shaver ('ʃeivə)   máquina de afeitar
  electric shaver (i'lektrik'ʃeivə)   máquina eléctrica de afeitar
shaving-brush   ('ʃeiviŋbrʌʃ)   brocha de afeitar
shaving-soap   ('ʃeiviŋsoup)   jabón de afeitar
strop   (strop)   suavizador (de navajas)
strop, to   (tə'strop)   suavizar (la navaja)

Tip   (tip)   propina
towel   ('tauəl)   toalla
trim   (trim)   arreglo de pelo
trim, to   (tə'trim)   arreglar el pelo

Wash-basin   ('woʃbeisin)   lavabo
whiskers   ('wiskəz)   patillas

11

| BATHROOM, A | UN CUARTO DE BAÑO (30) |

| ENGLISH | ESPAÑOL |

Bath   (bɑ:θ)   bañera
bathroom cupboard   ('bɑ:θrum'kʌbəd)   armario de baño
bathtub   ('bɑ:θtʌb)   bañera
bottle   ('botl)   frasco

Comb   (koum)   peine
curtain   ('kə:tən)   cortina

Hair-brush   ('heəbrʌʃ)   cepillo para el pelo

Jar   (dʒɑ:)   tarro

Lavatory-pan   ('lævətəri'pæn)   taza del «water»

BATHROOM, A — UN CUARTO DE BAÑO

Mirror	('mirə)	espejo
Pipe	(paip)	cañería
clean-water pipe	('kli:nwo:tə'paip)	tubería de agua clara
waste-water pipe	('weistwo:tə'paip)	tubería de desagüe
plug	(plʌg)	tapón del desagüe
plug-hole	('plʌghoul)	agujero del desagüe
Razor	('reizə)	máquina o navaja de afeitar
electric razor	(i'lektrik'reizə)	afeitadora eléctrica
safety-razor	('seiftireizə)	maquinilla de afeitar
razor-blade	('reizəbleid)	hoja de afeitar
rug	(rʌg)	alfombrilla
Shaving-brush	('ʃeiviŋbrʌʃ)	brocha de afeitar
shaving-cream	('ʃeiviŋkri:m)	crema de afeitar
shaving-lotion	('ʃeiviŋlouʃən)	loción para el afeitado
shaving-soap	('ʃeiviŋsoup)	jabón de afeitar
shelf	(ʃelf)	estante
shower	('ʃauə)	ducha
soap	(soup)	jabón
cake of soap	('keikəv'soup)	pastilla de jabón
soap-dish	('soupdiʃ)	jabonera
sponge	(spʌndʒ)	esponja
stool	('stu:l)	taburete
Tap	(tæp)	grifo
cold-water tap	('kouldwo:tə'tæp)	grifo de agua fría
hot-water tap	('hotwo:tə'tæp)	grifo de agua caliente
toilet-cover	('toilitkʌvə)	tapa del «water»
toilet-paper	('toilitpeipə)	papel higiénico
toilet-powder	('toilitpaudə)	polvos de talco
tooth-brush	('tu:θbrʌʃ)	cepillo de dientes
tooth-paste	('tu:θpeist)	dentífrico
towel	('tauəl)	toalla
towel rail	('tauəlreil)	toallero
tube	(tju:b)	tubo (de pasta, etc.)
Wash-basin	('woʃbeisin)	lavabo
water	('wo:tə)	agua
running water	('rʌniŋ'wo:tə)	agua corriente
water-closet	('wo:təklozit)	«water»
water-tank	('wo:tətæŋk)	cisterna

12

BICYCLE, A   **UNA BICICLETA (16)**

ENGLISH	ESPAÑOL
Air-pump ('eəpʌmp)	bomba de aire
Bell (bel)	timbre
bicycle ('baisik)	bicicleta
bike (baik)	«bici»
brake (breik)	freno
Chain (tʃein)	cadena
cross-bar ('krosbɑ:)	barra
cycle, to (tə'saikl)	ir en bicicleta
cycling ('saikliŋ)	ciclismo
cyclist ('saiklist)	ciclista
Frame (freim)	cuadro
Grips (grips)	agarraderos
Handle-bars ('hændəlbɑ:z)	manillar
Inner-tube ('inə'tju:b)	cámara
Lamp (læmp)	faro
front lamp ('frʌnt'læmp)	faro delantero
rear lamp ('riə'læmp)	faro trasero
Mudguard ('mʌdgɑ:d)	guardabarro
Pedal ('pedl)	pedal
Racing-bicycle ('reisiŋbaisikl)	bicicleta de carreras
reflector (ri'flektə)	luz trasera
Saddle ('sædl)	sillín
spokes (spouks)	radios
Tyre ('taiə)	cubierta
Valve (vælv)	válvula
Wheel (wi:l)	rueda
back wheel ('bæk'wi:l)	rueda trasera
front wheel ('frʌnt'wi:l)	rueda delantera

13

BIRDS **PAJAROS (75)**

ENGLISH	ESPAÑOL

Albatross ('ælbətros) — albatros
Bird (bə:d) — ave, pájaro
  wading bird ('weidiŋ'bə:d) — ave zancuda
  bird of paradise ('bə:dəv'pærədais) — ave del paraíso
  bird of passage ('bə:dəv'pæsidʒ) — ave de paso
  bird of prey ('bə:dəv'prei) — ave de rapiña
bittern ('bitən) — avetoro
blackbird ('blækbə:d) — mirlo
bullfinch ('bulfintʃ) — camachuelo

Canary (kə'neəri) — canario
chaffinch ('tʃæfintʃ) — pinzón
chicken ('tʃikən) — pollo
cock (kok) — gallo
cockatoo ('kokətu:) — cacatúa
cormorant ('ko:mərənt) — cormoran
crane (krein) — grulla
crow (krou) — corneja
cuckoo ('kuku:) — cuclillo

Dove (dʌv) — paloma
drake (dreik) — pato macho
duck (dʌk) — pato

Eagle ('i:gl) — águila

Falcon ('fo:lkən) — halcón
flamingo (flə'miŋgou) — flamenco

Geese (gi:s) — gansos
goldfinch ('gouldfintʃ) — jilguero
goose (gu:s) — ganso
grouse (graus) — perdiz blanca
gull (gʌl) — gaviota

Hawk (ho:k) — halcón, gavilán
hen (hen) — gallina
heron ('herən) — garza
humming-bird ('hʌmiŋ'bə:d) — colibrí

BIRDS — PÁJAROS

Jackdaw ('dʒækdo:)   grajilla
jay (dʒei)   arrendajo

Kestrel ('kestral)   cernícalo
kingfisher ('kiŋfiʃə)   martín pescador

Lark (lɑ:k)   alondra
  linnet ('linit)   pardillo

Macaw (mə'ko:)   guacamayo
magpie ('mægpai)   urraca
mallard ('mæləd)   ánade real

Nightingale ('naitiŋgeil) ruiseñor

Ostrich ('ostritʃ)   avestruz
owl (aul)   lechuza, búho
  little owl ('litl'aul)   mochuelo

Parakeet ('pærəki:t)   periquito
parrot ('pærət)   loro
partridge ('pɑ:tridʒ)   perdiz
peacock ('pi:kok)   pavo real
pelican ('pelikən)   pelícano
penguin ('peŋgwin)   pingüino
pheasant ('fezənt)   faisán
pigeon ('pidʒən)   pichón
plover ('plʌvə)   chorlito

Quail (kweil)   codorniz

Rail (reil)   rascón
raven ('reivən)   cuervo
robin ('robin)   petirrojo
robin redbreast
         ('robin'redbrest) petirrojo
rook (ruk)   grajo

Skylark ('skailɑ:k)   alondra
snipe (snaip)   agachadiza
song-bird ('soŋbə:d)   pájaro cantor
sparrow ('spærou)   gorrión
sparrowhawk. ('spærouho:k) gavilán
starling ('stɑ:liŋ)   estornino
stork (sto:k)   cigüeña
swan (swon)   cisne
swallow ('swolou)   golondrina

Thrush (θrʌʃ)   zorzal
turkey ('tə:ki)   pavo

BIRDS		PÁJAROS
toucan	('tu:kæn)	tucán
Vulture	('vʌltʃə)	buitre
Woodpecker	('wudpekə)	pájaro carpintero

14

BONES AND MUSCLES / HUESOS Y MUSCULOS (51)

ENGLISH		ESPAÑOL
Biceps	('baiseps)	biceps
breastbone	('brestboun)	esternón
Carpal bone	('kɑ:pəl'boun)	carpo
clavicle	('klævikl)	clavícula
coccyx	('koksis)	coxis
collarbone	('koləboun)	clavícula
Deltoid	('deltoid)	deltoides
Ethmoid	('eθmoid)	etmoides
Femur	('fi:mə)	fémur
fibula	('fibjulə)	fíbula
finger-bone	('fiŋgəboun)	falange
frontal-bone	('frʌntəl'boun)	hueso frontal
Humerus	('hju:mərəs)	húmero
Jaw	(dʒo:)	mandíbula
Knee-cap	('ni:kæp)	rótula
Metacarpal bone	(metə'kɑ:pəl'boun)	metacarpo
metatarsal bone	(metə'tɑ:səl'boun)	metatarso
maxillary bone	(mək'siləri'boun)	maxilar
Occipital bone	(ək'sipitəl'boun)	occipital

BONES AND MUSCLES	HUESOS Y MÚSCULOS
Parietal bone (pə'raiətəl'boun)	parietal
pectoral muscle ('pektərəl'mʌsl)	pectoral
pelvis ('pelvis)	pelvis
phalanges (fə'lændʒiz)	falanges
phalanx ('fælæŋks)	falange
plain muscle ('plein'mʌsl)	músculo plano
pubis ('pju:bis)	pubis
Radius ('reidiəs)	radio
Sacrum ('seikrəm)	sacro
shoulder-blade ('ʃouldəbleid)	omóplato
sphenoid ('sfi:noid)	esfenoides
spinal column ('spainəl'koləm)	columna vertebral
striated muscle (strai'eitid'mʌsl)	músculo estriado
Tarsal bone ('tɑ:səl'boun)	tarso
temporal bone ('tempərəl'boun)	temporal
tendon ('tendən)	tendón
Achilles tendon (ə'kili:z'tendən)	tendón de Aquiles
tibia ('tibiə)	tibia
triceps ('traiseps)	triceps
toe-bone ('touboun)	falange (de un dedo del pie)
Ulna ('ʌlnə)	cúbito

15

BUSINESS AND TRADE	LOS NEGOCIOS Y EL COMERCIO (71)
ENGLISH	ESPAÑOL
Advertise, to (tu'ædvətaiz)	anunciar
advertisement (əd'və:tizmənt)	anuncio
Bank (bæŋk)	banco
bargain ('bɑ:gən)	ganga
bargain, to (tə'bɑ:gən)	regatear
branch (brɑ:ntʃ)	sucursal
business letter ('biznisletə)	carta comercial

BUSINESS — LOS NEGOCIOS

business-man ('biznismæn) — hombre de negocios
buy, to (tə'bai) — comprar
buyer ('baiə) — comprador

Clerk (klɑ:k) — empleado
company ('kʌmpəni) — compañía
consumer (kən'sju:mə) — consumidor

Discount ('diskaunt) — descuento

Export, to (tuiks'pɔ:t) — exportar
exports ('ekspɔ:ts) — exportaciones

Factory ('fæktəri) — fábrica
firm (fə:m) — empresa

Goods (gudz) — mercancías

Import, to (tuim'pɔ:t) — importar
imports ('impɔ:ts) — importaciones
invoice ('invois) — factura

Manager ('mænidʒə) — director
manufacture, to (təmænju'fæktʃə) — fabricar
manufacturer (mænju'fæktʃərə) — fabricante
manufacturing (mænju'fæktʃəriŋ) — fabricación
market ('mɑ:kit) — mercado
middleman ('midəlmæn) — intermediario

Office* ('ofis) — oficina
head office ('hedofis) — oficina principal

Price (prais) — precio
fixed-price ('fikst'prais) — precio fijo
price-list ('praislist) — lista de precios
produce, to (təprə'dju:s) — producir
producer (prə'dju:sə) — productor
product ('prodʌkt) — producto
purchase ('pə:tʃəs) — compra

Relaiter (ri:'teilə) — minorista

Sale (seil) — venta
salesman ('seilzmən) — vendedor
secretary ('sekrətəri) — secretaria
sell, to (tə'sel) — vender
shop* (ʃop) — tienda
shop-assistant ('ʃopəsistənt) — **dependiente**
shop-keeper ('ʃopki:pə) — tendero

| BUSINESS | LOS NEGOCIOS |

stock   (stok)
stores   (sto:z)

existencias
grandes almacenes

Trade (treid)
  foreign trade   ('forin'treid)
  home trade   ('houmtreid)
  retail trade   ('ri:teiltreid)
  wholesale trade
           ('houlseil'treid)

comercio
comercio exterior
comercio interior
comercio al por menor

comercio al por mayor

Wharehouse ('weəhaus)
wholesaler ('houlseilə)

almacén
mayorista

16

CAR, A — UN COCHE (22)

ENGLISH — **ESPAÑOL**

Accelerator (ək'seləreitə)
axle ('æksəl)
  front axle ('frʌnt'æksəl)
  rear axle   ('riər'æksəl)

acelerador
eje
eje delantero
eje trasero

Battery ('bætəri)
body   ('bodi)
bonnet   ('bonit)
boot   (bu:t)
brake   (breik)
  hand-brake ('hændbreik)
  foot-brake ('futbreik)
bumper   ('bʌmpə)

batería
carrocería
capó
portaequipajes
freno
freno de mano
freno de pie
parachoques

Choke (tʃouk)

estrangulador

Dashboard ('dæʃbo:d)
door   (do:)
driving-mirror ('draiviŋmirə)

salpicadero
puerta
espejo retrovisor

Engine   ('endʒin)
exhaust (ig'zo:st)

motor
tubo de escape

Fog-lamp ('foglæmp)

lámpara anti-niebla

Gears (giəz)	marchas
first gear ('fə:st'giə)	primera
second gear ('sekənd'giə)	segunda
third gear ('θə:d'giə)	tercera
gear-box ('giəboks)	caja de cambios
gear lever ('giəli:və)	palanca de cambio
Headlights ('hedlaits)	faros
horn (ho:n)	bocina
Mudguard ('mʌdgɑ:d)	guardabarros
Number plate ('nʌmbəpleit)	matrícula
Parking lights ('pɑ:kiŋlaits)	luces de posición
pedal ('pedl)	pedal
acceleration pedal (əkselə'reiʃənpedl)	pedal del acelerador
brake pedal ('breikpedl)	pedal del freno
clutch pedal ('klʌtʃpedl)	pedal del embrague
Radiator ('reidieitə)	radiador
rear lights ('riə'laits)	luces posteriores
reverse (ri'və:s)	marcha atrás
Seat (si:t)	asiento
back seat ('bæk'si:t)	asiento de atrás
front seat ('frʌnt'si:t)	easiento delantero
shock absorber ('ʃokəbzo:bə)	amortiguador
side lights ('saidlaits)	luces de situación
speedometer (spi:'domitə)	cuenta kilómetros
spring (spriŋ)	muelle, ballesta
starter ('stɑ:tə)	«starter»
steering-wheel ('stiəriŋwi:l)	volante
Tail-lights ('teillaits)	luces de situación (traseras)
tank (tæŋk)	depósito de gasolina
tyre ('taiə)	neumático
Wheel (wi:l)	rueda
back wheel ('bæk'wi:l)	rueda trasera
front wheel ('frʌnt'wi:l)	rueda delantera
window ('windou)	ventanilla
wind-screen ('windskri:n)	parabrisas
wind-screen wiper ('windskri:n'waipə)	limpia parabrisas
wing (wiŋ)	aleta

17

CARDS   NAIPES (70)

ENGLISH	ESPAÑOL
Ace (eis)	as
Card (kɑ:d)	carta
bottom card ('botəm'kɑ:d)	carta de abajo
top card ('top'kɑ:d)	carta de arriba
clubs (klʌbz)	tréboles, bastos
cut, to (tə'kʌt)	cortar
Deal, to (tə'di:l)	dar
dealer ('di:lə)	el que da las cartas
diamonds ('daiəməndz)	rombos, oros
Game (geim)	juego
Hand (hænd)	mano
hearts (hɑ:ts)	corazones, copas
Jack (dʒæk)	sota
joker ('dʒoukə)	comodín
King (kiŋ)	rey
knave (neiv)	sota
Pack (pæk)	baraja
pack of cards ('pækəv'kɑ:dz)	baraja
partner ('pɑ:tnə)	compañero
player ('pleiə)	jugador
Queen (kwi:n)	reina
Spades (speidz)	picos, espadas
suit (su:t)	palo
Trump (trʌmp)	triunfo
turn-up ('tə:nʌp)	pinta

(See FRUITS, 36)

CEREALS

18

CHEMISTRY QUIMICA (85)

ENGLISH	ESPAÑOL
Acetate ('æsitit)	acetato
acetone ('æsitoun)	acetona
acid ('æsid)	ácido
boric acid ('bo:rik'æsid)	ácido bórico
carbonic acid (kɑ:'bonik'æsid)	ácido carbónico
citric acid ('sitrik'æsid)	ácido cítrico
nitric acid ('naitrik'æsid)	ácido nítrico
sulphuric acid (sʌl'fjuərik'æsid)	ácido sulfúrico
aluminium (ælju'miniəm)	aluminio
arsenic ('ɑ:snik)	arsénico
atmosphere ('ætməsfiə)	atmósfera
atom ('ætəm)	átomo
atomic (ə'tomik)	atómico
Barium ('beəriəm)	bario
boron ('bo:rən)	boro
bromide ('broumaid)	bromuro
bromine ('broumi:n)	bromo
Cadmium ('kæmiəm)	cadmio
calcium ('kælsiəm)	calcio
carbon ('kɑ:bən)	carbono
chemical ('kemikl)	químico (adj.)
chemical reaction ('kemikəlri'ækʃən)	reacción química
chemist ('kemist)	químico (sus.)
chlorine ('klo:ri:n)	cloro
chromium ('kroumiəm)	cromo
copper ('kopə)	cobre
Dioxide (dai'oksaid)	dióxido
Element ('eləmənt)	elemento
Flask ('flɑ:sk)	frasco de laboratorio
fluorine ('fluəri:n)	flúor
Gas (gæs)	gas
gaseous ('geiziəs)	gaseoso

CHEMISTRY — QUÍMICA

Helium ('hi:liəm) — helio
hydrogen ('haidrədʒən) — hidrógeno

Inorganic chemistry (ino:'gænik'kemistri) — química inorgánica
iodide ('aiədaid) — yoduro
iodine ('aiədi:n) — yodo
ions ('aiənz) — iones
iridium (ai'ridiəm) — iridio
iron ('aiən) — hierro

Laboratory (lə'borətəri) — laboratorio
lead (led) — plomo
liquid ('likwid) — líquido

Magnesium (mæg'ni:ziəm) — magnesio
matter ('mætə) — materia
mercury ('mə:kjuri) — mercurio
mix, to (tə'miks) — mezclar
molecule ('molikju:l) — molécula

Nitrate ('naitrit) — nitrato
nitrogen ('naitrədʒən) — nitrógeno

Organic chemistry (o:'gænik'kemistri) — química orgánica
oxide ('oksaid) — óxido
oxigen ('oksidʒən) — oxígeno

Particle ('pɑ:tikl) — partícula
phosphorus ('fosfərəs) — fosforo
potassium (pə'tæsiəm) — potasio

Radium ('reidiəm) — radio

Salt (so:lt) — sal
silicon ('silikən) — silicio
silver ('silvə) — plata
sodium ('soudiəm) — sodio
solid ('solid) — sólido
strontium ('stronʃiəm) — estroncio
substance ('sʌbstəns) — sustancia
sulphur ('sʌlfə) — azufre

Test-tube ('testju:b) — probeta
tin (tin) — estaño
titanium (tai'teiniəm) — titanio
tungsten ('tʌŋstən) — tungsteno

Valency ('veilənsi) — valencia

Zinc (ziŋk) — zinc

19

CHESS

AJEDREZ (4)

ENGLISH	ESPAÑOL
Bishop ('biʃəp)	alfil
board (bo:d)	tablero
Capture, to (tə'kæptʃə)	capturar
castle ('kɑ:sl)	torre
castle, to (ta'kɑ:sl)	enrocar
castling ('kɑ:sliŋ)	enroque
check (tʃek)	jaque
check, to (tə'tʃek)	dar jaque
checkmate ('tʃek'meit)	jaque mate
checkmate, to (tə'tfekmeit)	dar jaque mate
chess-board ('tʃesbo:d)	tablero de ajedrez
chess-man ('tʃesmæn)	ficha del ajedrez
chess-men ('tʃesmən)	fichas del ajedrez
chess-pieces ('tʃespi:siz)	fichas de ajedrez
chess-set ('tʃesset)	juego de ajedrez
Draw (dro:)	tablas
King (kiŋ)	rey
knight (nait)	caballo
Lose, to (tə'lu:z)	perder
Man (mæn)	ficha
men (men)	fichas
move (mu:v)	movimiento
move, to (tə'mu:v)	mover
Opponent (ə'pounənt)	contrincante
Pawn (po:n)	peón
piece (pi:s)	ficha
player ('pleiə)	jugador
Queen (kwi:n)	reina
Rook (ruk)	torre
Square (skweə)	cuadro
stalemate ('steilmeit)	tablas por ahogo

Take, to (tə'teik)	matar (una pieza)
tournament ('tuənəmənt)	torneo
Win, to (tu'win)	ganar
winner ('winə)	ganador

20

CINEMA AND THE THEATRE, THE

EL CINE Y EL TEATRO (20)

ENGLISH	ESPAÑOL
Act (ækt)	acto
first act ('fə:st'ækt)	primer acto
second act ('sekənd'ækt)	segundo acto
third act ('θə:d'ækt)	tercer acto
actor ('æktə)	actor
principal actor ('prinsipl'æktə)	protagonista (masculino)
actress ('æktris)	actriz
principal actress ('prinsipl'æktris)	protagonista (femenino)
adults only ('ædʌlts'ounli)	sólo para mayores
aisle ('ail)	pasillo
applaud, to (tuə'plo:d)	apaudir
applause (ə'plo:z)	aplauso
audience ('o:diəns)	público
author ('o:θə)	autor
Background ('bækgraund)	foro
ballet ('bælei)	ballet
baritone ('bæritoun)	barítono
bass (beis)	bajo
boo, to (tə'bu:)	abuchear
booing ('bu:iŋ)	abucheo
booking-clerk ('bukiŋkla:k)	taquillero, a
booking-office ('bukiŋofis)	taquilla
box (boks)	palco
Camera ('kæmərə)	cámara
cast (ka:st)	reparto
cinema-goer ('sinəməgouə)	persona asidua al cine

cloak-room ('kloukrum)	guardarropa
coffee-bar ('kofibɑ:)	bar
comedy ('kɔmədi)	comedia
light comedy ('lait'kɔmədi)	comedia ligera
musical comedy ('mju:zikəl'kɔmədi)	comedia musical
company ('kʌmpəni)	compañía
curtain ('kə:tən)	telón
Dancer ('dɑ:nsə)	bailarín
direct, to (tədai'rekt)	dirigir
director (dai'rektə)	director
drama ('drɑ:mə)	drama
dramatist ('dræmətist)	dramaturgo
dress-circle ('dressə:kl)	entresuelo
dressing-room ('dresiŋrum)	camerino
Entertainments guide (entə'teinmənts'gaid)	cartelera de espectáculos
Film (film)	película
black and white film ('blækən'wait'film)	película en blanco y negro
colour film ('kʌləfilm)	película en color
documentary film (dɔkju'mentəri'film)	película documental
feature film ('fi:tʃəfilm)	largometraje
short film ('ʃɔ:t'film)	cortometraje
silent film ('sailənt'film)	película muda
sound-film ('saundfilm)	película sonora
talking film ('tɔ:kiŋ'film)	película sonora
film-star ('filmstɑ:)	estrella de cine
finale (fi'nɑ:li)	cuadro final
fly (flay)	bambalina
footlights ('futlaits)	candilejas
Gallery ('gæləri)	galería (localidades en piso alto)
Hero ('hiərou)	protagonista (masculino)
heroine ('herouin)	protagonista (femenino)
Image ('imidʒ)	imagen
intermission (intə'miʃən)	descanso, entreacto
interval ('intəvəl)	descanso, entreacto
Leading lady ('li:diŋ'leidi)	primera actriz
leading man ('li:diŋ'mæn)	primer actor
Music ('mju:zik)	música
music-hall ('mju:zikhɔ:l)	teatro de variedades

| CINEMA, THE | EL CINE |

musician   (mju'ziʃən)   músico
movie   ('mu:vi)   película

Newsreel   ('nju:sri:l)   noticiario

Opera   ('opərə)   ópera
opera house   ('opərəhaus)   teatro de la ópera
orchestra   ('o:kistrə)   orquesta

Part   (pɑ:t)   papel
pantomime   ('pæntəmaim)   representación para niños
passage   ('pæsidʒ)   pasillo (entre butacas)
performance   (pə'fo:məns)   función
  continuous performance
        (kən'tinjuəspə'fo:məns)   sesión continua
  first performance
        ('fə:stpə'fo:məns)   estreno
pianist   ('piənist)   pianista
picture   ('piktʃə)   película
  motion picture
        ('mouʃənpiktʃə)   película
pit   (pit)   patio de butacas
play   (plei)   obra de teatro
playwright   ('pleirait)   dramaturgo
producer   (prə'dju:sə)   director de escena
programme   ('prougræm)   programa
project, to   (təprə'dʒekt)   proyectar
prompt, to   (tə'promt)   apuntar
prompter   ('promtə)   apuntador
prompter's box
        ('promtəzboks)   concha del apuntador
props-man   ('propsmən)   tramoyista

Rehearse, to   (təri'hə:s)   ensayar
rehearsal   (ri'hə:sl)   ensayo
  dress rehersal
        ('dresrihə:sl)   ensayo general
row   (rou)   fila

Scene   (si:n)   escena
scenery   ('si:nəri)   decorado
screen   (skri:n)   pantalla
script   (skript)   guión
seat   (si:t)   asiento
show   (ʃou)   representación, espectáculo
  late show   ('leitʃou)   último pase
  variety show   (və'raiətiʃou)   espectáculo de variedades
singer   ('siŋgə)   cantante
slow motion   ('slou'mouʃən)   cámara lenta

CINEMA, THE   EL CINE

solo ('soulou)   solo (de un artista)
soprano (sə'prɑ:nou)   soprano
sound (saund)   sonido
sound track ('saundtræk)   pista sonora
stage (steidʒ)   escenario
stall (sto:l)   butaca

Tenor ('tenə)   tenor
theatre-goer ('θiətəgouə)   persona asidua al teatro
thriller ('θrilə)   obra de «suspense»
ticket ('tikit)   entrada
tour (tuə)   turné
tragedy ('trædʒədi)   tragedia
treble ('trebl)   tiple

Understudy ('ʌndəstʌdi)   sustituto
upper circle ('ʌpə'sə:kl)   anfiteatro
usher ('ʌʃə)   acomodador
usherette (ʌʃə'ret)   acomodadora

Wings (wiŋz)   bastidores

21

CLOCKS AND WATCHES   RELOJES (87)

ENGLISH   ESPAÑOL

Chimes (tʃaimz)   carrillón
clock (klok)   reloj (no de pulsera o bolsillo)
  alarm clock (ə'lɑ:mklok)   reloj despertador
  cuckoo clock ('kuku:klok)   reloj de cuco
  chiming clock ('tʃaimiŋ'klok) reloj de carrillón
  grandfather clock
          ('grændfɑ:ðəklok)   reloj de pie
  long-case clock
          ('loŋkeis'klok)   reloj de pie
  mantel clock ('mæntəlklok)   reloj de sobremesa
  time clock ('taimklok)   reloj para fábrica u oficina
  tower clock ('tauəklok)   reloj de torre
  travelling clock
          ('trævəliŋklok)   reloj de petaca

CLOCKS AND WATCHES — RELOJES

wall clock ('wo:lklok) — reloj de pared
clock-dial ('klokdaiəl) — esfera del reloj
clock-face ('klokfeis) — esfera del reloj
clockmaker ('klokmeikə) — relojero
clock weight ('klokweit) — pesa
clockwise ('klokwaiz) — movimiento de las agujas del reloj

anticlockwise ('ænti'klokwaiz) — movimiento contrario a las agujas del reloj
clockwork ('klokwə:k) — mecanismo de relojería
Fast (fɑ:st) — adelantado
Hand (hænd) — manilla
  hour-hand ('auəhænd) — manilla de las horas
  minute-hand ('minithænd) — manilla de los minutos
  second-hand ('sekəndhænd) — manilla de los segundos
Pendulum ('pendjuləm) — péndulo
Slow (slou) — atrasado
strike the hours, to (tə'straikði'auəz) — dar las horas
striking-mechanism ('straikiŋ'mekənizm) — sonería
sand-glass ('sændglɑ:s) — reloj de arena
sun-dial ('sʌndaiəl) — reloj de sol
Watch (wotʃ) — reloj (de pulsera o bolsillo)
  key watch ('ki:wotʃ) — reloj de cuerda
  keyless watch ('ki:liswotʃ) — reloj automático
  pocket watch ('pokitwotʃ) — reloj de bolsillo
  stop-watch ('stopwotʃ) — cronómetro
  wrist-watch ('ristwotʃ) — reloj de pulsera
  watch case ('wotʃkeis) — caja de reloj
  watchmaker ('wotʃmeikə) — relojero
  watchwork ('wotʃwə:k) — mecanismo de relojería
  wind, to (tu'waind) — dar cuerda

22

CLOTHING — VESTIMENTA (98)

ENGLISH — ESPAÑOL

Apron ('eiprən) — delantal

| CLOTHING | VESTIMENTA |

Bath-robe ('bɑ:θroub) — albornoz
belt (belt) — cinturón
bib (bib) — babero
blazer ('bleizə) — americana escolar
blouse ('blauz) — blusa
  sailor blouse ('seiləblauz) — blusa marinera
bow (bou) — lazo de pajarita
bra (brɑ:) — sostén
braces ('breisiz) — tirantes (GB)
brassière ('bræsiə) — sostén
breeches ('britʃiz) — calzones
  riding-breeches ('raidiŋbritʃiz) — pantalones de montar
brief(s) (bri:f(s)) — «slip» de caballero
  bikini brief (bi'ki:ni'bri:f) — braga bikini

Cape (keip) — capa
cardigan ('kɑ:digən) — rebeca
cloak (klouk) — capa
clothes (klouðz) — ropa
  cool clothes ('ku:l'klouðz) — ropa de verano
  mourning-clothes ('mo:niŋklouðz) — ropa de luto
  ready-made clothes ('redimeid'klouð,z) — ropa de confección
  warm clothes ('wo:m'klouðz) — ropa de invierno
coat (kout) — chaqueta, abrigo
  dress-coat ('dres'kout) — frac
  fur-coat ('fə:'kout) — abrigo de piel
  great-coat ('greit'kout) — capote
  leopard-skin coat ('lepədskin'kout) — abrigo de piel de leopardo
  morning-coat ('mo:niŋ'kout) — chaqué
  tail-coat ('teil'kout) — frac
collar ('kolə) — cuello
  soft collar ('soft'kolə) — cuello blando
  stiff collar ('stif'kolə) — cuello duro
corset ('ko:sit) — corsé
costume ('kostju:m) — traje
  bathing-costume ('beiðiŋkostju:m) — traje de baño
  regional costume ('ri:dʒənəl'kostju:m) — traje regional

Dress (dres) — vestido
  battledress ('bætəldres) — uniforme de campaña
  evening-dress ('i:vniŋdres) — traje de noche (femenino),
  full dress ('ful'dres) — traje de gala

CLOTHING — VESTIMENTA

night-dress ('naitdres) — camisón
print dress ('printdres) — vestido estampado

Footwear* ('futweə) — calzado
frock (frok) — vestido

Garment ('gɑ:mənt) — prenda
  close-fitting garment ('klousfitiŋ'gɑ:mənt) — prenda ajustada
  inner garment ('inə'gɑ:mənt) — prenda interior
  loose garment ('lu:s'gɑ:mənt) — prenda suelta
garter ('gɑ:tə) — liga
glove (glʌv) — guante
  chamois gloves ('ʃæmwɑ:'glʌvz) — guantes de gamuza
  kid gloves ('kid'glʌvz) — guantes de cabritilla
  a pair of gloves (ə'peərəv'glʌvz) — un par de guantes
gown (gaun) — bata, toga
  dressing-gown ('dresiŋgaun) — bata
  evening-gown ('i:vniŋgaun) — vestido de noche

Head-dress* ('heddres) — prendas de cabeza

Jacket ('dʒækit) — chaqueta
  dinner-jacket ('dinədʒækit) — chaqueta «smoking»
  sports jacket ('spo:tsdʒækit) — chaqueta de «sport»
jersey ('dʒə:zi) — jersey con mangas
jumper ('dʒʌmpə) — jersey suelto

Kilt (kilt) — falda escocesa
kimono (ki'mounou) — kimono
knot (not) — nudo (de corbata)

Linen ('linən) — ropa blanca

Mittens ('mitənz) — mitones
muff (mʌf) — manguito

Necktie ('nektai) — corbata
nightie ('naiti) — camisón
  shortie nightie ('ʃo:ti'naiti) — «picardías»

Overalls ('ouvəro:lz) — mono de trabajo
overcoat ('ouvəkout) — abrigo

Panties ('pæntiz) — bragas

pants ('pænts)	pantalones (USA), calzoncillos (GB)
petticoat ('petikout)	enagua
pinafore ('pinəfo:)	delantal de niño
pullover ('pulouvə)	chaleco de punto
put on, to (tə'put'on)	ponerse (una prenda)
pyjamas (pi'dʒɑ:məz)	pijama
Raincoat ('reinkout)	gabardina
Sash (sæʃ)	faja (banda)
scarf (skɑ:f)	pañuelo para el cuello
shirt (ʃə:t)	camisa
polo shirt ('poulouʃə:t)	camisa de deporte
tee-shirt ('ti:ʃə:t)	camisa de deporte
shirt-front ('ʃə:tfrʌnt)	pechera
shorts (ʃo:ts)	pantalón corto
skirt (skə:t)	falda
gored skirt ('go:d'skə:t)	falda al bies
pleated skirt ('pli:tid'skə:t)	falda plisada
slacks (slæks)	pantalones
slip (slip)	enagua
sock (sok)	calcetín
a pair of socks (ə'peərəv'soks)	un par de calcetines
sock-suspenders ('soksəspendəz)	ligas de caballero
stocking ('stokiŋ)	media
a pair of stockings (ə'peərəv'stokiŋz)	un par de medias
spats (spæts)	botines
suit (su:t)	traje
bathing-suit ('beiðiŋsu:t)	traje de baño
diving-suit ('daiviŋsu:t)	traje de buzo
made-to-measure suit ('meidtə'meʒə'su:t)	traje a la medida
navy blue suit ('neivi'blu:'su:t)	traje azul marino
Prince of Wales check suit ('prinsəv'weilz'tʃeksu:t)	traje de Príncipe de Gales
pyjama suit (pi'dʒɑ:məsu:t)	pijama
ready-made suit ('redimeid'su:t)	traje de confección
tailored suit ('teiləd'su:t)	traje sastre de señora
suit made to measure ('su:t'meidtə'meʒə)	traje a la medida
suit of clothes ('su:təv'klouðz)	traje
suspenders (səs'pendəz)	tirantes (USA), liguero (GB)

CLOTHING

sweater ('swetə)
Take off, to (tə'teik'of)
tie (tai)
  bow tie ('boutai)
tights (taits)
trousers ('trauzəz)
  a pair of trousers
        (ə'peərəv'trauzəz)
try on, to (tə'trai'on)
tunic ('tju:nik)
tuxedo (tʌk'si:dou)

Underclothes ('ʌndəklouðz)
underclothing ('ʌndəklouðiŋ)
undergarment ('ʌndəgɑ:mənt)
underpants ('ʌndəpænts)
undershirt ('ʌndəʃə:t)
underskirt ('ʌndəskə:t)
underwear ('ʌndəweə)
uniform ('ju:nifo:m)
  full-dress uniform
        ('fuldres'ju:nifo:m)

Veil (veil)
vest (vest)

Waiscoat ('weistkout)
wear, to (tu'weə)

VESTIMENTA

jersey ajustado
quitarse (una prenda)
corbata
cuello de pajarita
leotardos
pantalones

un par de pantalones
probarse (una prenda)
túnica, guerrera
chaqueta «smoking» (USA)

ropa interior
ropa interior
prenda interior
calzoncillos (USA)
camiseta (USA)
enagua (USA)
ropa interior
uniforme

uniforme de gala

velo
camiseta (GB), chaleco (USA)

chaleco (GB)
llevar (una prenda)

23

COLOURS   COLORES (24)

ENGLISH   ESPAÑOL

Black (blæk)
  coal black ('koul'blæk)
  ink black ('iŋk'blæk)
blackish ('blækiʃ)
blue (blu:)
  dark blue ('dɑ:k'blu:)
  electric blue (i'lektrik'blu:)

negro
negro carbón
negro tinta
negruzco
azul
azul oscuro
azul eléctrico

COLOURS — COLORES

light blue ('lait'blu:) — azul claro
navy blue ('neivi'blu:) — azul marino
sky blue ('skai'blu:) — azul celeste
bluish ('blu:iʃ) — azulado
brown (braun) — marrón
  chestnut brown ('tʃestnʌt'braun) — castaño
  dark brown ('dɑ:k'braun) — marrón oscuro
  light brown ('lait'braun) — marrón claro

Canary-coloured (kə'neərikʌləd) — de color canario

Dun-coloured ('dʌnkʌləd) — pardo

Gilt (gilt) — dorado
gold-coloured ('gouldkʌləd) — dorado
green (gri:n) — verde
  bottle green ('botəl'gri:n) — verde botella
  dark green ('dɑ:k'gri:n) — verde oscuro
  grass green ('grɑ:s'gri:n) — verde hierba
  light green ('lait'gri:n) — verde claro
  olive green ('oliv'gri:n) — verde aceituna
greenish ('gri:niʃ) — verdoso
grey (grei) — gris
  dark grey ('dɑ:k'grei) — gris oscuro
  light grey ('lait'grei) — gris claro
greyish ('greiiʃ) — grisáceo

Indigo ('indigou) — azul añil

Orange-coloured ('orindʒkʌləd) — anaranjado

Pink (piŋk) — rosa
purple ('pə:pl) — morado

Red (red) — rojo
  blood red ('blʌd'red) — rojo sangre
  brick red ('brik'red) — color ladrillo
reddish ('rediʃ) — rojizo

Violet ('vaiəlit) — morado

White (wait) — blanco
  snow white ('snou'wait) — blanco nieve
  milk white ('milk'wait) — blanco leche
whitish ('waitiʃ) — blanquecino

Yellow ('jelou) — amarillo
yellowish ('jelouiʃ) — amarillento

24

COOKERY   **ARTE CULINARIO (10)**

ENGLISH   ESPAÑOL

Bake, to (tə'beik)   asar al horno
baked (beikt)   asado al horno
batter ('bætə)   pasta culinaria
bay (bei)   laurel
boil, to (tə'boil)   cocer, hervir
boiled (boild)   cocido, hervido
  hard-boiled ('hɑ:d'boild)   cocido (huevo)
  soft-boiled ('soft'boild)   pasado por agua (huevo)
boiling-point ('boiliŋpoint)   punto de ebullición
bread-crumbs ('bred'krʌmz)   pan rallado
breaded ('bredid)   empanado
broth (broθ)   caldo
brown, to (tə'braun)   dorar
butter ('bʌtə)   mantequilla
  melted butter ('meltid'bʌtə)   mantequilla derretida

Cake (keik)   pastel
  sponge cake ('spʌndʒkeik)   bizcocho
capers ('keipəz)   alcaparras
cinnamon ('sinəmən)   canela
clove (klouv)   clavo
cook (kuk)   cocinero
cook, to (tə'kuk)   guisar
croquettes (krou'kets)   croquetas
cuts of fish ('kʌtsəv'fiʃ)   medallones de pescado

Dessertspoonful (di'zə:tspu:nful)   cucharada de postre
dress, to (tə'dres)   aderezar
dressed (drest)   aderezado

Egg (eg) huevo
  white of an egg ('waitəvən'eg)   clara de huevo

Fat (fæt)   grasa
flavour ('fleivə)   sabor
flavour, to (tə'fleivə)   sazonar
flour ('flauə)   harina
fried (fraid)   frito
froth (froθ)   espuma

Garlic ('gɑ:lik)	ajo
clove of garlic ('klouəv'gɑ:lik)	diente de ajo
ginger ('dʒindʒə)	jengibre
golden brown ('gouldən'braun)	dorado (al fuego)
grate, to (tə'greit)	rallar (p. ej. queso)
grill (grill)	parrilla
grill, to (tə'gril)	asar a la parrilla
grilled (grild)	a la parrilla
gravy ('greivi)	salsa (jugo)
Handful ('hændful)	puñado
heat (hi:t)	calor
brisk heat ('brisk'hi:t)	fuego vivo
gentle heat ('dʒentəl'hi:t)	fuego lento
heat, to (tə'hi:t)	calentar
Insipid (in'sipid)	insípido
Juicy ('dʒu:si)	jugoso
Lard (lɑ:d)	manteca
Margarine (mɑ:dʒə'ri:n)	margarina
mayonnaise (meiə'neiz)	mayonesa
mustard ('mʌstəd)	mostaza
Nutmeg ('nʌtmeg)	nuez moscada
Oil (oil)	aceite
olive oil ('oliv'oil)	aceite de oliva
peanut oil ('pi:nʌt'oil)	aceite de cacahuete
soyabean oil ('soiəbi:n'oil)	aceite de soja
Parsley ('pɑ:sli)	perejil
patty ('pæti)	empanadilla
peel, to (tə'pi:l)	pelar
pepper ('pepə)	pimienta
peppercorn ('pepəko:n)	grano de pimienta
pickled ('pikəld)	aliñado
Recipe ('resipi)	receta
roast, to (tə'roust)	asar
roasted ('roustid)	asado
Saffron ('sæfrən)	azafrán
salt (so:lt)	sal
salted codfish ('so:ltid'kodfiʃ)	bacalao
salty ('so:lti)	salado
sauce (so:s)	salsa
season, to, (tə'si:zən)	sazonar

seasoning ('si:zəniŋ)	aliño, condimento
simmer, to (tə'simə)	hervir a fuego lento
slice (slais)	rebanada
soup (su:p)	sopa
spice (spais)	especia
sprinkle, to (tə'spriŋkl)	rociar
stew (stju:)	guisado
stuffed (stʌft)	relleno
sugar ('ʃugə)	azúcar
Tablespoonful ('teibəlspu:nful)	cucharada grande
taste, to (tə'teist)	catar
tasteless ('teistlis)	soso
tasty ('teisti)	sabroso
teasponful ('ti:spu:nful)	cucharadita de té
tender ('tendə)	tierno
thyme (taim)	tomillo
toasted ('toustid)	tostado
tough (tʌf)	duro
Underdone ('ʌndə'dʌn)	poco hecha (la carne)
Vanilla (və'nilə)	vainilla
vinegar ('vinigə)	vinagre
Well-done ('wel'dʌn)	bien hecha (la carne)
wormwood ('wə:mwud)	ajenjo
Yeast (ji:st)	levadura
yoke (jouk)	yema

25

COSMETICS   COSMETICOS (27)

ENGLISH	ESPAÑOL
Bath salts ('bɑ:θso:lts)	sales de baño
brilliantine (briliən'ti:n)	brillantina
Cologne (kə'loun)	colonia

eau-de-cologne ('oudəkə'loun)	agua de colonia
cologne water (kə'loun'wo:tə)	agua de colonia
cream (kri:m)	crema
beauty cream ('bju:tikri:m)	crema de belleza
brushless shaving-cream ('brʌʃlis'ʃeiviŋkri:m)	crema de afeitar sin brocha
cleansing-cream ('klenziŋkri:m)	crema limpiadora
cold-cream ('kould'kri:m)	crema suavizadora
day cream ('deikri:m)	crema de día
face-cream ('feiskri:m)	crema para la cara
foundation cream (faun'deiʃənkri:m)	crema base
hair cream ('heəkri:m)	fijador para el pelo
hand cream ('hændkri:m)	crema para las manos
night cream ('naitkri:m)	crema de noche
shaving cream ('ʃeiviŋkri:m)	crema de afeitar
sun-tan cream ('sʌntænkri:m)	crema bronceadora
Dentifrice ('dentifris)	dentífrico
deodorant (di'oudərənt)	desodorante
depilatory (di'pilətəri)	depilatorio
wax depilatory ('wæksdi'pilətəri)	depilatorio a la cera
Eyebrow pencil ('aibrau'pensəl)	lápiz para las cejas
Hair-dye ('heədai)	tinte para el pelo
hair-fixative ('heəfiksətiv)	fijapelo
hair-lacquer ('heəlækə)	laca para el pelo
hair-oil ('heəroil)	brillantina
hair-restorer ('heəristo:rə)	crecepelo
hair-tonic ('heətonik)	tónico para el pelo
Lavender water ('lævəndəwo:tə)	colonia de lavanda
lipstick ('lipstick)	lápiz de labios
lotion ('louʃən)	loción
after-shave lotion ('ɑ:ftəʃeiv'louʃən)	loción para después del afeitado
pre-shave lotion ('pri:ʃeiv'louʃən)	loción para antes del afeitado
shaving lotion ('ʃeiviŋlouʃən)	loción para el afeitado
Make-up ('meikʌp)	maquillaje

COSMETICS   COSMÉTICOS

mouth wash ('mauθwoʃ)   elixir para la boca

Nail varnish ('neilvɑ:niʃ)   esmalte para uñas
nail-varnish remover
        ('neilvɑ:niʃri'mu:və)   quita esmalte

Perfume ('pə:fju:m)   perfume
powder ('paudə)   polvos
  face powder ('feispaudə)   polvos para la cara
  talcum powder
             ('tælkəmpaudə)   polvos de talco

Rouge (ru:ʒ)   colorete

Scent (sent)   perfume
  a bottle of scent
             (ə'botələv'sent)   un frasco de perfume
shampoo (ʃæm'pu:)   champú
shaving-stick ('ʃeiviŋstik)   jabón en barra para afeitar
soap ('soup)   jabón
  medicated soap
           ('medikeitid'soup)   jabón medicinal
  shaving soap ('ʃeiviŋsoup)   jabón de afeitar
  toilet soap ('toilitsoup)   jabón de tocador

Toilet powder ('toilitpaudə)   polvos de talco
toilet water ('toilitwo:tə)   agua de colonia
toothpaste ('tu:θpeist)   crema dental

26

DOCTOR AND THE HOSPITAL, THE	**EL DOCTOR Y EL HOSPITAL (32)**
ENGLISH	ESPAÑOL

Ache (eik)   dolor
  backache ('bækeik)   dolor de espalda
  earache ('iəreik)   dolor de oídos
  headache ('hedeik)   dolor de cabeza
    stomachache ('stʌməkeik)   dolor de estómago
  toothache ('tu:θeik)   dolor de muelas
ambulance ('æmbjuləns)   ambulancia
anaesthesia (ænis'θi:ziə)   anestesia

antibiotic ('æntibai'otik)
appendicitis (əpendi'saitis)
aspirin ('æspirin)
asphyxia (əs'fiksiə)

Bacillus (bə'siləs)
bacteria (bæk'tiəriə)
bandage ('bændidʒ)
bile (bail)
bistoury ('bistəri)
blister ('blistə)
blood-donor ('blʌddounə)
blood group ('blʌdgru:p)
blood pressure ('blʌdpreʃə)
blood stream ('blʌdstri:m)
blood test ('blʌdtest)
blood transfusion
    ('blʌdtræns'fju:ʒən)
blood vessel ('blʌdvesl)
bone* (boun)
breathing ('bri:ðiŋ)
bruise ('bru:z)
bunion ('bʌniən)
burn (bə:n)

Clinic ('klinik)
coma ('koumə)
contagion (kən'teidʒən)
contagious (kən'teidʒəs)
corn (ko:n)
corpuscles ('ko:pʌslz)
   red corpuscles
            ('red'ko:pʌslz)
   white corpuscles
            ('wait'ko:pʌslz)
cough (kof)
cough, to (tə'kof)
cough-lozenges ('koflozəndziz)
cough mixture ('kofmikstʃə)
cramp (kræmp)
crutches ('krʌtʃiz)
cure ('kjuə)
cure, to (tə'kjuə)
cyst (sist)
   sebaceous cyst
            (si'beiʃəs'sist)

Dentist ('dentist)
diagnose, to (tə'daiəgnouz)
diagnosis (daiəg'nousis)

antibiótico
apendicitis
aspirina
asfixia

bacilo
bacterias
venda
bilis
bisturí
ampolla
donador de sangre
grupo sanguíneo
tensión de la sangre
corriente sanguínea
análisis de sangre

transfusión de sangre
vaso sanguíneo
hueso
respiración
cardenal
juanete
quemadura

clínica
coma
contagio
contagioso
callo
glóbulos

glóbulos rojos

glóbulos blancos
tos
toser
pastillas para la tos
jarabe para la tos
calambre
muletas
cura
curar
quiste

quiste sebáceo

dentista
diagnosticar
diagnóstico

digestion (di'dʒestʃən)	digestión
disease (di'zi:z)	enfermedad
chronic disease ('kronikdi'zi:z)	enfermedad crónica
infectious disease (in'fekʃəsdi'zi:z)	enfermedad infecciosa
diet ('daiət)	dieta
doctor ('doktə)	doctor
family doctor ('fæmilidoktə)	médico de cabecera
dose (dous)	dosis
Electrocardiogram (i'lektrou'kɑ:diougræm)	electrocardiograma
Faint (feint)	desmayo
faint, to (tə'feint)	desmayarse
fever ('fi:və)	fiebre
first aid ('fə:st'eid)	primeros auxilios
fit (fit)	ataque
fracture ('fræktʃə)	fractura
Ganglion ('gæŋgliən)	ganglio
gastric juice ('gæstrik'dʒu:s)	jugo gástrico
general practitioner ('dʒənərəlpræk'tiʃənə)	médico de medicina general
germ (dʒə:m)	germen
gland (glænd)	glándula
Health (helθ)	salud
heart failure ('hɑ:tfeiliə)	fallo cardíaco
hemorrhage ('heməridʒ)	hemorragia
hiccough ('hikʌp)	hipo
hospital ('hospitl)	hospital
mental hospital ('mentəl'hospitl)	manicomio
Ill (il)	enfermo (adj.)
illness* ('ilnis)	enfermedad
indigestion (indi'dʒestʃən)	indigestión
infection (in'fekʃən)	infección
inflammation (inflə'meiʃən)	inflamación
injection (in'dʒekʃən)	inyección
injury ('indʒəri)	herida
irritation (iri'teiʃən)	irritación
itching ('itʃiŋ)	picor
Laboratory (lə'borətəri)	laboratorio
lameness ('leimnis)	cojera
lesion ('li:ʒən)	lesión
leucocyte ('lju:kəsait)	leucocito

limp (limp)	cojera
Matron ('meitrən)	jefe de enfermeras
medical assistant ('medikələ'sistant)	practicante, ATS.
medicine ('medsin)	medicina
membrane ('membrein)	membrana
metabolism (mə'tæbəlizəm)	metabolismo
muscle* ('mʌsl)	músculo
Nerves (nə:vz)	nervios
nervous system ('nə:vəs'sistəm)	sistema nervioso
nurse (nə:s)	enfermera
nursing home ('nə:siŋhoum)	clínica
Oinment ('ointmənt)	ungüento
operate, to (tu'opəreit)	operar
operation (opə'reiʃən)	operación
organ ('o:gən)	órgano
respiratory organs (ris'paiətəri'o:gənz)	aparato respiratorio
organism ('o:gənizəm)	organismo
Pain (pein)	dolor
patient ('peiʃənt)	paciente, enfermo (sus.)
penicillin (peni'silin)	penicilina
perspiration (pə:spə'reiʃən)	sudor
plasma ('plæzmə)	plasma
pleura ('pluərə)	pleura
prescription (pris'kripʃən)	receta
pulse (pʌls)	pulso
pus (pʌs)	pus
Radiograph ('reidiougrɑ:f)	radiografía
respiration (respi'reiʃən)	respiración
Saliva (sə'laivə)	saliva
scab (skæb)	costra
shock (ʃok)	choque (postración nerviosa)
sick (sik)	enfermo (adj.)
sore (so:)	llaga
sore throat ('so:'θrout)	anginas
specialist ('speʃəlist)	especialista
sprain (sprein)	esguince
stethoscope ('steθəskoup)	estetoscopio
stiff neck ('stif'nek)	tortícolis
streptomycin (streptou'maisin)	estreptomicina
stretcher ('stretʃə)	camilla
stretcher-bearer ('stretʃəbeərə)	camillero

sunstroke ('sʌnstrouk)	insolación
surgeon ('sə:dʒən)	cirujano
surgery ('sə:dʒəri)	cirugía
symptoms ('simtəmz)	síntomas

Temperature ('tempərətʃə) — fiebre
therapy ('θerəpi) — terapia
thermometer (θə'momitə) — termómetro
tissue ('tiʃju:) — tejido
tonsils ('tonsəlz) — amígdalas
treament ('tri:tmənt) — tratamiento

Urine ('juərin) — orina

Vaccinate, to (tə'væksineit) — vacunar
vaccination (væksi'neiʃən) — vacuna
vertigo ('və:tigou) — vértigo
virus ('vaiərəs) — virus

Ward (wo:d) — sala de hospital
weakness ('wi:knis) — debilidad
wound ('wu:nd) — herida
  infected wound (in'fektid'wu:nd) — herida infectada

X-rays ('eks'reiz) — rayos X
X-ray examination ('eksreiigzæmi'neiʃən) — exploración por rayos X

DOMESTIC ANIMALS   (See MAMMALS, 58)

DRESSMAKER, THE   (See THE TAILOR, 86)

27

DRINKS   **BEBIDAS (15)**

ENGLISH   ESPAÑOL

Ale (eil) — cerveza
  ginger ale ('dʒindʒə'reil) — cerveza de jengibre

DRINKS — BEBIDAS

light ale ('lait'eil) — cerveza ligera
anisette (æni'zet) — anís

Beer (biə) — cerveza
  bottled beer ('botəld'biə) — cerveza embotellada
  ginger beer ('dʒindʒə'biə) — cerveza de jengibre
  beer on draught ('biəron'drɑ:ft) — cerveza de barril
beverage ('bevəridʒ) — bebida
brandy ('brændi) — coñac

Champagne (ʃæm'pein) — champán
cider ('saidə) — sidra
claret ('klærət) — clarete
cocoa ('koukou) — cacao
coffee ('kofi) — café
  black coffee ('blæk'kofi) — café solo
  white coffee ('wait'kofi) — café con leche
coke (kouk) — coca-cola

Drink (driŋk) — bebida
  alcoholic drink (ælkə'holik'driŋk) — bebida alcohólica
  cold drink ('kould'driŋk) — bebida fría
  hot drink ('hot'driŋk) — bebida caliente
  soft drink ('soft'drink) — bebida no alcohólica
drink, to (tə'driŋk) — beber

Gin (dʒin) — ginebra

Juice (dʒu:s) — zumo
  fruit juice ('fru:t'dʒu:s) — zumo de fruta
  lemon juice ('lemən'dʒu:s) — zumo de limón
  orange juice ('orindʒ'dʒu:s) — zumo de naranja
  tomato juice (tə'mɑ:tou'dʒu:s) — zumo de tomate

Lemonade ('lemə'neid) — limonada, gaseosa
liqueur (li'kjuə) — licor aromático
liquor ('likə) — licor

Milk (milk) — leche

Orangeade ('orin'dʒeid) — naranjada

Plonk (ploŋk) — vino corriente
port (po:t) — oporto
punch (pʌntʃ) — ponche

Rum (rʌm) — ron
rum and coke ('rʌmən'kouk) — «cuba libre»

Sherry ('ʃeri) — jerez
  dry sherry ('drai'ʃeri) — jerez seco
  sweet sherry ('swi:t'ʃeri) — jerez dulce

DRINKS — BEBIDAS

spirits   ('spirits)   bebidas alcohólicas
Tea   (ti:)   té
Vermouth   ('və:məθ)   vermut
Water   ('wo:tə)   agua
  ice water   ('aiswo:tə)   agua fría
  mineral water
          ('minərəl'wo:tə)   agua mineral
  soda-water   ('soudəwo:tə)   agua de seltz
whisky   ('wiski)   whisky
wine   (wain)   vino
  dry wine   ('drai'wain)   vino seco
  local wine   ('loukəl'wain)   vino del país
  red wine   ('red'wain)   vino tinto
  sparkling wine
          ('spɑ:kliŋ'wain)   vino espumoso
  sweet wine   ('swi:t'wain)   vino dulce
  white wine   ('wait'wain)   vino blanco

28

ELECTRICITY — ELECTRICIDAD (34)

ENGLISH   ESPAÑOL

Ampere   ('æmpeə)   amperio
arc   (ɑ:k)   arco

Battery   ('bætəri)   batería, pila
bulb   (bʌlb)   bombilla

Circuit   ('sə:kit)   circuito
circuit-breaker   ('sə:kitbreikə)   interruptor automático
conductor   (kən'dʌktə)   conductor
current   ('kʌrənt)   corriente
  alternating current
          ('o:ltəneitiŋ'kʌrənt)   corriente alterna
  direct current
          (di'rekt'kʌrənt)   corriente continua
  electric current
          (i'elektrik'kʌrənt)   corriente eléctrica

ELECTRICITY — ELECTRICIDAD

Dynamo ('dainəmou) — dinamo
Electric(al) (i'lektrik(əl)) — eléctrico
electrical appliances (i'lektrikələ'plaiənsiz) — electrodomésticos
electric energy (i'lektrik'enədʒi) — energía eléctrica
electric fire (i'lektrik'faiə) — hornillo eléctrico
electrify, to (tui'lektrifai) — electrificar
electrician (ilek'triʃən) — electricista
electric shock (i'lektrik'ʃok) — calambre
electric supply (i'lektriksə'plai) — suministro de energía eléctrica
electric wave (i'lektrik'weiv) — onda eléctrica

Flex (fleks) — flexible
fuse (fju:z) — fusible
fuse box ('fju:zboks) — caja de fusibles
fuse wire ('fju:zwaiə) — alambre para fusibles

Generator ('dʒenəreitə) — generador

Insulating-tape ('insjuleitiŋteip) — cinta aislante
insulation (insju'leiʃən) — aislamiento
insulator ('insjuleitə) — aislador

Kilowatt ('kiləwot) — kilovatio

Lamp (læmp) — lámpara
lampholder ('læmphouldə) — portalámparas
light (lait) — luz
electric light (i'lektrik'lait) — luz eléctrica
lighting ('laitiŋ) — alumbrado

Magnetic field (mæg'netik'fi:ld) — campo magnético
meter ('mi:tə) — contador

Phase (feiz) — fase
plug (plʌg) — enchufe (clavija)
power-station ('pauəsteiʃən) — central eléctica

Resistor (ri'zistə) — resistencia

Short-circuit ('ʃo:t'sə:kit) — corto circuito
socket ('sokit) — enchufe (receptáculo)
switch (switʃ) — interruptor
main switch ('mein'switʃ) — interruptor general
switch off, to (tə'switʃ'of) — apagar
switch on, to (tə'switʃ'on) — encender

ELECTRICITY		ELECTRICIDAD

Turn off, to (tə'tə:n'of) — apagar
turn on, to (tə'tə:n'on) — encender
Volt (voult) — voltio
voltage ('voultidʒ) — voltaje
  high voltage ('hai'voultidʒ) — alta tensión

Watt (wot) — vatio
wire ('waiə) — cable
  earth wire ('ə:θwaiə) — cable de tierra
  live wire ('laiv'waiə) — cable con corriente
  neutral wire ('nju:trəl'waiə) — cable neutro
wiring ('waiəriŋ) — instalación eléctrica

29

FAMILY, THE	LA FAMILIA (37)
ENGLISH	ESPAÑOL

Aunt (ɑ:nt) — tía

Baby ('beibi) — bebé
bride (braid) — novia (en la boda)
bridegroom ('braidgrum) — novio (en la boda)
brother ('brʌðə) — hermano
brother-in-law ('brʌðərinlo:) — cuñado

Child (tʃaild) — niño, a
children ('tʃildrən) — niños, as
cousin ('kʌzin) — primo, a

Daughter ('do:tə) — hija
daughter-in-law ('do:tərinlo:) — nuera

Father ('fɑ:ðə) — padre
father-in-law ('fɑ:ðərinlo:) — suegro
fiancé (fi'ɑ:nsei) — novio
fiancée (fi'ɑ:nsei) — novia

FAMILY, THE — LA FAMILIA

Godchild ('godtʃaild) — ahijado,a
god-daughter ('goddo:tə) — ahijada
godfather ('godfɑ:ðə) — padrino
godmother ('godmʌðə) — madrina
godson ('godsʌn) — ahijado
grandchild ('græntʃaild) — nieto, a
granddaughter ('grændo:tə) — nieta
grandfather ('grænfɑ:ðə) — abuelo
grandma ('grænmɑ:) — abuelita
grandmother ('grænmʌðə) — abuela
grandpa ('grænpɑ:) — abuelito
grandson ('grænsʌn) — nieto

Husband ('hʌzbənd) — marido, esposo

Mother ('mʌðə) — madre
mother-in-law ('mʌðərinlo:) — suegra

Nephew ('nevju:) — sobrino
niece (ni:s) — sobrina

Orphan ('o:fən) — huérfano

Parent ('peərənt) — padre o madre
parents ('peərənts) — padres (padre y madre)

Relative ('relətiv) — pariente

Sister ('sistə) — hermana
sister-in-law ('sistərinlo:) — cuñada
son (sʌn) — hijo
son-in-law ('sʌninlo:) — yerno
step-brother ('stepbrʌðə) — hermanastro
step-child ('steptʃaild) — hijastro, a
step-daughter ('stepdo:tə) — hijastra
step-father ('stepfɑ:ðə) — padrastro
step-mother ('stepmʌðə) — madrastra
step-sister ('stepsistə) — hermanastra
step-son ('stepsʌn) — hijastro

Uncle ('ʌŋkəl) — tío

Widow ('widou) — viuda
widower ('widouə) — viudo
wife (waif) — esposa

30

FARM, A

UNA GRANJA (46)

ENGLISH

ESPAÑOL

Barn (bɑ:n) — granero
bees (bi:z) — abejas
bee-hive ('bi:haiv) — colmena

Cart (kɑ:t) — carro
cattle ('kætl) — ganado
cheese (tʃi:z) — queso
chicken ('tʃikən) — polluelo o pollo
cock (kok) — gallo
corn (ko:n) — grano
cow (kau) — vaca

Dog (dog) — perro
  sheep-dog ('ʃi: pdog) — perro pastor
donkey ('doŋki) — asno, burro
dove (dʌv) — paloma
duck (dʌk) — pato

Eggs (egz) — huevos

Farmer ('fɑ:mə) — granjero
farmhand ('fɑ:mhænd) — peón de granja
farmhouse ('fɑ:mhaus) — granja
farm-worker ('fɑ:mwə:kə) — peón de granja
farmyard ('fɑ:mjɑ:d) — corral
feed (fi:d) — pienso
feed, to (tə'fi:d) — dar de comer
fence (fens) — cerca, valla
field (fi:ld) — campo
flock (flok) — rebaño

Garden ('gɑ:dən) — jardín
  fruit garden ('fru:tgɑ:dən) — huerto
  kitchen garden ('kitʃən'gɑ:dən) — huerta
  vegetable garden ('vedʒətəbəlgɑ:dən) — huerta
gate (geit) — puerta de verja
geese ('gi:s) — gansos

FARM, A — UNA GRANJA

goat (gout) — cabra
goose (gu:s) — ganso
grain (grein) — grano
grass (grɑ:s) — hierba
grow, to (tə'grou) — cultivar, crecer

Harvest ('hɑ:vist) — cosecha
hay (hei) — paja de heno
hen (hen) — gallina
hen-coop ('henku:p) — gallinero
herd (hə:d) — piara, manada
hoe (hou) — azada
honey ('hʌni) — miel
horse (ho:s) — caballo

Mare (meə) — yegua
milk (milk) — leche
milk, to (tə'milk) — ordeñar
mill (mil) — molino
mule (mju:l) — mula

Orchard ('o:tʃəd) — huerto
ox (oks) — buey

Pail (peil) — cubo
pig (pig) — cerdo
pigeon ('pidʒən) — pichón, paloma
pichfork ('pitʃfo:k) — horquilla
plant* (plɑ:nt) — planta
plant, to (tə'plɑ:nt) — plantar
plough (plau) — arado
plough, to (tə'plau) — arar
pond (pond) — estanque

Rabbit ('ræbit) — conejo
rain (rein) — lluvia
rain, to (tə'rein) — llover
rake (reik) — rastrillo
root (ru:t) — raíz

Sack (sæk) — saco
scarecrow ('skeəkrou) — espantapájaros
scythe (saið) — guadaña
season ('si:zən) — estación del año
seed (si:d) — simiente
shear, to (tə'ʃiə) — esquilar
shearing ('ʃiəriŋ) — esquileo
shed (ʃed) — cobertizo
sheep (ʃi:p) — oveja, ovejas
sheep-fold ('ʃi:pfould) — redil

FARM, A   UNA GRANJA

shovel ('ʃʌvəl) pala
sickle ('sikl) hoz
snow (snou) nieve
snow, to (tə'snou) nevar
soil (soil) suelo
sow, to (tə'sou) sembrar
spade (speid) pala para cavar
spring (spriŋ) primavera
stable ('steibl) establo, cuadra
straw (stro:) paja
summer ('sʌmə) verano
sun (sʌn) sol

Tractor ('træktə) tractor
tree* (tri:) árbol

Vine (vain) parra

Water, to (tu'wo:tə) regar
weather ('weðə) tiempo atmosférico
weed (wi:d) hierbajo
well (wel) pozo
wheat (wi:t) trigo
wheelbarrow ('wi:lbærou) carretilla
winter ('wintə) invierno
wool (wul) lana

Yard (jɑ:d) patio

FESTIVITIES

(See HOLIDAYS, 45)

31

FISH AND MOLLUSCS   PECES Y MOLUSCOS (76)

ENGLISH   ESPAÑOL

Anchovy ('æntʃəvi) anchoa
  fresh anchovy
        ('freʃ'æntʃəvi) boquerón

Barbel ('bɑ:bl) barbo

FISH AND MOLLUSCS — PECES Y MOLUSCOS

barnacle   ('bɑ:nəkl)   percebe
barracuda (bærə'ku:də)   barracuda
bass   (bæs)   perca
   black bass   ('blæk'bæs)   perca negra
   striped bass ('straipt'bæs)   lobina

Carp   (kɑ:p)   carpa
clam   (klæm)   almeja
cod   (kod)   bacalao
conger eel   ('koŋgər'i:l)   congrio
crab   (kræb)   cangrejo
large crab ('lɑ:dz 'kræb)   centollo

Dolphin   ('dolfin)   delfín
dory   ('do:ri)   gallo

Eel   (i:l)   anguila

Fish   (fiʃ)   pez, pescado
   catfish   ('kætfiʃ)   barbo
   codfish   ('kodfiʃ)   bacalao
   crawfish ('kro:fiʃ)   cangrejo de río
   crayfish ('kreifiʃ)   cangrejo de río
   cuttlefish   ('kʌtəlfiʃ)   sepia
   dogfish ('dogfiʃ)   perro marino
   flying fish   ('flaiiŋ'fiʃ)   pez volador
   shellfish   ('ʃelfiʃ)   marisco
   starfish ('stɑ:fiʃ)   estrella de mar
   swordfish ('so:dfiʃ)   pez espada
flounder   ('flaundə)   lenguado

Haddock   ('hædək)   róbalo
hake   (heik)   merluza
herring   ('heriŋ)   arenque

Lamprey   ('læmpri)   lamprea
lobster   ('lobstə)   langosta

Mackerel   ('mækərəl)   caballa
mullet   ('mʌlit)   salmonete
   red mullet   ('red'mʌlit)   salmonete
mussel   ('mʌsl)   mejillón

Octopus   ('oktəpəs)   pulpo
oyster   ('oistə)   ostra

Perch   (pə:tʃ)   perca
pike   (paik)   lucio
plaice   (pleis)   platija
prawn   (pro:n)   langostino

FISH AND MOLLUSCS	PECES Y MOLUSCOS

Ray (rei) — raya
Salmon ('sæmən) — salmón
sardine (sɑːˈdiːn) — sardina
sea-bream ('siːbriːm) — besugo
sea horse ('siːhoːs) — caballito de mar
shark (ʃɑːk) — tiburón
shell (ʃel) — caracola, concha, pechina
shrimp (ʃrimp) — gamba
skate (skeit) — raya
snail (sneil) — caracol
sole (soul) — lenguado
squid (skwid) — calamar
sturgeon ('stəːdʒən) — esturión

Tench (tentʃ) — tenca
trout (traut) — trucha
tuna ('tjuːnə) — atún
tunny ('tʌni) — atún
  striped tunny ('straiptˈtʌni) — bonito
turbot ('təːbət) — rodaballo

Whale (weil) — ballena
  sperm whale ('spəːmweil) — cachalote
whiting ('waitiŋ) — pescadilla

32

FISHING — LA PESCA (79)

ENGLISH	ESPAÑOL

Angler ('æŋglə) — pescador de caña
angling ('æŋgliŋ) — pesca con caña

Bait (beit) — cebo
beach (biːtʃ) — playa
boat (bout) — bote

Catch (kætʃ) — captura
coast (koust) — costa

Fish* (fiʃ) — pescado, pez
fish, to (təˈfiʃ) — pescar
fisherman ('fiʃəmən) — pescador

FISHING / LA PESCA

fish hatchery ('fiʃhætʃəri) — piscifactoría
fish-hook ('fiʃhuk) — anzuelo
fishing-bait ('fiʃiŋbeit) — cebo
fishing-boat ('fiʃiŋbout) — barco de pesca
fishing by line ('fiʃiŋbai'lain) — pesca con caña
fishing by nets ('fiʃiŋbai'nets) — pesca con red
fishing-fleet ('fiʃiŋfli:t) — flota pesquera
fishing industry ('fiʃiŋindəstri) — industria pesquera
fishing-line ('fiʃiŋlain) — sedal
fishing-net ('fiʃiŋnet) — red para pescar
fishing-tackle ('fiʃiŋtækl) — avíos de pesca
fishing-rod ('fiʃiŋrod) — caña de pescar
fish market ('fiʃmɑ:kit) — mercado del pescado
fishmonger ('fiʃmʌŋgə) — pescadero
fishmonger's shop ('fiʃmʌŋgəzʃop) — pescadería
fish-pond ('fiʃpond) — vivero

Harbour ('hɑ:bə) — puerto
harpoon (hɑ:'pu:n) — arpón

Lake (leik) — lago
line (lain) — sedal

Net (net) — red

Oyster bed ('oistəbed) — vivero de ostras

Port (po:t) — puerto

River ('rivə) — río

Sea (si:) — mar
shoal (ʃoul) — banco de peces

Tide (taid) — marea
  high tide ('hai'taid) — marea alta
  low tide ('lou'taid) — marea baja
trawling ('tro:liŋ) — pesca a la rastra

Water ('wo:tə) — agua
  deep water ('di:p'wo:tə) — agua profunda
  shallow water ('ʃælou'wo:tə) — agua poco profunda
  territorial waters (teri'toriəl'wo:təz) — aguas jurisdiccionales

FLOWERS

(See TREES, 94)

33

FOOTBALL	FUTBOL (42)
ENGLISH	ESPAÑOL

Back (bæk) — defensa
ball (bo:l) — balón

Centre forward ('sentə'fo:wəd) — delantero centro
centre half back ('sentə'hɑ:f'bæk) — defensa central
clearance ('kliərəns) — despeje
corner ('ko:nə) — esquina
corner-kick ('ko:nəkik) — saque de esquina
cross-bar ('krosbɑ:) — larguero

Goal ('goul) — portería
goal-keeper ('goulki:pə) — portero

Football ('futbo:l) — balón

Inside left ('insaid'left) — interior izquierda
inside right ('insaid'rait) — interior derecha

Kick-off ('kikof) — saque
kick off, to (tə'kik'of) — sacar

League (li:g) — liga
left back ('left'bæk) — defensa lateral izquierdo
left half back ('left'hɑ:f'bæk) — medio volante izquierdo
linesman ('lainzmən) — juez de línea

Match (mætʃ) — encuentro

Net (net) — red
Outside left ('autsaid'left) — extremo izquierda
outside right ('autsaid'rait) — extremo derecha

Referee (refə'ri:) — árbitro
right back ('rait'bæk) — defensa lateral derecho
right half back ('rait'hɑ:f'bæk) — medio volante derecho

Score, to (tə'sko:) — marcar

Team (ti:m) — equipo

34

FOOTWEAR   CALZADO (18)

ENGLISH	ESPAÑOL
Boot (buːt)	bota
a pair of boots (əˈpeərəvˈbuːts)	un par de botas
climbing-boots (ˈklaimiŋbuːts)	botas de alpinista
lace-up boots (ˈleisʌpˈbuːts)	botas con cordones
long boots (ˈlɔŋˈbuːts)	botas altas
riding-boots (ˈraidiŋbuːts)	botas de montar
bootlace (ˈbuːtleis)	cordón de bota
Clogs (klogz)	zuecos
Eyelet (ˈailit)	ojete
Galoshes (gəˈlɔʃiz)	chanclos
Heel (hiːl)	tacón
Insole (ˈinsoul)	plantilla
Legging (ˈlegiŋ)	polaina
Sandal (ˈsændəl)	sandalia
shoe (ʃuː)	zapato
a pair of shoes (əˈpeərəvˈʃuːz)	un par de zapatos
high-heeled shoes (ˈhaihiːldˈʃuːz)	zapatos de tacón alto
house-shoes (ˈhausʃuːz)	zapatillas
low-heeled shoes (ˈlouhiːldˈʃuːz)	zapatos de tacón bajo
patent-leather shoes (ˈpeitəntleðəˈʃuːz)	zapatos de charol
suede shoes (ˈsweidˈʃuːz)	zapatos de ante
shoelace (ˈʃuːleis)	cordón de zapato
slipper (ˈslipə)	zapatilla
a pair of slippers (əˈpeərəvˈslipəz)	un par de zapatillas
carpet slippers (ˈkɑːpitslipəz)	zapatillas de paño

FOOTWEAR	**95**	CALZADO

sole (soul)   suela
   inner sole ('inə'soul)   plantilla
Welt (welt)   ribete (de un zapato)

35

FRUIT   FRUTA (40)

ENGLISH	ESPAÑOL
Apple ('æpl)	manzana
custard-apple ('kristəd'æpl)	chirimoya
apricot ('eiprikot)	albaricoque
Banana (bə'nɑ:nə)	plátano
blackberry ('blækbəri)	mora
blackcurrant ('blæk'kʌrənt)	grosella negra
Cherry ('tʃeri)	cereza
currant ('kʌrənt)	grosella
Date (deit)	dátil
Fig (fig)	higo, breva
dried fig ('draid'fig)	higo seco
Gooseberry ('guzbəri)	uva espina
grapefruit ('greipfru:t)	pomelo
grapes (greips)	uvas
Lemon ('lemən)	limón
lime (laim)	lima
Melon ('melən)	melón
water-melon ('wo:təmelən)	sandía
Orange ('orindʒ)	naranja
Peach (pi:tʃ)	melocotón
pear (peə)	pera
prickly pear ('prikli'peə)	higo chumbo
pineapple ('painæpl)	piña américana
plum (plʌm)	ciruela

FRUIT		FRUTA
pomegranate ('pomgrænit)		granada
prune (pru:n)		ciruela pasa
Raisins ('reizinz)		uvas pasas
raspberry ('rɑ:zbəri)		frambuesa
Strawberry ('stro:bəri)		fresa
Tangerine (tændʒə'ri:n)		mandarina

36

FRUITS, VEGETABLES, CEREALS

FRUTOS, HORTALIZAS, LEGUMBRES, CEREALES (41)

ENGLISH	ESPAÑOL
Almond ('ɑ:mənd)	almendra
artichoke ('ɑ:titʃouk)	alcachofa
asparagus (əs'pærəgəs)	espárragos
aubergine ('oubədʒi:n)	berenjena
Barley ('bɑ:li)	cebada
bean (bi:n)	judía
broad bean ('bro:d'bi:n)	haba
French bean ('frentʃ'bi:n)	judía verde
beet (bi:t)	remolacha
Brussels-sprouts ('brʌsəls'sprauts)	coles de bruselas
Cabbage ('kæbidʒ)	col
carrot ('kærət)	zanahoria
cauliflower ('koliflauə)	coliflor
celery ('seləri)	apio
chestnut ('tʃestnʌt)	castaña
chick-pea ('tʃikpi:)	garbanzo
coconut ('koukənʌt)	coco
corn (ko:n)	maíz (USA); trigo (GB)
Indian corn ('indiən'ko:n)	maíz
cucumber ('kju:kəmbə)	pepino
Egg-plant ('egplɑ:nt)	berenjena
endive ('endaiv)	endibia
Garlic ('gɑ:lik)	ajo

| FRUITS, VEGETABLES, ETC. | FRUTOS, HORTALIZAS, ETC. |

gherkin ('gə:kin) — pepinillo
gourd (guəd) — calabaza
green pea ('gri:n'pi:) — guisante

Hazel-nut ('heizəlnʌt) — avellana

Leek (li:k) — puerro
lentil ('lentil) — lenteja
lettuce ('letis) — lechuga

Maize (meiz) — maíz
marrow ('mærou) — calabacín
millet ('milit) — mijo
mushroom ('mʌʃrum) — champiñón, seta

Oats (outs) — avena
onion ('ʌniən) — cebolla

Parsley ('pɑ:sli) — perejil
parsnip ('pɑ:snip) — chirivía
peanut ('pi:nʌt) — cacahuete
peas (pi:z) — guisantes
pepper ('pepə) — pimiento
pine-cone ('painkoun) — piña (del pino)
pine-nut ('painnʌt) — piñón
potato (pə'teitou) — patata
potatoes (pə'teitouz) — patatas
pumpkin ('pʌmpkin) — calabaza

Radish ('rædiʃ) — rábano
rice (rais) — arroz
rye (rai) — centeno

Spinach ('spinidʒ) — espinacas
squash (skwoʃ) — calabaza

Tomato (tə'mɑ:tou) — tomate
tomatoes (tə'mɑ:touz) — tomates
truffle ('trʌfl) — trufa
turnip ('tə:nip) — nabo
 turnip tops ('tə:niptops) — grelos

Walnut ('wo:lnʌt) — nuez
watercress ('wo:təkres) — berro
wheat (wi:t) — trigo

Yam (jæm) — batata

37

FURNITURE   MOBILIARIO (67)

ENGLISH	ESPAÑOL
Arm-chair ('ɑ:m'tʃeə)	sillón
Bed (bed)	cama
divan bed (di'vænbed)	cama turca
double bed ('dʌbəl'bed)	cama de matrimonio
folding bed ('fouldiŋ'bed)	cama plegable
four-poster bed ('fo:poustə'bed)	cama con dosel
single bed ('siŋgəl'bed)	cama de un cuerpo
bench (bentʃ)	banco
bookcase ('bukkeis)	librería
Cabinet ('kæbinit)	vitrina
cocktail cabinet ('kokteilkæbinit)	mueble bar
filing cabinet ('failiŋkæbinit)	archivador
carpet ('kɑ:pit)	alfombra
chair (tʃeə)	silla, sillón
cane chair ('kein'tʃeə)	silla de mimbre
foilding chair ('fouldiŋ'tʃeə)	silla plegable
upholstered chair (ʌp'houlstəd'tʃeə)	sillón tapizado
chandelier (ʃændi'liə)	lámpara de brazos
chest (tʃest)	arcón
chest-of-drawers ('tʃestəv'dro:əz)	cómoda
clock (klok)	reloj
cooker ('kukə)	cocina
electric-cooker (i'lektrik'kukə)	cocina eléctrica
gas-cooker ('gæskukə)	cocina de gas
cupboard ('kʌbəd)	armario
bathroom cupboard ('bɑ:θrumkʌbəd)	armario de baño
kitchen cupboard ('kitʃənkʌbəd)	armario de cocina
curtain ('kə:tən)	cortina
Davenport ('dævənpo:t)	sofá (USA); escritorio (GB)

FURNITURE

desk (desk)	escritorio
dish-washer ('diʃwoʃə)	lavavajillas
drawer (dro:)	cajón
dresser ('dresə)	aparador
Fridge (fridʒ)	refrigerador
furniture ('fə:nitʃə)	muebles
a piece of furniture	
(ə'pi:səv'fə:nitʃə)	un mueble
Lamp (læmp)	lámpara
floor-lamp ('flo:læmp)	lámpara de pie
reading-lamp ('ri:diŋlæmp)	lámpara de mesa
Mirror ('mirə)	espejo
full-length mirror	
('ful'leŋθ'mirə)	espejo de cuerpo entero
Piano ('pjɑ:nou)	piano
grand piano	
('grænd'pjɑ:nou)	piano de cola
upright piano	
('ʌprait'pjɑ:nou)	piano vertical
picture ('piktʃə)	cuadro
pier-glass ('piəglɑ:s)	espejo de cuerpo entero
Radio set ('reidjouset)	aparato de radio
refrigerator (ri'fridʒəreitə)	refrigerador
Settee (sə'ti:)	sofá
shelf (ʃelf)	estante
shelves (ʃelvz)	estantes
sideboard ('saidbo:d)	aparador
sofa ('soufə)	sofá
stool (stu:l)	taburete
Table ('teibl)	mesa
bedside-table	
('bedsaid'teibl)	mesilla de noche
coffee-table ('kofiteibl)	mesita de centro
console-table	
('konsoul'teibl)	consola
dressing-table ('dresiŋteibl)	coqueta, tocador
tall-boy ('to:lboi)	cómoda alta
tapestry ('tæpistri)	tapiz
television set ('televiʒənset)	aparato de televisión
Wardrobe ('wo:droub)	armario
washing-machine	
('woʃiŋməʃi:n)	lavadora

GAMES

(See SPORTS, 84)

38

GARAGE, AT THE   EN EL GARAJE (43)

ENGLISH	ESPAÑOL
Accelerate, to (tuək'seləreit)	acelerar
anti-freeze ('æti'fri:z)	anticongelante
Brake, to (tə'breik)	frenar
brake fluid ('breikflu:id)	líquido de frenos
Cam shaft ('kæmʃa:ft)	árbol de levas
car* (ka:)	coche
carburettor ('ka:bjuretə)	carburador
clutch (klʌtʃ)	embrague
disk clutch ('diskklʌtʃ)	embrague de disco
compression (kəm'preʃən)	compresión
cylinder ('silində)	cilindro
cylinder head ('silindəhed)	culata
Dent (dent)	abolladura
differential gear (difə'renʃəl'giə)	diferencial
distributor ('distribjutə)	delco
distributor-head ('distribjutəhed)	tapa del delco
dynamo ('dainəmou)	dinamo
Engine ('endʒin)	motor
air-cooled engine ('eəku:ld'endʒin)	motor refrigerado por aire
water-cooled engine ('wo:təku:ld'endʒin)	motor refrigerado por agua
exhaust (ig'zo:st)	escape
Fanbelt ('fænbelt)	correa del ventilador
Gear (giə)	engranaje
to throw into gear (tə'θrouintə'giə)	embragar
to throw out of gear (tə'θrouautəv'giə)	desembragar

| GARAGE, AT THE | EN EL GARAJE |

gear-box ('giəboks)   caja de cambios
gear-wheel ('giəwi:l)   rueda dentada
grease, to (tə'gri:s)   engrasar
greasing ('gri:siŋ)   engrase

Horse power ('ho:spauə)   caballos de fuerza

Induction (in'dʌkʃən)   admisión
inner-tube ('inə'tju:b)   cámara del neumático

Jack (dʒæk)   gato para levantar pesos

Lathe (leið)   torno
level ('levəl)   nivel
   oil level ('oil'levəl)   nivel del aceite
lorry ('lori)   camión

Mechanic (mi'kænik)   mecánico
motor ('moutə)   motor
motor-car ('moutəka:)   coche
motor-cycle ('moutəsaikl)   moto

Oil (oil)   aceite
   to change the oil (tə'tʃeindʒði'oil)   cambiar el aceite

Petrol ('petrəl)   gasolina
petrol can ('petrəlkæn)   bidón de gasolina
petrol pump ('petrəlpʌmp)   bomba de la gasolina
piston ('pistən)   émbolo
pulley ('puli)   polea
puncture ('pʌŋktʃə)   pinchazo

Radiator ('reidieitə)   radiador
repair, to (təri'peə)   reparar

Spare parts ('speə'pa:ts)   recambios
sparking plug ('spa:kiŋ'plʌg)   bujía
spring (spriŋ)   muelle, ballesta
start, to (tə'sta:t)   poner en marcha
starter ('sta:tə)   motor de arranque
stroke (strouk)   carrera del émbolo
suspension (səs'penʃən)   suspensión

Transmission (træns'miʃən)   transmisión
transmission shaft (træns'miʃənʃa:ft)   árbol de transmisión
truck (trʌk)   camión
tyre ('taiə)   neumático
   flat tyre ('flæt'taiə)   neumático pinchado
   tyre pressure ('taiəpreʃə)   presión de los neumáticos

GARAGE, AT THE	EN EL GARAJE
Van (væn)	furgoneta
valve (vælv)	válvula
vice (vais)	tornillo (para sujetar piezas)
Wheel (wi:l)	rueda
work, to (tuˈwəːk)	funcionar

39

GARDEN, A   UN JARDIN (56)

ENGLISH	ESPAÑOL
Bench (bentʃ)	banco
berry (ˈberi)	baya
bough (bau)	rama
bouquet (ˈbukei)	ramo
branch (brɑːntʃ)	rama
bud (bʌd)	capullo
bulb (bʌlb)	bulbo
bunch (bʌntʃ)	manojo
bush (buʃ)	arbusto
Corolla (kəˈrolə)	corola
creeper (ˈkriːpə)	enredadera
cutting (ˈkʌtiŋ)	esqueje
Dig, to (təˈdig)	cavar
Earth (əːθ)	tierra
Faucet (ˈfoːsit)	boca de riego
fence (fens)	valla
fertiliser (ˈfəːtilaizə)	fertilizante
flower* (ˈflauə)	flor
flower-beed (ˈflauəbed)	macizo de flores
flower-pot (ˈflauəpot)	tiesto
flower, to (təˈflauə)	florecer
foliage (ˈfouliidʒ)	follaje
fountain (ˈfauntən)	fuente
drinking-fountain (ˈdriŋkiŋfauntən)	fuente para beber agua
fruit* (fruːt)	fruto

Grow, to	(tə'grou)	crecer, cultivar
gardener	('gɑ:dənə)	jardinero
gardening	('gɑ:dəniŋ)	jardinería
garland	('gɑ:lənd)	guirnalda
gate	(geit)	puerta de la verja
graft	(grɑ:ft)	injerto
graft, to	(tə'grɑ:ft)	injertar
grass	(grɑ:s)	hierba
green-house	('gri:nhaus)	invernadero
Hedge	(hedʒ)	seto
hoe	(hou)	azadón
hose	(houz)	manguera
hothouse	('hothaus)	invernadero
Insecticide	(in'sektisaid)	insecticida
Lawn	(lo:n)	césped
lawn-mower	('lo:nmouə)	máquina para cortar el césped
leaf	(li:f)	hoja
leaves	(li:vz)	hojas
Manure	(mə'njuə)	abono
rotten manure	('rotənmə'njuə)	mantillo
mow, to	(tə'mou)	cortar el cesped
Offshoot	('ofʃu:t)	vástago
Path	(pɑ:θ)	vereda
petal	('petl)	pétalo
pistil	('pistil)	pistilo
plant*	(plɑ:nt)	planta
annual plant	('ænjuəl'plɑ:nt)	planta que dura un año
climbing plant	('klaimiŋ'plɑ:nt)	planta trepadora
evergreen plant	('evəgri:n'plɑ:nt)	planta siempre verde
perennial plant	(pə'reniəl'plɑ:nt)	planta perenne
trailing plant	('treiliŋ'plɑ:nt)	planta que se arrastra
plant, to	(tə'plɑ:nt)	plantar
pond	(pond)	estanque
posy	('pouzi)	ramillete
pot	(pot)	tiesto
pothook	('pothuk)	garabato
prune, to	(tə'pru:n)	podar
pruning	('pru:niŋ)	poda
pruning-knife	('pru:niŋnaif)	cuchillo para podar
pruning-shears	('pru:niŋʃiəz)	tijeras para podar

GARDEN, A	UN JARDÍN
Rake (reik)	rastrillo
root (ru:t)	raíz
rosebud ('rouzbʌd)	capullo de rosa
rose garden ('rouzgɑ:dən)	rosaleda
Sap (sæp)	savia
scent (sent)	perfume
seed (si:d)	semilla
shrub (ʃrʌb)	arbusto
soil (soil)	terreno
sow, to (tə'sou)	sembrar
spade (speid)	pala para cavar
sprout (spraut)	brote
sprout, to (tə'spraut)	brotar
stalk (sto:k)	tallo
stem (stem)	tallo
stock (stok)	tronco
summerhouse ('sʌməhaus)	cenador
Tree* (tri:)	árbol
trim, to (tə'trim)	podar
thorn (θo:n)	espina
Vase (vɑ:z)	jarrón
Walk (wo:k)	paseo (avenida)
water, to (tu'wo:tə)	regar
watering-can ('wo:təriŋkæn)	regadera
wheel-barrow ('wi:lbærou)	carretilla
wreath (ri:θ)	corona, guirnalda

40

GEOGRAPHY

GEOGRAFIA (44)

ENGLISH

ESPAÑOL

Archipelago (ɑ:ki'peligou)   archipiélago

Basin ('beisin)   cuenca
bay (bei)   bahía
beach (bi:tʃ)   playa
bight (bait)   ensenada

GEOGRAPHY — GEOGRAFÍA

Cape (keip)	cabo
cataract ('kætərækt)	catarata
cave (keiv)	cueva, caverna
channel ('tʃænəl)	canal
cliff (klif)	acantilado
coast (koust)	costa
coastline ('koustlain)	litoral
continent ('kontinənt)	continente
cove (kouv)	caleta
crater ('kreitə)	cráter
Delta ('deltə)	delta
desert ('dezət)	desierto
Earth (ə:θ)	tierra
east (i:st)	este
Fault (fo:lt)	falla
field (fi:ld)	campo
forest ('forist)	selva
Glacier ('glæsiə)	glaciar
gorge (go:dʒ)	desfiladero
gulf (gʌlf)	golfo
Hill (hil)	colina
Island ('ailənd)	isla
isle (ail)	isla
isthmus ('isməs)	istmo
Jungle ('dʒʌŋgəl)	jungla
Key (ki:)	cayo
Lagoon (lə'gu:n)	albufera
lake (leik)	lago
land (lænd)	tierra
highland ('hailənd)	región montañosa
lowland ('loulənd)	tierra baja
landscape ('lændskeip)	paisaje
Map (mæp)	mapa
relief map (ri'li:fmæp)	mapa en relieve
mountain ('mauntən)	montaña
the foot of a mountain (ðə'futəvə'mauntən)	el pie de una montaña
the top of a mountain (ðə'topəvə'mauntən)	la cima de una montaña
mountain chain ('mauntəntʃein)	cordillera

GEOGRAPHY	GEOGRAFÍA
mountain pass ('mauntənpɑ:s)	puerto de montaña
mountain range ('mauntənreindʒ)	cordillera
mouth (mauθ)	desembocadura
North (no:θ)	norte
Oasis (ou'eisis)	oasis
ocean ('ouʃən)	océano
Peninsula (pə'ninsjulə)	península
plain (plein)	llanura
precipice ('presipis)	precipicio
Ravine (rə'vi:n)	barranco
region ('ri:dʒən)	región
ridge (ridʒ)	loma
rivulet ('rivjulit)	riachuelo
river ('rivə)	río
Savannah (sə'vænə)	sabana
sea (si:)	mar
seaside ('si:'said)	costa
shore (ʃo:)	costa
slope (sloup)	ladera
south (sauθ)	sur
strait (streit)	estrecho
stream (stri:m)	arroyo
summit ('sʌmit)	cima
Table-land ('teibəl'lænd)	meseta
torrent ('torənt)	torrente
tundra ('tʌndrə)	tundra
Valley ('væli)	valle
vegetation (vedʒi'teiʃən)	vegetación
volcano (vəl'keinou)	volcán
Waterfall ('wo:təfo:l)	catarata
west (west)	oeste
wood (wud)	bosque

41

GEOMETRY

ENGLISH

GEOMETRIA (45)

ESPAÑOL

Altitude ('æltitju:d) altura
angle ('æŋgəl) ángulo

GEOMETRY — GEOMETRÍA

acute angle (ə'kju:t'æŋgəl)	ángulo agudo
obtuse angle (əb'tju:s'æŋgəl)	ángulo obtuso
right angle ('rait'æŋgəl)	ángulo recto
arc (ɑ:k)	arco
area ('eəriə)	área
axis ('æksis)	eje
Base (beis)	base
breadth (bredθ)	anchura
Centre ('sentə)	centro
chord (ko:d)	cuerda
circle ('sə:kl)	círculo
circumference (sə'kʌmfərəns)	circunferencia
cone (koun)	cono
cube (kju:b)	cubo
curve (kə:v)	curva
Diagonal (dai'ægənəl)	diagonal
diameter (dai'æmitə)	diámetro
dimension (dai'menʃən)	dimensión
Ellipse (i'lips)	elipse
equilateral (i:kwi'lætərəl)	equilátero
Geometrical figure (dʒiə'metrikəl'figə)	figura geométrica
Horizontal (hori'zontəl)	horizontal
hyperbola (hai'pə:bələ)	hipérbola
hypotenuse (hai'potinju:z)	hipotenusa
Intersection (intə'sekʃən)	intersección
isosceles (ai'sosəli:z)	isósceles
Length (leŋθ)	longitud
line (lain)	línea
convergent lines (kən'və:dʒənt'lainz)	líneas convergentes
curved line ('kə:vd'lain)	línea curva
divergent lines (dai'və:dʒənt'lainz)	líneas divergentes
parallel lines ('pærələl'lainz)	líneas paralelas
straight line ('streit'lain)	línea recta
Parabola (pa'ræbələ)	parábola
parallel ('pærəlel)	paralelo
parallelogram (pærə'leləgræm)	paralelogramo

GEOMETRY	GEOMETRÍA
perpendicular (pə:pən'dikjulə)	perpendicular
plane (plein)	plano
point (point)	punto
polygon ('poligən)	polígono
prism ('prizəm)	prisma
projection (prə'dʒekʃən)	proyección
Quadrangle ('kwodræŋgəl)	cuadrángulo
quadrilateral (kwodri'lætərəl)	cuadrilátero
Radius ('reidiəs)	radio
rectangle ('rektæŋgəl)	rectángulo
rectangular (rek'tæŋgjulə)	rectangular
revolution (revə'lu:ʃən)	desarrollo
rhomb (rom)	rombo
rhomboid ('romboid)	romboide
rhombus ('rombəs)	rombo
round (raund)	redondo
Scalene ('skeili:n)	escaleno
secant ('si:kənt)	secante
section ('sekʃən)	sección
segment ('segmənt)	segmento
semicircle ('semisə:kl)	semicírculo
side (said)	lado
space (speis)	espacio
sphere (sfiə)	esfera
spiral ('spaiərəl)	espiral
square (skweə)	cuadrado, cuadro
surface ('sə:fəs)	superficie
symmetry ('simitri)	simetría
Tangent ('tændʒənt)	tangente
thickness ('θiknis)	grosor
trapezium (trə'pi:ziəm)	trapecio
trapezoid ('træpizoid)	trapezoide
triangle ('traiæŋgəl)	triángulo
equilateral triangle (i:kwi'lætərəl'traiæŋgəl)	triángulo equilátero
triangular (trai'æŋgjulə)	triangular
Vertex ('və:teks)	vértice
vertical ('və:tikl)	vertical

42

AT THE LADIES' HAIRDRESSER'S	EN LA PELUQUERIA DE SEÑORAS (77)
ENGLISH	ESPAÑOL

Bun (bʌn)   moño

Cape (keip)   peinador
comb (koum)   peine
comb, to (tə'koum)   peinar
curl (kə:l)   rizo, bucle
curlers ('kə:ləz)   rulos
curling tongs ('kə:liŋtoŋz)   tenacillas

Depilatory (di'pilətəri)   depilatorio
dye, to (tə'dai)   teñir

Ends (endz)   puntas

Hair (heə)   pelo, cabello
  brown hair ('braun'heə)   pelo castaño
  curly hair ('kə:li'heə)   pelo rizado
  dark hair ('dɑ:k'heə)   pelo moreno
  dry hair ('drai'heə)   pelo seco
  fair hair ('feə'heə)   pelo rubio
  greasy hair ('gri:zi'heə)   pelo graso
  grey hair ('grei'heə)   pelo canoso
  straight hair ('streit'heə)   pelo liso
  wavy hair ('weivi'heə)   pelo ondulado
hair-brush ('heəbrʌʃ)   cepillo para el pelo
hair-comb ('heəkoum)   peinecillo
hair-curlers ('heəkə:ləz)   rulos
hair-do ('heədu:)   peinado
hair-dryer ('heədraiə)   secador
hair-dye ('heədai)   tinte para el cabello
hair-lacquer ('heəlækə)   laca para el pelo
hairpin ('heəpin)   horquilla
hair-net ('heənet)   redecilla
hair-style ('heəstail)   peinado

Irons ('aiənz)   tenazas

Manicure ('mænikjuə)   manicura (servicio)
manicurist ('mænikjuərist)   manicura (persona)

Nail-file ('neilfail)   lima para uñas

nail-scissors ('neilsizəz)	tijeras para las uñas
nail-varnish ('neilvɑ:niʃ)	laca para las uñas
nail-varnish remover ('neilvɑ:niʃri'mu:və)	quitaesmalte
Parting ('pɑ:tiŋ)	raya (del pelo)
perm (pə:m)	permanente
Shampoo (ʃæm'pu:)	champú
Wash (woʃ)	lavado de cabeza
wash, to (tu'woʃ)	lavar
wave (weiv)	onda
permanent wave ('pə:mənənt'weiv)	permanente

43

HEAD-DRESS

PRENDAS DE CABEZA (82)

ENGLISH	ESPAÑOL
Bearskin ('beəskin)	morrión
Beret ('berei)	boína
bonnet ('bonit)	gorra escocesa
bowler ('boulə)	sombrero hongo
brim (brim)	ala de sombrero
Cap (kæp)	gorra, gorro
cloth cap ('kloθ 'kæp)	gorra de paño
peaked cap (pi:kt'kæp)	gorra de visera
Fez (fez)	fez
Hat (hæt)	sombrero
bowler-hat ('bouləhæt)	sombrero hongo
felt hat ('felt'hæt)	sombrero de fieltro
straw hat ('stro:'hæt)	sombrero de paja
three-cornered hat ('θri:ko:nəd'hæt)	sombrero de tres picos
top hat ('top'hæt)	sombrero de copa
broad straw hat ('bro:d 'stro: 'hæt)	pamela
headscarf ('hedskɑ:f)	pañuelo de cabeza

HEAD-DRESS	PRENDAS DE CABEZA (82)
helmet ('helmit)	casco
sun-helmet ('sʌnhelmit)	salacot
hood (hud)	capucha
Kepi ('keipi)	quepis
nightcap ('naitkæp)	gorro de dormir
Peak (pi:k)	visera
Sombrero (som'breərou)	sombrero tejano
Topper ('topə)	chistera
turban ('tə:bən)	turbante

44

HISTORY / HISTORIA (49)

ENGLISH — **ESPAÑOL**

Allies ('ælaiz)	aliados
Anglo-Saxons ('æŋglou'sæksənz)	anglo-sajones
Arabs ('ærəbz)	árabes
archduke ('a:tʃ'dju:k)	archiduque
Armada, the (ðia:'ma:də)	la Armada Invencible
army ('a:mi)	ejército
Baron ('bærən)	barón
battle ('bætl)	batalla
sea battle ('si:bætl)	batalla naval
besiege, to (təbi'si:dʒ)	sitiar
Bronze Age, the (ðə'bronzeidʒ)	la Edad del Bronce
Carthaginians (ka:θə'dʒiniənz)	cartagineses
castle ('ka:sl)	castillo
catholic ('kæθəlik)	católico
century ('sentʃəri)	siglo
colonists ('kolənists)	colonizadores
conquer, to (tə'koŋkə)	conquistar
conqueror ('koŋkərə)	conquistador
conquest ('koŋkwest)	conquista
coronation (korə'neiʃən)	coronación
council ('kaunsəl)	concilio

HISTORY / HISTORIA

Counter-Reformation, the (ðəˈkauntərefəˈmeiʃən) — la Contrarreforma
coup d'etat (ˈkuːdeiˈtɑː) — golpe de estado
court (koːt) — corte
crown (kraun) — corona
crown, to (təˈkraun) — coronar
crusaders (kruːˈseidəz) — cruzados
Crusades, the (ðəkruːˈseidz) — las Cruzadas

Defeat (diˈfiːt) — derrota
defeat, to (tədiˈfiːt) — derrotar
duke (djuːk) — duque
dynasty (ˈdinəsti) — dinastía

Edict (ˈiːdikt) — edicto
emperor (ˈempərə) — emperador
empire (ˈempaiə) — imperio
empress (ˈempris) — emperatriz
enemy (ˈenəmi) — enemigo
execute, to (tuˈeksəkjuːt) — ejecutar
execution (eksiˈkjuːʃən) — ejecución

Feudalism (ˈfjuːdəlizəm) — feudalismo
fleet (fliːt) — flota
found, to (təˈfaund) — fundar
frontier (ˈfrʌntiə) — frontera

General (ˈdʒenərəl) — general
government (ˈgʌvənmənt) — gobierno
Greece (griːs) — Grecia
Greek (griːk) — griego

Hegemony (hiːˈgeməni) — hegemonía
heir (eə) — heredero
herald (ˈherəld) — heraldo
heraldry (ˈherəldri) — heráldica
heresy (ˈherəsi) — herejía
heretic (ˈherətik) — hereje
hero (ˈhiərou) — héroe
heroine (ˈherouin) — heroína
historian (hisˈtoːriən) — historiador
historic (hisˈtorik) — histórico
history (ˈhistəri) — historia
Holy See, the (ðəˈhouliˈsiː) — la Santa Sede

Inquisition, the (ðiinkwiˈziʃən) — la Inquisición
invade, to (tuinˈveid) — invadir
invaders (inˈveidəz) — invasores
invasion (inˈveiʒən) — invasión

King (kiŋ) — rey

HISTORY	HISTORIA
kingdom ('kiŋdəm)	reino
knight (nait)	caballero
Leader ('li:də)	jefe
league (li:g)	liga
lists (lists)	liza
Magna Carta ('mægnə'kɑ:tə)	Carta Magna
mediaeval (medi'i:vəl)	medieval
Middle Ages, the (ðə'midl'eidʒiz)	la Edad Media
minister ('ministə)	ministro
prime minister ('praim'ministə)	primer ministro
monarch ('monək)	monarca
monarchy ('monəki)	monarquía
monastery ('monəsteri)	monasterio
Nation ('neiʃən)	nación
navy ('neivi)	armada
Parliament ('pɑ:ləmənt)	parlamento
patriot ('peitriot)	patriota
peace (pi:s)	paz
Phoenicians (fi'niʃənz)	fenicios
policy ('polisi)	política
Pope, the (ðə'poup)	el Papa
possessions (pə'zeʃənz)	posesiones
power ('pauə)	potencia
prince (prins)	príncipe
princess ('prin'ses)	princesa
Protestant ('protistənt)	protestante
Queen (kwi:n)	reina
Rebel ('rebl)	rebelde
rebel, to (təri'bel)	rebelarse
rebellion (ri'beliən)	rebelión
reconquest ('ri:'koŋkwest)	reconquista
Reformation, the (ðərefə'meiʃən)	la Reforma
reign (rein)	reinado
reign, to (ðə'rein)	reinar
Renaissance, the (ðəri'neisəns)	el Renacimiento
republic (ri'pʌblik)	república
restoration (restə'reiʃən)	restauración
restore, to (təris'to:)	restaurar

| HISTORY | | HISTORIA |

revolution (revə'lu:ʃən)   revolución
Rome (roum)   Roma
Romans ('roumənz)   Romanos
rule (ru:l)   gobierno
rule, to (tə'ru:l)   gobernar
ruler ('ru:lə)   gobernante

Sack, to (tə'sæk)   saquear
Saracens ('særəsənz)   sarracenos
schism ('sizəm)   cisma
senate ('senit)   senado
settlement ('setəlmənt)   colonia
settlers ('setləz)   colonizadores
siege (si:dʒ)   sitio
slave (sleiv)   esclavo
slavery ('sleivəri)   esclavitud
sovereign ('sovrin)   soberano
state (steit)   estado
statesman ('steitsmən)   hombre de estado
Stone Age, the (ðə'stouneidʒ)   la Edad de Piedra
struggle ('strʌgl)   lucha
succeed, to (təsək'si:d)   suceder
succesion (sək'seʃən)   sucesión
supremacy (sju'preməsi)   supremacía
surrender (sə'rendə)   rendición
surrender, to (təsə'rendə)   rendirse

Throne (θroun)   trono
tournament ('tuənəmənt)   torneo
traitor ('treitə)   traidor
treason ('tri:zən)   traición
treaty ('tri:ti)   tratado
tribe (traib)   tribu

Unity ('ju:niti)   unidad

Victory ('viktəri)   victoria

War (wo:)   guerra
  civil war ('sivil'wo:)   guerra civil
  Hundred Years War, the (ðə'hʌndridjiəz'wo:)   la guerra de los Cien Años
  Peninsular Ward, the (ðəpə'ninsjulə'wo:)   la guerra de la Independencia (española)

45

HOLIDAYS AND FESTIVITIES

FIESTAS Y FESTIVIDADES (38)

ENGLISH	ESPAÑOL
All-Fools'-Day ('o:l'fu:lzdei)	Día de los Inocentes (1.° de abril)
All-Hallows ('o:l'hælouz)	Día de Todos los Santos
All-Saints'-Day ('o:l'seintsdei)	Día de Todos los Santos
Ascension Day (ə'senʃəndei)	Día de la Ascensión
Assumption Day (ə'sʌmpʃəndei)	Día de la Asunción
Ash Wednesday ('æʃ'wenzdi)	Miércoles de Ceniza
Birthday ('bə:θdei)	cumpleaños
Boxing-Day ('boksiŋdei)	Día del Aguinaldo (26 de diciembre)
Christmas ('krisməs)	Navidad
Christmas Day ('Krisməs'dei)	Día de Navidad
Christmas Eve ('krisməs'i:v)	Nochebuena
Christmas holidays ('krisməs'holidiz)	vacaciones de Navidad
Columbus Day (kə'lʌmbəsdei)	Día de la Raza (12 de octubre)
Corpus Christi ('ko:pəs'kristi)	Corpus Christi
Easter ('i:stə)	Pascua
Easter Monday ('i:stə'mʌndi)	Lunes de Pascua
Good Friday ('gud'fraidi)	Viernes Santo
Holy Thursday ('houli'θə:zdi)	Jueves Santo
Holy Week ('houliwi:k)	Semana Santa
Lent (lent)	Cuaresma
New Year ('nju:'jiə)	Año Nuevo
New Year's Day ('nju:'jiəz'dei)	Día de Año Nuevo
New Year's Eve ('nju:'jiəz'i:v)	Nochevieja
Palm Sunday ('pɑ:m'sʌndi)	Domingo de Ramos
Saint's day ('seints'dei)	día del santo (de una persona)
Shrove Tuesday ('ʃrouv'tju:zdi)	Martes de Carnaval
summer holidays ('sʌməholidiz)	vacaciones de verano

| HOLIDAYS AND FESTIVITIES | 116 | FIESTAS Y FESTIVIDADES |

Twelfth Night ('twelfθnait)　　　Noche de Reyes

Whitmonday ('wit'mʌndi)　　　Lunes de Pentecostés
Whitsunday ('wit'sʌndi)　　　Domingo de Pentecostés
Whitsuntide ('witsəntaid)　　　Fiesta del Espíritu Santo

HOME　　　(See LIFE AT HOME, 55)

HOSPITAL　　　(See THE DOCTOR, 26)

46

| HOTEL, A | UN HOTEL (50) |

| ENGLISH | ESPAÑOL |

Accommodation
　　　(əkomə'deiʃən)　　　alojamiento

Baggage ('bægidʒ)　　　equipaje (USA)
bar (bɑ:)　　　bar
barman ('bɑ:mən)　　　barman
bath (bɑ:θ)　　　baño
bathroom ('bɑ:θrum)　　　cuarto de baño
bed (bed)　　　cama
bedroom ('bedrum)　　　dormitorio
　double bedroom
　　　('dʌbəl'bedrum)　　　habitación doble
　single bedroom
　　　('siŋgəl'bedrum)　　　habitación individual
bell (bel)　　　timbre
bellboy ('belboi)　　　botones
bill (bil)　　　factura
board and lodging
　　　('bo:dən'lodʒiŋ)　　　pensión completa
breakfast ('brekfəst)　　　desayuno

Chamber-maid ('tʃeimbəmeid)　　　camarera
cook (kuk)　　　cocinero
corridor ('koridɔ:)　　　pasillo

Dining-room ('dainiŋrum)　　　comedor

HOTEL, A	UN HOTEL

dinner ('dinə) — cena
Full board ('ful'bo:d) — pensión completa
Hall porter ('ho:lpo:tə) — portero
headwaiter ('hedweitə) — maitre
hotel (hou'tel) — hotel
  five-star hotel ('faivsta:hou'tel) — hotel de cinco estrellas
  four-star hotel ('fo:sta:hou'tel) — hotel de cuatro estrellas
  luxurious hotel (lʌg'zjuəriəshou'tel) — hotel lujoso
  one-star hotel ('wʌnsta:hou'tel) — hotel de una estrella
  three-star hotel ('θri:sta:hou'tel) — hotel de tres estrellas
  two-star hotel ('tu:sta:hou'tel) — hotel de dos estrellas

Key (ki:) — llave
kitchen ('kitʃən) — cocina
kitchen boy ('kitʃənboi) — pinche

Laundry ('lo:ndri) — lavandería
lavatory ('lævətəri) — W.C.
lift (lift) — ascensor
linen ('linən) — ropa blanca
lodge, to (tə'lodʒ) — hospedarse
lounge (laundʒ) — sala de estar
luggage ('lʌgidʒ) — equipaje (GB)
lunch (lʌntʃ) — almuerzo

Manager ('mænədʒə) — gerente
meal (mi:l) — comida

Number ('nʌmbə) — número

Porter ('po:tə) — portero

Reception desk (ri'sepʃəndesk) — recepción
receptionist (ri'sepʃənist) — recepcionista
restaurant ('restərənt) — restaurante
room (rum) — habitación
  double room ('dʌbəl'rum) — habitación doble
  single room ('siŋgəl'rum) — habitación individual
  running water ('rʌniŋ'wo:tə) — agua corriente

Soap (soup) — jabón
shower ('ʃauə) — ducha
stay (at a hotel), to (tə'stei(ətəhou'tel)) — hospedarse (en un hotel)

HOTEL, A		UN HOTEL

suitcase   ('su:tkeis) maleta
Tip   (tip)   propina
towel   ('tauəl)   toalla
Voucher   ('vautʃə)   bono
Waiter   ('weitə)   camarero
waitress   ('weitris)   camarera

47

HOUSE, A	UNA CASA (19)
ENGLISH	ESPAÑOL

Air-conditioning
            ('eəkəndiʃəniŋ)   aire acondicionado
attic   ('ætik)   ático
Balcony   ('bælkəni)   balcón
balaustrade   (bæləs'treid)   balaustrada
banister   ('bænistə)   barandilla
basement   ('beismənt)   sótano
bath   (bɑ:θ)   bañera
blinds   (blaindz)   persianas
bolt   (boult)   cerrojo
Ceiling   ('si:liŋ)   techo
cellar   ('selə)   sótano
  coal-cellar   ('koulselə)   carbonera
  wine-cellar   ('wainselə)   bodega
chimney   ('tʃimni)   chimenea (en el tejado)
closet   ('klozit)   armario
cornice   ('ko:nis)   cornisa
corridor   ('korido:)   corredor
cupboard   ('kʌbəd)   armario

Door   (do:)   puerta
  back door   ('bæk'do:)   puerta trasera
  front door   ('frʌnt'do:)   puerta de la calle
door-bell   ('do:bel)   timbre de la puerta
door-handle   ('do:hændəl)   tirador de la puerta

HOUSE, A   UNA CASA

door-frame ('dɔ:freim)	marco de la puerta
door-knocker ('dɔ:nɔkə)	aldaba
drainage ('dreinidʒ)	desagüe
Eaves (i:vz)	alero
electricity (ilek'trisiti)	electricidad
entrance ('entrəns)	entrada
exit ('eksit)	salida
Fence (fens)	valla
fire-place ('faiəpleis)	chimenea (de salón)
flexible cord ('fleksibəl'kɔ:d)	flexible (cable)
flight of stairs ('flaitəv'steəz)	tramo de escalera
floor (flɔ:)	piso
first floor ('fə:st'flɔ:)	primer piso
ground floor ('graund'flɔ:)	planta baja
second floor ('sekənd'flɔ:)	segundo piso
third floor ('θə:d'flɔ:)	tercer piso
top floor ('tɔp'flɔ:)	último piso
front (frʌnt)	fachada
Garden ('gɑ:dən)	jardín
garret ('gærət)	buhardilla
gas (gæs)	gas
gate (geit)	puerta del jardín
Hall (hɔ:l)	entrada, vestíbulo, sala
hand-rail ('hændreil)	pasamanos
heating ('hi:tiŋ)	calefacción
central heating ('sentrəl'hi:tiŋ)	calefacción central
hinge (hindʒ)	bisagra
Kitchen ('kitʃən)	cocina
Larder ('lɑ:də)	despensa
latch (lætʃ)	picaporte
lavatory ('lævətəri)	«water»
lift (lift)	ascensor
light (lait)	luz
lightning-rod ('laitniŋrɔd)	pararrayos
lock (lɔk)	cerradura
Nursery ('nə:səri)	cuarto de los niños
Paint (peint)	pintura
pane (pein)	cristal de ventana
pantry ('pæntri)	despensa
parlour ('pɑ:lə)	salita
plumbing ('plʌmiŋ)	instalación de fontanería
porch (pɔ:tʃ)	porche

| HOUSE, A | UNA CASA |

Radiator   ('reidieitə)   radiador
roof   (ru:f)   tejado
  flat roof   ('flæt'ru:f)   terraza
  slate roof   ('sleit'ru:f)   tejado de pizarra
  tile roof   ('tail'ru:f)   tejado de teja
room   (rum)   habitación
  bathroom   ('bɑ:θrum)   cuarto de baño
  bedroom   ('bedrum)   dormitorio
  box-room   ('boksrum)   cuarto trastero
  dining-room   ('dainiŋrum)   comedor
  drawing-room   ('dro:iŋrum)   sala de estar
  living-room   ('liviŋrum)   sala de estar
  sitting-room   ('sitiŋrum)   sala de estar
  washroom   ('woʃrum)   lavabo

Shower   ('ʃauə)   ducha
shutter   ('ʃʌtə)   contraventana
skirting-board   ('skə:tiŋbo:d)   rodapié
socket   ('sokit)   enchufe
stair-case   ('steəkeis)   hueco de escalera
stair-case landing
    ('steəkeis'lændiŋ)   descansillo de escalera
stairs   (steəz)   escalera
  back stairs   ('bæk'steəz)   escalera de servicio
step   (step)   escalón
stove   (stouv)   cocina (mueble)
  electric stove
    (i'lektrik'stouv)   cocina eléctrica
  gas-stove   ('gæsstouv)   cocina de gas
study   ('stʌdi)   cuarto de estudio
switch   (switʃ)   interruptor

Tap   (tæp)   grifo
television aerial
    ('televiʒəneəriəl)   antena de televisión
threshold   ('θreʃould)   umbral
toilet   ('toilit)   inodoro
towel-rail   ('tauəlreil)   toallero

Wall   (wo:l)   pared
wall-paper   ('wo:lpeipə)   papel pintado
wash basin   ('woʃbeisin)   lavabo
water   ('wo:tə)   agua
  hot running water
    ('hot'rʌniŋ'wo:tə)   agua caliente central
  running water   ('rʌniŋ'wo:tə)   agua corriente
water-closet   ('wo:təklozit)   «water»
water-heater   ('wo:təhi:tə)   calentador de agua
window   ('windou)   ventana
window-frame   ('windoufreim)   marco de ventana

HOUSE, A	UNA CASA

window-sill ('windousil)   alféizar
wiring ('waiəriŋ)   instalación eléctrica

48

HOUSE BUILDING	CONSTRUCCION DE UN EDIFICIO (25)
ENGLISH	ESPAÑOL

English	Español
Architect ('ɑːkitekt)	arquitecto
Beam (biːm)	viga
brick (brik)	ladrillo
bricklayer ('brikleiə)	albañil
build, to (tə'bild)	construir
builder ('bildə)	constructor
building ('bildiŋ)	edificio
building materials ('bildiŋmətiəriəlz)	materiales de construcción
Carpenter ('kɑːpintə)	carpintero
cement (si'ment)	cemento
concrete ('konkriːt)	hormigón
concrete mixer ('konkriːtmiksə)	hormigonera
crane (krein)	grúa
Door frame ('doːfreim)	marco de puerta
door-post ('doːpoust)	jamba
Flat (flæt)	piso (vivienda)
foundations (faun'deiʃənz)	cimientos
front (frʌnt)	fachada
Girder ('gəːdə)	viga de hierro
gravel ('grævəl)	grava
Labourer ('leibərə)	peón
lime (laim)	cal
lintel ('lintəl)	dintel
Marble ('mɑːbl)	mármol
mason ('meisən)	cantero
mortar ('moːtə)	mortero

HOUSE BUILDING — CONST. DE UN EDIFICIO

Painter ('peintə)	pintor
partition (pɑ:'tiʃən)	tabique
pipe ('paip)	cañería
pillar ('pilə)	pilar
plan (plæn)	plano
planning ('plæniŋ)	distribución
plaster ('plɑ:stə)	yeso
plumber ('plʌmə)	fontanero
Rafter ('rɑ:ftə)	viga
Sand (sænd)	arena
scaffolding ('skæfəldiŋ)	andamio
slate (sleit)	pizarra
stone (stoun)	piedra
storey ('sto:ri)	planta
Tile (tail)	teja, baldosa
glazed tile ('gleizd'tail)	baldosín
Wall (wo:l)	pared
main wall ('mein'wo:l)	pared maestra
partition wall (pɑ:'tiʃənwo:l)	pared medianera
window-frame ('windoufreim)	marco de ventana
wiring ('waiəriŋ)	instalación eléctrica

49

HUMAN BODY, THE — EL CUERPO HUMANO (29)

ENGLISH	ESPAÑOL
Abdomen ('æbdəmən)	abdomen
Adam's apple ('ædəmz'æpl)	nuez
alimentary canal (æli'mentərikə'næl)	tubo digestivo
ankle ('æŋkəl)	tobillo
aorta (ei'o:tə)	aorta
arm (ɑ:m)	brazo
forearm ('fo:rɑ:m)	antebrazo
armpit ('ɑ:mpit)	axila
artery ('ɑ:təri)	arteria

HUMAN BODY, THE / EL CUERPO HUMANO

Back (bæk)	espalda
backbone ('bækboun)	columna vertebral
beard (biəd)	barba
beauty-spot ('bju:tispot)	lunar
belly ('beli)	vientre
bladder ('blædə)	vejiga
gall bladder ('go:lblædə)	vesícula biliar
urinary bladder ('juərinəri'blædə)	vejiga de la orina
blood (blʌd)	sangre
body ('bodi)	cuerpo
bone* (boun)	hueso
bowels ('bauəlz)	intestinos
brain (brein)	cerebro
breast (brest)	pecho (seno)
breath (breθ)	aliento
bronchial tubes ('broŋkiəl'tju:bz)	bronquios
brow (brau)	frente
bust (bʌst)	busto
Calf (kɑ:f)	pantorrilla
cartilage ('kɑ:tilidʒ)	cartílago
cheek (tʃi:k)	mejilla
cheekbone ('tʃi:kboun)	pómulo
chest (tʃest)	pecho (tórax)
chest cavity ('tʃestkæviti)	cavidad torácica
chin (tʃin)	barbilla
colon ('koulən)	colon
cornea ('ko:niə)	cornea
cranium ('kreiniəm)	cráneo
Diaphragm ('daiəfræm)	diafragma
duodenum (djuə'di:nəm)	duodeno
Ear (iə)	oreja, oído
elbow ('elbou)	codo
extremities (iks'tremitiz)	extremidades
eye (ai)	ojo
eye-ball ('ailbo:l)	globo del ojo
eyebrow ('aibrau)	ceja
eyelash ('ailæʃ)	pestaña
eye-lid ('ailid)	párpado
eyesight ('aisait)	vista
eye-socket ('aisokit)	cuenca del ojo
Face (feis)	cara
feet (fi:t)	pies
finger ('fiŋgə)	dedo
fore finger ('fo:fiŋgə)	dedo índice

| HUMAN BODY, THE | EL CUERPO HUMANO |

middle finger ('midəl'fiŋgə)   dedo corazón
ring finger ('riŋfiŋgə)   dedo anular
little finger ('litəl'fiŋgə)   dedo meñique
finger-bone ('fiŋgəboun)   falange de un dedo de la mano
fist (fist)   puño
flesh (fleʃ)   carne
foot (fut)   pie
forehead ('forid)   frente

Gall (go:l)   hiel
gland (glænd)   glándula
groin (groin)   ingle
gullet ('gʌlit)   esófago
gum (gʌm)   encía

Hair (heə)   pelo
hand (hænd)   mano
head (hed)   cabeza
hearing ('hiəriŋ)   oído
heart (ha:t)   corazón
heel (hi:l)   talón
hip (hip)   cadera

Instep ('instep)   empeine
intestine (in'testin)   intestino
  large intestine
    ('la:dʒin'testin)   intestino grueso
  small intestine
    ('smo:lin'testin)   intestino delgado
iris ('aiəris)   iris

Jaw (dʒo:)   mandíbula
joint ('dʒoint)   articulación
jugular ('dʒʌgjulə)   yugular

Kidney ('kidni)   riñón
knee (ni:)   rodilla
knuckle ('nʌkl)   nudillo

Larynx ('læriŋks)   laringe
leg (leg)   pierna
limb (lim)   miembro
lip (lip)   labio
liver ('livə)   hígado
lobe (loub)   lóbulo
loins (loinz)   lomo
lung (lʌŋ)   pulmón

Marrow ('mærou)   médula
mole (moul)   lunar

| HUMAN BODY, THE | EL CUERPO HUMANO |

moustache (məs'tɑːʃ) bigote
mouth (mauθ) boca
muscle* ('mʌsl) músculo

Nail (neil) uña
nape (neip) nuca
nasal cavity ('neizəl'kæviti) cavidad nasal
navel ('neivəl) ombligo
neck (nek) cuello
nerve (nəːv) nervio
nose (nouz) nariz
nostril ('nostril) ventana de la nariz

Organ ('oːgən) órgano

Palate ('pælət) paladar
palm (pɑːm) palma de la mano
pancreas ('pæŋkriəs) pancreas
pharynx ('færiŋks) faringe
pulmonary cavity
 ('pʌlmənəri'kæviti) cavidad pulmonar
pulse (pʌls) pulso
pupil ('pjuːpil) pupila

Retina ('retinə) retina
rib (rib) costilla
 false rib ('foːls'rib) costilla falsa
 floating rib ('floutiŋ'rib) costilla flotante

Saliva (sə'laivə) saliva
shin (ʃin) espinilla
shoulder ('ʃouldə) hombro
side (said) costado
sight (sait) vista
sinew ('sinjuː) tendón
skeleton ('skelitən) esqueleto
skin (skin) piel
skull (skʌl) cráneo
smell (smel) olfato
sole (soul) planta del pie
spine (spain) columna vertebral
spleen (spliːn) bazo
sternum ('stəːnəm) esternón
stomach ('stʌmək) estómago
sweat (swet) sudor

Taste (teist) gusto
tear (tiə) lágrima
teeth (tiːθ) dientes, muelas
temple ('tempəl) sien

| HUMAN BODY, THE | EL CUERPO HUMANO |

tendon ('tendən)
thigh (θai)
thorax ('θo:ræks)
throat (θrout)
thumb (θʌm)
toe (tou)
tongue (tʌŋ)
tonsil ('tonsəl)
tooth (tu:θ)
  eye tooth ('aitu:θ)
  milk tooth ('milktu:θ)
  wisdom tooth ('wizdəmtu:θ)
touch (tʌtʃ)
trunk (trʌŋk)

Uvula ('ju:vjulə)

Vein (vein)
vertebra ('və:tibrə)
vocal cords ('voukəl'ko:dz)

Waist (weist)
wart (wo:t)
whiskers ('wiskəz)
windpipe ('windpaip)
wrinkle ('riŋkəl)
wrist (rist)

tendón
muslo
tórax
garganta
dedo pulgar
dedo del pie
lengua
amígdala
diente, muela
colmillo
diente de leche
muela del juicio
tacto
tronco

úvula

vena
vértebra
cuerdas vocales

cintura
verruga
patillas
tráquea
arruga
muñeca

50

ILLNESSES ENFERMEDADES (35)

ENGLISH ESPAÑOL

Acne ('ækni)
adenoids ('ædinoidz)
allergy ('ælədʒi)
amnesia (æm'ni:ziə)
anaemia (ə'ni:miə)
anthrax ('ænθræks)
apoplexy ('æpəpleksi)
appendicitis (əpendi'saitis)

acné
vegetaciones
alergia
amnesia
anemia
antrax
apoplejía
apendicitis

| ILLNESSES | ENFERMEDADES |

arterio-sclerosis
        (ɑ:'tiərousklie'rousis)   arterioesclerosis
arthritis   (ɑ:'θraitis)   artritis
asthma   ('æsmə)   asma

Blindness   ('blaindnis)   ceguera
  colour blindness
        ('kʌləblaindnis)   daltonismo
bloodpoisoning   ('blʌdpoizəniŋ)   septicemia
blood pressure   ('blʌdpreʃə)   tensión de la sangre
  high blood pressure
        ('hai'blʌdpreʃə)   tensión alta
  low blood pressure
        ('lou'blʌdpreʃə)   tensión baja
bronchitis   (broŋ'kaitis)   bronquitis

Cancer   ('kænsə)   cáncer
cataract   ('kætərækt)   catarata
catarrh   (kə'tɑ:)   catarro
chicken-pox   ('tʃikənpoks)   varicela
chilblains   ('tʃilbleinz)   sabañones
cholera   ('kolərə)   cólera
cirrhosis   (si'rousis)   cirrosis
claustrophobia
        (klo:strə'foubiə)   claustrofobia
cold   (kould)   resfriado
colic   ('kolik)   cólico
colitis   (kə'laitis)   colitis
collapse   (kə'læps)   colapso
conjunctivitis
        (kəndʒʌnti'vaitis)   conjuntivitis
constipation   (konsti'peiʃən)   estreñimiento
consumption   (kən'sʌmpʃən)   tuberculosis
  galloping consumption
        ('gæləpiŋkən'sʌmpʃən)   tuberculosis galopante

Deaf-mutism   ('def'mju:tizəm)   sordomudez
deafness   ('defnis)   sordera
dermatitis   (də:mə'taitis)   dermatitis
diabetes   (daiə'bi:ti:z)   diabetes
diphtheria   (dif'θiəriə)   difteria
disease   (di'zi:z)   enfermedad
  allergic disease
        (ə'lə:dʒikdi'zi:z)   enfermedad alérgica
  blood disease   ('blʌddizi:z)   enfermedad de la sangre
  chronic disease
        ('kronikdi'zi:z)   enfermedad crónica
  endemic disease
        (en'demikdi'zi:z)   enfermedad endémica

ILLNESSES		ENFERMEDADES

heart disease ('hɑ:tdizi:z)   enfermedad del corazón
kidney disease ('kidnidizi:z)   enfermedad del riñón
mental disease
        ('mentəldi'zi:z)   enfermedad mental
nervous disease
        ('nə:vəsdi'zi:z)   enfermedad de los nervios
skin disease ('skindizi:z)   enfermedad de la piel
venereal disease
        (vi'niəriəldi'zi:z)   enfermedad venérea
dumbness ('dʌmnis)   mudez
dysentery ('disəntri)   disentería
dyspepsia (dis'pepsiə)   dispepsia

Eczema ('eksimə)   eczema
epilepsy ('epilepsi)   epilepsia

Favus ('feivəs)   tiña
fever ('fi:və)   fiebre
  hay fever ('heifi:və)   fiebre del heno
  intermittent fever
        (intə'mitənt'fi:və)   fiebre intermitente
  malignant fever
        (mə'lignənt'fi:və)   fiebre perniciosa
  Mediterranean fever
        (meditə'reiniən'fi:və)   fiebre de Malta
  paratyphoid fever
        ('pærətaifoid'fi:və)   fiebre paratífica
  rheumatic fever
        (ru'mætik'fi:və)   fiebre reumática
  scarlet fever ('skɑ:lit'fi:və)   escarlatina
  typhoid fever ('taifoid'fi:və)   fiebre tifoidea
  yellow fever ('jelou'fi:və)   fiebre amarilla
flat foot ('flæt'fut)   pie plano
flatulence ('flætjuləns)   flatulencia
flu (flu:)   gripe

Gall-stone ('go:lstoun)   cálculo hepático
gangrene ('gæŋgri:n)   gangrena
gastritis (gæs'traitis)   gastritis
goitre ('goitə)   bocio
gout (gaut)   gota

Hepatitis (hepə'taitis)   hepatitis
hernia ('hə:niə)   hernia
hives (haivz)   urticaria
hydrophobia (haidrou'foubiə)   hidrofobia
hypertension (haipə'tenʃən)   hipertensión
hypochondria (haipou'kondriə)   hipocondria
hipotension (haipou'tenʃən)   hipotensión
hysteria (his'tiəriə)   histeria

ILLNESSES		ENFERMEDADES

Influenza (influ'enzə) — gripe
insanity (in'sæniti) — locura
insomnia (in'somniə) — insomnio

Jaundice ('dʒo:ndis) — ictericia

Laryngitis (lærin'dʒaitis) — laringitis
leprosy ('leprəsi) — lepra
leukemia (lju'ki:miə) — leucemia
lumbago (lʌm'beigou) — lumbago

Madness ('mædnis) — locura
malaria (mə'leəriə) — malaria, paludismo
meningitis (menin'dʒaitis) — meningitis
measles ('mi:zəlz) — sarampión
   German measles ('dʒə:mən'mi:zəlz) — rubeola
mumps (mʌmps) — paperas
myopia (mai'oupiə) — miopía

Neuralgia (njuə'rældʒə) — neuralgia
neurosis (njuə'rousis) — neurosis

Obesity (ou'bi:siti) — obesidad

Paralysis (pə'rælisis) — parálisis
pharyngitis (færin'dʒaitis) — faringitis
phlebitis (fli'baitis) — flebitis
piles (pailz) — almorranas
pleurisy ('pluərisi) — pleuresía
pneumonia (nju'mouniə) — pulmonía
polio ('pouljou) — polio
poliomyelitis ('pouljoumaiə'laitis) — poliomielitis

Rabies ('reibii:z) — rabia
rheumatism ('ru:mətizəm) — reumatismo
rickets ('rikits) — raquitismo
rubella (ru'belə) — rubéola
rupture ('rʌptʃə) — hernia

Scabies ('skeibii:z) — sarna
schizophrenia (skitsou'fri:niə) — esquizofrenia
sclerosis (skliə'rousis) — esclerosis
sickness ('siknis) — enfermedad
sinusitis (sainə'saitis) — sinusitis
sleeping sickness ('sli:piŋsiknis) — enfermedad del sueño
smallpox ('smo:lpoks) — viruela

ILLNESSES	ENFERMEDADES

sore ears ('sɔːr'iəz)	mal de oídos
sore eyes ('sɔːr'aiz)	mal de ojos
sore throat ('sɔː'θrout)	mal de garganta
squint (skwint)	estrabismo
stammering ('stæməriŋ)	tartamudez
stuttering ('stʌtəriŋ)	tartamudez
St. Vitus' dance (sənt'vaitəsiz'dɑːns)	baile de San Vito
syphilis ('sifilis)	sífilis
TB ('tiː'biː)	tuberculosis
tetanus ('tetənəs)	tétanos
thombosis (θrom'bousis)	trombosis
coronary thrombosis ('korənəriθrom'bousis)	trombosis coronaria
tonsillitis (tonsi'laitis)	anginas
tuberculosis (tjubəːkju'lousis)	tuberculosis
typhus ('taifəs)	tifus
tumour ('tjuːmə)	tumor
benign tumour (bi'nain'tjuːmə)	tumor benigno
malignant tumour (mə'lignənt'tjuːmə)	tumor maligno
Ulcer ('ʌlsə)	úlcera
duodenal ulcer (djuə'diːnəl'ʌlsə)	úlcera duodenal
gastric ulcer ('gætrik'ʌlsə)	úlcera gástrica
stomach ulcer ('stʌməkʌlsə)	úlcera de estómago
Varicose veins ('værikous'veinz)	varices
Whooping cough ('huːpiŋkof)	tos ferina

51

INSECTS, ARACHNIDS AND ANNELIDS	INSECTOS, ARACNIDOS Y ANELIDOS (54)
ENGLISH	ESPAÑOL

Ant (ænt)	hormiga
Bee (biː)	abeja
bumblebee ('bʌmbəlbiː)	abejarrón

INSECTS, ARACHNIDS, ETC. INSECTOS, ARACNIDOS, ETC.

queen bee ('kwi:n'bi:) abeja reina
working bee ('wə:kiŋ'bi:) abeja obrera
beetle ('bi:tl) escarabajo
bluebottle ('blu:botl) moscardón
bug (bʌg) chinche
  bed bug ('bedbʌg) chinche
butterfly ('bʌtəflai) mariposa

Caterpillar ('kætəpilə) oruga
centipede ('sentipi:d) ciempiés
cicada (si'kɑ:də) cigarra
cockroach ('kokroutʃ) cucaracha
cricket ('krikit) grillo

Dragonfly ('drægənflai) libélula

Firefly ('faiəflai) luciérnaga
flea (fli:) pulga
fly (flai) mosca

Grasshopper ('grɑ:shopə) saltamontes

Ladybird ('leidibə:d) mariquita
leech (li:tʃ) sanguijuela
lice (lais) piojos
locust ('loukəst) langosta
louse (laus) piojo
  crab louse ('kræblaus) ladilla

Mantis ('mæntis) mantis
mosquito (məs'ki:tou) mosquito
moth (moθ) polilla

Scorpion ('sko:piən) escorpión, alacrán
spider ('spaidə) araña

Tarantula (tə'ræntjulə) tarántula
termite ('tə:mait) termita

Wasp (wosp) avispa
worm (wə:m) gusano
  earthworm ('ə:θwə:m) lombriz
  glow-worm ('glouwə:m) luciérnaga
  silkworm ('silkwə:m) gusano de seda
  tapeworm ('teipwə:m) solitaria

INSTRUMENTS (See TOOLS, 89; See MUSICAL INSTRUMENTS, 65)

52

JEWELLERY	JOYERIA (57)
ENGLISH	ESPAÑOL

Agate ('ægət) — ágata
aquamarine (ækwəmə'ri:n) — aguamarina
amber ('æmbə) — ámbar
amethyst ('æmiθist) — amatista

Bracelet ('breislit) — pulsera
brilliant ('briliənt) — piedra preciosa tallada
brooch (broutʃ) — broche

Cameo ('kæmiou) — camafeo
carat ('kærət) — quilate

Diamond ('daləmənd) — diamante, brillante

Earring ('iəriŋ) — pendiente
emerald ('emərəld) — esmeralda
enamel (i'næməl) — esmalte
enamelled (i'næməld) — esmaltado

Gem (dʒem) — gema
gemstone ('dʒemstoun) — gema
gold (gould) — oro
goldsmith ('gouldsmiθ) — orfebre

Jade (dʒeid) — jade
jewel ('dʒu:əl) — joya
jeweller ('dʒu:ələ) — joyero

Mount (maunt) — montura

Necklace ('nekləs) — collar

Opal ('oupl) — ópalo

Pearl (pə:l) — perla
pendent ('pendənt) — colgante
platinum ('plætinəm) — platino

Ring (riŋ) — sortija, anillo
  diamond ring ('daiəmənd'riŋ) — sortija de brillantes
  finger ring ('fiŋgəriŋ) — sortija

JEWELLERY   JOYERÍA

wedding-ring	('wediŋriŋ)	anillo de boda
signet ring	('signitriŋ)	sortija de sello
ruby	('ru:bi)	rubí
Sapphire	('sæfaiə)	zafiro
set, to	(tə'set)	engastar
silver	('silvə)	plata
solitaire	('soli'teə)	solitario
stone	(stoun)	piedra
precious stone	('preʃəs'stoun)	piedra preciosa
semi-precious stone	('semi'preʃəs'stoun)	piedra semi-preciosa
Topaz	('toupæz)	topacio
turquoise	('tə:kwɑ:z)	turquesa

53

KITCHEN, A   UNA COCINA (23)

ENGLISH   ESPAÑOL

Baking-tin	('beikiŋtin)	chapa de enhornar
bottle-opener	('botl oupənə)	abrebotellas
bowl	(boul)	tazón, ensaladera
breadbin	('bredbin)	recipiente para el pan
Cap-lifter	('kæpliftə)	abrebotellas
casserole	('kæsəroul)	cacerola
chopping-board	('tʃopiŋbo:d)	tabla de picar
cook	(kuk)	cocinero
cooker	('kukə)	cocina (mueble)
pressure cooker	('preʃəkukə)	olla de presión
colander	('kʌləndə)	colador
corkscrew	('ko:kskru:)	sacacorchos
Dishwasher	('diʃwoʃə)	lavavajillas
draining-board	('dreiniŋbo:d)	escurreplatos
Fridge	(fridʒ)	frigorífico
frying-pan	('fraiiŋpæn)	sartén

KITCHEN, A — UNA COCINA

funnel ('fʌnəl) — embudo
Gas-ring ('gæsriŋ) — hornillo de gas
geyser ('gi:zə) — termo de agua caliente
Heater ('hi:tə) — calentador, hornillo
 electric heater (i'lektrik'hi:tə) — hornillo eléctrico
 water-heater ('wo:təhi:tə) — calentador de agua
Jar (dʒa:) — tarro
Kettle ('ketl) — marmita
kitchen-cupboard ('kitʃənkʌbəd) — armario de cocina
kitchen implements ('kitʃənimplimənts) — utensilios de cocina
kitchen sink ('kitʃən'sink) — fregadero
kitchen range ('kitʃən'reindʒ) — fogón
kitchen scales ('kitʃənskeilz) — balanza
kitchen stove ('kitʃənstouv) — cocina (mueble)
kitchen utensils ('kitʃənju:'tensilz) — utensilios de cocina
kitchenware ('kitʃənweə) — batería de cocina
Ladle ('leidl) — cazo
 soup ladle ('su:pleidl) — cazo
larder ('la:də) — despensa
lemon squeezer ('lemənskwi:zə) — esprimelimones
lid (lid) — tapadera
Mincer ('minsə) — picador de carne
mixer ('miksə) — batidora
 electric mixer (i'lektrik'miksə) — batidora eléctrica
Oven ('ʌvən) — horno
Pan (pæn) — cazuela
pantry ('pæntri) — despensa
plug (plʌg) — tapón del desagüe
pot (pot) — cacerola, puchero
Range (reindʒ) — fogón
refrigerator (ri'fridʒəreitə) — frigorífico
refuse bin ('refju:sbin) — cubo de la basura
rolling-pin ('rouliŋpin) — rodillo (para amasar)
Saucepan ('so:spən) — cazuela
sink (siŋk) — fregadero
skewer ('skju:ə) — broqueta

| KITCHEN, A | UNA COCINA |

skillet ('skilit)	cacerola de mango largo
skimmer ('skimə)	espumadera
stove (stouv)	cocina (mueble)
electric stove (i'lektrik'stouv)	cocina eléctrica
gas-stove ('gæsstouv)	cocina de gas
strainer ('streinə)	colador
pointed strainer ('pointid'streinə)	colador en forma de cono
Tap (tæp)	grifo
tin-opener ('tinoupənə)	abrelatas
toaster ('toustə)	tostador
Washer ('woʃə)	lavadora
washing-machine ('woʃiŋməʃi:n)	lavadora
whisk (wisk)	batidor

54

LAW, THE   LA LEY (58)

ENGLISH	ESPAÑOL
Accusation (ækju'zeiʃən)	acusación
accuse, to (tuə'kju:z)	acusar
accused, the (ðiə'kju:zd)	el acusado
accuser (ə'kju:zə)	acusador
advocate ('ædvəkit)	letrado
arrest (ə'rest)	arresto
under arrest ('ʌndərə'rest)	arrestado
arrest, to (tuə'rest)	arrestar
attorney (ə'tə:ni)	apoderado, abogado
attorney at law (ə'tə:niət'lo:)	procurador
Barrister ('bæristə)	abogado
burglar ('bə:glə)	ladrón
burglary ('bə:gləri)	robo
Code (koud)	código
confess, to (təkən'fes)	confesar
constable ('kʌnstəbl)	guardia

| LAW, THE | LA LEY |

counsel for the defence
('kaunsəlfəðədi'fens) — abogado defensor
court (ko:t) — tribunal de justicia
courthouse ('ko:thaus) — palacio de justicia
court martial ('ko:t'ma:ʃəl) — consejo de guerra
court of justice
('ko:təv'dʒʌstis) — sala de justicia
crime (kraim) — delito
criminal ('kriminəl) — delincuente

Damages ('dæmidʒiz) — daños y perjuicios
defence (di'fens) — defensa
defend, to (tədi'fend) — defender
dock (dok) — banquillo de los acusados
duty ('dju:ti) — deber

Fine (fain) — multa
fine to (tə'fain) — multar

Gaol (dʒeil) — cárcel

Illegal (i'li:gəl) — ilegal
indemnification
(indemnifi'keiʃən) — indemnización
indemnify, to (tuin'demnifai) — indemnizar

Jail (dʒeil) — cárcel
judge (dʒʌdʒ) — juez
jurist ('dʒuərist) — jurista
jury ('dʒuəri) — jurado

Law (lo:) — ley
natural law ('nætʃərəl'lo:) — ley natural
law-breaker ('lo:breikə) — transgresor de la ley
lawful ('lo:ful) — legal
law-maker ('lo:meikə) — legislador
law of nations ('lo:əv'neiʃənz) — derecho internacional
law student ('lo:stju:dənt) — estudiante de derecho
law-suit ('lo:su:t) — pleito
lawyer ('lo:jə) — abogado
legal ('li:gəl) — legal
legal adviser ('li:gələd'vaizə) — asesor jurídico
legislate, to (tə'ledʒisleit) — legislar
legislation (ledʒis'leiʃən) — legislación

Magistrate ('mædʒistrit) — magistrado
murder ('mə:də) — homicidio

murderer ('mə:dərə)	homicida
Notary ('noutəri)	notario
Police, the (ðəpə'li:s)	la policía
policeman (pə'li:smən)	guardia, policia
police-officer (pə'li:sofisə)	agente de policia
police-station (pə'li:ssteiʃən)	comisaría
policewoman (pə'li:swumən)	mujer policía
prison ('prizən)	prisión
prisoner ('prizənə)	detenido
prosecute, to (tə'prosikju:t)	procesar
prosecution (prosi'kju:ʃən)	procesamiento
prosecutor ('prosikju:tə)	demandante
public prosecutor ('pʌblik'prosikju:tə)	fiscal
punish, to (tə'pʌniʃ)	castigar
punishment ('pʌniʃmənt)	castigo
Rob, to (tə'rob)	robar (en un lugar, a una persona)
robbery ('robəri)	robo
Sentence ('sentəns)	sentencia
sentence, to (tə'sentəns)	sentenciar
solicitor (sə'lisitə)	procurador
stand (stænd)	estrado de los testigos
steal, to (tə'sti:l)	robar (un objeto)
sue, to (tə'sju:)	demandar
suit (su:t)	pleito
Testify, to (tə'testifai)	testificar
theft (θeft)	robo
thief (θi:f)	ladrón
trial ('traiəl)	juicio
Unlawful (ʌn'lo:fəl)	ilegal
Verdict ('və:dikt)	veredicto
Witness ('witnis)	testigo
witness for the defence ('witnis faðə di'fens)	testigo de descargo
witness, to (tu'witnis)	atestiguar, presenciar
witness for the prosecution ('witnis faðə prosi'kju:ʃən)	testigo de cargo

55

LIFE AT HOME LA VIDA EN EL HOGAR (100)

ENGLISH ESPAÑOL

Ash-tray ('æʃtrei) cenicero
Baby ('beibi) bebé
baby-carriage ('beibikæridʒ) cochecito de niño
basket ('bɑ:skit) cesto
  shopping-basket
              ('ʃopiŋbɑ:skit) cesto de la compra
  work-basket ('wə:kbɑ:skit) costurero
bag (bæg) bolso
  shopping-bag ('ʃopiŋbæg) bolsa de la compra
bed-clothes ('bedklouðz) ropa de cama
bedspread ('bedspred) colcha
blanket ('blæŋkit) manta
breakfast ('brekfəst) desayuno
broom (bru:m) escoba
brush (brʌʃ) cepillo
bucket ('bʌkit) cubo
bulb (bʌlb) bombilla
button ('bʌtən) botón

Carpet ('kɑ:pit) alfombra
char-woman ('tʃɑ:wumən) asistenta
children ('tʃildrən) niños
clean, to (tə'kli:n) limpiar
clothes-basket ('klouðzbɑ:skit) cesto de la colada
clothes-brush ('klouðzbrʌʃ) cepillo de ropa
clothes-line ('klouðzlain) cuerda para tender la ropa
clothing* ('klouðiŋ) ropa
cook (kuk) cocinera
cook, to (tə'kuk) guisar
cot (kɔt) cuna
curtain ('kə:tən) cortina
cushion ('kuʃən) cojín

Dinner ('dinə) cena
dust, to (tə'dʌst) limpiar el polvo
duster ('dʌstə) gamuza, plumero
dustbin ('dʌstbin) cubo de basura
dustpan ('dʌstpæn) cogedor

Furniture* ('fə:nitʃə) muebles

LIFE AT HOME	LA VIDA EN EL HOGAR

Gas (gæs) — gas
gas-fire ('gæsfaiə) — estufa de gas
gas-ring ('gæsriŋ) — hornillo de gas
gas-stove ('gæsstouv) — cocina de gas

Heating ('hi:tiŋ) — calefacción
  central heating ('sentrəl'hi:tiŋ) — calefacción central
hook (huk) — percha
house-keeper ('hauski:pə) — ama de llaves
housewife ('hauswaif) — ama de casa
housework ('hauswə:k) — trabajo de la casa
husband ('hʌzbənd) — marido

Iron ('aiən) — plancha
iron, to (tu'aiən) — planchar

Key (ki:) — llave
kitchen* ('kitʃən) — cocina (habitación)
kitchenware ('kitʃənweə) — bateria de cocina

Linen ('linən) — ropa blanca
lunch (lʌntʃ) — almuerzo

Maid (meid) — criada
mat (mæt) — estera, felpudo
mattress ('mætris) — colchón
meal (mi:l) — comida
meter ('mi:tə) — contador
  electric meter (i'lektrik'mi:tə) — contador de la luz
  gas meter ('gæsmi:tə) — contador del gas
mirror ('mirə) — espejo
mop (mop) — fregasuelos

Neighbour ('neibə) — vecino
nurse (nə:s) — niñera

Pan (pæn) — cazuela
pantry ('pæntri) — despensa
parlour ('pɑ:lə) — sala
pillow ('pilou) — almohada
pillow-case ('piloukeis) — funda de almohada
play-pen ('pleipen) — parque (para un niño)
plug (plʌg) — enchufe
pram (præm) — cochecito de niño

Radio-set ('rediouset) — aparato de radio
record-player ('rekɔ:dpleiə) — tocadiscos
rent (rent) — renta
rubbish bin ('rʌbiʃbin) — cubo de basura

LIFE AT HOME

LA VIDA EN EL HOGAR

runner ('rʌnə)	tapete
Scrub, to (tə'skrʌb)	fregar (el suelo)
sew, to (tə'sou)	coser
sewing-machine ('souiŋməʃi:n)	máquina de coser
silverware ('silvəweə)	plata (objetos)
sheet (ʃi:t)	sábana
bed sheet ('bedʃi:t)	sábana
soap (soup)	jabón
stove (stouv)	cocina (mueble)
supper ('sʌpə)	cena
sweep, to (tə'swi:p)	barrer
Table-cloth ('teibəlkloθ)	mantel
tableware* ('teibəlweə)	vajilla
tapestry ('tæpistri)	tapiz
telephone ('telifoun)	teléfono
television-set ('teliviʒənset)	aparato de televisión
towel ('tauəl)	toalla
tray (trei)	bandeja
Vacuum cleaner ('vækjuəmkli:nə)	aspiradora
vase (vɑ:z)	florero
Wash, to (tu'woʃ)	lavar
wash-disher ('woʃdiʃə)	lavaplatos
washing-machine ('woʃiŋməʃi:n)	lavadora
wash up, to (tu'woʃ'ʌp)	fregar (la vajilla)
wife (waif)	esposa
window curtain ('windoukə:tən)	visillo
work-basket ('wə:kbɑ:skit)	costurero
work-box ('wə:kboks)	costurero

56

LIFE AT SCHOOL

LA VIDA EN LA ESCUELA (99)

ENGLISH	ESPAÑOL
Algebra ('ældʒibrə)	álgebra
arithmetic* (ə'riθmətik)	aritmética

LIFE AT SCHOOL — LA VIDA EN LA ESCUELA

Ball-pen ('bo:lpen) — bolígrafo
bench (bentʃ) — banco
blackboard ('blækbo:d) — encerado
boarder ('bo:də) — alumno interno
  day-boarder ('deibo:də) — pensionista
board of examiners ('bo:dəvig'zæminəz) — tribunal de examen
book (buk) — libro
  reference book ('refərənsbuk) — libro de consulta
  test-book ('tekstbuk) — libro de texto

Chalk (tʃo:k) — tiza
chemistry* ('kemistri) — química
class (klɑ:s) — clase
  to give a class (tə'givə'klɑ:s) — dar una clase
  to take a class (tə'teikə'klɑ:s) — tomar una clase
classroom ('klɑ:srum) — aula
college ('kolidʒ) — colegio universitario
pair of compasses, a (ə'peərəv'kʌmpəsiz) — un compás
copy-bock ('kopibuk) — cuaderno
correct, to (təkə'rəkt) — corregir
course (ko:s) — curso
crib (krib) — «chuleta»
crib, to (tə'krib) — copiar (de otro alumno), usar una "chuleta"

Degree (di'gri:) — título universitario
  doctor's degree ('doktəzdigri:) — doctorado
desk (desk) — pupitre
dictation (dik'teiʃən) — dictado
dictionary ('dikʃənəri) — diccionario
draw, to (tə'dro:) — dibujar
drawing ('dro:iŋ) — dibujo
duster ('dʌstə) — gamuza para limpiar el encerado

Essay ('esei) — redacción
exam (ig'zæm) — examen
examination (igzæmi'neiʃən) — examen
entrance examination ('entrənsigzæmi'neiʃən) — examen de admisión
to fail an examination (tə'feilənigzæmi'neiʃən) — suspender un examen

LIFE AT SCHOOL — LA VIDA EN LA ESCUELA

oral examination
    ('ɔrəligzæmi'neiʃən) — examen oral
to pass an examination
    (tə'pɑ:sənigzæmi'neiʃən) — aprobar un examen
to sit for an examination
    (tə'sitfərənigzæmi'neiʃən) — presentarse a examen
to take an examination
    (tə'teikənigzæmi'neiʃən) — examinarse
written examination
    ('ritənigzæmi'neiʃən) — examen escrito
examine, to (tuig'zæmin) — examinar
examinee (igzæmi'ni:) — examinando
examiner (ig'zæminə) — examinador
exam-paper (ig'zæmpeipə) — supuesto de examen
exercise ('eksəsaiz) — ejercicio
  to do an exercise
    (tə'du:ən'eksəsaiz) — hacer un ejercicio
exercise-book ('eksəsaizbuk) — cuaderno

Fail, to (tə'feil) — suspender
failed (feild) — suspenso

Geography* (dʒi'ɔgrəfi) — geografía
geometry* (dʒi'ɔmətri) — geometría
general knowledge
    ('dʒenərəl'nɔlidʒ) — cultura general
graduate ('grædjuit) — licenciado
grammar ('græmə) — gramática

Headmaster ('hed,mɑ:stə) — director
headmistress ('hed,mistris) — directora
history* ('histəri) — historia
  natural history
    ('nætʃərəl'histəri) — historia natural
holidays* ('hɔlidiz) — vacaciones
homework ('houmwə:k) — deberes para casa

Kindergarten ('kindəgɑ:tən) — escuela maternal

Lecture ('lektʃə) — conferencia
lecture-room ('lektʃərum) — sala de conferencias
lecturer ('lektʃərə) — conferenciante, catedrático
lesson ('lesən) — lección
letters ('letəz) — letras
librarian (lai'breəriən) — bibliotecario
library ('laibrəri) — biblioteca
  lending-library
    ('lendiŋ'laibrəri) — biblioteca de préstamo
literature* ('litərətʃə) — literatura

Map (mæp) — mapa

mark(s) (mɑːk(s))	nota(s)
to get a bad mark (təˈgetəˈbædˈmɑːk)	sacar mala nota
to get a good mark (təˈgetəˈgudˈmɑːk)	sacar buena nota
mathematics* (mæθəˈmætiks)	matemáticas
Note-book (ˈnoutbuk)	cuaderno
Pass, to (təˈpɑːs)	aprobar
passed (pɑːst)	aprobado
pen (pen)	pluma
pencil (ˈpensl)	lápiz
pencil-box (ˈpenselboks)	caja de lápices
physical-training (ˈfizikəlˈtreiniŋ)	educación física física
physics (ˈfiziks)	estrado
platform (ˈplæfoːm)	terreno de juego
play-ground (ˈpleigraund)	hacer novillos
play truant, to (təˈpleitruːənt)	profesor universitario
professor (prəˈfesə)	«soplar» (un alumno a otro)
prompt, to (təˈprompt)	
Reading (ˈriːdiŋ)	lectura
reading-book (ˈriːdiŋbuk)	libro de lectura
reading-room (ˈriːdiŋrum)	sala de lectura
rubber (ˈrʌbə)	goma de borrar
ruler (ˈruːlə)	regla
Satchel (ˈsætʃəl)	cartera de colegial
science (ˈsaiəns)	ciencia
exact sciences (igˈzæktˈsaiənsiz)	ciencias exactas
natural sciences (ˈnætʃərəlˈsaiənsiz)	ciencias naturales
school (skuːl)	escuela, colegio
boarding-school (ˈboːdiŋskuːl)	internado
boys' school (ˈboizskuːl)	escuela de niños
day-school (ˈdeiskuːl)	escuela diurna
girls' school (ˈgəːlzskuːl)	escuela de niñas
grammar school (ˈgræməskuːl)	escuela elemental
high school (ˈhaiskuːl)	escuela secundaria
infant school (ˈinfəntskuːl)	escuela maternal
mixed school (ˈmikstˈskuːl)	escuela mixta
night-school (ˈnaitskuːl)	escuela nocturna
primary-school (ˈpraiməriˈskuːl)	escuela primaria

LIFE AT SCHOOL

public school ('pʌblik'sku:l)	internado privado (GB)
secondary school ('sekəndəri'sku:l)	escuela secundaria
technical school ('teknikəl'sku:l)	escuela profesional
schoolboy ('sku:lboi)	colegial
school-fellow ('sku:lfelou)	condiscípulo
schoolgirl ('sku:lgə:l)	colegiala
school-master ('sku:lmɑ:stə)	maestro de escuela
school-mistress ('sku:lmistris)	maestra de escuela
spelling ('spelin)	ortografía
spelling mistake ('spelinmisteik)	falta de ortografía
student ('stju:dənt)	estudiante
day-student ('deistju:dənt)	estudiante externo
law-student ('lo:stju:dənt)	estudiante de derecho
medical-student ('medikəl'stju:dənt)	estudiante de medicina
study ('stʌdi)	estudio
study, to (tə'stʌdi)	estudiar
subject ('sʌbdʒikt)	asignatura
syllabus ('siləbəs)	programa de estudios
Teach, to (tə'ti:tʃ)	enseñar
teacher ('ti:tʃə)	profesor, profesora
art teacher ('ɑ:tti:tʃə)	profesor de arte
language teacher ('læŋgwidʒti:tʃə)	profesor de idiomas
man-teacher ('mæn'ti:tʃə)	profesor
music teacher ('mju:zikti:tʃə)	profesor de música
private teacher ('praivit'ti:tʃə)	profesor particular
woman-teacher ('wumən'ti:tʃə)	profesora
teaching ('ti:tʃiŋ)	enseñanza
test (test)	test
thesis ('θi:sis)	tesis
Undergraduate (ʌndə'grædjuit)	estudiante universitario
Vacation (və'keiʃən)	vacaciones
Writing ('raitiŋ)	escritura

57

LITERATURE   LITERATURA (59)

ENGLISH	ESPAÑOL
Allegory ('æligəri)	alegoría
anon (ə'non)	anónimo
anonymus (ə'noniməs)	anónimo
anthology (æn'θolədʒi)	antología
author ('o:θə)	autor
authoress ('o:θəris)	autora
Ballad ('bæləd)	balada
best seller ('best'selə)	libro de gran éxito
biographer (bai'ogrəfə)	biógrafo
biography (bai'ogrəfi)	biografía
book (buk)	libro
Canto ('kæntou)	canto (en un poema)
chapter ('tʃæptə)	capítulo
classical ('klæsikl)	clásico
comedy ('komədi)	comedia
compiler (kəm'pailə)	recopilador
copy ('kopi)	ejemplar
couplet ('kʌplit)	estrofa, copla
critic ('kritik)	crítico
Drama ('drɑ:mə)	teatro (género literario)
dramatist ('dræmətist)	dramaturgo
describe, to (tədis'kraib)	describir
description (dis'kripʃən)	descripción
Edition (i'diʃən)	edición
elegy ('elidʒi)	elegía
Elizabethan (ilizə'bi:θən)	isabelino
epic ('epik)	epopeya
epigram ('epigræm)	epigrama
epistle (i'pisl)	epístola
Hymn (him)	himno
Incomplete (inkəm'pli:t)	incompleto
influence ('influəns)	influencia
inspire, to (tuins'paiə)	inspirar

LITERATURE   LITERATURA

Languaje ('læŋgwidʒ)	lenguaje
Latin ('lætin)	latín
letter ('letə)	carta
literary ('litərəri)	literario
literary price ('litərəri'prais)	premio literario
literature ('litərətʃə)	literatura
lyric ('lirik)	poema lírico
lyrical ('lirikl)	lírico
lyrics ('liriks)	letra de una canción
Manuscript ('mænjuskript)	manuscrito
masterpiece ('mɑ:stəpi:s)	obra maestra
metaphor ('metəfə)	metáfora
poetic metaphor (pou'etik'metəfə)	metáfora poética
metre ('mi:tə)	metro
muse (mju:z)	musa
mystic ('mistik)	místico (sus. y adj.)
mysticism ('mistisizəm)	misticismo
Novel ('novl)	novela
novelist ('novəlist)	novelista
Ode (oud)	oda
Passage ('pæsidʒ)	párrafo
pen-name ('penneim)	pseudónimo
period ('piəriəd)	período
play (plei)	obra de teatro
playwright ('pleirait)	dramaturgo
poem ('pouim)	poema
poet ('pouit)	poeta
lyrical poet ('lirikəl'pouit)	poeta lírico
metaphysical poet (metə'fizikəl'pouit)	poeta metafísico
mystical poet ('mistikəl'pouit)	poeta místico
Romantic poet (rə'mæntik'pouit)	poeta romántico
poetess ('pouitis)	poetisa
poetic(al) (pou'etik(əl))	poético
poetry ('pouitri)	poesía
epic poetry ('epik'pouitri)	poesía épica
lyrical poetry ('lirikəl'pouitri)	poesía lírica
religious poetry (ri'lidʒəs'pouitri)	poesía religiosa
precursor (pri:'kə:sə)	precursor
print, to (tə print)	imprimir

LITERATURE — LITERATURA

print, in (in'print) — en prensa (un libro)
print, ouf of ('autəv'print) — agotado (un libro)
printer ('printə) — impresor
prose (prouz) — prosa
psalm (sɑ:m) — salmo
publish, to (tə'pʌbliʃ) — publicar
publisher ('pʌbliʃə) — editor

Read, to (tə'ri:d) — leer
reader ('ri:də) — lector
recital (ri'saitl) — recital
recite, to (təri'sait) — recitar
rhetoric ('retərik) — retórica
rhyme (raim) — rima
rhyme, to (tə'raim) — rimar
romance (rə'mæns) — romance
romantic (rə'mæntik) — romántico
romanticism (rə'mæntisizəm) — romanticismo

Satire ('sætaiə) — sátira
satirical (sə'tirikl) — satírico
satirist ('sætirist) — escritor satírico
school (sku:l) — escuela
script (skript) — guión
sermon ('sə:mən) — sermón
song (soŋ) — canción
sonnet ('sonit) — soneto
stanza ('stænzə) — estrofa
story ('sto:ri) — historia, narración
 short story ('ʃo:t'sto:ri) — historia corta
story teller ('sto:ritelə) — narrador
style (stail) — estilo
subject ('sʌbdʒikt) — tema

Tale (teil) — cuento
theme (θi:m) — tema
title ('taitl) — título
tragedy ('trædʒədi) — tragedia
translate, to (tətræns'leit) — traducir
translation (træns'leiʃən) — traducción

Verse (və:s) — verso
 blank verse ('blæŋk'və:s) — verso libre
 rhymed verse ('raimd'və:s) — verso rimado
volume ('volju:m) — volumen

Work(s) (wə:k(s)) — obra(s)
write, to (tə'rait) — escribir

writer ('raitə) escritor
writings ('raitiŋz) escritos
  prose writings
          ('prouzraitiŋz) escritos en prosa

58

MAMMALS — MAMIFEROS (60)

ENGLISH — ESPAÑOL

DOMESTIC ANIMALS — ANIMALES DOMESTICOS

Ass (æs) — burro

Calf (kɑ:f) — ternera
cat (kæt) — gato
colt (koult) — potro
cow (kau) — vaca

Dog (dog) — perro
  bulldog ('buldog) — perro de presa
  Newfoundland dog
          (nju'faundlənddog) — perro de Terranova
  police-dog (pə'li:sdog) — perro policía
  shepherd's dog
          ('ʃepədzdog) — perro pastor
  St. Bernard dog
          (sənt'bə:nəddog) — perro San Bernardo
  watch-dog ('wotʃdog) — perro guardián
donkey ('doŋki) — burro

Ewe (ju:) — oveja hembra

Filly (fili) — potranca
foal (foul) — potro

Goat (gout) — cabra
Great Dane ('greit'dein) — gran danés
greyhound ('greihaund) — galgo

Hack (hæk) — rocín

| MAMMALS | MAMÍFEROS |

heifer ('hefə)   vaquilla
hog (hog)   cerdo
horse (ho:s)   caballo
  draught-horse ('drɑ:ftho:s)   caballo de tiro
  race-horse ('reisho:s)   caballo de carreras
  saddle-horse ('sædəlho:s)   caballo de silla
  stud-horse ('stʌdho:s)   semental
hound (haund)   perro de caza

Kid (kid)   cabrito
kitten ('kitən)   gatito

Lamb (læm)   cordero

Mare (meə)   yegua
mastiff ('mæstif)   mastín
mule (mju:l)   mula, mulo

Ox (oks)   buey

Pig (pig)   cerdo
piglet ('piglit)   cerdito
pony ('pouni)   caballito
poodle ('pu:dl)   caniche
puppy ('pʌpi)   perrito, cachorro

Rabbit ('ræbit)   conejo
ram (ræm)   carnero

Sheep (ʃi:p)   oveja, s
sow (sau)   cerda
stallion ('stæliən)   semental
steed (sti:d)   corcel
swine (swain)   cerdo

WILD ANIMALS   ANIMALES SALVAJES

Ant-eater ('ænti:tə)   oso hormiguero
ape (eip)   mono
armadillo (ɑ:mə'dilou)   armadillo

Baboon (bə'bu:n)   mandril
badger ('bædʒə)   tejón
bat (bæt)   murciélago
bear (beə)   oso
  brown bear ('braun'beə)   oso pardo
  polar bear ('poulə'beə)   oso polar
bear cub ('beəkʌb)   osezno
beaver ('bi:və)   castor
bison ('baisən)   bisonte
boar ('bo:)   jabalí

MAMMALS	MAMÍFEROS
buck (bʌk)	gamo
buffalo ('bʌfəlou)	búfalo
bull (bul)	toro
Camel ('kæməl)	camello
chamois ('ʃæmwɑː)	ante
chimpanzee (tʃimpən'ziː)	chimpancé
cub (kʌb)	cachorro
Deer (diə)	ciervo
doe (dou)	hembra del gamo
dolphin ('dolfin)	delfín
dormouse ('doːmaus)	lirón
dromedary ('droməderi)	dromedario
duck-billed platypus ('dʌkbild'plætipəs)	ornitorrinco
Elephant ('elifənt)	elefante
elk (elk)	alce
Ferret ('ferit)	hurón
fox (foks)	zorro
Gazelle (gə'zel)	gacela
gibbon ('gibən)	gibón
giraffe (dʒi'rɑːf)	jirafa
Hare (heə)	liebre
hart (hɑːt)	venado
hedgehog ('hedʒhog)	erizo
hind (haind)	cierva
hippopotamus (hipə'potəməs)	hipopótamo
hyena (hai'iːnə)	hiena
Kangaroo (kæŋgə'ruː)	canguro
Leopard ('lepəd)	leopardo
lion ('laiən)	león
lioness ('laiənis)	leona
llama ('lɑːmə)	llama
lynx (liŋks)	lince
Marmot ('mɑːmət)	marmota
marten ('mɑːtin)	marta
mice (mais)	ratones
mink (miŋk)	visón
mole (moul)	topo
monkey ('mʌŋki)	mono
mouse (maus)	ratón
Ocelot ('ousilot)	ocelote
orang-outang ('oːrəŋ'uːtæŋ)	orangután
otter ('otə)	nutria

MAMMALS / MAMÍFEROS

Panther ('pænθə)	pantera
polecat ('poulkæt)	mofeta
porcupine ('po:kjupain)	puercoespín
porpoise ('po:pəs)	marsopa
puma ('pju:mə)	puma
Racoon (rə'ku:n)	mapache
rat (ræt)	rata
reindeer ('reindiə)	reno
rhinoceros (rai'nosərəs)	rinoceronte
Seal (si:l)	foca
sea lion ('si:laiən)	león marino
skunk (skʌŋk)	mofeta
sloth (slouθ)	perezoso
squirrel ('skwirəl)	ardilla
stag (stæg)	venado
Tapir ('teipə)	tapir
tiger ('taigə)	tigre
tigress ('taigris)	tigresa
Walrus ('wo:lrəs)	morsa
whale (weil)	ballena
sperm whale ('spə:mweil)	cachalote
wildboar ('waild'bo:)	jabalí
wildcat ('waild'kæt)	gato montés
wolf (wulf)	lobo
Yak (jæk)	yak
Zebra ('zi:brə)	cebra

MATHEMATICS   (See ARITHMETIC, 8)

MEASURES   (See WEIGHTS, 98)

59

MECHANICS / MECANICA (62)

ENGLISH	ESPAÑOL
Axle ('æksəl)	eje

| MECHANICS | MECÁNICA |

Ball-bearing   ('bo:lbeəriŋ) — cojinete de bolas
bolt   (boult) — perno

Crank   (kræŋk) — manivela
crank arm   ('kræŋk ɑ:m) — brazo de la manivela
cylinder   ('silində) — cilindro

Dynamics   (dai'næmiks) — dinámica

Equilibrium   (i:kwi'libriəm) — equilibrio

Force   (fo:s) — fuerza
fulcrum   ('fʌlkrəm) — fulcro

Gear   (giə) — engranaje
  worm gear   ('wə:mgiə) — tornillo sin fin
gearing   ('giəriŋ) — engranaje
gear tooth   ('giətu:θ) — diente de engranaje

Joint   (dʒoint) — articulación

Lever   ('li:və) — palanca

Motion   ('mouʃən) — movimiento

Nut   (nʌt) — tuerca

Pawl   (po:l) — trinquete
pulley   ('puli) — polea

Rod   (rod) — vástago
  connecting-rod   (kə'nektiŋrod) — biela

Screw   (skru:) — tornillo
shaft   ('ʃɑ:ft) — árbol

Wedge   (wedʒ) — cuña
weight   (weit) — peso
wheel   (wi:l) — rueda
  flywheel   ('flaiwi:l) — volante
  free wheel   ('fri:'wi:l) — rueda loça
  gear wheels   ('giəwi:lz) — juego de ruedas dentadas
  toothed wheel   ('tu:ðd'wi:l) — rueda dentada

60

METALLURGY   METALURGIA (64)

ENGLISH	ESPAÑOL
Alloy (ə'loi)	aleación
anvil ('ænvil)	yunque
Bar (bɑ:)	barra
Cast, to (tə'kɑ:st)	fundir
cool, to (tə'ku:l)	enfriar
cooling ('ku:liŋ)	enfriamiento
crucible ('kru:sibl)	crisol
Density ('densiti)	densidad
ductility (dʌk'tiliti)	ductibilidad
Flexibility (fleksi'biliti)	flexibilidad
flexible ('fleksibl)	flexible
forge (fo:dʒ)	fragua
foundry ('faundri)	fundición
iron foundry ('aiənfaundri)	fundición de hierro
furnace ('fə:nis)	horno
blast-furnace ('blɑ:st'fə:nis)	alto horno
fusibility (fju:zi'biliti)	fusibilidad
Hard (hɑ:d)	duro
to harden (tə'hɑ:dən)	endurecer(se)
hardness ('hɑ:dnis)	dureza
heat, to (tə'hi:t)	calentar
heating ('hi:tiŋ)	calentamiento
Ingot ('iŋgət)	lingote
iron ('aiən)	hierro
cast iron ('kɑ:st'aiən)	hierro colado
pig iron ('pigaiən)	hierro en lingotes
scrap iron ('skræpaiən)	chatarra
wrought iron ('ro:t'aiən)	hierro forjado
Lustre ('lʌstə)	lustre
Malleability (mæliə'biliti)	maleabilidad
malleable ('mæliəbl)	maleable
melt, to (tə'melt)	derretir(se)
metal ('metl)	metal
metallurgical (metə'lə:dʒikl)	metalúrgico (adj.)

| METALLURGY | | METALURGIA |

metallurgist (mə'tælədʒist) metalúrgico (sus.)
mineral ('minərəl) mineral

Ore (o:) mineral

Shape (ʃeip) forma
shape, to (tə'ʃeip) dar forma
sheet (ʃi:t) plancha (de metal)
smelt, to (tə'smelt) fundir
solder, to (tə'soldə) soldar
soldering ('soldəriŋ) soldadura
solidify (sə'lidifai) solidificarse

Weld, to (tu'weld) soldar
welding ('weldiŋ) soldadura
wire ('waiə) alambre

61

| METALS, MINERALS AND ALLOYS | METALES, MINERALES Y ALEACIONES (63) |

| ENGLISH | ESPAÑOL |

Aluminium (ælju'miniəm) aluminio
antimony ('æntiməni) antimonio
asbestos (æz'bestəs) asbesto
azurite ('æʒərait) azurita

Barytes (bə'raiti:z) barita
basalt ('bæso:lt) basalto
bauxite ('bo:ksait) bauxita
beryl ('beril) berilo
blende (blend) blenda
brass (brɑ:s) latón
bronze (bronz) bronce

Cadmium ('kædmiəm) cadmio
cassiterite (kə'sitərait) casiterita
chromium ('kroumiəm) cromo
cinnabar ('sinəbɑ:) cinabrio
coal (koul) carbón
copper ('kopə) cobre

Duralumin (djuə'ræljumin) duraluminio

| METALS, MINERALS, ETC. | METALES, MINERALES, ETC. |

Feldspar ('feldspɑ:)   feldespato
flint (flint)   pedernal

Galena (gə'li:nə)   galena
gold (gould)   oro
granite ('grænit)   granito
graphite ('græfait)   grafito

Iridium (ai'ridiəm)   iridio
iron ('aiən)   hierro

Kaolin ('keiəlin)   caolín

Lead (led)   plomo
lignite ('lignait)   lignito

Manganese (mæŋgə'ni:z)   manganeso
marble ('mɑ:bl)   mármol
mercury ('mə:kjuri)   mercurio
mica ('maikə)   mica

Nickel ('nikl)   níquel

Platinum ('plætinəm)   platino
pyrites (pai'raiti:z)   pirita

Quartz ('kwo:ts)   cuarzo

Radium ('reidiəm)   radio

Salt (so:lt)   sal
siderite ('saidərait)   siderita
silver ('silvə)   plata
steel (sti:l)   acero

Tin (tin)   estaño
titanium (tai'teiniəm)   titanio

Uranium (juə'reiniəm)   uranio

Zinc (ziŋk)   cinc

62

METEOROLOGY	METEOROLOGIA (65)
ENGLISH	ESPAÑOL

Air (eə)	aire
alto-cumulus	
('æltou'kju:mjuləs)	alto-cúmulo
alto-stratus ('æltou'streitəs)	alto-estrato
atmospheric conditions	
(ætməs'ferikkən'diʃənz)	condiciones atmosféricas
atmospheric pressure	
(ætməs'ferik'preʃə)	presión atmosférica
Barometer (bə'romitə)	barómetro
barometric pressure	
(bærə'metrik'preʃə)	presión barométrica
breeze (bri:z)	brisa
Calm (kɑ:m)	calma
cirro-cumulus	
('sirou'kju:mjuləs)	cirro-cúmulos
cirro-stratus ('sirou'streitəs)	cirroestratos
cirrus ('sirəs)	cirro
climate ('klaimit)	clima
cloud (klaud)	nube
cloudless ('klaudlis)	despejado
cloudy ('klaudi)	nublado
cold (kould)	frío
cumulo-nimbus	
('kju:mjulou'nimbəs)	cúmulo-nimbo
cumulus ('kju:mjuləs)	cúmulo
cyclone ('saikloun)	ciclón
Drizzle ('drizl)	llovizna
drizzle, to (tə'drizl)	lloviznar
Fog (fog)	niebla
foggy ('fogi)	nuboso
freeze, to (tə'fri:z)	helar
frost (frost)	escarcha
Gale (geil)	ventarrón
Hail (heil)	granizo
hail, to (tə'heil)	granizar

| METEOROLOGY | METEOROLOGÍA |

haze   (heiz)   bruma
heat   (hi:t)   calor
hurricane   ('hʌrikən)   huracán

Lightning   ('laitniŋ)   rayo, relámpago

Mist   (mist)   neblina
misty   ('misti)   nebuloso

Nimbus   ('nimbəs)   nimbo

Rain   (rein)   lluvia
rain, to   (tə'rein)   llover
rainbow   ('reinbou)   arco iris
rainfall   ('reinfo:l)   aguacero
rainy   ('reini)   lluvioso
rough sea   ('rʌf'si:)   mar gruesa

Shower   ('ʃauə)   chaparrón
sky   (skai)   cielo
smooth sea   ('smu:θ'si:)   mar rizada
snow   (snou)   nieve
snow, to   (tə'snou)   nevar
storm   (sto:m)   tormenta
sunny   ('sʌni)   soleado

Temperature   ('temprətʃə)   temperatura
thermometer   (θə'momitə)   termómetro
thunder   ('θʌndə)   trueno
thunder, to   (tə'θʌndə)   tronar
thunder-storm   ('θʌndəsto:m)   tormenta

Vortex   ('vo:teks)   vórtice

Wave   ('weiv)   ola
weather   ('weðə)   tiempo atmosférico
weather forecast   ('weðəfo:ka:st)   predicción del tiempo
weather-man   ('weðamæn)   hombre del tiempo
weather-map   ('weðəmæp)   mapa del tiempo
weather-ship   ('weðəʃip)   barco meteorológico
wind   (wind)   viento
   whirlwind   ('wə:lwind)   remolino

MINERALS   (See METALS, 1)

63

MINING   MINERIA (66)

ENGLISH	ESPAÑOL
Blasting-cartridge ('blɑːstiŋ'kɑːtridʒ)	barreno
Cage (keidʒ)	ascensor
coal (koul)	carbón
coalfield ('koulfiːld)	yacimiento de carbón
coalmine ('koulmain)	mina de carbón
coal-pit ('koulpit)	mina de carbón
coal-seam ('koulsiːm)	veta de carbón
coke (kouk)	coque
collier ('koliə)	minero de carbón
Davy-lamp ('deivilæmp)	lámpara de seguridad
diamond ('daiəmənd)	diamante
dig, to (tə'dig)	cavar
drill, to (tə'dril)	perforar
driller ('drilə)	perforadora
dynamite ('dainəmait)	dinamita
Extract, to (tuiks'trækt)	extraer
Falling-in ('foːliŋ'in)	derrumbamiento
firedamp ('faiədæmp)	grisú
Gallery ('gæləri)	galería
gold (gould)	oro
Hewer ('hjuə)	obrero que pica en una mina
hoist (hoist)	ascensor
Iron ('aiən)	hierro
iron-ore ('aiən'oː)	mineral de hierro
Layer ('leiə)	capa
lead (led)	plomo
lode (loud)	filón
Mercury ('məːkjuri)	mercurio
metal* ('metl)	metal
mine (main)	mina
mine, to (tə'main)	extraer minerales
mine-car ('mainkɑː)	vagoneta
miner ('mainə)	minero

MINING		MINERÍA

mineral* ('minərəl)   mineral
mining-engineer ('mainiŋindʒiniə)   ingeniero de minas
Nugget ('nʌgit)   pepita
  gold nugget ('gould'nʌgit)   pepita de oro
Open-cast workings ('oupənkɑ:st'wə:kiŋz)   explotación a cielo abierto
ore (o:)   mineral
Pick (pik)   pico
pit (pit)   pozo de mina
pit props ('pitprops)   entibado
Safety-lamp ('seiftilæmp)   lámpara de seguridad
shaft (ʃɑ:ft)   pozo
shovel ('ʃʌvəl)   pala
silver ('silvə)   plata
surface ('sə:fəs)   superficie
Tin (tin)   estaño
truck (trʌk)   vagoneta
tunnel ('tʌnəl)   túnel
Underground workings ('ʌndəgraund'wə:kiŋz)   explotación subterránea
Vein (vein)   veta

MOLLUSCS   (See FISH, 31)

MUSCLES   (See BONES, 14)

64

MUSIC   MUSICA (69)

ENGLISH	ESPAÑOL

A (ei)   la
B (bi:)   si
baritone ('bæritoun)   barítono
bass (beis)   bajo
baton ('bætən)   batuta

MUSIC	MÚSICA
brass band ('bræs'bænd)	banda
C (si:)	do
choir (kwaiə)	coro
chorus ('korəs)	coro
composer (kəm'pouzə)	compositor
concert ('konsət)	concierto (programa)
concert hall ('konsətho:l)	sala de conciertos
concerto (kən'tʃeətou)	concierto (pieza)
conductor (kən'dʌktə)	director de orquesta
contralto (kən'træltou)	contralto
D (di:)	re
E (i:)	mi
F (ef)	fa
G (dʒi:)	sol
guitarist (gi'ta:rist)	guitarrista
guitar player (gi'ta:pleiə)	guitarrista
Harmony ('ha:məni)	armonía
Jazz (dʒæz)	jazz
Key (ki:)	tecla
keyboard ('ki:bo:d)	teclado
key-note ('ki:nout)	nota musical
Major ('meidʒə)	mayor
march (ma:tʃ)	marcha
melody ('melədi)	melodía
minor ('mainə)	menor
music ('mju:zik)	música
chamber music ('tʃeimbəmju:zik)	música de cámara
classical music ('klæsikəl'mju:zik)	música clásica
music lover ('mju:ziklʌvə)	amante de la música
music rest ('mju:zikrest)	atril de piano
musical ('mju:zikəl)	musical
musical instrument* ('mju:zikəl'instrəmənt)	instrumento musical
musician (mju'ziʃən)	músico
music-stand ('mju:zikstænd)	atril
music stool ('mju:ziksto:l)	taburete para tocar el piano
music teacher ('mju:zikti:tʃə)	profesor de música
Note (nout)	nota
Octave ('oktiv)	octava

MUSIC		MÚSICA

opera   ('opərə)
orchestra   ('ɔːkistrə)
overture   ('ouvətjuə)

Pianist   ('piənist)
play, to   (tə'plei)

Quartet   (kwoː'tet)
quintet   (kwin'tet)

Refrain   (ri'frein)
rhythm   ('riðəm)

Scale   (skeil)
score   (skoː)
sing, to   (tə'siŋ)
song   (soŋ)
　folksong   ('foukson)
soprano   (sə'prɑːnou)
sound   (saund)
staff (stɑːf)
stave (steiv)
string   (striŋ)
symphony   ('simfəni)

Tenor   ('tenə)
treble   ('trebl)
tune   (tjuːn)
　marching tune
　　　('mɑːtʃiŋtjuːn)
tune, to   (tə'tjuːn)

Violinist   ('vaiəlinist)
voice   (vois)

Waltz   (wɔːlts)

ópera
orquesta
obertura

pianista
tocar

cuarteto
quinteto

estribillo
ritmo

escala
partitura
cantar
canción
canción folklórica
soprano
sonido
pentagrama
pentagrama
cuerda
sinfonía

tenor
tiple
melodía

marcha
afinar

violinista
voz

vals

65

MUSICAL INSTRUMENTS	INSTRUMENTOS MUSICALES (55)
ENGLISH	ESPAÑOL

Accordion   (ə'kɔːdiən)
Banjo   ('bændʒou)

acordeón
banjo

MUSICAL INSTRUMENTS — INSTRUMENTOS MUSICALES

bassoon (bə'suːn) — fagot
bass viol ('beis'vaiəl) — violón
bugle ('bjuːgl) — cornetín

Castanets (kæstə'nets) — castañuelas
cello ('tʃelou) — violoncelo
clarinet (klæri'net) — clarinete
clavichord ('klævikoːd) — clavicordio
contrabass ('kontrə'beis) — contrabajo
cornet ('koːnit) — corneta
cymbals ('smibəlz) — platillos

Double-bass ('dʌbəl'beis) — contrabajo
drum (drʌm) — tambor
  bass drum ('beis'drʌm) — bombo
  kettle drum ('ketəldrʌm) — timbal

Flute (fluːt) — flauta

Guitar (gi'tɑː) — guitarra
  steel guitar ('stiːlgi'tɑː) — guitarra eléctrica

Harp (hɑːp) — arpa
harpsicord ('hɑːpsikoːd) — arpicordio
horn (hoːn) — trompa
  bass horn ('beis'hoːn) — tuba

Instrument ('instrəmənt) — instrumento
  brass instrument ('brɑːs'instrəmənt) — instrumento de metal
  percussion instrument (pə'kʌʃəninstrəmənt) — instrumento de percusión
  stringed instrument ('striŋd'instrəmənt) — instrumento de cuerda
  wind-instrument ('windinstrəmənt) — instrumento de viento
  wood-wind instrument ('wudwind'instrəmənt) — instrumento de viento de madera

Mandolin ('mændəlin) — mandolina
mouth-organ ('mauθoːgən) — armónica
mouthpiece ('mauθpiːs) — boquilla
musical box ('mjuːzikəlboks) — caja de música

Oboe ('oubou) — oboe
organ ('oːgən) — órgano
electric organ (i'lektrik'oːgarən) — órgano eléctrico

Pedal ('pedl) — pedal

MUSICAL INSTRUMENTS	INSTRUMENTOS MUSICALES
piano ('pjɑ:nou)	piano
grand piano ('grænd'pjɑ:nou)	piano de cola
upright piano ('ʌprait'pjɑ:nou)	piano vertical
Saxophone ('sæksəfoun)	saxofón
spinet (spi'net)	espineta
Tambourine (tæmbə'ri:n)	pandereta
trombone ('trom'boun)	trombón
trumpet ('trʌmpit)	trompeta
tuba ('tju:bə)	tuba
Ukelele (jukə'leili)	ukelele
Viola ('vaiələ)	viola
violin (vaiə'lin)	violín
first violin ('fə:stvaiə'lin)	primer violín
second violin ('sekəndvaiə'lin)	segundo violín
Xilophone ('zailəfoun)	xilófono

66

NAMES / NOMBRES (72)

ENGLISH / **ESPAÑOL**

MEN'S NAMES / NOMBRES MASCULINOS

Adam ('ædəm)	Adán
Adrian ('eidriən)	Adrián
Albert ('ælbət)	Alberto
Alexander (ælig'zændə)	Alejandro
Alfred ('ælfrid)	Alfredo
Ambrose ('æmbrouz)	Ambrosio
Andrew ('ændru:)	Andrés
Andy ('ændi)	Dim. de Andrés
Anthony ('æntəni / 'ænθəni)	Antonio
Archibald ('ɑ:tʃibəld)	Archibaldo
Arthur ('ɑ:θə)	Arturo
Augustus (o'gʌstəs)	Augusto

Bartholomew (ˈbɑːˈθoləmjuː)	Bartolomé
Basil (ˈbæzil)	Basilio
Ben (ben)	Dim. de Benjamín
Benjamin (ˈbendʒəmin)	Benjamín
Bernard (ˈbəːned)	Bernardo
Bill (bill)	Dim. de William
Billy (ˈbili)	Dim. de William
Bob (bob)	Dim. de Robert
Bobby (ˈbobi)	Dim. de Robert
Charles (tʃɑːlz)	Carlos
Christopher (ˈkristəfə)	Cristóbal
Cecil (ˈsesil)	Cecilio
Claude (kloːd)	Claudio
Conrad (ˈkonræd)	Conrado
Cyril (ˈsiril)	Cirilo
Daniel (ˈdæniəl)	Daniel
David (ˈdeivid)	David
Davy (ˈdeivi)	Dim. de David
Dennis (ˈdenis)	Dionisio
Edmund (ˈedmənd)	Edmundo
Edward (ˈedwəd)	Eduardo
Ernest (ˈəːnist)	Ernesto
Ferdinand (ˈfəːdinənd)	Fernando
Francis (ˈfrɑːnsis)	Francisco
Frank (fræŋk)	Dim. de Francis
Fred (fred)	Dim. de Frederick
Freddie (ˈfredi)	Dim. de Frederick
Frederick (ˈfredrik)	Federico
George (dʒoːdʒ)	Jorge
Gerard (ˈdʒerɑːd)	Gerardo
Gilbert (ˈgilbət)	Gilberto
Gregory (ˈgregəri)	Gregorio
Harry (ˈhæri)	Dim. de Henry
Henry (ˈhenri)	Enrique
Hillary (ˈhiləri)	Hilario
Horace (ˈhorəs)	Horacio
Hugh (hjuː)	Hugo
Humbert (ˈhʌmbət)	Humberto
Jack (dʒæk)	Dim. de John
James (dʒeimz)	Jaime
Jasper (ˈdʒæspə)	Gaspar
Jerome (dʒəˈroum)	Jerónimo
Jim (dʒim)	Dim. de James
Jimmy (ˈdʒimi)	Dim. de James
Joe (dʒou)	Dim. de Joseph

NAMES	NOMBRES
Joey ('dʒoui)	Dim. de Joseph
John (dʒon)	Juan
Johnny ('dʒoni)	Dim. de John
Joseph ('dʒouzif)	José
Julian ('dʒu:liən)	Julián
Larry ('læri)	Dim. de Lawrence
Lawrence ('lo:rəns)	Lorenzo
Len (len)	Dim. de Leonard
Leo ('li:ou)	León
Leonard ('lenəd)	Leonardo
Lewis ('lu:is)	Luis
Luke (lu:k)	Lucas
Mark (mɑ:k)	Marcos
Martin ('mɑ:tin)	Martín
Matthew ('mæθju:)	Mateo
Maurice ('moris)	Mauricio
Michael ('maikl)	Miguel
Micky ('miki)	Dim. de Michael
Mike (maik)	Dim. de Michael
Ned (ned)	Dim. de Edward
Nicholas ('nikələs)	Nicolás
Nick (nik)	Dim. de Nicholas
Oliver ('olivə)	Oliverio
Pat (pæt)	Dim. de Patrick
Patrick ('pætrik)	Patricio
Paul (po:l)	Pablo
Pete (pi:t)	Dim. de Peter
Peter ('pi:tə)	Pedro
Phil (fil)	Dim. de Philip
Philip ('filip)	Felipe
Ralph (reif/rælf)	Rodolfo
Raymond ('reimənd)	Ramón
Richard ('ritʃəd)	Ricardo
Rob (rob)	Dim. de Robert
Robert ('robət)	Roberto
Robin ('robin)	Dim. de Robert
Roger ('rodʒə)	Rogelio
Sam (sæm)	Dim. de Samuel
Sammy ('sæmi)	Dim. de Samuel
Samuel ('sæmjuəl)	Samuel
Stephen ('sti:vən)	Esteban
Teddie ('tedi)	Dim. de Edward
Thomas ('toməs)	Tomás
Tim (tim)	Dim. de Timothy

Timmy ('timi)	Dim. de Timothy
Timothy ('timəθi)	Timoteo
Tom (tom)	Dim. de Thomas
Tommy ('tomi)	Dim. de Thomas
Tony ('touni)	Dim. de Anthony
Vincent ('vinsənt)	Vicente
Will (wil)	Dim. de William
William ('wiliəm)	Guillermo
Willie ('wili)	Dim. de William
Willy ('wili)	Dim. de William

WOMEN'S NAMES — NOMBRES FEMENINOS

Adelaide ('ædileid)	Adelaida
Adeline ('ædili:n)	Adelina
Agatha ('ægəθə)	Agueda
Agnes ('ægnis)	Inés
Aileen ('eili:n)	Elena
Alexandra (ælig'zɑ:ndrə)	Alejandra
Alice ('ælis)	Alicia
Alison ('ælisən)	Eloísa
Amelia (ə'mi:liə)	Amelia
Angela ('ændʒilə)	Angela
Ann (æn)	Ana
Anne (æn)	Ana
Barbara ('bɑ:bərə)	Bárbara
Beatrice ('biətris)	Beatriz
Becky ('beki)	Dim. de Rebecca
Bertha ('bə:θə)	Berta
Bess (bes)	Dim. de Elizabeth
Bessie ('besi)	Dim. de Elizabeth
Bet (bet)	Dim. de Elizabeth
Betsy ('betsi)	Dim. de Elizabeth
Betty ('beti)	Dim. de Elizabeth
Bridget ('bridʒit)	Brígida
Carol ('kærəl)	Carolina
Caroline ('kærəlain)	Carolina
Carrie ('kæri)	Dim. de Caroline
Catherine ('kæθərin)	Catalina
Cecily ('sisili)	Cecilia
Charlotte ('ʃɑ:lət)	Carlota
Christine (kris'ti:n)	Cristina
Diana (dai'ænə)	Diana
Dolly ('doli)	Dim. de Dorothy
Dorothy ('dorəθi)	Dorotea

NAMES		NOMBRES
Eleonor	('elinə)	Leonor
Elizabeth	(i'lizəbəθ)	Isabel
Ellen	('elin)	Elena
Elsa	('elsə)	Alicia
Emily	('emili)	Emilia
Emma	('emə)	Emma
Esther	('estə/'esθə)	Ester
Eve	(i:v)	Eva
Evelyn	('evlin)	Evelina
Fanny	('fæni)	Dim. de Frances
Florence	('florəns)	Florencia
Frances	('frɑ:nsis)	Francisca
Genevieve	(dʒenə'vi:v)	Genoveva
Geraldine	('dʒerəldi:n)	Gerarda
Gertrude	('gə:tru:d)	Gertrudis
Grace	(greis)	Engracia
Gwendolen	('gwendəlin)	Genoveva
Harriet	('hæriət)	Enriqueta
Helen	('helən)	Elena
Henrietta	(henri'etə)	Enriqueta
Isabella	(izə'belə)	Isabel
Jane	(dʒein)	Juana
Janet	('dʒænit)	Juana
Jean	(dʒi:n)	Dim. de Jane
Jennie	('dʒeni)	Dim. de Jane
Jenny	('dʒeni)	Dim. de Jane
Joan	(dʒoun)	Juana
Josephine	('dʒouzifi:n)	Josefina
Kate	(keit)	Dim. de Catherine
Katie	('keiti)	Dim. de Catherine
Kit	(kit)	Dim. de Catherine
Kitty	('kiti)	Dim. de Catherine
Laura	('lo:rə)	Laura
Liz	(liz)	Dim. de Elizabeth
Lizzy	('lizi)	Dim. de Elizabeth
Louise	(lu'i:z)	Luisa
Lucy	('lu:si)	Lucía
Magdalen	('mægdəlin)	Magdalena
Margaret	('mɑ:gərit)	Margarita

Marian ('meəriən)	Mariana
Marion ('meəriən)	Mariana
Marjory ('mɑːdʒəri)	Dim. de Margaret
Martha ('mɑːθə)	Marta
Mary ('meəri)	María
May (mei)	Dim. de Mary
Mollie ('moli)	Dim. de Mary
Molly ('moli)	Dim. de Mary
Monica ('monikə)	Mónica
Nan (næn)	Dim. de Ann
Nancy ('nænsi)	Dim. de Ann
Nel (nel)	Dim. de Helen
Nellie ('neli)	Dim. de Helen
Nora ('noːrə)	Nora
Pam (pæm)	Dim. de Pamela
Pamela ('pæmilə)	Pamela
Pat (pæt)	Dim. de Patricia
Patricia (pə'triʃə)	Patricia
Pauline (poː'liːn)	Paulina
Peg (peg)	Dim. de Margaret
Peggy ('pegi)	Dim. de Margaret
Penelope (pə'neləpi)	Penélope
Penny ('peni)	Dim. de Penelope
Rachel ('reitʃəl)	Raquel
Rebecca (ri'bekə)	Rebeca
Rita ('riːtə)	Rita
Rose (rouz)	Rosa
Rosemary ('rouzməri)	Rosa María
Ruth (ruːθ)	Ruth
Sally ('sæli)	Dim. de Sarah
Sarah ('seərə)	Sara
Sophia (sə'faiə)	Sofía
Sue (suː)	Dim. de Susan
Susan ('suːzən)	Susana
Susanna (suːˈzænə)	Susana
Susie ('suːzi)	Dim. de Susan
Tessie ('tesi)	Dim. de Theresa
Theresa (tə'riːzə)	Teresa
Vicky ('viki)	Dim. de Victoria
Victoria (vik'toːriə)	Victoria

67

OCCUPATIONS   PROFESIONES (83)

ENGLISH	ESPAÑOL
Accoutant (ə'kauntənt)	contable
actor ('æktə)	actor
actress ('æktris)	actriz
air-hostess ('eəhoustis)	azafata
announcer (ə'naunsə)	locutor
radio announcer ('reidjouənaunsə)	locutor de radio
television announcer ('teliviʒənənaunsə)	locutor de televisión
architect ('a:kitekt)	arquitecto
army officer ('a:miofisə)	oficial del ejército
artist ('a:tist)	artista
author ('o:θə)	autor
Baker ('beikə)	panadero
barber ('ba:bə)	barbero
barman ('ba:mən)	barman
bartender ('ba:tendə)	barman
bell boy ('belboi)	botones
blacksmith ('blæksmiθ)	herrero
bookbinder ('bukbaində)	encuadernador
bookkeeper ('bukki:pə)	tenedor de libros
bookseller ('buksele)	librero
bootblack ('bu:tblæk)	limpiabotas
bricklayer ('brikleiə)	albañil
builder ('bildə)	constructor
butcher ('butʃə)	carnicero
butler ('bʌtlə)	mayordomo
Carpenter ('ka:pintə)	carpintero
cashier (kæ'ʃiə)	cajero
charwoman ('tʃa:wumən)	asistenta
chauffeur ('ʃoufə)	chófer
chef (ʃef)	cocinero
chemist ('kemist)	farmacéutico, químico
chimney-sweep ('tʃimniswi:p)	deshollinador
clerk (kla:k)	empleado
bank clerk ('bæŋkla:k)	empleado de banca
composer (kəm'pouzə)	compositor
compositor (kəm'pozitə)	cajista

| OCCUPATIONS | PROFESIONES |

conductor   (kən'dʌktə)

confectioner   (kən'fekʃənə)
cook   (kuk)

Dancer   ('dɑ:nsə)
director   (di'rektə)
doctor   ('doktə)
dressmaker   ('dresmeikə)
driver   ('draivə)
  bus-driver   ('bʌsdraivə)
  lorry-driver   ('loridraivə)
  taxi-driver   ('tæksidraivə)

Electrician   (ilek'triʃən)
engineer   (endʒi'niə)
  train engineer
        ('treinendʒiniə)

Farmer   ('fɑ:mə)
fisherman   ('fiʃəmən)
florist   ('florist)
foreman   ('fo:mən)
fruiterer   ('fru:tərə)

Gardener   ('gɑ:dənə)
goldsmith   ('gouldsmiθ)
greengrocer   ('gri:ngrousə)
grocer   ('grousə)
guitar-player   (gi'tɑ:pleiə)

Haberdasher   ('hæbədæʃə)
hairdresser   ('heədresə)
hatter   ('hætə)
hawker   ('ho:kə)
housewife   ('hauswaif)

Interpreter   (in'tə:pritə)

Jeweller   ('dʒu:ələ)
journalist   ('dʒə:nəlist)
judge   (dʒʌdʒ)

Labourer   ('leibərə)
lawyer   ('lo:jə)
liftman   ('liftmən)
lion-tamer   ('laiənteimə)

Maid   (meid)
maid-servant   ('meidsə:vənt)
manager   ('mænədʒə)

cobrador de autobús, director de orquesta
pastelero
cocinero

bailarín, bailarina
director
doctor
modista
conductor
conductor de autobús
camionero
taxista

electricista
ingeniero

conductor de tren

granjero
pescador
florista
capataz
frutero

jardinero
orfebre
verdulero
tendero de ultramarinos
guitarrista

mercero
peluquero
sombrerero (de caballeros)
vendedor ambulante
ama de casa

intérprete

joyero
periodista
juez

peón
abogado
ascensorista
domador de leones

criada
criada
gerente

| OCCUPATIONS | PROFESIONES |

manicurist ('mænikjuərist) — manicura
man-servant ('mænsə:vənt) — criado
manufacturer (mænju'fæktʃərə) — fabricante
mason ('meisən) — cantero
mechanic (mə'kænik) — mecánico
merchant ('mə:tʃənt) — comerciante
milkman ('milkmən) — lechero
miller ('milə) — molinero
milliner ('milinə) — sombrerero (de señoras)
miner ('mainə) — minero
motor repairman ('moutəri'peəmæn) — mecánico de coches
musician (mju'ziʃən) — músico

News-agent ('nju:seidʒənt) — vendedor de periódicos y revistas
news-boy ('nju:zboi) — vendedor de periódicos
newspaper-man ('nju:speipəmæn) — periodista
nurse (nə:s) — enfermera

Painter ('peintə) — pintor
paperhanger ('peipəhæŋgə) — empapelador
pedlar ('pedlə) — vendedor ambulante
photographer (fə'togrəfə) — fotógrafo
pianist ('piənist) — pianista
pilot ('pailət) — piloto
ploughman ('plaumən) — labrador
plumber ('plʌmə) — fontanero
poet ('pouit) — poeta
policeman (pə'li:smən) — guardia
porkbutcher ('po:kbutʃə) — salchichero
porter ('po:tə) — portero
postman ('poustmən) — cartero
postmaster ('poustma:stə) — administrador de correos
printer ('printə) — impresor
proof-reader ('pru:f ri:də) — corrector de pruebas
publisher ('pʌbliʃə) — editor

Receptionist (ri'sepʃənist) — recepcionista
reporter (ri'po:tə) — reportero

Sailor ('seilə) — marinero
sales-girl ('seilzgə:l) — vendedora
sales-man ('seilzmən) — vendedor
sales-woman ('seilzwumən) — vendedora
sculptor ('skʌlptə) — escultor
secretary ('sekrətəri) — secretario, a
shepherd ('ʃepəd) — pastor

shoemaker   ('ʃu:meikə)   zapatero
shop-assistant   ('ʃopəsistənt)   dependiente
shop-boy   ('ʃopboi)   chico de tienda
shop-girl   ('ʃopgə:l)   vendedora
shopkeeper   ('ʃopki:pə)   comerciante
shopman   ('ʃopmən)   comerciante
silvermith   ('silvəsmiθ)   platero
singer   ('siŋgə)   cantante
soldier   ('souldʒə)   soldado
stationer   ('steiʃənə)   dueño de una papelería
station master
      ('steiʃənmɑ:stə)   jefe de estación de ferrocarril
steward   ('stjuəd)   camarero de un buque
surgeon   ('sə:dʒən)   cirujano

Tailor   ('teilə)   sastre
teacher   ('ti:tʃə)   profesor
technician   (tek'niʃən)   técnico
  electrical technician
      (i'lektrikəltek'niʃən)   técnico electricista
teller   ('telə)   cajero (de un banco)
tobacconist   (tə'bækənist)   estanquero
ticket-collector   ('tikitkəlektə)   revisor
translator   (træns'leitə)   traductor
typist   ('taipist)   mecanógrafo,a
  shorthand typist
      ('ʃo:thænd'taipist)   taquimecanógrafo,a

Violinist   ('vaiəlinist)   violinista

Waiter   ('weitə)   camarero
  head-waiter   ('hedweitə)   camarero jefe
waitress   ('weitris)   camarera
watchmaker   ('wotʃmeikə)   relojero
watchman   ('wotʃmən)   vigilante
wine-merchant
      ('wainmə:tʃənt)   comerciante de vinos
woodsman   ('wudzmən)   leñador
writer   ('raitə)   escritor

68

OFFICE, AN   UNA OFICINA (74)

ENGLISH   ESPAÑOL

Adding-machine
      ('ædiŋməʃi:n)   sumadora

address (ə'dres)	dirección
Ball-pen ('bo:lpen)	bolígrafo
Calculating-machine ('kælkjuleitiŋməʃi:n)	calculadora
calculator ('kælkjuleitə)	calculadora
copy (Ikopi)	copia
copying-machine ('kopiiŋməʃi:n)	multicopista
correspondence (koris'pondəns)	correspondencia
Department (di'pɑ:tmənt)	departamento
desk (desk)	mesa de trabajo
dictate, to (tədik'teit)	dictar
drawing-pin ('dro:iŋpin)	chincheta
Envelope ('envəloup)	sobre
File, to (tə'fail)	archivar
files (failz)	archivos
filing-cabinet ('failiŋkæbinit)	archivo (mueble)
filing-card ('failiŋkɑ:d)	ficha
Ink (iŋk)	tinta
Letter ('letə)	carta
business letter ('biznisletə)	carta comercial
circular letter ('sə:kjulə'letə)	circular
official letter (ə'fiʃəl'letə)	oficio
Office-manager ('ofismænidʒə)	jefe de oficina
Paper ('peipə)	papel
carbon paper ('kɑ:bənpeipə)	papel carbón
sheet of paper ('ʃi:təv'peipə)	hoja de papel
writing paper ('raitiŋpeipə)	papel para cartas
paper-weight ('peipəweit)	pisapapeles
pen (pen)	pluma
pencil ('pensəl)	lápiz
propelling-pencil (prə'peliŋ'pensəl)	lápiz mecánico
pencil-sharpener ('pensəlʃɑ:pnə)	sacapuntas
photo copier ('foutoukopiə)	fotocopiadora

OFFICE, AN　　　　　　　**174**　　　　　　　UNA OFICINA

photo-copying machine
　　　('foutou'kopiiŋməʃi:n)　　　　fotocopiadora

Records　('reko:dz)　　　　archivo
　　　　　　　　　　　　　　　　(documentos archivados)
report　(ri'po:t)　　　　informe
ribbon　('ribən)　　　　cinta para la máquina de
　　　　　　　　　　　　　　escribir
rubber　('rʌbə)　　　　goma de borrar

Sealing-wax　('si:liŋwæks)　　　lacre
secretary　('sekrətəri)　　　secretario, a
shorthand　('ʃo:thænd)　　　taquigrafía
shorthand typist
　　　('ʃo:thænd'taipist)　　　taquimecanógrafo, a
stamp　(stæmp)　　　sello de correos
staples　('steipəlz)　　　grapas
stapler　('steiplə)　　　grapadora
switch-board　('switʃbo:d)　　　centralita del teléfono

Telephone　('telifoun)　　　teléfono
type, to　(tə'taip)　　　escribir a máquina
typewriter　('taipraitə)　　　máquina de escribir
typist　('taipist)　　　mecanógrafo, a

Waste-paper basket
　　　('weistpeipə'ba:skit)　　　cesto de los papeles

69

PAINTING AND SCULPTURE　　　PINTURA Y ESCULTURA (81)

ENGLISH　　　　　　　　ESPAÑOL

Abstract　('æbstrækt)　　　abstracto
alabaster　('æləba:stə)　　　alabastro
art　(a:t)　　　arte
artist　('a:tist)　　　artista

Background　('bækgraund)　　　fondo
bas-relief　('bæsrili:f)　　　bajo relieve
bronze　(bronz)　　　bronce
brush　(brʌʃ)　　　pincel, brocha

PAINTING AND SCULPTURE — PINTURA Y ESCULTURA

paint-brush ('peintbrʌʃ)	pincel
bust (bʌst)	busto
Canvas ('kænvəs)	lienzo
carve, to (tə'kɑ:v)	tallar
carving ('kɑ:viŋ)	talla
cast, to (tə'kɑ:st)	fundir
chisel ('tʃizl)	cincel
clay (klei)	arcilla
colour ('kʌlə)	color
cubism ('kju:bizəm)	cubismo
Easel ('i:zl)	caballete
Follower ('folouə)	seguidor
Impressionism (im'preʃənizəm)	impresionismo
Landscape ('lændskeip)	paisaje
Marble ('mɑ:bl)	mármol
model ('modl)	modelo
model, to (tə'modl)	modelar
Oil-colour ('oilkʌlə)	óleo (pintura)
oil painting ('oilpeintiŋ)	pintura al óleo (forma de pintar y cuadro)
Paint (peint)	pintura (para pintar)
paint, to (tə'peint)	pintar
paint box ('peintboks)	caja de colores
painter ('peintə)	pintor
painting ('peintiŋ)	cuadro
palette ('pælit)	paleta
perspective (pəs'pektiv)	perspectiva
picture ('piktʃə)	pintura (cuadro)
portrait ('po:trit)	retrato
Realism ('riəlizəm)	realismo
School (sku:l)	escuela
sculptor ('skʌlptə)	escultor
sea-piece ('si:pi:s)	marina
shadow ('ʃædou)	sombra
statue ('stætju:)	estatua
equestrian statue (i'kwestriən'stætju:)	estatua ecuestre
statuette (stætju'et)	estatuilla
still life ('stil laif)	bodegón
stone (stoun)	piedra

PAINTING AND SCULPTURE   **176**   PINTURA Y ESCULTURA

style   (stail)   estilo
surrealism   (sə'riəlizəm)   surrealismo
Water-colour   ('wo:tɘkʌlə)   acuarela (forma de pintar y cuadro)

70

PERSON, A   UNA PERSONA (78)

ENGLISH   ESPAÑOL

Absent-minded
         ('æbsənt'maindid)   distraído

Badly-dressed   ('bædli'drest)   mal vestido
badly-mannered
         ('bædli'mænəd)   mal educado
bald   (bo:ld)   calvo
beautiful   ('bju:tiful)   hermosa
big   (big)   grande
black   (blæk)   negro
blind   (blaind)   ciego
blue-eyed   ('blu:'aid)   de ojos azules
broad-shouldered
         ('bro:d'ʃouldəd)   de espaldas anchas
brown-haired   ('braun'heəd)   de pelo castaño

Chubby   ('tʃʌbi)   regordete
clever   ('klevə)   listo
crazy   ('kreizi)   chiflado
crippled   ('kripəld)   mutilado

Dark   (dɑ:k)   moreno
dark-haired   ('dɑ:k'heəd)   de pelo moreno
deaf   (def)   sordo
dumb   (dʌm)   mudo

Elegant   ('eligənt)   elegante

Fair   (feə)   rubio
fair-haired   ('feə'heəd)   de pelo rubio
fat   (fæt)   grueso
flat-nosed   ('flæt'nouzd)   chato
foolish   ('fu:liʃ)   tonto

PERSON, A		UNA PERSONA

Good-looking ('gud'lukiŋ) — bien parecido

Healthy ('helθi) — sano

Ill (il) — enfermo
impolite (impə'lait) — descortés
intelligent (in'telidʒənt) — inteligente

Lame (leim) — cojo
long-armed ('loŋ'a:md) — de brazos largos
long-legged ('loŋ'legd) — de piernas largas
long-necked ('loŋ'nekt) — de cuello largo

Mad (mæd) — loco

Nervous ('nə:vəs) — nervioso
nimble ('nimbəl) — ágil

Old (ould) — viejo
one-armed ('wʌn'a:md) — manco
one-eyed ('wʌn'aid) — tuerto
one-handed ('wʌn'hændid) — manco
one-legged ('wʌn'legd) — cojo (con una sola pierna)

Pale (peil) — pálido
plump (plʌmp) — rollizo
pock-marked ('pok'ma:kt) — picado de viruelas
polite (pə'lait) — cortés
poor (puə) — pobre
portly ('po:tli) — corpulento
pretty ('priti) — guapa

Rich (ritʃ) — rico
robust (rə'bʌst) — robusto
rude (ru:d) — grosero, tosco

Sad (sæd) — triste
sane (sein) — cuerdo
sensible ('sensibl) — sensato
sensitive ('sensitiv) — sensible
short (ʃo:t) — bajo
short-armed ('ʃo:t'a:md) — de brazos cortos
short-legged ('ʃo:t'legd) — de piernas cortas
short-necked ('ʃo:t'nekt) — de cuello corto
sick (sik) — enfermo
silly ('sili) — tonto
skinny ('skini) — muy delgado
slender ('slendə) — esbelto
slim (slim) — delgado
small (smo:l) — pequeño

stout (staut)	corpulento
strong (stroŋ)	fuerte
stubborn ('stʌbən)	terco
sturdy ('stə:di)	fuerte
Tall (to:l)	alto
thin (θin)	delgado
Ugly ('ʌgli)	feo
Well-dressed ('wel'drest)	bien vestido
well-educated ('wel'edjukeitid)	culto
well-mannered ('wel'mænəd)	de buenos modales
white (wait)	blanco
Young (jʌŋ)	joven

71

PERSONAL BELONGINGS   OBJETOS PERSONALES (73)

ENGLISH   ESPAÑOL

Bag (bæg)	bolso, cartera de mano
belt (belt)	cinturón
book (buk)	libro
box of matches ('boksəv'mætʃiz)	caja de cerillas
bracelet ('breislit)	pulsera
brush (brʌʃ)	cepillo
hair-brush ('heəbrʌʃ)	cepillo para el pelo
shaving-brush ('ʃeiviŋbrʌʃ)	brocha de afeitar
bus-ticket ('bʌstikit)	billete de autobús
button ('bʌtən)	botón
Cigarette-case (sigə'retkeis)	pitillera
cigarette-holder (sigə'rethouldə)	boquilla
collar-stud ('koləstʌd)	pasador de la camisa
comb ('koum)	peine
cuff-links ('kʌfliŋks)	gemelos
Diary ('daiəri)	agenda
dressing-case ('dresiŋkeis)	neceser

| PERSONAL BELONGINGS | OBJETOS PERSONALES |

Ear-rings   ('iəriŋz)　　　　　　　　　　pendientes
eye-lash curlers
　　　　　('ailæʃ'kə:ləz)　　　　　rizapestañas
Glasses   ('glɑ:siz)　　　　　　　　　gafas
　sun-glasses   ('sʌnglɑ:siz)　　　gafas de sol

Hairpin   ('heəpin)　　　　　　　　　horquilla
hair-tonic   ('heətonik)　　　　　　tónico para el pelo
handbag   ('hændbæg)　　　　　　　　bolso
handkerchief   ('hæŋketʃif)　　　　pañuelo

Identity card   (ai'dentitikɑ:d)　　tarjeta de identidad

Key-holder   ('ki:houldə)　　　　　llavero
key-ring   ('ki:riŋ)　　　　　　　　llavero
keys   (ki:z)　　　　　　　　　　　llaves

Lighter   ('laitə)　　　　　　　　　mechero
lipstick   ('lipstik)　　　　　　　lápiz de labios

Magazine   (mægə'zi:n)　　　　　　　revista
mirror   ('mirə)　　　　　　　　　　espejo

Nail clipper   ('neilklipə)　　　　cortauñas
nail file   ('neilfail)　　　　　　lima de uñas
necklace   ('neklis)　　　　　　　　collar

Packet of cigarettes
　　　　　('pækitəvsigə'rets)
passport   ('pɑ:spo:t)　　　　　　　paquete de cigarrillos
pen   (pen)　　　　　　　　　　　　pasaporte
　ball-pen   ('bo:lpen)　　　　　　pluma
　ball-point pen　　　　　　　　　　bolígrafo
　　　　　　('bo:lpoint'pen)
　　fountain pen   ('fauntənpen)　bolígrafo
pencil   ('pensl)　　　　　　　　　estilográfica
penknife   ('pennaif)　　　　　　　lápiz
perfume   ('pə:fju:m)　　　　　　　navaja
pipe   (paip)　　　　　　　　　　　perfume
pin   (pin)　　　　　　　　　　　　pipa
　bobby pin   ('bobi'pin)　　　　alfiler
　hairpin   ('heəpin)　　　　　　　horquilla pasador
　hatpin   ('hætpin)　　　　　　　horquilla invisible
　safety-pin   ('seiftipin)　　　alfiler de sombrero
　powder-box   ('paudəboks)　　　imperdible
　powder-puff   ('paudəpʌf)　　　polvera
purse   (pə:s)　　　　　　　　　　borla para polvos
　　　　　　　　　　　　　　　　　　portamonedas

Razor   ('reizə)　　　　　　　　　　máquina de afeitar
　electric razor
　　　　　(i'lektrik'reizə)　　　máquina de afeitar eléctrica

PERSONAL BELONGINGS   OBJETOS PERSONALES

safety-razor ('seiftireizə) — maquinilla de afeitar
razor blade ('reizəbleid) — hoja de afeitar
ring (riŋ) — anillo, sortija
Shoe-polish ('ʃu:poliʃ) — crema del calzado
stick of shaving-soap ('stikəv'ʃeiviŋsoup) — barra de jabón de afeitar
Tablet of soap ('tæblitəv'soup) — pastilla de jabón
ticket ('tikit) — billete (entrada)
tobacco pouch (tə'bækoupautʃ) — petaca
toilet water ('toilitwo:tə) — colonia
tooth-brush ('tu:θbrʌʃ) — cepillo de dientes
tooth-paste ('tu:θpeist) — pasta de dientes
towel ('tauəl) — toalla
transistor radio (træn'sistəreidjou) — transistor
Umbrella (ʌm'brelə) — paraguas
Walking-stick ('wo:kiŋstik) — bastón
wallet (wolit) — cartera (billetera)
watch (wotʃ) — reloj de pulsera o bolsillo

72

PHOTOGRAPHY   FOTOGRAFIA (39)

ENGLISH   ESPAÑOL

Background ('bækgraund) — segundo plano

Camera ('kæmərə) — cámara
camera-man ('kæmərəmæn) — cámara (persona)
cine-camera ('sinikæmərə) — tomavistas
close-up ('klousʌp) — primer plano
colour ('kʌlə) — color

Dark-room ('dɑ:krum) — cuarto oscuro
develop, to (tədi'veləp) — revelar
development (di'veləpmənt) — revelado
distance ('distəns) — distancia

Emulsion (i'mʌlʃən) — emulsión

PHOTOGRAPHY — FOTOGRAFIA

enlarge, to (tuin'lɑ:dʒ) — ampliar
enlargement (in'lɑ:dʒmənt) — ampliación
exposure (iks'pouʒə) — exposición

Film (film) — película
filter ('filtə) — filtro
flash (flæʃ) — «flash»
　electronic flash (ilek'tronik'flæʃ) — «flash» electrónico
flashbulb ('flæʃbʌlb) — lámpara «flash»
focus ('foukəs) — foco
　in focus (in'foukəs) — enfocado
　out of focus ('autəv'foukəs) — desenfocado
focus, to (tə'foukəs) — enfocar
foreground ('fo:graund) — primer plano

Image ('imidʒ) — imagen

Lens (lenz) — lente
light (lait) — luz

Negative ('negətiv) — negativo

Photo ('foutou) — foto
photo-dealer's ('foutoudi:ləz) — tienda de artículos fotográficos
photogenic (foutə'dʒenik) — fotogénico
photograph ('foutəgrɑ:f) — fotografía
　to take a photograph (tə'teikə'foutəgrɑ:f) — hacer una foto
photographer (fə'togrəfə) — fotógrafo
photographic (foutə'græfik) — fotográfico
photometer (fə'tomitə) — fotómetro
positive print ('pozitiv'print) — positivo
print (print) — positivo

Roll (roul) — rollo de película

Shutter ('ʃʌtə) — obturador
snapshot ('snæpʃot) — instantánea
speed (spi:d) — velocidad

Tripod ('traipod) — trípode

PLANTS (See TREES, 94)

73

POST, THE — EL CORREO (26)

ENGLISH	ESPAÑOL
Address (ə'dres)	dirección
address, to (tuə'dres)	dirigir (una carta)
Delivery (di'liveri)	reparto
payment on delivery ('peiməntondi'livəri)	pago contra reembolso
Envelope ('envəloup)	sobre
Form (fo:m)	impreso para rellenar
Letter ('letə)	carta
registered letter ('redʒistəd'letə)	carta certificada
letter-box ('letəboks)	buzón
Mail (meil)	correo
air-mail ('eəmeil)	correo aéreo
mail-bag ('meilbæg)	saca de correos
mail-order ('meilo:də)	pedido hecho por correo
mail-train ('meiltrein)	tren correo
money-order ('mʌnio:də)	giro
postal money-order ('poustəl'mʌnio:də)	giro postal
telegraph money-order ('teligrɑ:f'mʌnio:də)	giro telegráfico
Packet ('pækit)	paquete
post, to (tə'poust)	echar al correo
postage ('poustidʒ)	franqueo
post-bag ('poustbæg)	valija
postbox ('poustboks)	apartado de correos
postcard ('poustkɑ:d)	tarjeta postal
post-free ('poust'fri:)	franco de porte
postmark ('poustmɑ:k)	matasellos
postmaster ('poustmɑ:stə)	administrador de correos
post-office ('poustofis)	estafeta de correos
post-office box ('pustofis'boks)	apartado de correos
post-office savings bank ('poustofis'seiviŋzbæŋk)	caja postal de ahorros

POST, THE		EL CORREO

post-paid ('poust'peid)   franqueo pagado
poste restante ('post res'tɑ:nt)   lista de correos
printed matter ('printid'mætə)   impresos

Register, to (tə'redʒistə)   certificar

Send, to (tə'send)   enviar
sender ('sendə)   remitente
stamp (stæmp)   sello
  postage-stamp ('poustidʒstæmp)   sello

74

PRINTING   LA IMPRENTA (52)

ENGLISH   ESPAÑOL

Bind, to (tə'baind)   encuadernar
binder ('baində)   encuadernador
book (buk)   libro

Capitals ('kæpitəlz)   versales
  small capitals ('smɔ:l'kæpitəlz)   versalitas
compositor (kəm'positə)   cajista
copy ('kopi)   copia
copy, to (tə'kopi)   copiar
correct, to (təkə'rekt)   corregir

Engrave, to (tuin'greiv)   grabar
engraving (in'greiviŋ)   grabado (sus.)
etching ('etʃiŋ)   grabado al agua fuerte

Format ('fo:mæt)   formato

Galley proof ('gælipru:f)   galerada
galleys ('gæliz)   galeradas

Illustration (iləs'treiʃən)   ilustración
ink (ink)   tinta

Letter ('letə)   letra
  capital letter ('kæpitəl'letə)   letra mayúscula
  small letter ('smɔ:l'letə)   letra minúscula

line (lain)	línea
linotype ('lainətaip)	linotipia
lithograpy (li'θogrəfi)	litografía
lower case ('louə'keis)	caja baja
Magazine (mægə'zi:n)	revista
manuscript ('mænjuskript)	manuscrito
margin ('mɑ:dʒin)	margen
matrix ('mætriks)	matriz
Minerva machine (mi'nə:vəmə'ʃi:n)	minerva
misprint ('misprint)	errata
mistake (mis'teik)	error
monotype ('mounətaip)	monotipia
Newspaper ('nju:speipə)	periódico
Page (peidʒ)	página
paper ('peipə)	papel
indian paper ('indiən'peipə)	papel biblia
photogravure (foutəgrə'vjuə)	fotograbado
picture ('piktʃə)	grabado, dibujo, ilustración
press (pres)	prensa
print, to (tə'print)	imprimir
printer ('printə)	impresor
printing machine ('printiŋməʃi:n)	máquina de imprimir
printing press ('printiŋpres)	rotativa
print shop ('printʃop)	imprenta
proof (pru:f)	prueba
proof-reader ('pru:f ri:də)	lector de pruebas
publish, to (tə'pʌbliʃ)	publicar
publisher ('pʌbliʃə)	editor
publishing firm ('pʌbliʃiŋfə:m)	editorial
punctuation (pʌŋktju'eiʃən)	puntuación
Quire ('kwaiə)	mano (de papel)
Ream (ri:m)	resma
Sheet (ʃi:t)	hoja de papel
stereotype ('stiərətaip)	estereotipia
Type (taip)	tipo
bold-faced type ('bouldfeist'taip)	letra negrita
italic type (i'tælik'taip)	letra cursiva
Roman type ('roumən'taip)	letra redonda

PRINTING   LA IMPRENTA

typesetter ('taipsetə) cajista
typographer (tai'pogrəfə) tipógrafo
typography (tai'pogrəfi) tipografía
Upper case ('ʌpə'keis) caja alta

RADIO (See TELEVISION, 87)

75

RAILWAY STATION, A   UNA ESTACION DE FERROCARRIL (36)

ENGLISH	ESPAÑOL
Arrival (ə'raivl)	llegada
Baggage ('bægidʒ)	equipaje (USA)
berth (bə:θ)	litera
booking-office ('bukiŋofis)	taquilla
bookstall ('buksto:l)	quiosco de periódicos
Carriage ('kæridʒ)	coche
case (keis)	maleta
coach (koutʃ)	coche
passenger coach ('pæsəndʒəkoutʃ)	coche de viajeros
railway coach ('reilweikoutʃ)	vagón de ferrocarril
compartment (kəm'pa:tmənt)	compartimento
Departure (di'pa:tʃə)	partida
dining-car ('dainiŋka:)	coche restaurante
Engine ('endʒin)	locomotora
shunting engine ('ʃʌntiŋendʒin)	máquina de maniobras
engine-driver ('endʒindraivə)	maquinista
engine shed ('endʒinʃed)	depósito de máquinas
entrance ('entrəns)	entrada
exit ('eksit)	salida
express (iks'pres)	exprés
First class ('fə:st'kla:s)	primera clase
Guard (ga:d)	factor

Left-luggage office
  ('leftlʌgidʒ'ofis)   consigna
lines (lainz)   vías
local train ('loukəl'trein) tren local
locomotive ('loukəmoutiv) locomotora
  diesel locomotive
    ('di:zəl loukəmoutiv)   locomotora diesel
  electric locomotive
    (i'lektrik'loukəmoutiv) locomotora eléctrica
  steam locomotive
    ('sti:mloukəmoutiv)   locomotora de vapor
luggage ('lʌgidʒ)   equipaje (GB)
luggage trolley ('lʌgidʒtroli) carretilla de equipajes
luggage van ('lʌgidʒvæn)   vagón de equipajes
Passenger ('pæsəndʒə)   pasajero
platform ('plætfo:m)   andén
pointsman ('pointsmən)   guardaagujas
porter ('po:tə)   mozo

Rack (ræk)   rejilla para el equipaje
rail (reil)   rail
rails (reilz)   raíles
railway ('reilwei)   ferrocarril
railway man ('reilweimæn) ferroviario
railway station
  ('reilweisteiʃən)   estación de ferrocarril
refreshment room
  (ri'freʃmənt rum)   bar, cantina
Seat (si:t)   asiento
second class ('sekənd'kla:s) segunda clase
signals ('signəlz)   semáforo
sleeper ('sli:pə)   departamento cama
sleeping-car ('sli:piŋka:) coche cama
station ('steiʃən)   estación
station master
  ('steiʃənma:stə)   jefe de estación
stoker ('stoukə)   fogonero
subway ('sʌbwei)   paso subterráneo
suitcase ('su:tkeis)   maleta

Taxi-rank ('tæksiræŋk)   parada de taxis
tender ('tendə)   ténder
ticket ('tikit)   billete
  return ticket (ri'tə:ntikit) billete de ida y vuelta
  single ticket ('siŋgəl'tikit) billete de ida
ticket collector ('tikitkəlektə) revisor
ticket office ('tikitofis) taquilla
time-table ('taimteibl)   horario
tracks (træks)   vías

RAILWAY STATION, A — ESTACIÓN DE FERROCARRIL

train (trein) — tren
electric train (i'lektrik'trein) — tren eléctrico
express train (iks'pres'trein) — tren expreso
fast train ('fɑ:st'trein) — tren rápido
goods-train ('gudztrein) — tren de mercancías
mail-train ('meiltrein) — tren correo
passenger train ('pæsəndʒətrein) — tren de viajeros
steam train ('sti:mtrein) — tren de vapor
traveller ('trævələ) — viajero
truck (trʌk) — vagón de carga
trunk (trʌŋk) — baúl

Van (væn) — furgón

Wagon ('wægən) — vagón
open wagon ('oupən'wægən) — vagón abierto
tank wagon ('tænkwægən) — vagón cisterna
waiting-room ('weitiŋrum) — sala de espera
way in ('wei'in) — entrada
way out ('wei'aut) — salida
window ('windou) — ventanilla

76

RELIGION / RELIGION (86)

ENGLISH — ESPAÑOL

Abel ('eibəl) — Abel
Adam ('ædəm) — Adán
altar-piece ('o:ltəpi:s) — retablo
angel ('eindʒəl) — ángel
apostle (ə'posl) — apóstol
atheism ('eiθiizəm) — ateísmo
atheist ('eiθiist) — ateo

Baptism ('bæptizəm) — bautismo
baptize, to (təbæp'taiz) — bautizar
beliefs (bi'li:fs) — creencias
Bible, the (ðə'baibl) — la Biblia
bless, to (tə'bles) — bendecir

blessed ('blesid)	bendito
brethren ('breðrən)	hermanos
Buddha ('budə)	Buda
Buddism ('budizəm)	budismo
Cain (kein)	Caín
cathedral (kə'θi:drəl)	catedral
Catholic ('kæθəlik)	católico
catholicism (kə'θolisizəm)	catolicismo
Christ (kraist)	Cristo
Christian ('kristiən)	cristiano
christanism ('kristiənizəm)	cristianismo
church (tʃə:tʃ)	iglesia
Roman Catholic Church ('roumən'kæθəlik'tʃə:tʃ)	Iglesia Católica, Apostólica y Romana
clergy ('klə:dʒi)	clero
clergyman ('kə:dʒimən)	clérigo
convent ('konvənt)	convento
creation (kri'eiʃən)	creación
creed (kri:d)	credo
cross (kros)	cruz
Deity ('di:iti)	divinidad
demon ('di:mən)	demonio
devil ('devəl)	diablo
dogma ('dogmə)	dogma
Doomsday ('du:mzdei)	Día del Juicio Final
Eve (i:v)	Eva
evil ('i:vəl)	mal
Faith (feiθ)	fe
Father ('fɑ:ðə)	Padre
God (god)	Dios
good (gud)	bien
Heaven ('hevən)	cielo
hell (hel)	infierno
heresy ('herəsi)	herejía
heretic ('herətik)	hereje
Hinduism ('hinduizəm)	hinduismo
holy ('houli)	santo
Holy Ghost ('houli'goust)	Espíritu Santo
Holy Land ('houli'lænd)	Tierra Santa
Holy Writ ('houli'rit)	Sagrada Escritura
Holy-Week ('houliwi:k)	Semana Santa
hymn (him)	himno
Inquisition (iŋkwi'ziʃən)	Inquisición

RELIGION

Jesus ('dʒi:zəs) — Jesús
Jesus Christ ('dʒi:zəs'kraist) — Jesucristo
Judaism ('dʒu:deiizəm) — judaísmo

Last Supper, the (ðə'lɑ:st'sʌpə) — La Ultima Cena
Lord, the (ðə'lo:d) — El Señor

Mahomet (mə'homit) — Mahoma
miracle ('mirəkl) — milagro
missionary ('miʃənəri) — misionero
monk (mʌŋk) — monje
Moses ('mouziz) — Moisés

Nun (nʌn) — monja

Pagan ('peigən) — pagano
paganism ('peigənizəm) — paganismo
parable ('pærəbl) — parábola
Pope, the (ðə'poup) — el Papa
pray, to (tə'prei) — rezar
prayer (preə) — oración
priest (pri:st) — sacerdote
procession (prə'seʃən) — procesión
prophet ('profit) — profeta
Protestant ('protistənt) — protestante
punish, to (tə'pʌniʃ) — castigar
punishment ('pʌniʃmənt) — castigo

Redeemer (ri'di:mə) — Redentor
Redemption (ri'dempʃən) — Redención
reward (ri'wo:d) — recompensa
reward, to (təri'wo:d) — recompensar
rite (rait) — rito

Sacred ('seikrid) — sagrado
saint (seint) — santo
Satan ('seitən) — Satán
Scriptures ('skriptʃəz) — Escrituras
sin (sin) — pecado
sin, to (tə'sin) — pecar
sinner ('sinə) — pecador
Son (sʌn) — Hijo
soul (soul) — alma

Testament, The New (ðə'nju:'testəmənt) — El Nuevo Testamento
Testament, The Old (ði'ould'testəmənt) — El Antiguo Testamento

Ten Commandments, The   Los Diez Mandamientos
    (ðə'tenkə'mɑːndments)
Virgin ('vəːdʒin)   Virgen

Worship ('wəːʃip)   adoración
worship, to (tu'wəːʃip)   adorar

77

REPTILES AND AMPHIBIANS   REPTILES Y ANFIBIOS (88)

ENGLISH   ESPAÑOL

Adder ('ædə)   víbora
alligator ('æligeitə)   caimán

Boa ('bouə)   boa

Chameleon (kə'miːliən)   camaleón
cobra ('koubrə)   cobra
crocodile ('krokədail)   cocodrilo

Frog (frog)   rana

Iguana (i'gwɑːnə)   iguana

Lizard ('lizəd)   lagarto
  small lizard ('smoːl'lizəd)   lagartija

Newt (njuːt)   tritón

Python ('paiθən)   pitón

Salamander ('sæləmændə)   salamandra
snake (sneik)   serpiente, culebra
  coral snake ('korəlsneik)   serpiente coralillo
  rattlesnake ('rætəlsneik)   serpiente de cascabel

Toad (toud)   sapo
tortoise ('toːtəs)   tortuga
turtle ('təːtl)   tortuga de mar

Viper ('vaipə)   víbora

78

RESTAURANT, AT THE   EN EL RESTAURANTE (89)

ENGLISH	ESPAÑOL

Appetite ('æpitait) — apetito
apple pie ('æpəl'pai) — tarta de manzana

Bacon and eggs ('beikənən'egz) — huevos con bacón
baked apple ('beikt'æpl) — manzana asada
beefsteak ('bi:f'steik) — bistec
bill (bil) — cuenta, nota
biscuit ('biskit) — galleta
bread (bred) — pan
bread and butter ('bredən'bʌtə) — pan con mantequilla
breakfast ('brekfəst) — desayuno
butter ('bʌtə) — mantequilla
buttered toast ('bʌtəd'toust) — tostada con mantequilla

Cake (keik) — pastel, tarta
caramel custard ('kærəməl'kʌstəd) — flan
cheese (tʃi:z) — queso
chicken ('tʃikən) — pollo
chips (tʃips) — patatas fritas
chop (tʃop) — chuleta
  lamb chop ('læm'tʃop) — chuleta de cordero lechal
  mutton chop ('mʌtən'tʃop) — chuleta de cordero
  pork chop ('po:k'tʃop) — chuleta de cerdo
cutlet ('kʌtlit) — chuleta
  lamb cutlet ('læm'kʌtlit) — chuleta de cordero
  veal cutlet ('vi:l'kʌtlit) — chuleta de ternera
coffee ('kofi) — café
  black coffee ('blæk'kofi) — café solo
  instant coffee ('instənt'kofi) — café instantáneo
  white coffee ('wait'kofi) — café con leche
cook (kuk) — cocinero
cook, to (tə'kuk) — guisar
course (ko:s) — plato (de una comida)
crisps (krisps) — patatas fritas a la inglesa
custard ('kʌstəd) — natillas
customer ('kʌstəmə) — cliente

RESTAURANT, AT THE   EN EL RESTAURANTE

Dessert (di'zə:t) — postre
diet ('daiət) — dieta
dinner ('dinə) — cena
dish (diʃ) — plato
  cold dish ('kould'diʃ) — plato frío
  vegetarian dish (vedʒi'teəriən'diʃ) — plato vegetariano

Egg (eg) — huevo
  boiled egg ('boild'eg) — huevo pasado por agua
  fried egg ('fraid'eg) — huevo frito
  hard-boiled egg ('hɑ:dboild'eg) — huevo duro
  poached eggs ('poutʃt'egz) — huevos revueltos
  scrambled eggs ('skræmbəld'egz) — huevos escalfados

Fish* (fiʃ) — pescado
fruit* (fru:t) — fruta
  stewed fruit ('stju:d'fru:t) — compota
  tinned fruit ('tind'fru:t) — fruta en conserva

Game (geim) — caza
garnish ('gɑ:niʃ) — guarnición
glass (glɑ:s) — vaso
  wine-glass ('wainglɑ:s) — copa
gravy ('greivi) — salsa (jugo)
greens (gri:nz) — verduras

Ham (hæm) — jamón
hors d'oeuvres ('o:'də:vr) — entremeses

Ice (ais) — hielo
ice-cream ('ais'kri:m) — helado

Jam (dʒæm) — mermelada
  cherry jam ('tʃeri'dʒæm) — mermelada de cerezas
  gooseberry jam ('guzbəri'dʒæm) — mermelada de frambuesa
  strawberry jam ('stro:bəri'dʒæm) — mermelada de fresa
jug (dʒʌg) — jarra
  water-jug ('wo:tədʒʌg) — jarra de agua

Kidneys ('kidniz) — riñones
knife (naif) — cuchillo

Lamb (læm) — cordero
lemon juice ('lemən'dʒu:s) — zumo de limón
liver ('livə) — hígado
loaf (louf) — panecillo
lunch (lʌntʃ) — almuerzo

set lunch ('set'lʌntʃ)	cubierto
Marmalade ('mɑ:məleid)	mermelada de naranja
mayonnise (meiə'neiz)	mayonesa
meal (mi:l)	comida
cold meal ('kould'mi:l)	comida fría
hot meal ('hot'mi:l)	comida caliente
meat (mi:t)	carne
cold meat ('kould'mi:t)	fiambre
roast meat ('roust'mi:t)	carne asada
meat balls ('mi:t'bo:lz)	albóndigas
meat dish ('mi:tdiʃ)	plato de carne
menu ('menju:)	menú
mustard ('mʌstəd)	mostaza
mutton ('mʌtən)	cordero
Napkin ('næpkin)	servilleta
Oil (oil)	aceite
olives ('olivz)	aceitunas
stuffed olives ('stʌft'olivz)	aceitunas rellenas
omelette ('omlit)	tortilla
plain omelette ('plein'omlit)	tortilla a la francesa
Spanish omelette ('spæniʃ'omlit)	tortilla a la española
order, to (tu'o:də)	encargar
Pastry ('peistri)	pastelería (pasteles)
pepper ('pepə)	pimienta
pickled onions ('pikəld'ʌniənz)	cebolletas en vinagre
pie (pai)	pastel
porridge ('poridʒ)	sopa de avena
portion ('po:ʃən)	ración
potatoes (pə'teitouz)	patatas asadas
baked potatoes ('beiktpə'teitouz)	patatas asadas
chipped potatoes ('tʃiptpə'teitouz)	patatas fritas
mashed potatoes ('mæʃtpə'teitouz)	puré de patatas
roast potatoes ('roustpə'teitouz)	patatas asadas
poultry ('poultri)	aves de corral
pudding ('pudiŋ)	«pudin»
Quince jelly ('kwins'dʒeli)	membrillo
Restaurant ('restərənt)	restaurante
self-service restaurant ('selfsə:vis'restərənt)	restaurante de autoservicio

rice (rais)	arroz
roast-beef ('roust'bi:f)	«rosbif»
roast kid ('roust'kid)	cabrito asado
roast lamb ('roust'læm)	cordero lechal asado
roast suckling-pig ('roust'sʌkliŋ'pig)	cochinillo asado
roll (roul)	panecillo
Salad ('sæləd)	ensalada
green salad ('gri:n'sæləd)	ensalada variada
lettuce salad ('letis'sæləd)	ensalada de lechuga
Russian salad ('rʌʃən'sæləd)	ensaladilla rusa
salt (so:lt)	sal
salted almonds ('so:ltid'ɑ:məndz)	almendras saladas
sandwich ('sændwidʒ)	bocadillo
cheese sandwich ('tʃi:z'sændwidʒ)	bocadillo de queso
ham sandwich ('hæm'sændwidʒ)	bocadillo de jamón
sauce (so:s)	salsa
green sauce ('gri:n'so:s)	salsa verde
tomato sauce (tə'mɑ:tou'so:s)	salsa de tomate
vinegar sauce ('vinigə'so:s)	salsa vinagreta
saucer ('so:sə)	platillo (de taza)
serve, to (tə'sə:v)	servir
shell-fish ('ʃelfiʃ)	marisco
sirloin ('sə:loin)	solomillo
smoked eel ('smoukt'i:l)	anguila ahumana
smoked salmon ('smoukt'sæmən)	salmón ahumado
soup (su:p)	sopa
clear soup ('kliə'su:p)	consomé
fish-soup ('fiʃ'su:p)	sopa de pescado
lentil soup ('lentil'su:p)	puré de lentejas
onion soup ('ʌniən'su:p)	sopa de cebolla
oxtail soup ('o:ksteil'su:p)	sopa de rabo de buey
thick soup ('θik'su:p)	puré
tomato soup (tə'mɑ:tou'su:p)	sopa de tomate
steak (steik)	filete
stew (stju:)	estofado
sugar ('ʃugə)	azúcar
sugar-basin ('ʃugəbeisin)	azucarero
sugar-bowl ('ʃugəboul)	azucarero
supper ('sʌpə)	cena

| RESTAURANT, AT THE | EN EL RESTAURANTE |

sweet (swi:t)   postre

Table ('teibl)   mesa
  to book a table (tə'bukə'teibl)   reservar una mesa
table-cloth ('teibəlkloθ)   mantel
tableware* ('teibəlweə)   vajilla
tea-strainer ('ti:streinə)   colador para el té
tip (tip)   propina
toast (toust)   tostada
toothpick ('tu:θpik)   mondadientes
tray (trei)   bandeja

Veal (vi:l)   ternera
vegetables* ('vedʒitəbəlz)   verduras, legumbres
vermicelli noodles (və:mi'seli'nu:dəlz)   fideos
vinegar ('vinigə)   vinagre

Waiter ('weitə)   camarero
waitress ('weitris)   camarera
water ('wo:tə)   agua
  mineral water ('minərəl'wo:tə)   agua mineral
wine (wain)   vino
wine-list ('wainlist)   lista de vinos

SCHOOL

(See LIFE AT SCHOOL, 56)

SCULPTURE

(See PAINTING, 63)

79

| SEA PORT, A | UN PUERTO DE MAR (84) |

| ENGLISH | ESPAÑOL |

Boat (bout)   bote, barca
bollard ('boləd)   noray
breakwater ('breikwo:tə)   rompeolas

Cargo ship ('kɑ:gouʃip)   buque de carga

SEA-PORT, A — UN PUERTO DE MAR

crane (krein)	grúa
Disembark, to (tədisim'bɑ:k)	desembarcar
dock (dok)	dique, muelle
dry dock ('drai'dok)	dique seco
dockage ('dokidʒ)	derechos de dique
docker ('dokə)	estibador
Embark, to (tuim'bɑ:k)	embarcar
Fender ('fendə)	defensas (para evitar golpes)
fishing-boat ('fiʃiŋbout)	barco de pesca
Harbour ('hɑ:bə)	puerto
inner harbour ('inə'hɑ:bə)	puerto interior
outer harbour ('autə'hɑ:bə)	puerto exterior
harbour pilot ('hɑ:bəpailət)	práctico de puerto
Jetty ('dʒeti)	malecón
Liner ('lainə)	transatlántico
load, to (tə'loud)	cargar
Moor, to (tə'muə)	amarrar
mooring ('muəriŋ)	amarra
Naval base ('neivəl'beis)	base naval
Oil installations ('oilinstəleiʃənz)	instalaciones petrolíferas
Pier (piə)	escollera
port (po:t)	puerto
free port ('fri:'po:t)	puerto franco
promenade (promi'nɑ:d)	paseo marítimo
Quay (ki:)	muelle, desembarcadero
Seagulls ('si:gʌlz)	gaviotas
ship* (ʃip)	buque
Tanker ('tæŋkə)	petrolero
timber yard ('timbəjɑ:d)	depósito para madera
tug (tʌg)	remolcador
tow, to (tə'tou)	remolcar
Unload, to (tuʌn'loud)	descargar
Wharf (wo:f)	tinglado, muelle de carga y descarga

80

SEASIDE, AT THE   EN LA COSTA (28)

ENGLISH	ESPAÑOL

Air mattress ('eəmætris) — colchón de aire
Bathe (beið) — baño
bathe, to (tə'beið) — bañarse
bather ('beiðə) — bañista
bath robe ('bɑ:θroub) — albornoz
bathing-cap ('beiðiŋkæp) — gorro de agua
bathing-costume ('beiðiŋkostju:m) — traje de baño
  two-piece bathing-costume ('tu:pi:s'beiðiŋkostju:m) — traje de baño de dos piezas
bathing-hut ('beiðiŋhʌt) — caseta de baño
beach (bi:tʃ) — playa
  sandy beach ('sændi'bi:tʃ) — playa arenosa
  stony beach ('stouni'bi:tʃ) — playa pedregosa
beach chair ('bi:tʃtʃeə) — silla de playa
bikini (bi'ki:ni) — bikini
boat (bout) — barca, bote
buoy (boi) — boya

Camping-site ('kæmpiŋsait) — «camping»
canvas ('kænvəs) — toldo.
caravan ('kærəvæn) — remolque vivienda
caravan park ('kærəvænpɑ:k) — «camping» para remolques.
coast (koust) — costa

Deck-chair ('dektʃeə) — hamaca
dive, to (tə'daiv) — zambullirse
diving-board ('daiviŋbo:d) — trampolín
dune (dju:n) — duna

Edge (edʒ) — orilla (del mar)

Fish, to (tə'fiʃ) — pescar
fishing-boat ('fiʃiŋbout) — barco de pesca
fishing-rod ('fiʃiŋrod) — caña de pescar
fishing-village ('fiʃiŋvilidʒ) — pueblo de pescadores
flippers ('flipəz) — aletas para nadar
folding chair ('foudiŋ'tʃeə) — silla plegable

Goggles ('gogəlz)	gafas de buceo
Holiday-makers ('holidimeikez)	veraneantes
hotel* (hou'tel)	hotel
Life-belt ('laifbelt)	cinturón salvavidas
lighthouse ('laithaus)	faro
Rescue ('reskju:)	salvamento
rock ('rok)	roca
row, to (tə'rou)	remar
rowing-boat ('rouiŋbout)	bote de remos
Sailing-boat ('seiliŋbout)	bote de vela
sand (sænd)	arena
to lie on the sand (tə'laionðə'sænd)	tumbarse en la arena
sandals ('sændəlz)	sandalias
sandcastle ('sænd'kɑ:sl)	castillo de arena
sea (si:)	mar
seaside holidays ('si:said'holidiz)	vacaciones en la playa
seaside town ('si:said'taun)	ciudad costera
sea-view ('si:vju:)	vistas al mar
shade (ʃeid)	sombra
shell (ʃel)	concha
ship* (ʃip)	barco
shore (ʃo:)	costa
sky (skai)	cielo
spade (speid)	pala
splash, to (tə'splæʃ)	salpicar
summer holidays ('sʌməholidiz)	vacaciones de verano
summer resort ('sʌmərizo:t)	lugar de veraneo
sun (sʌn)	sol
to lie in the sun (tə'laiinðə'sʌn)	tumbarse al sol
sunbathe, to (tə'sʌnbeið)	tomar baños de sol
sunburnt ('sʌnbə:nt)	tostado por el sol
sunglasses ('sʌnglɑ:siz)	gafas de sol
sunshade ('sʌnʃeid)	sombrilla
sunstroke ('sʌnstrouk)	insolación
sun-tan lotion ('sʌntæn'louʃən)	loción para broncear
sun umbrella ('sʌnʌmbrelə)	sombrilla
swim, to (tə'swim)	nadar
swimmer ('swimə)	nadador
swimming ('swimiŋ)	natación
swimming-pool ('swimiŋpu:l)	piscina

Tide (taid)	marea
full tide ('ful'taid)	pleamar
high tide ('hai'taid)	marea alta
low tide ('lou'taid)	marea baja
towel ('tauəl)	toalla
Under-water fishing ('ʌndəwo:tə'fiʃiŋ)	pesca submarina
Water skiing ('wo:təski:iŋ)	esquí acuático
wave (weiv)	ola

81

SHIP, A   UN BARCO (14)

ENGLISH	ESPAÑOL
Anchor ('æŋkə)	ancla
Berth (bə:θ)	litera
boiler ('boilə)	caldera
boiler-room ('boilərum)	sala de calderas
bow (bau)	proa
bowsprit ('bousprit)	bauprés
breadth (bredθ)	manga
bridge (bridʒ)	puente
navigating-bridge ('nævigeitiŋbridʒ)	puente de navegación
bulwark ('bulwək)	amurada
Cabin ('kæbin)	camarote
capstan ('kæpstən)	cabrestante
cowl ventilador ('kaulventileitə)	ventilador
crow's nest ('krouznest)	cofa de vigía
Deck (dek)	cubierta
derrick ('derik)	cabria
draught (drɑ:ft)	calado
Engine ('endʒin)	máquina
engine-room ('endʒinrum)	sala de máquinas

Forecastle ('fouksəl)	castillo de proa
funnel ('fʌnəl)	chimenea
Gangway ('gæŋwei)	escalerilla
Hatch (hætʃ)	escotilla
helm (helm)	timón (rueda)
hold (hould)	bodega
depth of hold ('depθəv'hould)	puntal
hull (hʌl)	casco
Keel (ki:l)	quilla
Length (leŋθ)	eslora
Mast (mɑ:st)	mástil
foremast ('fo:məst)	palo de trinquete
mainmast ('meinməst)	palo mayor
mooring ('muəriŋ)	amarra
Oar (o:)	remo
Poop (pu:p)	popa
port (po:t)	babor
porthole ('po:thoul)	portilla
propeller (prə'pelə)	hélice
prow (prau)	proa
Rudder ('rʌdə)	timón
Sail (seil)	vela
sail, to (tə'seil)	navegar
screw (skru:)	hélice
spar (spɑ:)	verga
starboard ('stɑ:bəd)	estribor
steer, to (tə'stiə)	gobernar (un buque)
stem (stem)	tajamar
stern (stə:n)	popa
Water line ('wo:təlain)	línea de flotación
wheel (wi:l)	timón (rueda)
wheelhouse ('wi:lhaus)	timonera

82

SHIPS, TYPES OF	TIPOS DE BUQUES (17)
ENGLISH	ESPAÑOL

Aircraft carrier ('eəkrɑːftkæriə)   portaaviones
Barge (bɑːdʒ)   gabarra
battleship ('bætəlʃip)   acorazado
boat (bout)   bote, barca, lancha, barco
  antisubmarine boat ('ænti'sʌbməriːnbout)   lancha antisubmarina
  cargo-boat ('kɑːgoubout)   carguero
  ferry-boat ('feribout)   transbordador
  fishing-boat ('fiʃiŋbout)   barco de pesca
  gun-boat ('gʌnbout)   cañonero
  life-boat ('laifbout)   bote salvavidas
  motor-boat ('moutəbout)   lancha motora
motor gun-boat ('moutə'gʌnbout)   lancha cañonera
  outboard motor-boat ('autboːd'moutəbout)   lancha fuera borda
  paddle-boat ('pædəlbout)   barco de ruedas
  rowing-boat ('rouiŋbout)   bote de remos
  sailing-boat ('seiliŋbout)   barco de vela
  speed-boat ('spiːdbout)   lancha rápida
  torpedo-boat (təˈpiːdoubout)   lancha torpedera
  tugboat ('tʌgbout)   remolcador
  whale-boat ('weilbout)   ballenera
brig (brig)   bergantín
brigantine ('brigəntain)   bergantín

Canoe (kəˈnuː)   canoa
caravel ('kærəvel)   carabela
catamaran (kætəməˈræn)   patín a vela
Chinese junk ('tʃainiːzˈdʒʌŋk)   junco chino
clipper ('klipə)   velero de línea
coaster ('koustə)   buque de cabotaje
cruiser ('kruːzə)   crucero
  battle cruiser ('bætəlkruːzə)   crucero de batalla
  heavy cruiser ('heviˈkruːzə)   crucero pesado
  light cruiser ('laitˈkruːzə)   crucero ligero
cutter ('kʌtə)   falúa

Destroyer (disˈtroiə)   destructor

SHIPS, TYPES OF — TIPOS DE BUQUES

torpedo-boat destroyer (təˈpiːdouboutdisˈtroiə) — cazatorpedero
dinghy (ˈdiŋgi) — bote
Frigate (ˈfrigit) — fragata
Galleon (ˈgæliən) — galeón
galley (ˈgæli) — galera
gig (gig) — falúa
gondola (ˈgondələ) — góndola
Kayak (ˈkaiæk) — cayac
ketch (ketʃ) — queche
Landing craft (ˈlændiŋkrɑːft) — lancha de desembarco
launch (loːntʃ) — lancha
  motor-launch (ˈmoutəloːntʃ) — lancha motora
liner (ˈlainə) — transatlántico
  ocean liner (ˈouʃənlainə) — transatlántico
lighter (ˈlaitə) — gabarra
lugger (ˈlʌgə) — lugre
Man-of-war (ˈmænəvˈwoː) — buque de guerra
merchantman (ˈməːtʃəntmən) — buque mercante
mine layer (ˈmainleiə) — minador
mine sweeper (ˈmainswiːpə) — dragaminas
Raft (ˈrɑːft) — balsa
revenue-cutter (ˈrevinjuːkʌtə) — guardacostas
Schooner (ˈskuːnə) — goleta
ship* (ʃip) — barco, buque
  cargo ship (ˈkɑːgouʃip) — buque de carga
  coastguard ship (ˈkoustgɑːdʃip) — guardacostas
  flagship (ˈflægʃip) — buque insignia
  fruit-ship (fruːtʃip) — buque frutero
  lightship (ˈlaitʃip) — buque faro
  merchant ship (ˈməːtʃənt ʃip) — buque mercante
  passenger-ship (ˈpæsəndʒəʃip) — buque de pasajeros
  sailing-ship (ˈseiliŋʃip) — velero
  sister ship (ˈsistəʃip) — buque gemelo
  steamship (ˈstiːmʃip) — buque de vapor
  training-ship (ˈtreiniŋʃip) — buque escuela
  warship (ˈwoːʃip) — buque de guerra
skiff (skif) — esquife
sloop (sluːp) — balandro
sloop of war (ˈsluːpəvˈwoː) — corbeta
smack (smæk) — queche
steamer (ˈstiːmə) — vapor

SHIPS, TYPES OF	TIPOS DE BUQUES
paddle-steamer ('pædəlsti:mə)	vapor de ruedas
submarine ('sʌbməri:n)	submarino
atomic-driven submarine (ə'tomikdrivən'sʌbməri:n)	submarino atómico
Tanker ('tæŋkə)	petrolero
tramp (træmp)	vapor volandero
tramp steamer ('træmpsti:mə)	vapor volandero
trawler ('tro:lə)	barco de pesca al arrastre
tug (tʌg)	remolcador
ocean-going tug ('ouʃəngouiŋ'tʌg)	remolcador de alta mar
Vessel ('vesl)	buque
cargo vessel ('kɑ:gou'vesəl)	buque de carga
merchant vessel ('mə:tʃənt'vesəl)	buque mercante
sailing vessel ('seiliŋvesl)	buque de vela
Yacht (jot)	yate
yawl (jo:l)	yola

83

SHOPS — TIENDAS (93)

ENGLISH	ESPAÑOL
Baker's (beikəz)	panadería
bakery ('beikəri)	tahona
barber's ('bɑ:bəz)	barbería
bookseller's ('bukseləz)	librería
bookstall ('buksto:l)	quiosco de libros y periódicos
butcher's ('butʃəz)	carnicería
Café ('kæfei)	cafetería
chemist's ('kemists)	farmacia
cleaner's ('kli:nəz)	tintorería
confectioner's (kən'fekʃənəz)	confitería, pastelería
counter ('kauntə)	mostrador
customer ('kʌstəmə)	cliente
Dairy ('deəri)	lechería

| SHOPS | TIENDAS |

department (di'pɑ:tmənt) — sección
department store (di'pɑ:tməntsto:) — almacenes
draper's ('dreipəz) — tienda de tejidos
drug store ('drʌgsto:) — droguería, perfumería

Fishmonger's ('fiʃmʌŋgəz) — pescadería
florist's ('florists) — floristería
fruiterer's ('fru:tərəz) — frutería

Greengrocer's ('gri:ngrousəz) — verdulería
grocer's ('grousəz) — tienda de comestibles
Haberdasher's ('hæbədæʃəz) — mercería
hairdresser's ('heədresəz) — peluquería

Ironmonger's ('aiənmʌŋgəz) — ferretería

Jeweller's ('dʒu:ələz) — joyería

Laundry ('lo:ndri) — lavandería

Newsagent's ('nju:zeidʒənts) — puesto de periódicos

Optician (op'tiʃən) — óptico
outfitter's ('autfitəz) — camisería

Pastry-cook's ('peistrikuks) — pastelería

Shop (ʃop) — tienda
  antique shop (æn'ti:kʃop) — tienda de antigüedades
  book shop ('bukʃop) — librería
  cake shop ('keikʃop) — pastelería
  ceramics shop (si'ræmiksʃop) — tienda de objetos de cerámica
  hardware shop ('hɑ:dweəʃop) — ferretería
  pet-shop ('petʃop) — tienda de animales domésticos
  radio-shop ('reidjouʃop) — tienda de aparatos de radio
  shoe-shop ('ʃu:ʃop) — zapatería
  toy-shop ('toiʃop) — juguetería
shop-assistant ('ʃopəsistənt) — dependiente
shopkeeper ('ʃopki:pə) — tendero
shop window ('ʃop'windou) — escaparate
stationer's ('steiʃənəz) — papelería
stores (sto:z) — grandes almacenes
supermarket ('sju:pəmɑ:kit) — supermercado

Tailor's ('teiləz) — sastrería
tobacconist's (tə'bækənists) — estanco

Watchmaker's ('wotʃmeikəz) — relojería

84

SPORTS AND GAMES   DEPORTES Y JUEGOS (31)

ENGLISH	ESPAÑOL
Amateur ('æmətjuə)	aficionado
angling ('æŋgliŋ)	pesca con caña
archery ('ɑːtʃəri)	tiro con arco
athlete ('æθliːt)	atleta
Ball (boːl)	balón, pelota
baseball ('beisboːl)	pelota base
basketball ('bɑːskitboːl)	baloncesto
billiards ('biliədz)	billar
boating ('boutiŋ)	navegación
motor-boating ('moutəboutiŋ)	navegación a motor
bowling ('bouliŋ)	bolos
boxer ('boksə)	boxeador
boxing ('boksiŋ)	boxeo
bridge ('bridʒ)	juego del «bridge»
Cards* (kɑːdz)	cartas
champion ('tʃæmpiən)	campeón
championship ('tʃæmpiənʃip)	campeonato
chess* (tʃes)	ajedrez
climbing ('klaimiŋ)	escalada
cricket (krikit)	juego del criquet
croquet ('kroukei)	juego del croquet
cycling ('saikliŋ)	ciclismo
motor cycling ('moutəsaikliŋ)	motorismo
Darts (dɑːts)	dardos
diving ('daiviŋ)	buceo
dominoes ('dominouz)	dominó
draughts (drɑːfts)	damas
Fencing ('fensiŋ)	esgrima
fishing* ('fiʃiŋ)	pesca
football* ('futboːl)	fútbol, balón
Game (geim)	juego
card game ('kɑːdgeim)	juego de naipes
indoor games ('indoːʹgeimz)	juegos en pista cubierta

SPORTS AND GAMES — DEPORTES Y JUEGOS

Olympic games (ə'limpik'geimz) — juegos Olímpicos
outdoor games ('autdo:'geimz) — juegos al aire libre
golf (golf) — golf
golf link ('golfliŋk) — campo de golf
greyhound racing ('greihaund'reisiŋ) — carreras de galgos
gymnastics (dʒim'næstiks) — juegos gimnásticos

Hockey ('hoki) — «hockey»
  ice-hockey ('aishoki) — «hockey» sobre hielo
horse-racing ('ho:sreisiŋ) — carreras de caballos
hunting (hʌntiŋ) — caza mayor

Jump (dʒʌmp) — salto
  long jump ('loŋ'dʒʌmp) — salto de longitud
  high jump ('hai'dʒʌmp) — salto de altura
jumping ('dʒʌmpiŋ) — salto

Leg (leg) — manga

Marbles ('mɑ:bəlz) — canicas
match (mætʃ) — encuentro
motor-racing ('moutəreisiŋ) — carreras de coches
motor-boat racing ('moutəbout'reisiŋ) — carreras de lanchas motoras
motor-cycle racing ('moutəsaikəl'reisiŋ) — carreras de motos
mountaineering (mauntə'niəriŋ) — alpinismo

Olympiad (ə'limpiæd) — Olimpiada

Pole vault ('poulvo:lt) — salto con pértiga

Race (reis) — carrera
  horse-race ('ho:sreis) — carrera de caballos
  hurdle-race ('hə:dəlreis) — carrera de vallas
  obstacle-race ('obstəkəlreis) — carrera de obstáculos
riding ('raidiŋ) — equitación
rowing ('rouiŋ) — remo
rugby ('rʌgbi) — «rugby»
runner ('rʌnə) — corredor
running ('rʌniŋ) — carrera

Sailing ('seiliŋ) — navegación a vela
shooting ('ʃu:tiŋ) — caza menor
skating ('skeitiŋ) — patinaje
  ice-skating ('aisskeitiŋ) — patinaje sobre hielo
  roller-skating ('rouləskeitiŋ) — patinaje en pista

SPORTS AND GAMES	DEPORTES Y JUEGOS
ski-ing ('ski:iŋ)	esquí
water ski-ing ('wo:təski:iŋ)	esquí acuático
skittles ('skitəlz)	bolos
soccer ('sokə)	fútbol
swimming ('swimiŋ)	natación
under-water swimming ('ʌndəwo:tə'swimiŋ)	buceo
Tennis ('tenis)	tenis
lawn tennis ('lo:n'tenis)	tenis
table tennis ('teibəltenis)	ping pong
tennis court ('tenisko:t)	pista de tenis
throwing the discus ('θrouiŋðə'diskəs)	lanzamiento de disco
throwing the hammer ('θrouiŋðə'hæmə)	lanzamiento de martillo
throwing the javelin ('θrouiŋðə'dʒævlin)	lanzamiento de jabalina
track (træk)	pista
Volleyball ('volibo:l)	balón volea
Weight-lifting ('weitliftiŋ)	levantamiento de pesos
wrestling ('resliŋ)	lucha

85

TABLEWARE	VAJILLA (97)
ENGLISH	ESPAÑOL
Beaker ('bi:kə)	jarra con pitorro
bowl (boul)	tazón
Coffee-pot ('kofipot)	cafetera
crockery ('krokəri)	loza
cup (kʌp)	taza
coffee-cup ('kofikʌp)	taza para café
tea-cup ('ti:kʌp)	taza para té
cutlery ('kʌtəlri)	cubertería
Dish (diʃ)	fuente
Fork (fo:k)	tenedor

| TABLEWARE | VAJILLA |

Glass ('glɑːs)
  wine-glass ('wainglɑːs)
  glassware ('glɑːsweə)

Jug (dʒʌg)

Knife (naif)

knives (naivz)

Ladle ('leidl)

Mug (mʌg)

Plate (pleit)
  dessert-plate (di'zəːtpleit)
  dinner-plate ('dinəpleit)
  soup-plate ('suːpleit)
  sweet-plate ('swiːtpleit)

Salad-bowl ('sælədboul)
saltcellar ('soːltselə)
saucer ('soːsə)
soup-tureen ('suːptəriːn)
spoon (spuːn)
  dessert-spoon (di'zəːtspuːn)
  soup-spoon ('suːpspuːn)
  table-spoon ('teibəlspuːn)
  tea-spoon ('tiːspuːn)
sugar-bowl ('ʃugəboul)
sugar-tongs ('ʃugətoŋz)

Tableware ('teibəlweə)
teapot ('tiːpot)
tray (trei)

vaso
copa
cristalería

jarra

cuchillo

cuchillos

cazo

jarra sin pitorro

plato
plato de postre
plato llano
plato sopero
plato de postre

ensaladera
salero
platillo para taza
sopera
cuchara
cucharilla de postre
cuchara sopera
cuchara grande
cucharilla
azucarero
tenacillas para el azúcar

vajilla
tetera
bandeja

86

TAILOR AND THE DRESSMAKER, THE

EL SASTRE Y LA MODISTA (90)

ENGLISH

ESPAÑOL

Belt (belt)
bobbin ('bobin)
bodice ('bodis)

cinturón
bobina (de hilo)
cuerpo de un vestido

buckle ('bʌkl)	hebilla
buckram ('bʌkrəm)	entretela
button ('bʌtən)	botón
buttonhole ('bʌtənhoul)	ojal
Calico ('kælikou)	percal, retor
chalk (tʃo:k)	jaboncillo
checked (tʃekt)	a cuadros (tela)
cheviot ('tʃeviət)	cheviot
cloak (klouk)	capa
close-fitting ('klous'fitiŋ)	ajustado (una prenda)
cloth (kloθ)	tela, paño
roll of cloth ('rouləv'kloθ)	pieza de tela
coat (kout)	americana
collar ('kolə)	cuello (de una prenda)
cotton ('kotən)	hilo de algodón
crease (kri:s)	raya (del pantalón), arruga
cretonne (kre'ton)	cretona
cuff (kʌf)	puño (de una prenda)
cut (kʌt)	corte
Darn, to (tə'dɑ:n)	zurcir zurcido (sus.)
dress (dres)	vestido
dressmaker ('dresmeikə)	modista
Embroider, to (tuim'broidə)	bordar
embroidery (im'broidəri)	bordado (sus.)
Fabric ('fæbrik)	tejido
felt (felt)	fieltro
fit, to (tə'fit)	sentar bien (una prenda)
fitting ('fitiŋ)	prueba
fitting-room ('fitiŋrum)	probador
flannel ('flænəl)	franela
Garment ('gɑ:mənt)	prenda
Hemstitch ('hemstitʃ)	vainica
Iron ('aiən)	plancha
iron, to (tu'aiən)	planchar
Jacket ('dʒækit)	chaqueta
double-breasted jacket ('dʌbəlbrestid'dʒækit)	chaqueta de dos filas
single-breasted jacket ('siŋgəlbrestid'dʒækit)	chaqueta de una fila
sports jacket ('spo:stsdʒækit)	chaqueta de «sport»
Knitted ('nitid)	de punto (tejido)

| TAILOR, THE | EL SASTRE |

Lace (leis) — puntilla, encaje
lapel (lə'pel) — solapa
leather ('leðə) — cuero
lengthen, to (tə'leŋθən) — alargar (una prenda)
let out, to (tə'let'aut) — sacar (una prenda)
linen ('linən) — tela de hilo
lining ('lainiŋ) — forro
loose (lu:s) — suelto (una prenda)
low neck ('lou'nek) — escote bajo

Mannequin bust ('mænikinbʌst) — maniquí de sastre o modista
material (mə'tiəriəl) — paño
measure ('meʒə) — medida
 made to measure ('meidtə'meʒə) — a la medida
measure, to (tə'meʒə) — medir
measurement ('meʒəmənt) — medida
mirror ('mirə) — espejo

Needle ('ni:dl) — aguja
nylon ('nailən) — nylón

Overcoat ('ouvəkout) — abrigo

Pattern ('pætən) — patrón, dibujo (de la tela)
pin (pin) — alfiler
 safety-pin ('seiftipin) — imperdible
pincushion ('pinkuʃən) — acerico
pleat (pli:t) — pliegue
pleating ('pli:tiŋ) — plisado (sus.)
plush (plʌʃ) — felpa, pana
pocket ('pokit) — bolsillo
 breast pocket ('brestpokit) — bolsillo de pecho
 inside pocket ('insaid'pokit) — bolsillo interior
 side pocket ('saidpokit) — bolsillo de costado
press, to (tə'pres) — planchar
put on, to (tə'put'on) — ponerse (una prenda)

Ready-made ('redi'meid) — de confección
reel (ri:l) — carrete
ribbon ('ribən) — cinta

Satin ('sætin) — satín
scissors ('sizəz) — tijeras
seam (si:m) — costura
seamstress ('semstris) — sastra
sew, to (tə'sou) — coser
sewing-machine ('souiŋməʃi:n) — máquina de coser
sewn (soun) — cosido

hand-sewn ('hænd'soun)	cosido a mano
machine-sewn (mə'ʃi:n'soun)	cosido a máquina
shorten, to (tə'ʃo:tən)	acortar (una prenda)
silk (silk)	seda
artificial silk ('ɑ:tifiʃəl'silk)	seda artificial
natural silk ('nætʃərəl'silk)	seda natural
skirt (skə:t)	falda
sleeve (sli:v)	manga
long sleeve ('loŋ'sli:v)	manga larga
short sleeve ('ʃo:t'sli:v)	manga corta
snap fastener ('snæpfɑ:sənə)	automático
striped (straipt)	a rayas
suede (sweid)	ante
Tailor ('teilə)	sastre
take in, to (tə'teik'in)	meter (una prenda)
take off, to (tə'teik'of)	quitarse (una prenda)
tape (teip)	cinta de algodón
tape measure ('teipmeʒə)	cinta métrica
thimble ('θimbəl)	dedal
thread (θred)	hilo
tight (tait)	ajustado
skin tight ('skin'tait)	muy ajustado
train (trein)	cola de un vestido
trousers ('trauzəz)	pantalón
trouserleg ('trauzəleg)	pernera del pantalón
try on, to (tə'trai'on)	probarse (una prenda)
tuck (tʌk)	frunce
tulle (tul)	tul
tweed (twi:d)	tela de «tweed»
Velvet ('velvit)	terciopelo
V-shaped neck ('vi:ʃeipt'nek)	escote puntiagudo
Waist (weist)	cintura
wear, to (tu'weə)	llevar puesta (una prenda)
well-cut ('wel'kʌt)	bien cortado
wool (wul)	lana
work-basket ('wə:kbɑ:skit)	costurero
worsted ('wustid)	estambre
wristband ('ristbænd)	bocamanga
Yoke (jouk)	canesú

87

TELEVISION AND RADIO   TELEVISION Y RADIO (91)

ENGLISH	ESPAÑOL

Acoustic signals
        (ə'ku:stik'signəlz)   señales acústicas
aerial   ('eəriəl)   antena
airwaves   ('eəweivz)   ondas de radio
amplifier   ('æmplifaiə)   amplificador
amplify, to   (tu'æmplifai)   amplificar

Battery   ('bætəri)   batería
broadcast, to   (tə'bro:dkɑ:st)   transmitir

Camera   ('kæmərə)   cámara
cathode-ray tube
        ('kæθoud rei'tju:b)   tubo de rayos catódicos
circuit   ('sə:kit)   circuito

Electrical impulses
        (i'lektrikəl'impʌlsiz)   impulsos eléctricos
electro-magnetic waves
      (i'lektroumæg'netik'weivz)   ondas electromagnéticas
electron   (i'lektron)   electrón

Film   (film)   película
  silent film   ('sailənt'film)   película muda
  sound film   ('saundfilm)   película sonora
frequency   ('fri:kwənsi)   frecuencia
  Ultra High Frequency
        ('ʌltrə'hai'fri:kwənsi)   U. H. F.
  Very High Frequency
        ('veri'hai'fri:kwensi)   V. H. F.

Image   ('imidʒ)   imagen

Kilocycles   ('kilousaikəlz)   kilociclos
knob   (nob)   mando (de un aparato)

Long wave   ('loŋ'weiv)   onda larga
loudspeaker   ('laud'spi:kə)   altavoz

Medium wave   ('mi:diəm'weiv)   onda media
megacycles   ('megəsaikəlz)   megaciclos
Morse code   ('mo:skoud)   alfabeto Morse

TELEVISION AND RADIO — TELEVISIÓN Y RADIO

Picture ('piktʃə) — imagen
  talking picture ('tɔ:kiŋ'piktʃə) — película sonora

Radio receiver ('reidjourisi:və) — receptor de radio
radio set ('reidjouset) — aparato de radio
radio station ('reidjousteiʃən) — estación de radio
radio transmitter ('reidjoutrænsmitə) — transmisor de radio
receive, to (təri'si:v) — recibir
receiver (ri'si:və) — receptor

Screen (skri:n) — pantalla
short wave ('ʃo:t'weiv) — onda corta
signal ('signəl) — señal
sound (saund) — sonido
sound effects ('saundifekts) — efectos de sonido
sound-track ('saundtræk) — pista de sonido
sound-wave ('saundweiv) — onda de sonido
synchronize, to (tə'siŋkrənaiz) — sincronizar

Television set ('təliviʒənset) — aparato de televisión
transformer (træns'fo:mə) — transformador
transistor (træn'sistə) — transistor
transmission (træns'miʃən) — transmisión
transmit, to (tətræns'mit) — transmitir
transmitting station (træns'mitiŋsteiʃən) — estación transmisora

Valve (vælv) — válvula
voltage ('voultidʒ) — voltaje
volume ('volju:m) — volumen
volume control ('volju:mkəntroul) — control del volumen

Wave (weiv) — onda
wireless set ('waiəlisset) — aparato de radio

THEATRE, THE   (See THE CINEMA, 20)

88

TIME	EL TIEMPO (92)
ENGLISH	ESPAÑOL

Afternoon ('a:ftə'nu:n)   tarde (sus.)
age* (eidʒ)   edad
almanac ('o:lmənæk)   almanaque
April (eipril)   abril
August ('o:gəst)   agosto
autumn ('o:təm)   otoño

Calendar ('kælində)   calendario
   block calendar
       ('blokkælində)   calendario de taco
century ('sentʃəri)   siglo
clock* (klok)   reloj (no de pulsera o bolsillo)

Date (deit)   fecha
day (dei)   día
decade ('dekeid)   década
December (di'sembə)   diciembre

Early (ə:li)   temprano
epoch ('i:pok)   época
era ('iərə)   era
eternity (i'tə:niti)   eternidad
evening ('i:vniŋ)   tarde (sus.)

February ('februəri)   febrero
fortnight ('fo:tnait)   quincena
friday ('fraidi)   viernes
future ('fju:tʃə)   futuro

Hour ('auə)   hora
   a quarter of an hour
       (ə'kwo:tərəvən'auə)   un cuarto de hora
   half an hour ('ha:fən'auə)   media hora

Instant ('instənt)   instante

January ('dʒænjuəri)   enero
July (dʒu'lai)   julio
June (dʒu:n)   junio

TIME — EL TIEMPO

Late (leit) — tarde (adv.)
leap-year ('li:pjiə) — año bisiesto

March (mɑ:tʃ) — marzo
May (mei) — mayo
midday ('middei) — medio día
midnight ('midnait) — media noche
minute ('minit) — minuto
moment ('moumənt) — momento
Monday ('mʌndi) — lunes
month (mʌnθ) — mes
morning ('mo:niŋ) — mañana (sus.)

Night (nait) — noche
November (nou'vembə) — noviembre

October (ək'toubə) — octubre

Past (pɑ:st) — pasado
period ('piəriəd) — período
present ('prezənt) — presente

Saturday ('sætədi) — sábado
season ('si:zən) — estación, temporada
second ('sekənd) — segundo
September (sep'tembə) — septiembre
spring (spriŋ) — primavera
summer ('sʌmə) — verano
  Indian Summer ('indiən'sʌmə) — veranillo de San Martín
Sunday ('sʌndi) — domingo

Term (tə:m) — trimestre
Thursday ('θə:zdi) — jueves
time, to (tə'taim) — cronometrar
time-table ('taimteibl) — horario
today (tə'dei) — hoy
tomorrow (tə'morou) — mañana (adv.)
  the day after tomorrow (ðə'deiɑ:ftətə'morou) — pasado mañana
tonight (tə'nait) — esta noche
Tuesday ('tju:zdi) — martes

Watch (wotʃ) — reloj (de pulsera o bolsillo)
wednesday ('wenzdi) — miércoles
week (wi:k) — semana
week-end ('wi:k'end) — fin de semana
winter ('wintə) — invierno

TIME 216 EL TIEMPO

Year (jiə) año
yesterday ('jestədi) ayer
  the day before yesterday
          (ðə'deibifo:'jestədi) anteayer

89
TOOLS AND INSTRUMENTS   HERRAMIENTAS E INSTRUMENTOS (48)

ENGLISH	ESPAÑOL
Anvil ('ænvil)	yunque
axe (æks)	hacha
awl (o:l)	lezna
Bit (bit)	broca
blowlamp ('bloulæmp)	lámpara de soldar
brace (breis)	berbiquí
Callipers ('kælipəz)	calibrador
chisel ('tʃizl)	cincel, escoplo, formón
cold chisel ('kould'tʃizl)	cortafrío
clamp (klæmp)	prensa de tornillo
compasses, a pair of (ə'peərəv'kʌmpəsiz)	un compás
cramp (kræmp)	prensa de tornillo
crampon ('kræmpən)	tenazas de garfios
crane (krein)	grúa
Drill (dril)	taladro
File (fail)	lima
fork (fo:k)	horquilla
Gauge (geidʒ)	calibrador
gimlet ('gimlit)	barrena
grease gun ('gri:sgʌn)	pistola de engrase
Hammer ('hæmə)	martillo
hoe (hou)	azadón

| TOOLS, ETC. | HERRAMIENTAS, ETC. |

Jack (dʒæk) — gato (para levantar pesos)
Lathe (leið) — torno
level ('levl) — nivel
  spirit level ('spiritlevl) — nivel de burbuja

Mallet ('mælit) — mazo
milling tool ('miliŋtu:l) — fresa

Oil-can ('oilkæn) — aceitera

Pick (pik) — pico, punzón
pickaxe ('pikæks) — zapapico
pincers ('pinsəz) — tenazas
pitchfork ('pitʃfo:k) — horquilla
plane (plein) — cepillo de carpintero
pliers ('plaiəz) — alicates
plumb line ('plʌmlain) — plomada

Rake (reik) — rastrillo
rule (ru:l) — metro plegable

Saw (so:) — sierra
  band saw ('bændso:) — sierra circular
  circular saw ('sə:kjulə'so:) — sierra circular
  frame saw ('freimso:) — sierra de bastidor
  fretsaw ('fretso:) — sierra de marquetería
  hacksaw ('hækso:) — sierra para metales
  hand saw ('hændso:) — serrucho
  scissors ('sizəz) — tijeras
  scoop (sku:p) — pala de mango corto
  screwdriver ('skru:draivə) — destornillador
  scythe (saið) — guadaña
  shears (ʃiəz) — tijeras de jardín
  shovel ('ʃʌvəl) — pala de mango largo
  sickle ('sikl) — hoz
  soldering-iron ('soldəriŋaiən) — soldador
  spade (speid) — pala para cavar
  spanner ('spænə) — llave de tuercas
  square (skweə) — escuadra

Tongs (toŋz) — tenazas
tool (tu:l) — herramienta
trowel ('trauəl) — llana, paleta
tweezers ('twi:zəz) — pinzas

Vice (vais) — tornillo (para sujetar piezas)

Wrench (rentʃ) — llave inglesa

90

TOURISM AND TRAVELLING   TURISMO Y VIAJES (96)

ENGLISH   ESPAÑOL

Airhostess ('eəhoustis)   azafata
air line ('eəlain)   compañía de aviación
airport* ('eəpo:t)   aeropuerto
air-sick ('eəsik)   mareado (en avión)
air-sickness ('eəsiknis)   mareo (en avión)
arrival (ə'raivəl)   llegada

Baggage ('bægidʒ)   equipaje (USA)
berth (bə:θ)   litera
boarding-house ('bo:diŋhaus)   pensión
boat (bout)   barco
book, to (tə'buk)   reservar
booking-office ('bukiŋofis)   taquilla
bus (bʌs)   autobús

Cabin ('kæbin)   camarote
camping-site ('kæmpiŋsait)   «camping»
car* (kɑ:)   coche
carriage ('kæridʒ)   vagón
case (keis)   maleta
class (klɑ:s)   clase
   first class ('fə:st'klɑ:s)   primera clase
   luxury class ('lʌkʃərriklɑ:s)   clase de lujo
   second class ('sekənd'klɑ:s)   segunda clase
   third class ('θə:d'klɑ:s)   tercera clase
   tourist class ('tuəristklɑ:s)   clase turista
coach (koutʃ)   coche de línea
comparment (kəm'pɑ:tmənt)   compartimento
connection (kə'nekʃən)   transbordo
crew (kru:)   tripulación
crossing ('krosiŋ)   travesía
Customs ('kʌstəmz)   Aduana
Customs duty ('kʌstəmzdju:ti)   derechos de Aduana
Customs House ('kʌstəmzhaus)   edificio de la Aduana
Customs-officer ('kʌstəmzofisə)   oficial de Aduanas

Departure (di'pɑ:tʃə)   partida
dining-car ('dainiŋkɑ:)   coche restaurante

TOURISM	TURISMO
disembark, to (tədisim'bɑːk)	desembarcar
drive, to (tə'draiv)	conducir
Embark, to (tuim'bɑːk)	embarcar
Fare (feə)	precio del viaje
half fare ('hɑːf'feə)	medio billete
flight (flait)	vuelo
fly, to (tə'flai)	volar
frontier ('frʌntiə)	frontera
Guest-house ('gesthaus)	pensión
guide (gaid)	guía (persona)
railway-guide ('reilweigaid)	guía de ferrocarriles
guide-book ('gaidbuk)	guía (libro)
Hotel* (hou'tel)	lugar de vacaciones
Inn (in)	fonda
Inquiry office (iŋ'kwaiəri'ofis)	oficina de información
itinerary (ai'tinirəri)	itinerario
Journey ('dʒəːni)	viaje por tierra o aire
Left-luggage office ('leflʌgidʒ'ofis)	consigna
liner ('lainə)	transatlántico
luggage ('lʌgidʒ)	equipaje (GB)
luggage-rack ('lʌgidʒræk)	rejilla del equipaje
Map (mæp)	mapa
monuments ('monjuments)	monumentos
motor-car ('moutəkɑː)	coche
Non-smoker ('non'smoukə)	departamento para no fumadores
Passage ('pæsidʒ)	travesía
passenger ('pæsəndʒə)	pasajero
passport ('pɑːspoːt)	pasaporte
plane (plein)	avión
platform ('plætfoːm)	andén
port (poːt)	puerto
porter ('poːtə)	mozo
Quay (kiː)	muelle (desembarcadero)
Railway ('reilwei)	ferrocarril
railway-station* ('reilweisteiʃən)	estación de ferrocarril

refreshment room
           (ri'freʃmənt rum)   cantina
registration slip
           (redʒis'treiʃənslip)   talón de facturación de equipajes
restaurant*   ('restərənt)   restaurante
restaurant car   ('restərəntkɑ:) coche restaurante
road   (roud)   carretera
route   (ru:t)   ruta

Safety-belt   ('seiftibelt)   cinturón de seguridad
sail, to   (tə'seil)   zarpar, navegar
sea-sick   ('si:sik)   mareado (en barco)
sea-sickness   ('si:siknis)   mareo (en barco)
seat   (si:t)   asiento
service   ('sə:vis)   servicio
  regular service
            ('regjulə'sə:vis)   servicio regular
ship*   (ʃip)   barco
sight-seeing   ('saitsi:iŋ)   visita a una ciudad
sleeper   ('sli:pə)   coche cama
smoker   ('smoukə)   departamento para fumadores
speed   (spi:d)   velocidad
station   ('steiʃən)   estación
stay   (stei)   estancia
steamer   ('sti:mə)   buque de vapor
steamship company
            ('sti:mʃip'kʌmpəni) compañía de navegación
stewardess   ('stjuədis)   azafata
stop   (stop)   parada
suitcase   ('su:tkeis)   maleta

Taxi   ('tæksi)   taxi
terminus   ('tə:minəs)   estación terminal
ticket   ('tikit)   billete
  air-ticket   ('eətikit)   billete de avión
  return ticket   (ri'tə:ntikit) billete de ida y vuelta
  single ticket   ('siŋgəl'tikit) billete de ida
ticket collector   ('tikitkəlektə) revisor
ticket-office   ('tikitofis)   taquilla
time-table   ('taimteibl)   horario
toilet case   ('toilitkeis)   neceser
tourist   ('tuərist)   turista
train   (trein)   tren
  express train
            (iks'prestrein)   tren expreso
  fast train   ('fɑ:st'trein)   tren rápido
  slow train   ('slou'trein)   tren ómnibus
  through train   ('θru:'trein) tren directo

transportation	(trænspo:'teiʃən)	transporte
travel, to	(tə'trævəl)	viajar
travel agency	('trævəleidʒənsi)	agencia de viajes
travel by air, to	(tə'trævəlbai'eə)	viajar en avión
travel by car, to	(tə'trævəlbai'kɑ:)	viajar en coche
travel by rail, to	(tə'trævəlbai'reil)	viajar en tren
travel by sea, to	(tə'trævəlbai'si:)	viajar por mar
traveller	('trævələ)	viajero
trip	(trip)	viaje
trunk	(trʌŋk)	baúl
Visa	('vi:zə)	visado
entry visa	('entri'vi:zə)	visado de entrada
exit visa	('eksit'vi:zə)	visado de salida
voyage	('voiidʒ)	viaje por mar
Waiting-room	('weitiŋrum)	sala de espera
way	(wei)	camino

91

TOWN, A   UNA CIUDAD (21)

ENGLISH   **ESPAÑOL**

Advertisement	(əd'və:tizmənt)	anuncio
air pollution	('eəpəlu:ʃən)	contaminación atmosférica
airport*	('eəpo:t)	aeropuerto
arch	(ɑ:tʃ)	arco
avenue	('ævinju:)	avenida
Bank	(bæŋk)	banco (casa de banca)
barracks	('bærəks)	cuartel
bench	(bentʃ)	banco (para sentarse)
block	(blok)	manzana de casas
block of flats	('blokəv'flæts)	casa de pisos
bookstall	('buksto:l)	quiosco de periódicos y libros

TOWN, A	UNA CIUDAD

bridge (bridʒ) — puente
building ('bildiŋ) — edificio
  public building ('pʌblik'bildiŋ) — edificio público
bull-ring ('bulriŋ) — plaza de toros
bus (bʌs) — autobús
bus line ('bʌslain) — línea de autobuses
bus stop ('bʌsstop) — parada de autobús

Café ('kæfei) — cafetería
canal (kə'næl) — canal
car (kɑ:) — coche
castle ('kɑ:sl) — castillo
cathedral (kə'θi:drəl) — catedral
cemetery ('semitri) — cementerio
centre, the (ðə'sentə) — el centro
church (tʃə:tʃ) — iglesia
cinema ('sinəmə) — cine
city ('siti) — ciudad
  garden city ('gɑ:dən'siti) — ciudad jardín
consulate ('konsjulit) — consulado
corner ('ko:nə) — esquina
crossroads ('krosroudz) — cruce
crowd (kraud) — multitud

District ('distrikt) — distrito, barrio
dustcart ('dʌstkɑ:t) — coche de recogida de basura
dustman ('dʌstmən) — basurero, barrendero

Embassy ('embəsi) — embajada

Factory ('fæktəri) — fábrica
fire-brigade ('faiəbrigeid) — brigada de bomberos
fire-department ('faiədipɑ:tmənt) — servicio de incendios
fire-engine ('faiərendʒin) — coche de bomberos
firemen ('faiəmen) — bomberos
flyover ('flaiouvə) — paso elevado
fountain ('fauntən) — fuente

Garage ('gærɑ:ʒ) — garaje
garden* ('gɑ:dən) — jardín
gutter ('gʌtə) — arroyo de la calle

Hospital* ('hospitl) — hospital
hotel* (hou'tel) — hotel
house* (haus) — casa

Island ('ailənd) — isleta para peatones

Kerb (kə:b) bordillo de la acera
kiosk ('ki:osk) quiosco

Lamp-post ('læmpoust) farola
lane (lein) callejón
letter-box ('letəboks) buzón
library ('laibrəri) biblioteca
  public library
        ('pʌblik'laibrəri) biblioteca pública
lost property office
        ('lost'propəti'ofis) oficina de objetos perdidos

Market ('mɑ:kit) mercado
market-place ('mɑ:kitpleis) plaza del mercado
memorial (mə'moriəl) monumento conmemorativo
military post ('militəri'poust) puesto militar
monument ('monjumənt) monumento
museum (mju'ziəm) museo

Naval base ('neivəl'beis) base naval
neon lights ('ni:ən'laits) anuncios luminosos
newspaper-boy
        ('nju:speipəboi) vendedor de periódicos
newspaper-stall
        ('nju:speipəsto:l) quiosco de periódicos

Opera-house ('operəhaus) teatro de la ópera
outskirts, the (ði'autskə:ts) las afueras
overpass ('ouvəpɑ:s) paso elevado

Palace ('pæləs) palacio
paper-boy ('peipəboi) vendedor de periódicos
park (pɑ:k) parque
  amusement park
        (ə'mju:zməntpɑ:k) parque de atracciones
  car park ('kɑ:pɑ:k) aparcamiento
pavement ('peivmənt) acera (GB)
pedestrian (pə'destriən) peatón
policeman (pə'li:smən) guardia
port (po:t) puerto
poster ('poustə) cartel
post-office ('poustofis) estafeta de correos
postman ('pousmən) cartero
prison ('prizən) cárcel
promenade (promi'nɑ:d) paseo marítimo

Quarter ('kwo:tə) barrio

Restaurant* ('restərənt) restaurante
river ('rivə) río

| TOWN, A | UNA CIUDAD |

road   (roud)   calzada
roadway   ('roudwei)   calzada
School   (sku:l)   escuela
sewer   ('sjuə)   alcantarilla
sewerage   ('sjuəridʒ)   alcantarillado
shop*   (ʃop)   tienda
shop-window   ('ʃop'windou)   escaparate
sidewalk   ('saidwo:k)   acera (USA)
site   (sait)   solar
skyscraper   ('skaïskreipə)   rascacielos
square   (skweə)   plaza
station   ('steiʃən)   estación
  fire-station   ('faiəsteiʃən)   parque de bomberos
  petrol station
        ('petrəlsteiʃən)   estación de gasolina
  police station
        (pə'li:ssteiʃən)   comisaría
  railway station
        ('reilweisteiʃən)   estación de ferrocarril
  underground station
        ('ʌndəgraundsteiʃən)   estación del metro
statue   ('stætju:)   estatua
stop   (stop)   parada (de autobús, etc.)
stores   (sto:z)   almacenes
street   (stri:t)   calle
  high street   ('hai'stri:t)   gran vía
  main street   ('mein'stri:t)   calle principal
street corner   ('stri:tko:nə)   esquina de la calle
suburbs, the   (ðə'sʌbə:bz)   las afueras
sweeper   ('swi:pə)   barrendero
Taxi   ('tæksi)   taxi
taxi-rank   ('tæksirænk)   parada de taxis
telegraph office
        ('teligrɑ:fofis)   oficina de telégrafos
telephone   ('telifoun)   teléfono
  public telephone
        ('pʌblik'telifoun)   teléfono público
  telephone booth
        ('telifounbu:θ)   cabina telefónica
  telephone box   ('telifounboks)   cabina telefónica
theatre   ('θiətə)   teatro
thoroughfare   ('θʌrəfeə)   vía pública
tourist office   ('tuəristofis)   oficina de turismo
tower   ('tauə)   torre
town   (taun)   ciudad
  industrial town
        (in'dʌstriəl'taun)   ciudad industrial

TOWN, A		UNA CIUDAD

seaside town ('si:said'taun)	ciudad costera
town council ('taunkaunsil)	ayuntamiento (corporación)
town hall ('taunho:l)	ayuntamiento (edificio)
traffic* ('træfik)	tráfico
tram (træm)	tranvía
tram stop ('træmstop)	parada del tranvía
transport ('trænspo:t)	transporte
means of transport ('mi:nzəv'trænspo:t)	medios de transporte
tree* (tri:)	árbol
trolley-bus ('trolibʌs)	trolebús
turning ('tə:niŋ)	bocacalle
Underground ('ʌndəgraund)	metro
university (juni'və:siti)	universidad
Villa ('vilə)	chalet
Wall (wo:l)	muralla
Zoo (zu:)	parque zoológico
TRADE	(See BUSINESS, 15)

92

TRAFFIC · TRAFICO (94)

ENGLISH	ESPAÑOL
Accident ('æksidənt)	accidente
Bend (bend)	curva
double bend ('dʌbəl'bend)	doble curva
Car park ('kɑ:pɑ:k)	aparcamiento
crash, to (tə'kræʃ)	chocar
crossing ('krosiŋ)	cruce
children crossing ('tʃildrənkrosiŋ)	cruce de niños
pedestrian crossing (pə'destriənkrosiŋ)	cruce de peatones
zebra crossing ('zi:brəkrosiŋ)	cruce de cebra

TRAFFIC TRÁFICO

cross-roads ('krosroudz) — cruce
cyclist ('saiklist) — ciclista

Diversion (dai'vəːʃən) — desvío
drive, to (tə'draiv) — conducir
driver ('draivə) — conductor
  lorry-driver ('loridraivə) — camionero
driving licence ('draiviŋlaisəns) — permiso de conducir

Flyover ('flaiouvə) — paso elevado

Gates (geits) — barreras

Highway Code ('haiwei'koud) — Código de la circulación

Left ('left) — izquierda
  keep left ('kiːp'left) — manténgase a la izquierda
level-crossing ('levəl'krosiŋ) — paso a nivel
  guarded level-crossing ('gɑːdid'levəlkrosiŋ) — paso a nivel con barrera
  unguarded level-crossing (ʌn'gɑːdid'levəlkrosiŋ) — paso a nivel sin barrera

Motor-cyclist ('moutəsaiklist) — motorista
motorist ('moutərist) — automovilista
motorway ('moutəwei) — autopista

No parking ('nou'pɑːkiŋ) — se prohibe aparcar
no waiting ('nou'weitiŋ) — se prohibe estacionar

Park, to (tə'pɑːk) — aparcar
policeman (pə'liːsmən) — guardia
  traffic policeman ('træfikpə'liːsmən) — guardia urbano

Right (rait) — derecha
  keep right ('kiːp'rait) — manténgase a la derecha
road blocked ('roud'blokt) — carretera cortada
road junction ('rouddʒʌŋkʃən) — cruce de carreteras
road narrows ('roud'nærouz) — estrechamiento de calzada
road signs ('roudsainz) — señales de tráfico
roundabout ('raundəbaut) — giro en el centro de la glorieta

Sign (sain) — señal
slippery surface ('slipəri'səːfis) — calzada resbaladiza
speed limit ('spiːdlimit) — límite de velocidad

TRAFFIC		TRÁFICO

stop   (stop) — alto
stop, to   (tə'stop) — parar
street   (stri:t) — calle
  one-way street
       ('wʌnwei'stri:t) — calle de una dirección
  two-way street
       ('tu:wei'stri:t) — calle de doble dirección

Throroughfare   ('θʌrəfeə) — vía pública
  no thoroughfare
       ('nou'θʌrəfeə) — calle cortada
traffic   ('træfik) — tráfico
traffic congestion
       ('træfikkən'dʒestʃən) — congestión de tráfico
traffic control   ('træfikkəntroul) — regulación del tráfico
traffic-jam   ('træfikdʒæm) — atasco de tráfico
traffic lights   ('træfiklaits) — semáforo
traffic police   ('træfikpə'li:s) — policía de tráfico
traffic signs   ('træfiksainz) — señales de tráfico
turn   (tə:n) — giro
  no right turn   ('nou'rait'tə:n) — se prohibe el giro a la derecha
  no left turn   ('nou'left'tə:n) — se prohibe el giro a la izquierda

Underpass   ('ʌndəpɑ:s) — paso subterráneo
uneven surface
       (ʌn'i:vən'sə:fis) — calzada irregular

93

TRANSPORTATION   EL TRANSPORTE (95)

ENGLISH   ESPAÑOL

Aircraft*   ('eəkrɑ:ft) — aeronave
air-liner   ('eəlainə) — avión de pasajeros
ambulance   ('æmbjuləns) — ambulancia

Bicycle*   ('baisikl) — bicicleta
bus   (bʌs) — autobús

Camel   ('kæməl) — camello
car*   (kɑ:) — coche
cart   (kɑ:t) — carro

| TRANSPORTATION | EL TRANSPORTE |

chariot ('tʃæriət) carro romano
coach (koutʃ) coche de línea
  stage coach ('steidʒkoutʃ) diligencia
  state coach ('steitkoutʃ) carroza

Donkey ('dɔŋki) burro

Helicopter ('helikoptə) helicóptero
horse (hoːs) caballo

Jeep (dʒiːp) «jeep»
jet (dʒet) avión de reacción

Liner ('lainə) transatlántico
lorry ('lori) camión (GB)

Motor-car ('moutəkɑː) coche
motorcycle ('moutəsaikl) moto
motor-scooter ('moutəskuːtə) moto «escuter»
mule (mjuːl) mula

Plane (plein) avión
post-chaise ('poustʃeiz) silla de posta

Railway ('reilwei) ferrocarril

Sailing-boat ('seiliŋbout) barco de vela
sedan-chair (si'dæntʃeə) silla de manos
ship* (ʃip) barco
sleigh (slei) trineo
space-ship ('speisʃip) nave espacial
steamer ('stiːmə) vapor
submarine ('sʌbməriːn) submarino

Taxi ('tæksi) taxi
train (trein) tren
tram (træm) tranvía
tramcar ('træmkɑː) tranvía
trolley-bus ('trolibʌs) trolebús
truck (trʌk) camión (USA)

Underground ('ʌndəgraund) metro

Van (væn) furgoneta

Wheelbarrow ('wiːlbærou) carretilla

TRAVELLING (See TOURISM, 90)

94

TREES, PLANTS AND FLOWERS	ARBOLES, PLANTAS Y FLORES (6)
ENGLISH	ESPAÑOL

Acacia   (ə'keiʃə)   acacia
alder   ('o:ldə)   aliso
anemone   (ə'nemən i)   anémona
ash   (æʃ)   fresno
aspidistra (æspi'distrə)   aspidistra
aster   ('æstə)   aster
azalea   (ə'zeiliə)   azalea

Bamboo   (bæm'bu:)   bambú
beech   (bi:tʃ)   haya
birch   (bə:tʃ)   abedul
blackberry bush
          ('blækbəribuʃ)
bluebell ('blu:bel)   zarzal
bulrush   ('bulrʌʃ)   campánula azul
bush   (buʃ)   junco
buttercup ('bʌtəkʌp)   arbusto
                               botón de oro

Cactus   ('kæktəs)   cactus
camellia (kə'mi:liə)   camelia
camomile ('kæməmail)   manzanilla
carnation (kɑ:'neiʃən)   clavel
cedar   ('si:də)   cedro
chrysanthemum
          (kri'sænθəməm)   crisantemo
clover   ('klouvə)   trébol
cowslip   ('kauslip)   primavera
creeper   ('kri:pə)   enredadera
crocus   ('kroukəs)   azafrán
cultivate, to (tə'kʌltiveit)   cultivar
cyclamen ('sikləmən)   ciclamen
cypres   ('saipris)   ciprés

Daffodil ('dæfədil)   narciso
dahlia   ('deiliə)   dalia
daisy   ('deizi)   margarita
dandelion ('dændilaiən)   diente de león
dog-rose ('dog rouz)   escaramujo, rosal silvestre

Ebony   ('ebəni)   ébano

TREES, ETC. ÁRBOLES, ETC.

elder ('eldə) — saúco
elm (elm) — olmo
eucalyptus (ju:kə'liptəs) — eucalipto

Fennel ('fenəl) — hinojo
fern (fə:n) — helecho
fir (fə:) — abeto
flax (flæks) — lino
flower ('flauə) — flor
forget-me-not (fə'getminot) — no me olvides. miosotis.
foxglove ('foksglʌv) — dedalera
fuchsia ('fju:ʃə) — fucsia

Geranium (dʒi'reiniəm) — geranio
gladiolus (glæ'djouləs) — gladiolo
grape-vine ('greipvain) — vid
grass (grɑ:s) — hierba

Harebell ('heəbel) — campánula
hawthorn ('ho:θo:n) — espino
heather ('heðə) — brezo
hemlock ('hemlok) — cicuta
hemp (hemp) — cáñamo
holly ('holi) — acebo
holly-hock ('holihok) — malva loca
honeysuckle ('hʌnisʌkl) — madreselva
hyacinth ('haiəsinθ) — jacinto
hydrangea (hai'dreindʒə) — hortensia

Iris ('aiəris) — lirio
ivy ('aivi) — hiedra

Jasmin ('dʒæzmin) — jazmín
juniper ('dʒu:nipə) — enebro

Laburnum (lə'bə:nəm) — laburno, lluvia de oro
larch (lɑ:tʃ) — alerce
lavender ('lævəndə) — espliego
lilac ('lailək) — lila
lily ('lili) — lirio
   water-lily ('wo:təlili) — nenúfar
   white lily ('wait'lili) — azucena
lily of the valley ('liliəvðə'væli) — muguete

Magnolia (məg'nouliə) — magnolia
mahogany (mə'hogəni) — caoba
mallow ('mælou) — malva
maple ('meipl) — arce
marigold ('mærigould) — caléndula
marjoram ('mɑ:dʒərəm) — mejorana

TREES, ETC.   ÁRBOLES, ETC.

mimosa (mi'mouzə)   mimosa
mint (mint)   hierbabuena
mistletoe ('misəltou)   muérdago
moss (mos)   musgo
mushroom ('mʌʃrum)   champiñón, seta, hongo
myrtle ('mə:tl)   mirto

Narcissus (nɑ:'sisəs)   narciso
nasturtium (nəs'tə:ʃəm)   capuchina

Oak (ouk)   roble, encina
oleander (ouli'ændə)   adelfa
orchid ('o:kid)   orquidea

Palm (pɑ:m)   palmera
  cocoanut palm ('koukənʌtpɑ:m)   cocotero
  date-palm ('deitpɑ:m)   palmera datilera
pansy ('pænzi)   pensamiento
peony ('piəni)   peonía
periwinkle ('periwiŋkəl)   pervinca
petunia (pə'tju:niə)   petunia
pine (pain)   pino
pink (piŋk)   clavel
poplar ('poplə)   álamo, chopo
poppy ('popi)   amapola
primrose ('primrouz)   primavera
privet ('privit)   aligustre

Reed (ri:d)   caña
redwood ('redwud)   secoya
rhododendron (roudə'dendrən)   rododendro
rhubarb ('ru:bɑ:b)   ruibarbo
rose (rouz)   rosa
rosebush ('rouzbuʃ)   rosal
rosewood ('rouzwud)   palo de rosa
rush (rʌʃ)   junco

Seaweed ('si:wi:d)   alga marina
snapdragon ('snæpdrægən)   boca de dragón
snowdrop ('snoudrop)   campanilla blanca
sorrel ('sorəl)   acedera
spruce (spru:s)   picea
sunflower ('sʌnflauə)   girasol
sweet william ('swi:t'wiliəm)   minutisa
sycamore ('sikəmo:)   sicomoro

Tarragon ('tærəgən)   estragón
teak (ti:k)   teca
thistle ('θisl)   cardo

TREES, ETC.   ÁRBOLES, ETC.

thyme   (taim)   tomillo
tree   (tri:)   árbol
  almond-tree   ('ɑ:məndtri:)   almendro
  apple-tree   ('æpəltri:)   manzano
  apricot-tree   ('eiprikottri:)   albaricoquero
  banana-tree   (bə'nɑ:nətri:)   plátano (árbol)
  cherry-tree   ('tʃeritri:)   cerezo
  chestnut-tree   ('tʃesnʌttri:)   castaño
  coconut-tree   ('koukənʌttri:)   cocotero
  cork-tree   ('ko:ktri:)   alcornoque
  fig-tree   ('figtri:)   higuera
  hazelnut-tree   ('heizəlnʌttri:)   avellano
  lemon-tree   ('lemən tri:)   limonero
  lilac-tree   ('lailəktri:)   lilo
  linden-tree   ('lindəntri:)   tilo
  maple-tree   ('meipəltri:)   arce
  olive-tree   ('olivtri:)   olivo
  orange-tree   ('orindʒtri:)   naranjo
  palm-tree   ('pɑ:mtri:)   palmera
  peach-tree   ('pi:tʃtri:)   melocotonero
  pear-tree   ('peətri:)   peral
  pine-tree   ('paintri:)   pino
  plane-tree   ('pleintri:)   plátano
  plum-tree   ('plʌmtri:)   ciruelo
  quince-tree   ('kwinstri:)   membrillo
  rubber-tree   ('rʌbətri:)   árbol del caucho
  walnut-tree   ('wo:lnʌttri:)   nogal
tulip   ('tju:lip)   tulipán

Vine   (vain)   vid, parra
violet   ('vaiəlit)   violeta

Wallflower   ('wo:lflauə)   alhelí
willow   ('wilou)   sauce
  weeping willow
          ('wi:piŋ'wilou)   sauce llorón

Yew   (ju:)   tejo

95

TYPEWRITER, A   **UNA MAQUINA DE ESCRIBIR (61)**

ENGLISH   ESPAÑOL

Carriage   ('kæridʒ)   carro
copy   ('kopi)   copia

| TYPEWRITER, A | UNA MÁQUINA DE ESCRIBIR |

Key (ki:) — tecla
  back space key ('bækspeis'ki:) — tecla de retroceso
  margin release key ('mɑ:dʒinrili:s'ki:) — tecla para soltar el margen
  shift-key ('ʃiftki:) — tecla de mayúsculas
  tabulador set key ('tæbjuleitə'setki:) — tecla para fijar el tabulador
keyboard ('ki:bo:d) — teclado

Lever ('li:və) — palanca
  carriage release lever ('kæridʒrili:s'li:və) — palanca para dejar libre el carro
  line space lever ('lainspeis'li:və) — palanca para espacios
  paper release lever ('peipərili:s'li:və) — palanca para dejar libre el papel
letter ('letə) — letra
  capital letter ('kæpitəl'letə) — letra mayúscula
  small letter ('smo:l'letə) — letra minúscula

Margin ('mɑ:dʒin) — margen
margin setter ('mɑ:dʒinsetə) — colocador del margen

Ribbon ('ribən) — cinta
ribbon reverse ('ribənrivə:s) — dispositivo para hacer que vuelva la cinta

roller ('roulə) — rodillo

Segment ('segmənt) — segmento
shift lock ('ʃiftlok) — sujetador de mayúsculas
space (speis) — espacio
space bar ('speisbɑ:) — espaciador

Tabulator ('tæbjuleitə) — tabulador
type (taip) — tipo
typebar ('taipbɑ:) — palanca (con el tipo)
typewriter ('taipraitə) — máquina de escribir
  electric typewriter (i'lektrik'taipraitə) — máquina de escribir eléctrica
  office typewriter ('ofistaipraitə) — máquina de escribir de oficina
  portable typewriter ('po:təbəl'taipraitə) — máquina de escribir portátil

Variable line spacer ('veəriəbəl'lainspeisə) — dispositivo para variar los espacios

UNIVERSE, THE (See THE WORLD, 100)

VEGETABLES (See FRUITS, 36)

96

WARFARE   LA GUERRA (47)

ENGLISH   ESPAÑOL

Admiral ('ædmirəl)   almirante
admiralty ('ædmirəlti)   almirantazgo
air barrage ('eəbærɪdʒ)   barrera aérea
aircraft* ('eəkrɑ:ft)   avión
  bombing aircraft
      ('bomiŋeəkrɑ:ft)   avión de bombardeo
  fighter aircraft
      ('faitəeəkrɑ:ft)   avión de caza
aircraft squadron
      ('eəkrɑ:ftskwodrən)   escuadrilla de aviones
air superiority
      ('eəsjupiəri'oriti)   superioridad aérea
alarm (ə'lɑ:m)   alarma
  air raid alarm
      ('eəreidə'lɑ:m)   alarma aérea
ally (ə'lai)   aliado
ammunition (æmju'niʃən)   munición
armament ('ɑ:məmənt)   armamento
armour ('ɑ:mə)   blindaje
army ('ɑ:mi)   ejército
army-corps ('ɑ:miko:)   cuerpo de ejército
artillery (ɑ:'tiləri)   artillería
  antiaircraft artillery
      ('ænti'eəkrɑ:ftɑ:'tiləri)   artillería antiaérea
  antitank artillery
      ('ænti'tæŋkɑ:'tiləri)   artillería contra carros
  field artillery ('fi:ldɑ:'tiləri)   artillería de campaña
  heavy artillery
      ('heviɑ:'tiləri)   artillería pesada
  light artillery ('laitɑ:'tiləri)   artillería ligera
  long-range artillery
      ('loŋreindʒɑ:'tiləri)   artillería de largo alcance
  mountain artillery
      ('mauntənɑ:'tiləri)   artillería de montaña
attack (ə'tæk)   ataque
  air attack ('eərətæk)   ataque aéreo
attack, to (tuə'tæk)   atacar
aviation (eivi'eiʃən)   aviación

Barraks ('bærəks)   cuartel
barricade (bæri'keid)   barricada
base ('beis)   base
　air base ('eəbeis)   base aérea
　naval base ('neivəl'beis)   base naval
battalion (bə'tæliən)   batallón
　infantry battalion
　　　　　('infəntribətæliən)   batallón de infantería
battle ('bætl)   batalla
　air-battle ('eəbætl)   batalla aérea
　sea-battle ('si:bætl)   batalla naval
battledress ('bætəldres)   uniforme de campaña
battle-field ('bætəlfi:ld)   campo de batalla
battery ('bætəri)   batería
　coast battery
　　　　　('koustbætəri)   batería de costa
bombardment (bom'ba:dmənt)   bombardeo
bombing ('bomiŋ)   bombardeo
　dive bombing ('daivbomiŋ)   bombardeo en picado
brigade (bri'geid)   brigada
bugle band ('bju:gəlbænd)   banda de cornetas

Camouflage ('kæmufla:ʒ)   camuflaje
camp (kæmp)   campamento
　concentration camp
　　　　(konsən'treiʃənkæmp)   campo de concentración
campaign (kæm'pein)   campaña
captain ('kæptən)   capitán
casualties ('kæʒuəltiz)   bajas
cavalry ('kævəlri)   caballería
charge ('tʃa:dʒ)   carga (ataque)
　bayonet charge
　　　　　('beiənittʃa:dʒ)   ataque a la bayoneta
colonel ('kə:nəl)   coronel
column ('koləm)   columna
combat ('kombət)   combate
command (kə'ma:nd)   mando
　high command
　　　　　('haikə'ma:nd)   alto mando
commander (kə'ma:ndə)   comandante (jefe con mando)
company ('kʌmpəni)   compañía
corporal ('ko:pərəl)   cabo
counter-attack ('kauntərətæk)   contraataque
counter-offensive
　　　　('kauntərə'fensiv)   contraofensiva
curfew ('kə:fju:)   toque de queda

D-day ('di:dei)   día D

defence (di'fens) — defensa
detachment (di'tætʃmənt) — destacamento
division (di'viʒən) — división
  airborne division ('eəbo:ndi'viʒən) — división aerotransportada
  armoured division ('ɑ:məddi'viʒən) — división acorazada
  infantry division ('infəntridiviʒən) — división de infantería
  mechanized division ('mekənaizddi'viʒən) — división mecanizada
  motorized division ('moutəraizddi'viʒən) — división motorizada
drill (dril) — instrucción

Emplacement (im'pleismənt) — emplazamiento
  artillery emplacement (ɑ:'tiləriimpleismənt) — emplazamiento artillero
enemy ('enəmi) — enemigo
enlisted man (in'listid'mæn) — individuo de tropa
enlistment (in'listmənt) — alistamiento
  oath of enlisment ('ouθəvin'listmənt) — juramento de la bandera

Field dress ('fi:lddres) — uniforme de campaña
field hospital ('fi:ld'hospitl) — hospital de campaña
fight (fait) — lucha
fight, to (tə'fait) — luchar
flag (flæg) — bandera
flag bearer ('flægbeərə) — abanderado
flank (flæŋk) — flanco
fleet (fli:t) — flota
forces ('fo:siz) — fuerzas
front (frʌnt) — frente

General ('dʒenərəl) — general
guerrilla fighter (gə'riləfaitə) — guerrillero
gunner ('gʌnə) — artillero

Headquarters ('hed'kwo:təz) — cuartel general
hostilities (hos'tilitiz) — hostilidades

Infantry ('infəntri) — infantería

Lieutenant (lef'tenənt) — teniente
lieutenant colonel (lef'tenənt'kə:nəl) — teniente coronel
Major ('meidʒə) — comandante (grado)
manoeuvres (mə'nu:vəz) — maniobras

Marshal ('mɑ:ʃəl) — mariscal

| WARFARE | | LA GUERRA |

military academy ('militəriə'kædəmi) — academia militar
military service ('militəri'sə:vis) — servicio militar
military training ('militəri'treiniŋ) — instrucción militar
mine field ('mainfi:ld) — campo de minas
Objective (əb'dʒektiv) — objetivo
offensive (ə'fensiv) — ofensiva
officer ('ofisə) — oficial
  army officer ('a:miofisə) — oficial del ejército
outpost ('autpoust) — avanzadilla

Parade (pə'reid) — parada
paratroops ('pærətru:ps) — tropas paracaidistas
patrol (pə'troul) — patrulla
peace treaty ('pi:stri:ti) — tratado de paz
private ('praivit) — soldado raso

Rank (ræŋk) — grado (categoría), fila
rear (riə) — retaguardia
rearguard ('riəga:d) — retaguardia
reconnaissance (ri'konisəns) — reconocimiento
  air reconnaissance ('eərikonisəns) — reconocimiento aéreo
recruit (ri'kru:t) — recluta
recruiting centre (ri'kru:tiŋsentə) — centro de reclutamiento
reinforcements (ri:in'fo:smənts) — refuerzos
resistance (ri'zistəns) — resistencia
retreat (ri'tri:t) — retirada
retreat, to (təri'tri:t) — retirarse
regiment ('redʒimənt) — regimiento

Salute (sə'lu:t) — saludo
second lieutenant ('sekəndlef'tenənt) — alférez
sergeant ('sa:dʒənt) — sargento
siege (si:dʒ) — sitio
siege, to (tə'si:dʒ) — sitiar
soldier ('souldʒə) — soldado
  discharged soldier (dis'tʃa:dʒd'souldʒə) — soldado licenciado
  squadron ('skwodrən) — escuadrilla, escuadrón, escuadra

strategic (strə'ti:dʒik) — estratégico
strategy ('strætədʒi) — estrategia

WARFARE — LA GUERRA

stretcher bearer ('stretʃəbeərə) — camillero
supply (sə'plai) — abastecimiento, aprovisionamiento
surrender (sə'rendə) — rendición
surrender, to (təsə'rendə) — rendirse

Tactical ('tæktikl) — táctico
tactics ('tæktiks) — táctica
tent (tent) — tienda de campaña
training centre ('treiniŋsentə) — centro de instrucción
trench (trentʃ) — trinchera
troops (tru:ps) — tropas
 airborne troops ('eəbo:n'tru:ps) — tropas aerotransportadas
 mountain troops ('mauntəntru:ps) — tropas de montaña

Ultimatum (ʌlti'meitəm) — ultimatum
uniform ('ju:nifo:m) — uniforme
unit ('ju:nit) — unidad

Veteran ('vetərən) — veterano
volunteer (volən'tiə) — voluntario

War (wo:) — guerra
 declaration of war (deklə'reiʃənəv'wo:) — declaración de guerra
warrior ('woriə) — guerrero
weapon* ('wepən) — arma
withdraw, to (tuwið'dro:) — retirarse
withdrawal (wið'dro:əl) — retirada

WATCHES

(See CLOCKS, 21)

97

WEAPONS — ARMAS (8)

ENGLISH — ESPAÑOL

Arm (ɑ:m) — arma
 fire-arm ('faiərɑ:m) — arma de fuego

| WEAPONS | ARMAS |

side arm ('saidɑ:m)	machete o sable
small arm ('smo:l'ɑ:m)	arma portátil
armoured car ('ɑ:məd'kɑ:)	coche blindado
arrow ('ærou)	flecha

Bayonet ('beiənil) — machete
bazooka (bə'zu:kə) — bazoka
bomb (bom) — bomba
  aircraft bomb ('eəkrɑ:ft'bom) — bomba de aviación
  atomic bomb (ə'tomik'bom) — bomba atómica
  delayed-action bomb (di'leid'ækʃən'bom) — bomba de acción retardada
  incendiary bomb (in'sendiəri'bom) — bomba incendiaria
  smoke bomb ('smouk'bom) — bomba de humo
  tear-gas bomb ('tiəgæs'bom) — bomba lacrimógena
  time-bomb ('taimbom) — bomba de tiempo
bomb-trower ('bomθrouə) — lanzabombas
bomber ('bomə) — avión de bombardeo
bow (bou) — arco
blunderbuss ('blʌndəbʌs) — trabuco
bullet ('bulit) — bala
  explosive bullet (iks'plouziv'bulit) — bala explosiva
  tracer bullet ('treisəbulit) — bala trazadora

Calibre ('kælibə) — calibre
  large calibre ('lɑ:dʒ'kælibə) — grueso calibre
  small calibre ('smo:l'kælibə) — pequeño calibre
cannon ('kænən) — cañón
catapult ('kætəpʌlt) — catapulta
carbine ('kɑ:bain) — carabina
  machine carbine (mə'ʃi:nkɑ:bain) — fusil ametrallador
cartridge ('kɑ:tridʒ) — cartucho
crossbow ('krosbou) — ballesta
cutlass ('kʌtləs) — alfanje

Dagger ('dægə) — puñal
depth-charge ('depθtʃɑ:dʒ) — carga de profundidad
dynamite ('dainəmait) — dinamita

Explosive charge (iks'plouziv'tʃɑ:dʒ) — carga explosiva

Falchion ('fo:ltʃən) — alfanje
fighter ('faitə) — avión de caza
flame thrower ('fleimθrouə) — lanzallamas

WEAPONS — ARMAS

Grenade (grə'neid) — granada
  hand grenade ('hændgrəneid) — granada de mano
  grenade thrower (grə'neidθrouə) — lanzagranadas
gun (gʌn) — cañón
  antiaircraft gun ('ænti'eəkrɑ:ftgʌn) — cañón antiaéreo
  antitank gun ('ænti'tæŋkgʌn) — cañón contra carros
  automatic gun (o:tə'mætik'gʌn) — cañón automático
  machine gun (mə'ʃi:ngʌn) — ametralladora
gunpowder ('gʌnpaudə) — pólvora

Halberd ('hælbəd) — alabarda
howitzer ('hauitsə) — obús

Lance (lɑ:ns) — lanza

Mine (main) — mina
  antisubmarine mine ('ænti'sʌbməri:n'main) — mina antisubmarina
  antitank mine ('ænti'tæŋkmain) — mina contra carros
  land mine ('lændmain) — mina terrestre
  sea mine ('si:main) — mina marina
missile ('misail) — proyectil dirigido

Pistol ('pistl) — pistola
  automatic pistol (o:tə'mætik'pistl) — pistola automática
projectile ('prodʒiktail) — proyectil

Range (reindʒ) — alcance (de un arma)
rapier ('reipiə) — estoque
revolver (ri'volvə) — revólver
rifle ('raifl) — fusil

Sabre ('seibə) — sable
scimitar ('simitə) — cimitarra
shell (ʃel) — bala de cañón
spear (spiə) — lanza
sword (so:d) — espada
  hand-and-a-half sword ('hændəndə'ha:f'so:d) — espada de dos manos
  two-edged sword ('tu:edʒd'so:d) — espada de doble filo

Tank (tæŋk) — carro de combate

98

WEIGHTS AND MEASURES   **PESOS Y MEDIDAS (80)**

ENGLISH   ESPAÑOL

Acre ('eikə) — acre
altitude ('æltitju:d) — altitud
ampere ('æmpeə) — amperio
area ('eəriə) — superficie

Barometer (bə'romitə) — barómetro
boiling point ('boiliŋpoint) — punto de ebullición
breadth (bredθ) — anchura

Calorie ('kæləri) — caloría
centigrade ('sentigreid) — centígrado
centigramme ('sentigræm) — centígramo
centimetre ('sentimi:tə) — centímetro

Decibel ('desibel) — decibelio
decigramme ('desigræm) — decígramo
decilitre ('desili:tə) — decilitro
decimetre ('desimi:tə) — decímetro
degree (di'gri:) — grado
depth (depθ) — profundidad
dram (dræm) — dracma

Fahrenheit ('fɑ:rənhait) — Fahrenheit
fathom ('fæðəm) — braza
feet (fi:t) — pies
foot (fut) — pie
  cubic foot ('kju:bik'fut) — pie cúbico
  square foot ('skweə'fut) — pie cuadrado
freezing point ('fri:ziŋpoint) — punto de congelación

Gallon ('gælən) — galón
gill (dʒil) — cuarta parte de una pinta
gramme (græm) — gramo

Half (hɑ:f) — mitad
hectare ('hekteə) — hectárea
hectolitre ('hektouli:tə) — hectólitro
hectometre ('hektoumi:tə) — hectómetro
height (hait) — altura
horse-power ('ho:spauə) — caballo de vapor
hundredweight ('hʌndridweit) — quintal

| WEIGHTS, ETC. | PESOS, ETC. |

Inch (intʃ)
  cubic inch ('kju:bik'intʃ)
  square inch ('skweə'intʃ)

Kilogramme ('kiləgræm)
kilometre (ki'lomitə)
  square kilometre
        ('skweəki'lomitə)
knot (not)

League (li:g)
length (leŋθ)
litre ('li:tə)

Measure ('meʒə)
  cubic measures
        ('kju:bik'meʒəz)
  linear measures
        ('liniə'meʒəz)
  liquid measures
        ('likwid'meʒəz)
  square measures
        ('skweə'meʒəz)
measure, to (tə'meʒə)
measuring instrument
        ('meʒəriŋinstrəmənt)
meter ('mi:tə)
metre ('mi:tə)
  cubic metre ('kju:bik'mi:tə)
  square metre ('skweə'mi:tə)
metric system
        ('metrik'sistəm)
mile (mail)
  nautical mile ('nɔ:tikəl'mail)
  square mile ('skweə'mail)
millimetre ('milimi:tə)

Ohm (oum)
ounce (auns)

Pair of compasses, a
        (ə'peərəv'kʌmpəsiz)
pair of scales, a
        (ə'peərəv'skeilz)
pint (paint)
pound (paund)

Quart (kwɔ:t)
quarter, a (ə'kwɔ:tə)
quire ('kwaiə)

pulgada
pulgada cúbica
pulgada cuadrada

kilogramo
kilómetro

kilómetro cuadrado
nudo

legua
longitud
litro

medida

medidas cúbicas

medidas de longitud

medidas de líquidos

medidas de superficie
medir

instrumento de medida
medidor, contador
metro
metro cúbico
metro cuadrado

sistema métrico
milla
milla náutica
milla cuadrada
milímetro

ohmio
onza

un compás

una balanza
pinta
libra

dos pintas
una cuarta parte
mano de papel

| WEIGHTS, ETC. | PESOS, ETC. |

Ream (ri:m) — resma de papel
rule (ru:l) — regla
   folding rule ('foudiŋ'ru:l) — metro plegable
ruler ('ru:lə) — regla

Size (saiz) — tamaño
stone (stoun) — catorce libras

Tape measure ('teipmeʒə) — cinta métrica
temperature ('tempərətʃə) — temperatura
thermometer (θə'momitə) — termómetro
thickness ('θiknis) — espesor
ton (tʌn) — tonelada

Volt (voult) — voltio
volume ('volju:m) — volumen

Watt (wot) — watio
weigh, to (tu'wei) — pesar
weighing machine ('weiiŋməʃi:n) — báscula
weight (weit) — peso
width (widθ) — anchura

Yard (jɑ:d) — yarda
   square yard ('skweə'jɑ:d) — yarda cuadrada

Zero ('ziərou) — cero
   above zero (ə'bʌv'ziərou) — sobre cero
   below zero (bi'lou'ziərou) — bajo cero

WILD ANIMALS (See MAMMALS 58)

99

| **WOOD INDUSTRY** | **INDUSTRIA DE LA MADERA (53)** |

| ENGLISH | ESPAÑOL |

Afforestation (æfəris'teiʃən) — repoblación forestal
axe (æks) — hacha

Bark (bɑ:k) — corteza de árbol
board (bo:d) — tabla

Cabinetmaker ('kæbinitmeikə)	ebanista
cabinetmaking ('kæbinitmeikiŋ)	ebanistería (oficio)
carpenter ('kɑ:pintə)	carpintero
carpenter's shop ('kæpintəzʃop)	carpintería (taller)
carpentry ('kɑ:pintri)	carpintería (oficio)
chisel ('tʃizl)	formón
Ebony ('ebəni)	ébano
Fell, to (tə'fel)	talar
forest ('forist)	bosque
furniture* ('fə:nitʃə)	muebles
Glue (glu:)	cola
Hammer ('hæmə)	martillo
Inlaid work ('inleid'wə:k)	marquetería
Lathe (leið)	torno
log (log)	tronco
lumber ('lʌmbə)	madera aserrada
lumberman ('lʌmbəmæn)	maderero
lumber-yard ('lʌmbəjɑ:d)	depósito de maderas
Mahogany (mə'hogəni)	caoba
Nail (neil)	clavo
nail, to (tə'neil)	clavar
Oak (ouk)	roble
Pine (pain)	pino
plane (plein)	cepillo de carpintero
plank (plæŋk)	tablón
pollard, to (tə'poləd)	desmochar
poplar ('poplə)	chopo
prune, to (tə'pru:n)	podar
pulping-mill ('pʌlpiŋmil)	fábrica de pasta para papel
Sandpaper ('sændpeipə)	lija
sandpaper, to (tə'sændpeipə)	lijar
sap (sæp)	savia
saw (so:)	sierra
band saw ('bændso:)	sierra circular
handsaw ('hændso:)	serrucho
jigsaw ('dʒigso:)	sierra de vaivén
saw, to (tə'so:)	aserrar
sawdust ('so:dʌst)	serrín
sawmill ('so:mil)	serrería

WOOD INDUSTRY	INDUSTRIA DE LA MADERA

screw (skru:) — tornillo
  wood screw ('wudskru:) — tornillo para madera
  shavings ('ʃeiviŋz) — virutas

Timber ('timbə) — madera para la construcción
timber-yard ('timbəjɑːd) — fábrica de maderas
tongs (toŋz) — tenazas
tree* (triː) — árbol
trunk (trʌŋ) — tronco (de un árbol)

Varnish, to (tə'vɑːniʃ) — barnizar

Wood (wud) — madera, bosque
  hard wood ('hɑːd'wud) — madera dura
  soft wood ('soft'wud) — madera blanda
  wood-cutter ('wudkʌtə) — leñador
  wooden ('wudən) — de madera
  woodland ('wudlənd) — bosque
  wood-pulp ('wudpʌlp) — pulpa de madera
  woodsman ('wudzmən) — leñador
  woodwork ('wudwəːk) — obra de carpintería
  woodyard ('wudjɑːd) — depósito de madera

100

WORLD AND THE UNIVERSE, THE

EL MUNDO Y EL UNIVERSO (68)

ENGLISH	ESPAÑOL

Air (eə) — aire
asteroid ('æstəroid) — asteroide
atmosphere ('ætməsfiə) — atmósfera
atmospheric phenomena ('ætməs'ferikfə'nomənə) — fenómenos atmosféricos

Beam (biːm) — rayo (del sol, de luz)
Big Dipper ('big'dipə) — Osa Mayor (USA)

Climate ('klaimit) — clima
cloud (klaud) — nube
comet ('komit) — cometa
constellation (konstə'leiʃən) — constelación

Dawn (dɔ:n)	alba, aurora
day (dei)	día
daybreak ('deibreik)	amanecer
daylight ('deilait)	luz del día
dusk (dʌsk)	crepúsculo
Earth (ə:θ)	tierra
earthquake ('ə:θkweik)	terremoto
east (i:st)	este
eclipse (i'klips)	eclipse
elements, the (ði'elimənts)	los elementos
equator (i'kweitə)	ecuador
Fire (faiə)	fuego
first quarter ('fə:st'kwo:tə)	cuarto creciente (de la luna)
Galaxy ('gæləksi)	galaxia
Great Bear ('greit'beə)	Osa Mayor (GB)
Heat (hi:t)	calor
heavenly body ('hevənli'bodi)	astro
hemisphere ('hemisfiə)	hemisferio
horizon (hə'raizən)	horizonte
Jupiter ('dʒu:pitə)	Júpiter
Land (lænd)	tierra
last quarter ('la:st'kwo:tə)	cuarto menguante (de la luna)
latitude ('lætitju:d)	latitud
light (lait)	luz
lightning ('laitniŋ)	relámpago
light-year ('laitjiə)	año luz
Little Bear ('litəl'beə)	Osa Menor (GB)
Little Dipper ('litəl'dipə)	Osa Menor (USA)
longitude ('londʒitju:d)	longitud
Mars (ma:z)	Marte
meteor ('mi:tiə)	meteoro
Mercury ('mə:kjuri)	Mercurio
meridian (mə'ridiən)	meridiano
Milky Way ('milki'wei)	Vía Láctea
moon (mu:n)	luna
full moon ('ful'mu:n)	luna llena
new moon ('nju:'mu:n)	luna nueva
Nebula ('nebjulə)	nebulosa
Neptune ('neptju:n)	Neptuno
night (nait)	noche
north (no:θ)	norte
north-east ('no:θ'i:st)	nordeste
north-west ('no:θ'west)	noroeste

Observatory	(əb'zə:vətəri)	observatorio
ocean	('ouʃən)	océano
Parallel	('pærəlel)	paralelo
planet	('plænit)	planeta
Pluto	('plu:tou)	Plutón
pole-star	('poulstɑ:)	estrella polar
Ray	(rei)	rayo (del sol, de luz)
ring	(riŋ)	anillo (alrededor de un planeta)
Saturn	('sætən)	Saturno
sea	(si:)	mar
seismic	('saizmik)	sísmico
sky	(skai)	cielo
south	(sauθ)	sur
south-east	('sauθ'i:st)	sudeste
south-west	('sauθ'west)	sudoeste
sphere	(sfiə)	esfera
star	(stɑ:)	estrella, astro
storm	(sto:m)	tormenta
stratosphere	('strætəsfiə)	estratosfera
Southern Cross	('sʌðən'kros)	Cruz del Sur
sun	(sʌn)	sol
sunlight	('sʌnlait)	luz del sol
sunrise	('sʌnraiz)	salida del sol
sunset	('sʌnset)	puesta del sol
sunshine	('sʌnʃain)	luz del sol
sunspot	('sʌnspot)	mancha solar
Telescope	('teliskoup)	telescopio
thunder	('θʌndə)	trueno
thunderbolt	('θʌndəboult)	rayo (de una tormenta)
tide	(taid)	marea
tropic	('tropik)	trópico
troposphere	('troupəsfiə)	troposfera
twilight	('twailait)	crepúsculo
Uranus	('juərənəs)	Urano
Venus	('vi:nəs)	Venus
Water	('wo:tə)	agua
weather, the	(ðə'weðə)	el tiempo
west	(west)	oeste
wind	(wind)	viento
Zenith	('zeniθ)	cenit

SEGUNDA PARTE
ESPAÑOL - INGLES

1

AERONAVES, TIPOS DE   TYPES OF AIRCRAFT (4)

ESPAÑOL	ENGLISH
Aeroplano	plane, aeroplane (GB), airplane (USA)
avión	plane, aircraft
avión bimotor	twin-engined plane
avión biplaza	two-seater plane
avión birreactor	twin-jet plane
avión de bombardeo	bomber
avión de bombardeo en picado	dive bomber
avión de caza	fighter
avión de gran radio de acción	long-range plane
avión de pasajeros	air-liner
avión de reacción	jet-plane
avión de transporte	cargo plane, transport plane
avión escuela	training-plane
avión ligero de bombardeo	light bomber
avión monomotor	single-engined plane
avión monoplaza	single-seater plane
avión pesado de bombardeo	heavy bomber
avión polimotor	multi-engined plane
avión sin piloto	pilotless plane
avión trimotor	three-engined plane
avioneta	light plane
Biplano	biplane
Caza	fighter
caza-bombardero	fighter bomber
cohete	rocket
cuatrimotor	four-engined plane
Dirigible	airship
Globo	balloon
Hidroavión	flying-boat
hidroavión de flotadores	seaplane
helicóptero	helicopter
Monoplano	monoplane
monoplano de alta ala	high-wing monoplane
monoplano de ala baja	low-wing monoplane

AERONAVES, TIPOS DE   **252**   TYPES OR AIRCRAFT

monoplano de ala media	mid-wing monoplane
Nave espacial	spaceship
Planeador	glider
Reactor	jet
Triplano	triplane

2

AEROPUERTO, UN   AN AIRPORT (5)

ESPAÑOL	ENGLISH
Aduana, la	the Customs
aeropuerto intercontinental	inter-continental airport
altavoz	loudspeaker
aterrizaje	landing
aterrizaje forzoso	forced landing
aterrizar	to land
aviación civil	civil aviation
aviador	airman
avión*	aircraft
avión civil	civil aircraft
avión de pasajeros	air-liner
azafata	air-hostess
Billete	ticket
medio billete	half fare
billete de avión	air-ticket
billete de clase turistas	tourist-ticket
billete entero	full fare
Cafetería	refreshment-room
camarero	steward
camión cisterna	petrol lorry
canal de embarque	flight channel
clase turista	tourist class
corredor	gallery
Departamento de clase turista	tourist-class compartment

| AEROPUERTO, UN | AN AIRPORT |

departamento de primera clase
despegar
despegue

Entrada delantera (del avión)
entrada posterior (del avión)
equipaje
   exceso de equipaje
escalerillas (para subir al
   avión)
estación meteorológica

Hangar
hora de presentación de los
   pasajeros
horario

Información meteorológica

Líneas aéreas
lista de pasajeros

Llegada

Manga que indica la dirección
   del viento
mecánico de vuelo

Navegante

Oficina de Aduanas
oficina de billetes

Partida
pasajero
personal al servicio de los
   pasajeros
personal de tierra
piloto
pista
   luces de pista
pista de estacionamiento
pista de rodadura
primera clase

Radar
radio telegrafista
reserva
   aplazar una reserva
   cancelar una reserva
reserva de plaza
rodar (un avión) por la pista

first-class compartment
to take off
take-off

forward entrance
rear entrance
luggage
excess luggage

gangway
meteorological station

hangar

check-in time
time-table

meteorological information

airways, airlines
passenger list

arrival

wind sock
flying engineer

navigator

Customs-House
booking-office

departure
passenger

cabin staff
ground staff
pilot
runway
runway lights
apron
taxi-way
first class

radar
wireless operator
reservation
to defer a reservation
to cancel a reservation
seat reservation
to taxi

AEROPUERTO, UN	AN AIRPORT
ruta aérea	air-route
Sala de espera	waiting-room, lounge
señaleros de pista	tarmac marshallers
servicios de corta distancia	short-range services
servicios de larga distancia	long-range services
Tarjeta de embarque	boarding-card
terminal	terminal
torre de control	control tower
torre del aeropuerto	airport tower
transporte aéreo	air transport
tripulación	aircrew
Vestíbulo	concourse
viaje	trip
precio del viaje	fare
viaje aéreo	air trip
viaje de vuelta	return trip
visibilidad	visibility
mala visibilidad	poor visibility
volar	to fly
vuelo	flight
vuelo internacional	international flight
vuelo nacional	domestic flight
vuelo regular	regular flight

3

AGRICULTURA / AGRICULTURE (2)

ESPAÑOL	ENGLISH
Abono	manure
agavilladora	binder
agrícola	agricultural
arado	plough
reja del arado	ploughshare
arar	to plough
árbol*	tree
arboleda	grove
aperos de labranza	tillage implements
aventar	to winnow

AGRICULTURA — AGRICULTURE

Bosque — wood, forest

Campo — field
cereales* — cereals
cosecha — crop
cosechadora — harvester
crecer — to grow
cultivadora — cultivator
cultivar — to grow, to cultivate
cultivo — cultivation
    rotación de cultivos — rotation of crops

Desyerbadora — grubber
desyerbar — to grub

Espiga — ear
estiércol — dung

Fertilizante — fertilizer
forraje — fodder
frutos* — fruits

Ganado — cattle, livestock
gavilla — sheaf
gavillas — sheaves
grada — harrow
gradar — to harrow
granero — barn
granja* — farm
grano — grain

Heno — hay
hierba — grass
huerta — kitchen garden
huerto — orchard

Labrador — ploughman

Maduro — ripe
monte alto — forest
monte bajo — brushwood

Olivar — olive-grove

Pacer — to graze
paja — straw, chaff
pastos — pastures
pinar — pine-grove
planta* — plant
plantar — to plant
prado — meadow

AGRICULTURA	AGRICULTURE
Raíz	root
rastrojera	stubble-field
rastrojo	stubble
recoger	to pick up
recolección	harvest
regar	to water
riego	irrigation
robledal	oak-grove
Segador	reaper
segadora	reaping-machine
segar	to reap
sembrador	sower
sembrar	to sow
semilla	seed
semillero	seed-plot
siega	reaping
silvicultura	forestry
suelo	soil
surco	furrow
Terreno	ground
tiempo de siembra	seedtime
tierra	land
tierra de labranza	arable land
tierra de regadío	irrigated land
tierra de secano	unwatered land
tierra estéril	barren land
tierra fértil	fertile land
tractor	tractor
trigal	wheat-field
trilla	threshing
trilladora	thresher
trillar	to thresh
Viña	vineyard

4

AJEDREZ — CHESS (19)

ESPAÑOL	ENGLISH
Alfil	bishop
Caballo	knight

AJEDREZ	CHESS
capturar	to capture
contrincante	opponent
cuadro	square
Enrocar	to castle
enroque	castling
Ficha	man, piece
ficha del ajedrez	chess-man, chess-piece
fichas	men, pieces
fichas del ajedrez	chess-men, chess-pieces
Ganador	winner
ganar	to win
Jaque	check
dar jaque	to check
jaque mate	checkmate
dar jaque mate	to checkmate
juego de ajedrez	chess-set
jugador	player
Matar (una pieza)	to take
mover	to move
movimiento	move
Peón	pawn
perder	to lose
Reina	queen
rey	king
Tablas	draw
tablas por ahogo	stalemate
tablero	board
tablero de ajedrez	chess-board
torneo	tournament
torre	castle, rook

ALEACIONES (Véase METALES, MINERALES y ALEACIONES, 63)

ANÉLIDOS (Véase INSECTOS, ARACNIDOS y ANELIDOS, 54)

ANFIBIOS (Véase REPTILES, Y ANFIBIOS, 88)

5

ANIMAL, UN   AN ANIMAL (6)

ESPAÑOL	ENGLISH
Agallas	gills
ala	wing
aleta	fin
Boca	mouth
Cabeza	head
cola	tail
colmillo	tusk, fang
cresta	crest
crin	horse-hair
crines	mane
cuello	neck
cuerno	horn
Escamas	scales
espolón	spur
Garra	claw, paw
Herradura	horseshoe
hocico	muzzle
Lomo	back
Melena	mane
moco de pavo	crest of a turkey
molleja	gizzard
morro	snout
Ojos	eyes
ollares	nostrils
Palmípedo	web-footed
pata	leg
pellejo	skin, hide
pezuña	hoof
pico	bill, beak
piel	fur
pluma	feather
plumón	down

ANIMAL, UN		AN ANIMAL

Rabo tail
Trompa trunk
Ubre udder
Zarpa paw

ANIMALES DOMESTICOS (Véase MAMIFEROS, 60)

ANIMALES SALVAJES (Véase MAMIFEROS, 60)

ARÁCNIDOS (Véase INSECTOS, 54)

6

ÁRBOLES, PLANTAS Y FLORES **TREES, PLANTS AND FLOWERS (94)**

ESPAÑOL ENGLISH

Abedul birch
abeto fir
acacia acacia
acebo holly
acedera sorrel
adelfa oleander
álamo poplar
albaricoquero apricot-tree
alcornoque cork-tree
alerce larch
alga marina seaweed
alhelí wallflower
aligustre privet
alisio alder
almendro almond-tree
amapola poppy
anémona anemone
árbol tree
árbol del caucho rubber-tree
arbusto bush

ÁRBOLES, ETC.	TREES, ETC.
arce	maple-tree
aspidistra	aspidistra
aster	aster
avellano	hazelnut-tree
azafrán	crocus
azalea	azalea
azucena	white lily
Bambú	bamboo
berro	nasturtium
boca de dragón	snapdragon
botón de oro	buttercup
brezo	heather
Cactus	cactus
caléndula	marigold
camelia	camellia
campánula	harebell
campánula azul	bluebell,
campanilla blanca	snowdrop
caña	reed
cáñamo	hemp
caoba	mahogany
capuchina	nasturtium
cardo	thistle
castaño	chestnut-tree
cedro	cedar
cerezo	cherry-tree
ciclamen	cyclamen
cicuta	hemlock
ciprés	cypres
ciruelo	plum-tree
clavel	carnation, pink
cocotero	coconut-tree
crisantemo	chrysanthemum
CHampiñón	mushroom
chopo	poplar
Dalia	dahlia
dedalera	foxglove
diente de león	dandelion
Ébano	ebony
encina	oak
enebro	juniper
enredadera	creeper
escaramujo	dog-rose
espino	hawthorn
espliego	lavender
estragón	tarragon

| ÁRBOLES, ETC. | TREES, ETC. |

eucalipto — eucalyptus

Flor — flower
fresno — ash
fucsia — fuchsia

Geranio — geranium
girasol — sunflower
gladiolo — gladiolus

Haya — beech
helecho — fern
hiedra — ivy
hierba — grass
hierbabuena — mint
higuera — fig-tree
hinojo — fennel
hongo — mushroom
hortensia — hydrangea

Jacinto — hyacinth
jazmín — jasmin
junco — rush

Laburno — laburnum
lila — lilac
lilo — lilac-tree
limero — lime-tree
limonero — lemon-tree
lino — flax
lirio — lily

Madreselva — honeysuckle
magnolia — magnolia
malva — mallow
malva loca — holly-hock
manzanilla — camomile
manzano — apple-tree
margarita — daisy
mejorana — marjoram
melocotonero — peach-tree
membrillo — quince-tree
mimosa — mimosa
minutisa — sweet william
miositis — forget-me-not
mirto — myrtle
muérdago — mistletoe
muguete — lily of the valley

ÁRBOLES, ETC.	TREES, ETC.
musgo	moss
Naranjo	orange-tree
narciso	daffodil
nenúfar	water-lily
nogal	walnut-tree
nomeolvides	forget-me-not
Olivo	olive-tree
olmo	elm
orquídea	orchid
Palmera	palm-tree
palo de rosa	rosewood
parra	vine
pensamiento	pansy
peonía	peony
peral	pear-tree
petunia	petunia
picea	spruce
pino	pine
plátano	banana-tree
primavera	primrose, cowslip
Rododendro	rhododendron
roble	oak
rosa	rose
rosal	rosebush
ruibarbo	rhubarb
Sauce	willow
sauce llorón	weeping willow
sauco	elder
secoya	redwood
seta	mushroom
sicomoro	sycamore
Teca	teak
tejo	yew
tilo	linden-tree
tomillo	thyme
trébol	clover
tulipán	tulip
Vid	vine
violeta	violet
Zarzal	blackberry bush

7

ARITMÉTICA Y MATEMÁTICAS

ARITHMETIC AND MATHEMATICS (8)

ESPAÑOL	ENGLISH
Calcular	to calculate
cálculo infinitesimal	infinitesimal calculus
cantidad	quantity
centenas	hundreds
centenas de mil	hundreds of thousands
centenas de millón	hundreds of millions
cifra	figure
cociente	quotient
coma (decimal)	point
comprobar	to check
contar	to count
correcto	right
cuádruple	quadruple
cuarta parte	a quarter
Decenas	tens
decenas de mil	tens of thousands
decenas de millón	tens of millions
decimal	decimal
denominador	denominator
diferencia	difference
dividendo	dividend
dividir	to divide
divisible	divisible
división	division
divisor	divider
doble	double
Ecuación	equation
equivocado	wrong
exacto	exact
Factor	factor
Guarismo	numeral
Igual	equal
indefinido	indefinite
indivisible	non divisible
Logaritmo	logarithm

| ARITMÉTICA, ETC. | ARITHMETIC, ETC. |

Más
matemáticas
matemático

mitad
multiplicación
multiplicador
multiplicando
multiplicar
   tabla de multiplicar

Numerador
número
   bajar (un número)
   llevarse (un número)
número cardinal
número entero
número impar
número mixto
número ordinal
número par
número primo
números árabes
números romanos

Operación

Problema
producto
progresión aritmética
proporción

Quebrado
quíntuple

Regla
   la regla de tres
   las cuatro reglas
resolver
resta
restar
resto
resultado

Signo
signo aritmético
signo de igualdad
signo de la división
signo de la multiplicación
signo de la resta
signo de la suma

plus
mathematics
mathematical (adj.)
mathematician (sus.)
half
multiplication
multiplier
multiplicand
to multiply
multiplication table

numerator
number, numeral
to bring down
to carry
cardinal number
integral number
odd number
mixed number
ordinal number
even number
prime number
Arabic numbers
Roman numbers

operation

sum
product
arithmetical progression
proportion

fraction
quintuple

rule
the rule of three
the four elementary operations
to solve
subtraction
to subtract
remainder
result

sign
arithmetical sign
equal sign
division sign
multiplication sign
minus sign
plus sign

ARITMÉTICA, ETC.	ARITHMETIC, ETC.
solución	solution
suma	addition, sum
suma anterior	carry over
sumar	to add
Tercio, un	a third
total	total
triple	triple
Unidad	unit
unidades de mil	thousands
unidades de millón	millions

8

ARMAS — WEAPONS (97)

ESPAÑOL	ENGLISH
Alabarda	halberd
alcance (de un arma)	range
alfanje	cutlass, falchion
ametralladora	machine-gun
arco	bow
arma	arm, weapon
arma de fuego	fire-arm
arma portátil	small arm.
avión de bombardeo	bomber
avión de caza	fighter
Bala	bullet
bala de cañón	shell
bala explosiva	explosive bullet
bala trazadora	tracer bullet
ballesta	crossbow
bayoneta	bayonet
bomba	bomb
bomba atómica	atomic bomb
bomba de acción retardada	delayed-action bomb
bomba de aviación	aircraft bomb
bomba de humo	smoke bomb
bomba de tiempo	time-bomb
bomba incendiaria	incendiary bomb

ARMAS / WEAPONS

bomba lacrimógena	tear-gas bomb
bazoka	bazooka

Calibre — calibre
  grueso calibre — large calibre
  pequeño calibre — small calibre
cañón — gun
cañón antiaéreo — antiaircraft gun
cañón automático — automatic gun
cañón contra carros — antitank gun
carabina — carbine
carga de profundidad — depth-charge
carga explosiva — explosive charge
carro de combate — tank
cartucho — cartridge
catapulta — catapult
cimitarra — scimitar
coche blindado — armoured car

Dinamita — dynamite

Espada — sword
espada de doble fino — two-edged sword
espada de dos manos — hand-and-a-half sword
estoque — rapier

Flecha — arrow
fusil — rifle
fusil ametrallador — machine carbine

Granada — grenade
granada de mano. — hand grenade

Lanza — lance, spear
lanzabombas — bomb-thrower
lanzallamas — flame-thrower
lanzagranadas — grenade-thrower

Machete — bayonet
mina — mine
mina antisubmarina — antisumbarine mine
mina contra carros — antitank mine
mina marina — sea-mine
mina terrestre — land-mine

Obús — howitzer
pistola — pistol
pistola automática — automatic pistol
pólvora — gunpowder
proyectil — proyectile
proyectil dirigido — missile

ARMAS		WEAPONS

puñal dagger
Revólver revolver
Sable sabre
Trabuco blunderbuss

9

ARQUITECTURA / ARCHITECTURE (7)

ESPAÑOL — **ENGLISH**

Ábside — apse
acueducto — aqueduct
aguja (de una torre) — steeple, spire
anfiteatro — amphiteatre
arbotante — flying buttress
arcada — archway
arco — arch
arco adintelado — flat arch
arco apuntado — pointed arch
arco conopial — ogee arch
arco de herradura — horseshoe arch
arco de medio punto — round arch
arco gótico — Gothic arch
arco peraltado — stilted arch
arco triunfal — triumphal arch
arquitecto — architect
arquitectónico — architectural
arquitrabe — architrave
atlantes — atlantes

Basílica — basilican church
bóveda — vault
bóveda de cañón — barrel-vault
bóveda de nervios — ribbed vault

Campanario — belfry
capitel — capital
capitel románico — Romanesque capital

cariátide	caryatid
casa*	house
castillo	castle
catedral	cathedral
catedral gótica	Gothic cathedral
catedral románica	Romanesque cathedral
circo	circus
claustro	cloister
clave (de un arco)	keystone
colegiata	collegiate church
columna	column
columna corintia	Corinthian column
columna dórica	Doric column
columna jónica	Ionic column
contrafuerte	buttress
cornisa	cornice
crucero	transept
cúpula	dome
cúpula bizantina	Byzantine dome
Dovelas	voussoirs
Edificar	to build
edificio	building
entablamento	entablature
escocia (de una columna)	scotia
estadio	stadium
estilo	style
estilo barroco	Baroque style
estilo bizantino	Byzantine style
estilo gótico	Gothic style
estilo perpendicular	Perpendicular style
estilo románico	Romanesque style
Flecha (de un arco)	rise
friso	frieze
frontispicio	façade
fuste (de una columna)	shaft
Gárgola	gargoyle
Hojas de acanto	acanthus leaves
Iglesia	church
iglesia románica	Romanesque church
imposta	springer
intradós	intrados
Luz (de un arco)	span
Mansión	mansion

ARQUITECTURA	ARCHITECTURE
mausoleo	mausoleum
mezquita	mosque
minarete	minaret
monasterio	monastery
monumento	monument
monumento prehistórico	prehistoric monument
muralla	wall
muro	wall
Nave lateral	aisle
Obelisco	obelisk
Palacio	palace
panteón	pantheon
patio	courtyard
pilastra	pilaster
pirámide	pyramid
pórtico	portico
puente	bridge
Restaurar	to restore
rosetón	rose-window
Teatro	theatre
templo	temple
templo egipcio	Egyptian temple
templo griego	Greek temple
tímpano	tympanum
toro (de una columna)	torus
torre	tower
trasdós	extrados
Volutas	volutes

10

ARTE CULINARIO — COOKERY (24)

ESPAÑOL	ENGLISH
Aceite	oil
aceite de oliva	olive oil
aceite de cacahuete	peanut oil
aceite de soja	soyabean oil

ARTE CULINARIO	COOKERY
aderezado	dressed
aderezar	to dress
ajenjo	wormwood
ajo	garlic
diente de ajo	clove of garlic
alcaparras	capers
aliñado	seasoned
aliño	seasoning
asado	roasted
asado al horno	baked
asado a la parrilla	grilled
asar	to roast
asar a la parrilla	to grill
asar al horno	to bake
azafrán	saffron
azúcar	sugar
Bizcocho	sponge cake
Caldo	broth
calentar	to heat
canela	cinnamon
carne	meat
catar	to taste
clara de huevo	white of an egg
clavo	clove
cocer	to boil
cocido	boiled
cocido (huevo)	hard-boiled
cocinero	cook
condimento	seasoning
croquetas	croquettes
cucharada de postre	dessertspoonful
cucharada grande	tablespoonful
cucharadita de té	teaspoonful
Dorado (al fuego)	golden brown
dorar	to brown
duro	tough
Empanadilla	patty
empanado	breaded
especia	spice
espuma	froth
Frito	fried
fuego lento	gentle heat
fuego vivo	brisk heat
Grasa	fat
guisado (sus.)	stew

| ARTE CULINARIO | COOKERY |

guisar — to cook

Harina — flour
hecha (la carne) — well-done
  poco hecha (la carne) — underdone
hervido — boiled
hervir — to boil
hervir a fuego lento — to simmer
huevo — egg

Insípido — insipid

Jengibre — ginger
jugoso — juicy

Laurel — bay
levadura — yeast

Manteca — lard
mantequilla — butter
mantequilla derretida — melted butter
margarina — margarine
mayonesa — mayonnaise
medallones de pescado — cuts of fish
mostaza — mustard

Nuez moscada — nutmeg

Pan rallado — bread-crumbs
parrilla — grill
  a la parrilla — grilled
pasado por agua (huevo) — soft-boiled
pasta culinaria — batter
pastel — cake
pelar — to peel
perejil — parsley
pescado — fish
pimienta — pepper
  grano de pimienta — peppercorn
puñado — handful

Rebanada — slice
receta — recipe
relleno — stuffed
rociar — to sprinkle

Sabor — flavour
sabroso — tasty
sal — salt
salado — salty
salsa — sauce, gravy (jugo)
sazonar — to season
  — soup

ARTE CULINARIO	COOKERY
soso	tasteless
Tomillo	thyme
tierno	tender
tostado	toasted
Vainilla	vanilla
vinagre	vinegar
Yema	yoke

AVES (Véase PÁJAROS, 75)

11

AVIÓN, UN	AN AIRCRAFT (3)
ESPAÑOL	ENGLISH
Alas	wings
alerones	ailerons
aleta vertical de cola	fin
alojamiento del tren de aterrizaje	undercarriage bay
altímetro	altimeter
Borde de ataque (de un ala)	leading edge
borde de salida (de un ala)	trailing edge
brújula	compass
Cabina de pilotaje	control cabin
cabina del pasaje	passenger cabin
carlinga	cockpit
cola	tail
Depósito de combustible	fuel tank
Envergadura	wing span
estabilizador vertical	vertical stabilizer
«**F**laps»	flaps
fuselaje	fuselage
Hélice	propeller

| AVIÓN, UN | | AN AIRCRAFT |

Indicador de velocidad — speed indicator

Luz de situación — navegation light

Motor — engine
motor de reacción — jet-engine

Palanca de mando — control stick
piloto automático — automatic pilot

Rueda — wheel
rueda de morro — nose-wheel

Timón de dirección — rudder
timón de profundidad — elevator
tren de aterrizaje — undercarriage
tren de aterrizaje triciclo — tricycle undercarriage

12

BANCA, LA   BANKING (9)

ESPAÑOL	ENGLISH
Acción	share
accionista	stockholder, shareholder
acreedor	creditor
ahorrar	to save
Bancarrota	bankrupt
banco	bank
beneficio	profit
beneficio neto	net profit
billete de banco	bank-note
Bolsa de Comercio	Stock Exchange
bono	bond
Caja de ahorros	savings-bank
cajero	teller
corredor de Bolsa	stockbroker
crédito	credit
cuenta	account
abrir una cuenta	to open an account
cuenta corriente	current-account

cheque	cheque
cobrar un cheque	to cash a cheque
cruzar un cheque	to cross a cheque
endosar un cheque	to endorse a cheque

Deuda — debt
deudor — debtor
dinero — money
dinero en moneda — metallic currency
dividendo — dividend

Empleado de banca — bank-clerk
endosar — to endorse
endoso — endorsement

Fondo — fund

Garantía — guaranty
gerente de banco — bank-manager

Hipoteca — mortgage

Insolvencia — insolvency
interés — interest
inversión — investment
invertir — to invest

Letra de cambio — bill of exchange, draft
librado — drawee
librador — drawer

Moneda — coin (pieza), currency (moneda circulante en un país)
  papel moneda — paper money

Obligación — bond

Pagador — payer
pagar — to pay
pago — payment
portador — bearer
prestamista — lender
préstamo — loan
prestar — to lend
prestatario — borrower

Solvencia — solvency

Talonario — cheque-book

BAÑO, CUARTO DE

(Véase CUARTO DE BAÑO, 30)

13

BARBERÍA, EN LA   AT THE BARBER'S (10)

ESPAÑOL   ENGLISH

Afeitado — shave
afeitadora — razor
afeitar — to shave
arreglar el pelo — to trim
arreglo de pelo — trim
atomizador de colonia — scent sprayer
atomizador de polvos — powder sprayer

Barba — beard
barbilla — chin
bigote — moustache
brillantina — hair-oil
brocha de afeitar — shaving-brush

Cepillo para el pelo — hair-brush
colonia — cologne
cortar — to cut
corte de pelo — hair-cut
crecepelo — hair-restorer
cuello — neck

CHampú — shampoo
chamú al aceite — oil shampoo
champú en seco — dry shampoo

Enjabonar — to lather
espejo — mirror
espejo de mano — hand mirror

Fijador — hair-cream

Hoja afeitar — razor-blade

Jabón de afeitar — shaving-soap

Lavabo — wash-basin
loción — lotion
loción para antes del afeitado — pre-shave lotion
loción para después del afeitado — after-shave lotion

| BARBERÍA, EN LA | AT THE BARBER'S |

Maquinilla para cortar el pelo — hair-clippers
máquina eléctrica de afeitar — electric shaver
maquinilla de afeitar — safety razor

Navaja barbera — cut-throat razor

Patillas — whiskers
peinar — to comb
peine — comb
pelo — hair
peluquero — hairdresser
propina — tip

Raya del pelo — parting

Suavizador de navajas — strop
suavizar la navaja — to strop

Tijeras de peluquero — hair-scissors
toalla — towel
tónico para el pelo — hair-tonic

14

| BARCO, UN | A SHIP (81) |
| ESPAÑOL | ENGLISH |

Amarra — mooring
amurada — bulwark
ancla — anchor

Babor — port
bauprés — bowsprit
bodega — hold

Cabestrante — capstan
cabria — derrick
calado — draught
caldera — boiler
camarote — cabin
casco — hull
castillo de proa — forecastle

BARCO, UN — A SHIP

cofa de vigía	crow's nest
cubierta	deck
CHimenea	funnel
Escalerilla	gangway
escotilla	hatch
eslora	length
estribor	starboard
Gobernar (un buque)	to steer
Hélice	propeller
Línea de flotación	water-line
litera	berth, bunk
Manga	breadth
máquina	engine
mástil	mast
Navegar	to sail
Palo mayor	mainmast
palo de trinquete	foremast
popa	stern, poop
portilla	porthole
proa	bow, prow
puente	bridge
puente de navegación	navigating-bridge
puntal	depth of hold
Quilla	keel
Remo	oar
Sala de calderas	boiler-room
sala de máquinas	engine-room
Tajamar	stem
timón	helm (rueda), rudder
timonera	wheelhouse
Vela	sail
ventiladores	cowl ventilators
verga	spar

BARCOS, TIPOS DE (Véase BUQUES, TIPOS DE, 17)

15

BEBIDAS — DRINKS (27)

ESPAÑOL	ENGLISH
Agua	water
agua de seltz	soda-water
agua fría	cold water
agua mineral	mineral water
anís	anisette
Beber	to drink
bebida	drink, beverage
bebida alcohólica	alcoholic drink
bebida caliente	hot drink
bebida fría	cold drink
bebida no alcohólica	soft drink
bebidas alcohólicas	spirits
Cacao	cocoa
café	coffee
café con leche	white coffee
café solo	black coffee
cerveza	beer
cerveza de barril	beer on draught
cerveza de jengibre	ginger ale
cerveza embotellada	bottled beer
cerveza ligera	light ale
clarete	claret
coca-cola	coke
coñac	brandy
«cuba libre»	rum and coke
CHampán	champagne
Gaseosa	lemonade
ginebra	gin
Jerez	sherry
jerez dulce	sweet sherry
jerez seco	dry sherry
Leche	milk
licor	liquor
licor aromático	liqueur
limonada	lemonade

BEBIDAS	DRINKS
Naranjada	orangeade
Oporto	port
Ponche	punch
Ron	rum
Sidra	cider
Té	tea
Vermut	vermouth
vino	wine
vino blanco	white wine
vino corriente	plonk
vino del país	local wine
vino dulce	sweet wine
vino espumoso	sparkling wine
vino seco	dry wine
vino tinto	red wine
Whisky	whisky
Zumo	juice
zumo de fruta	fruit juice
zumo de limón	lemon juice
zumo de naranja	orange juice
zumo de tomate	tomato juice

16

BICICLETA, UNA   A BICYCLE (12)

ESPAÑOL	ENGLISH
Agarraderos	grips
Barra	cross-bar
«bici»	bike
bicicleta	bicycle
bicicleta de carreras	racing bicycle
ir en bicicleta	to cycle
bomba de aire	air-pump
Cadena	chain

BICICLETA, UNA　　　　　　　**280**　　　　　　　A BICYCLE

cámara　　　　　　　　　　　　inner-tube
ciclismo　　　　　　　　　　　cycling
ciclista　　　　　　　　　　　cyclist
cuadro　　　　　　　　　　　　frame
cubierta　　　　　　　　　　　tyre

Faro　　　　　　　　　　　　lamp
faro delantero　　　　　　　　front-lamp
faro trasero　　　　　　　　　rear lamp
freno　　　　　　　　　　　　brake

Guardabarro　　　　　　　　mudguard

Luz trasera　　　　　　　　reflector

Manillar　　　　　　　　　handle-bars

Pedal　　　　　　　　　　pedal

Radios　　　　　　　　　　spokes
rueda　　　　　　　　　　　　wheel
rueda delantera　　　　　　　front wheel
rueda trasera　　　　　　　　back wheel

Sillín　　　　　　　　　　saddle

Timbre　　　　　　　　　　bell

Válvula　　　　　　　　　valve

BUQUE, UN　　　　　　　　(Véase UN BARCO, 14)

17

BUQUES, TIPOS DE　　　　TYPES OF SHIPS (82)

ESPAÑOL　　　　　　　　　　ENGLISH

Acorazado　　　　　　　　battleship

Balandro　　　　　　　　　sloop
ballenera　　　　　　　　　　whale-boat
balsa　　　　　　　　　　　　raft
barca　　　　　　　　　　　　boat
barco　　　　　　　　　　　　ship, boat

BUQUES, TIPOS DE — TYPES OF SHIPS

barco de pesca	fishing-boat
barco de pesca al arrastre	trawler
barco de ruedas	paddle-boat
barco de vela	sailing-boat
bergantín	brigantine
bote	boat, dinghy
bote de remos	rowing-boat
bote salvavidas	life-boat
buque	ship, vessel
buque de cabotaje	coaster
buque de carga	cargo ship
buque de guerra	warship,
buque de pasajeros	passenger-ship
buque de vapor	steamship
buque escuela	training-ship
buque faro	lightship
buque frutero	fruit-ship
buque gemelo	sister ship
buque insignia	flagship
buque mercante	merchant ship, merchantman
Canoa	canoe
cañonero	gun-boat
carabela	caravel
carguero	cargo boat
cayac	kayak
cazatorpedero	torpedo-boat destroyer
corbeta	sloop of war
crucero	cruiser
crucero de batalla	battle cruiser
crucero ligero	light cruiser
crucero pesado	heavy criser
Destructor	destroyer
dragaminas	mine sweeper
Esquife	skiff
Falúa	gig, cutter
fragata	frigate
Gabarra	lighter, barge
galeón	galleon
galera	galley
goleta	schooner
góndola	gondola
guardacostas	coastguard ship
Junco chino	Chinese junk
Lancha	boat, launch

BUQUES, TIPOS DE	TYPES OF SHIPS
lancha antisubmarina	antisubmarine boat
lancha cañonera	motor gun-boat
lancha de desembarco	landing craft
lancha fuera borda	outboard motor-boat
lancha motora	motor-boat
lancha rápida	speed-boat
lancha torpedera	torpedo-boat
lugre	lugger
Minador	mine layer
Patín a vela	catamaran
petrolero	tanker
portaaviones	aircraft carrier
Queche	ketch
Remolcador	tugboat, tug
remolcador de alta mar	ocean-going tug
Submarino	submarine
submarino atómico	atomic-driven submarine
Transatlántico	ocean liner, liner
transbordador	ferry-boat
Vapor	steamer
vapor de ruedas	paddle-steamer
vapor volandero	tramp steamer
velero	sailing-ship
velero de línea	clipper
Yate	yacht
yola	yawl

18

CALZADO	FOOTWEAR (34)
ESPAÑOL	ENGLISH
Bota	boot
botas	boots
un par de botas	a pair of boots
botas altas	long boots

CALZADO	FOOTWEAR
botas con cordones	lace-up boots
botas de alpinista	climbing-boots
botas de montar	riding-boots
Cordón de bota	bootlace
cordón de zapato	shoelace
CHanclos	galoshes
Ojete	eyelet
Plantilla	insole
polaina	legging
Ribete (de un zapato)	welt
Sandalia	sandal
suela	sole
Tacón	heel
Zapatilla	slipper
zapatillas	slippers, house-shoes
un par de zapatillas	a pair of slippers
zapatillas de paño	carpet slippers
zapato	shoe
zapatos	shoes
un par de zapatos	a pair of shoes
zapatos de ante	suede shoes
zapatos de charol	patent-leather shoes
zapatos de tacón alto	high-heeled shoes
zapatos de tacón bajo	low-heeled shoes
zuecos	clogs

CARTAS, JUEGO DE   (Véase NAIPES, 70)

19

CASA, UNA — A HOUSE (47)

ESPAÑOL	ENGLISH
Agua caliente central	hot running water
agua corriente	running water
aire acondicionado	air-conditioning

aldaba	door-knocker
alero	eaves
alféizar	window-sill
armario	cupboard, closet
ascensor	lift
ático	attic
Balaustrada	balaustrade
balcón	balcony
bañera	bath
barandilla	banister
bisagra	hinge
bodega	wine-cellar
buhardilla	garret
Calefacción	heating
calefacción central	central heating
calentador de agua	water-heater
carbonera	coal-cellar
cerradura	lock
cerrojo	bolt
cocina* (habitación)	kitchen
cocina (mueble)	stove
cocina de gas	gas-stove
cocina eléctrica	electric stove
comedor	dining-room
contraventana	shutter
cornisa	cornice
corredor	corridor
cristal de ventana	pane
cuarto de baño*	bathroom
cuarto de estudio	study
cuarto de los niños	nursery
cuarto trastero	box-room
CHimenea (de salón)	fire-place
chimenea (en el tejado)	chimney
Desagüe	drainage
descansillo de escalera	stair-case landing
despensa	pantry, larder
dormitorio	bedroom
ducha	shower
Electricidad	electricity
enchufe	socket
entrada	hall, entrance
escalera	stairs
escalera de servicio	back stairs
escalón	step

Fachada	front
flexible (cable)	flexible cord
Garaje*	garage
grifo	tap
grifo del agua caliente	hot-water tap
grifo del agua fría	cold-water tap
Habitación	room
hueco de escalera	stair-case
Inodoro	toilet
instalación de fontanería	plumbing
instalación eléctrica	wiring
interruptor	switch
Jardín	garden
Lavabo	wash basin (aparato sanitario) washroom (habitación)
luz	light
Marco de puerta	door-frame
marco de ventana	window-frame
Papel pintado	wall-paper
pararrayos	lightning-rod
pared	wall
pasamanos	hand-rail
persianas	blinds
picaporte	latch
pintura	paint
piso	floor
primer piso	first floor
segundo piso	second floor
tercer piso	third floor
último piso	top floor
planta baja	ground-floor
porche	porch
puerta	door
puerta de la calle	front-door
puerta del jardín	gate
puerta trasera	back door
Radiador	radiator
rodapié	skirting-board
Sala de estar	sitting-room, living-room
salida	exit
salita	parlour
sótano	basement, cellar

Techo	ceiling
tejado	roof
tejado de pizarra	slate roof
tejado de teja	tile roof
terraza	flat roof
timbre de la puerta	door-bell
tirador de la puerta	door-handle
toallero	towel-rail
tramo de escalera	flight of stairs
Umbral	threshold
Valla	fence
ventana	window
vestíbulo	hall
«**W**ater»	water-closet, lavatory

CEREALES (Véase FRUTOS, 41)

20

CINE Y EL TEATRO, EL   THE CINEMA AND THE THEATRE (20)

ESPAÑOL	ENGLISH
Abuchear	to boo
abucheo	booing
acomodador	usher
acomodadora	usherette
acto	act
primer acto	first act
segundo acto	second act
tercer acto	third act
actor	actor
primer actor	leading man
actriz	actress
primera actriz	leading lady
anfiteatro	upper circle
aplaudir	to applaud
aplauso	applause

apuntador	prompter
asiento	seat
autor	author
Bailarín	dancer
bajo	bass
ballet	ballet
bambalina	fly
bar	coffee-bar
barítono	baritone
bastidores	wings
butaca	stall
Cámara	camera
cámara lenta	slow motion
camerino	dressing-room
candilejas	footlights
cantante	singer
cartelera de espectáculos	entertainments guide
comedia	comedy
comedia ligera	light comedy
comedia musical	musical comedy
compañía	company
concha del apuntador	prompter's box
cortometraje	short film
cuadro final	finale
Decorado	scenery
descanso	intermission, interval
director	director
director de escena	producer
dirigir	to direct
drama	drama
dramaturgo	playwright, dramatist
Ensayar	to rehearse
ensayo	rehearsal
ensayo general	dress rehearsal
entrada	ticket
entreacto	intermission, interval
entresuelo	dress-circle
escena	scene
escenario	stage
espectáculo	show
espectáculos de variedades	variety show
estrella de cine	film star
estreno	first performance
Fila	row
foro	background
función	performance

CINE, EL 288 THE CINEMA

Galería — gallery
guardarropa — cloak-room
guión — script

Imagen — image

Largometraje — feature film

Música — music
músico — musician

Noticiario — newsreel

Obra de teatro — play
ópera — opera
orquesta — orchestra

Palco — box
pantalla — screen
papel — part
pasillo — passage, aisle
patio de butacas — pit
película — picture, film, movie
película documental — documentary film
película en blanco y negro — black and white film
película en color — colour film
película muda — talking film, sound-film
película sonora — silent film
pianista — pianist
pista sonora — sound track
programa — programme
protagonista — principal actor, principal actress

proyectar — to project
público — audience

Reparto — cast
representación — show, performance

Sesión continua (en un cine) — continuous performance
solo — solo (artista)
sólo para mayores — adults only
sonido — sound
soprano — soprano
sustituto — understudy

Taquilla — booking-office
taquillero, a — booking-clerk
teatro de la ópera — opera house
teatro de variedades — music-hall
telón — curtain
tenor — tenor

CINE, EL		THE CINEMA

tiple — treble
tragedia — tragedy
tramoyista — props-man
turné — tour

Último pase (de una película) — late show

21

CIUDAD, UNA	A TOWN (91)
ESPAÑOL	ENGLISH

Acera — pavement (GB), sidewalk (USA)

aeropuerto* — airport
afueras, las — the outskirts, the suburbs
alcantarilla — sewer
alcantarillado — sewerage
almacenes — stores
anuncio — advertisement
anuncios luminosos — neon lights
aparcamiento — car park
árbol* — tree
arco — arch
arroyo de la calle — gutter
autobús — bus
avenida — avenue
ayuntamiento — town council (corporación), town hall (edificio)

Banco — bank (casa de banca), bench (para sentarse)

barrendero — dustman, sweeper
barrio — quarter, district
basurero — dustman
biblioteca pública — public library
bocacalle — turning
bomberos — firemen
   brigada de bomberos — fire-brigade
bordillo de la acera — kerb
buzón — letter-box

Cabina telefónica — telephone box, telephone booth

| CIUDAD, UNA | A TOWN |

cafetería — café
calle — street
calle principal — main street
callejón — lane
calzada — roadway
canal — canal
cárcel — prison
cartel — poster
cartero — postman
casa* — house
casa de pisos — block of flats
castillo — castle
catedral — cathedral
cementerio — cemetery
centro, el — the centre
cine* — cinema
ciudad costera — seaside town
ciudad industrial — industrial town
coche* — car
coche de bomberos — fire-engine
coche de recogida de basura — dustcart
comisaría — police station
consulado — consulate
contaminación atmosférica — air pollution
cruce — crossroads
cuartel — barracks

CHalet — villa

Distrito — district

Edificio — building
edificio público — public building
embajada — embassy
escaparate — shop-window
escuela* — school
esquina — corner
esquina de la calle — street corner
estación — station
estación de ferrocarril* — railway station
estación de gasolina — petrol station
estación del metro — underground station
estafeta de correos — post-office
estatua — statue

Fábrica — factory
farola — lamp-post
fuente — fountain

Garaje* — garage

gran vía	high street
guardia	policeman
Hospital*	hospital
hotel*	hotel
Iglesia	church
isleta para peatones	island
Jardín*	garden
Línea de autobuses	bus line
Manzana de casas	block
mercado	market
metro	underground
monumento	monument
monumento conmemorativo	memorial
muralla	wall
museo	museum
Oficina de objetos perdidos	lost property office
oficina de telégrafos	telegraph office
oficina de turismo	tourist office
Palacio	palace
parada de autobús	bus stop
parada de taxis	taxi-rank
parque	park
parque de atracciones	amusement park
parque de bomberos	fire-station
parque zoológico	zoo
paseo marítimo	promenade
paso elevado	overpass, flyover
paso subterráneo	underpass
peatón	pedestrian
plaza	square
plaza del mercado	market-place
plaza de toros	bull-ring
puente	bridge
puerto*	port
Quisco	kiosk
quiosco de periódicos	newspaper-stall
Rascacielos	skyscraper
restaurante*	restaurant
río	river
Servicio de incendios	fire-department
solar	site

CIUDAD, UNA A TOWN

Taxi — taxi
teatro* — theatre
teatro de la ópera — opera-house
teléfono público — public telephone
tienda* — shop
torre — tower
tráfico* — traffic
transporte* — transport
medios de transporte — means of transport
tranvía — tram
trolebús — trolley bus

Vendedor de periódicos — newspaper-boy
vía pública — thoroughfare

22

COCHE, UN — A CAR (16)

ESPAÑOL — ENGLISH

Acelerador — accelerator
aleta — wing
amortiguador — shock absorber
asiento — seat
asiento de atrás — back seat
asiento delantero — front seat

Ballesta — spring
batería — battery
bocina — horn

Caja de cambios — gear-box
capó — bonnet
carrocería — body
cuenta kilómetros — speedometer

Depósito — tank

Eje — axle
eje delantero — front axle
eje trasero — rear axle
espejo retrovisor — driving-mirror

COCHE, UN	A CAR
estrangulador	choke
Faros	head-lights
freno	brake
freno de mano	hand-brake
freno de pie	foot-brake
Guardabarro	mudguard
Lámpara anti-niebla	fog-lamp
limpia parabrisas	wind-screen wiper
luces de posición	parking lights
luces posteriores	rear lights
Marcha atrás	reverse
marchas	gears
matrícula	number plate
motor	engine
muelle	spring
Neumático	tyre
Palanca de cambio	gear lever
parabrisas	wind-screen
parachoques	bumper
pedal	pedal
pedal del acelerador	acceleration pedal
pedal del embrague	clutch pedal
pedal del freno	brake pedal
portaequipajes	boot
primera velocidad	first gear
puerta	door
Radiador	radiator
rueda	wheel
rueda delantera	front wheel
rueda trasera	back wheel
Salpicadero	dashboard
segunda velocidad	second gear
«starter»	starter
Tercera velocidad	third gear
tubo de escape	exhaust
Ventanilla	window
volante	steering-wheel

COCINA (Véase ARTE CULINARIO, 10)

23

COCINA, UNA	A KITCHEN (53)
ESPAÑOL	ENGLISH

Abrebotellas	cap-lifter, bottle-opener
abrelatas	tin-opener
armario de cocina	kitchen-cupboard
Balanza	kitchen scales
batería de cocina	kitchenware
batidor	whisk
batidora	mixer
batidora eléctrica	electric mixer
broqueta	skewer
Cacerola	casserole, pot
cacerola de mango largo	skillet
calentador de agua	water-heater
cazo	ladle
cazuela	saucepan, pan
cocina (mueble)	cooker
cocina de gas	gas-stove
cocina eléctrica	electric stove
cocinero	cook
colador	strainer
colador en forma de cono	pointed strainer
cubo de basura	refuse bin
CHapa de enhornar	baking-tin
Despensa	larder, pantry
Embudo	funnel
escurreplatos	draining-board
esprimelimones	lemon squeezer
espumadera	skimmer
Fogón	range, kitchen range
fregadero	sink, kitchen sink
frigorífico	refrigerator, fridge
Grifo	tap
Hornillo de gas	gas-ring
horno	oven

COCINA, UNA	A KITCHEN
Lavadora	washing-machine
lavavajillas	dishwasher
Marmita	kettle
Olla a presión	pressure cooker
Picador de carne	mincer
Recipiente para el pan	bread tin
rodillo (para amasar)	rolling-pin
Sacacorchos	corkscrew
sartén	frying-pan
Tabla de picar	chopping-board
tapadera	lid
tapón de desagüe	plug
tarro	jar
tazón	bowl
termo de agua caliente	geyser, water heater
tostador	toaster
Utensilios de cocina	kitchen utensils

24

COLORES / COLOURS (23)

ESPAÑOL	ENGLISH
Amarillento	yellowish
amarillo	yellow
anaranjado	orange-coloured
azul	blue
azul añil	indigo
azul celeste	sky blue
azul claro	light blue
azul eléctrico	electric blue
azul marino	navy blue
azul oscuro	dark blue
azulado	bluish
Blanco	white
blanco como la leche	milk white

COLORES	COLOURS
blanco nieve	snow white
blanquecino	whitish
Castaño	chestnut brown
color canario	canary-coloured
color ladrillo	brick red
Dorado	gold-coloured, gilt
Gris	grey
gris claro	light grey
gris oscuro	dark grey
grisáceo	greyish
Marrón	brown
marrón claro	light brown
marrón oscuro	dark brown
morado	violet, purple
Negro	black
negro carbón	coal black
negro tinta	ink black
negruzco	blackish
Pardo	dun-coloured
Rojizo	reddish
rojo	red
rojo sangre	blood red
rosa	pink
Verde	green
verde aceituna	olive green
verde botella	bottle green
verde claro	light green
verde hierba	grass green
verde oscuro	dark green
verdoso	greenish

COMERCIO, EL

(Véase LOS NEGOCIOS Y COMERCIO, 71)

25

CONSTRUCCION DE UN EDIFICIO	HOUSE-BUILDING (48)
ESPAÑOL	ENGLISH

Albañil — bricklayer
andamio — scaffolding
arena — sand
arquitecto — architect

Baldosa — tile
baldosín — glazed tile

Cal — lime
cantero — mason
cañería — pipe
carpintero — carpenter
cemento — cement
cimientos — foundations
constructor — builder
construir — to build

CHimenea — chimney

Dintel — lintel
distribución — planning

Edificio — building

Fachada — front
fontanero — plumber

Grava — gravel
grúa — crane

Hormigón — concrete
hormigonera — concrete mixer

Instalación eléctrica — wiring

Jamba — door-post

Ladrillo — brick

Marco de puerta — door frame
marco de ventana — window-frame
mármol — marble
materiales de construcción — building materials

CONSTRUCCIÓN EDIFICIO — HOUSE-BUILDING

mortero	mortar
Pared	wall
pared maestra	main wall
pared medianera	partition wall
peón	labourer
piedra	stone
pilar	pillar
pintor	painter
piso (vivienda)	flat
pizarra	slate
plano	plan
planta	storey
puerta	door
Suelo	floor
Tabique	partition
techo	ceiling
teja	tile
tejado	roof
Ventana	window
viga	beam
viga de hierro	girder
Yeso	plaster

26

CORREO, EL — THE POST (73)

ESPAÑOL — ENGLISH

Administrador de correos	postmaster
apartado de correos	post-office box
Buzón	letter-box
Caja postal de ahorros	post-office savings bank
carta	letter
carta certificada	registered letter
certificar (un envío)	to register
correo	post (GB), mail (USA)
correo aéreo	air-mail

CORREO, EL	THE POST
Dirección	address
dirigir (una carta)	to address
Echar al correo	to post (GB), to mail (USA)
enviar	to send
estafeta de correos	post-office
Franco de porte	post-free
franqueo	postage
franqueo pagado	post-paid
Giro	money-order
giro postal	postal money-order
giro telegráfico	telegraph money-order
Impreso (para rellenar)	form
impresos (envío)	printed matter
Lista de correos	poste restante
Matasellos	postmark
Pago contra reembolso	payment on delivery
paquete	parcel
pedido hecho por correo	mail-order
Remitente	sender
reparto	delivery
Saca de correos	mail-bag
sello	stamp
sobre	envelope
Tarjeta postal	postcard
tren correo	mail-train
Valija	post-bag

27

COSMETICOS   COSMETICS (25)

ESPAÑOL   ENGLISH

Agua de colonia	toilet water, cologne water
Brillantina	hair-oil, brilliantine

Colonia	cologne
colonia de lavanda	lavender water
colorete	rouge
crecepelo	hair-restorer
crema	cream
crema base	foundation cream
crema bronceadora	sun-tan cream
crema de afeitar	shaving-cream
crema de afeitar sin brocha	brushless shaving-cream
crema de belleza	beauty cream
crema de día	day cream
crema de noche	night cream
crema dental	toothpaste
crema limpiadora	cleansing-cream
crema para la cara	face-cream
crema para las manos	hand cream
crema suavizadora	cold-cream
CHampú	shampoo
Dentífrico	dentifrice
depilatorio	depilatory
depilatorio a la cera	wax depilatory
desodorante	deodorant
Elixir para la boca	mouth wash
esmalte para uñas	nail varnish
Fijador para el pelo	hair cream
fijapelo	hair-fixative
Jabón	soap
jabón de afeitar	shaving-soap
jabón en barra para afeitar	shaving-stick
jabón de tocador	toilet soap
jabón medicinal	medicated soap
Laca para el pelo	hair-lacquer
lápiz de labios	lipstick
lápiz para las cejas	eyebrow pencil
loción	lotion
loción para antes del afeitado	pre-shave lotion
loción para después del afeitado	after-shave lotion
loción para el afeitado	shaving-lotion
Maquillaje	make-up
Perfume	scent, perfume
un frasco de perfume	a bottle of scent
polvos	powder

COSMETICOS	COSMETICS
polvos de talco	talcum powder, toilet powder
polvos para la cara	face powder
Quitaesmalte	nail-varnish remover
Sales de baño	bath salts
Tinte para el pelo	hair-dye
tónico para el pelo	hair-tonic

28

COSTA, EN LA / AT THE SEASIDE (80)

ESPAÑOL	ENGLISH
Albornoz	bath robe
aletas para nadar	flippers
arena	sand
tumbarse en la arena	to lie on the sand
Bañarse	to bathe
bañista	bather
baño	bathe
barca	boat
barco*	ship
bikini	bikini
bote	boat
bote con motor fuera borda	outboard motorboat
bote de remos	rowing-boat
bote de vela	sailing-boat
boya	buoy
«camping»	camping-site
«camping» para remolques	caravan park
caña de pescar	fishing-rod
caseta de baño	bathing-hut
castillo de arena	sandcastle
cinturón salvavidas	life-belt
ciudad costera	seaside town
colchón de aire	air mattress
concha	shell
costa	coast, shore
cubo (de juguete)	bucket

Duna	dune
Esquí acuático	water ski-ing
Faro	lighthouse
Gafas de buceo	goggles
gafas de sol	sunglasses
gorro de baño	bathing-cap
Hamaca	deck-chair
hotel*	hotel
Insolación	sunstroke
Lancha de motor	motorboat
loción para broncear	sun-tan lotion
lugar de veraneo*٧	summer resort
Mar	sea
marea	tide
marea alta	high tide
marea baja	low tide
Nadador	swimmer
nadar	to swim
natación	swimming
Ola	wave
orilla (del mar)	edge
Pala (de juguete)	spade
paseo marítimo	promenade
pesca submarina	under-water fishing
pescar	to fish
pleamar	full tide
playa	beach
playa arenosa	sandy beach
playa pedregosa	stony beach
pueblo de pescadores	fishing-village
puerto de mar*	sea-port
Remar	to row
remolque vivienda	caravan
roca	rock
Salvamento	rescue
sandalias	sandals
silla de playa	beach chair
sol	sun
tomar baños de sol	to sunbathe
tostado por el sol	sunburnt

COSTA, EN LA		AT THE SEASIDE

tumbarse al sol — to lie in the sun
sombra — shade
sombrilla — sun umbrella

Toalla — towel
toldo — canvas
traje de baño — bathing-costume

Vacaciones de verano — summer holidays
vacaciones en la playa — seaside holidays
veraneantes — holiday-makers
vistas al mar — sea-view

Zambullirse — to dive

29

CUERPO HUMANO, EL   THE HUMAN BODY (49)

ESPAÑOL   ENGLISH

Abdomen — abdomen
aliento — breath
amígdala — tonsil
aorta — aorta
arruga — wrinkle
arteria — artery
articulación — joint
axila — armpit

Barba — beard
barbilla — chin
bazo — spleen
bigote — moustache
boca — mouth
brazo — arm
   antebrazo — forearm
bronquios — bronchial tubes
busto — bust

Cabeza — head
cadera — hip
cara — face
carne — flesh

cartílago	cartilage
cavidad nasal	nasal cavity
cavidad pulmonar	pulmonary cavity
cavidad torácica	chest cavity
ceja	eyebrow
cerebro	brain
cintura	waist
codo	elbow
colmillo	eye-tooth
colon	colon
columna vertebral	backbone
corazón	heart
córnea	cornea
costado	side
costilla	rib
costilla falsa	false rib
costilla flotante	floating rib
cráneo	skull, cranium
cuello	neck
cuerdas vocales	vocal cords
cuerpo	body
Dedo	finger
dedo anular	ring finger
dedo corazón	middle finger
dedo del pie	toe
dedo índice	forefinger
dedo meñique	little finger
dedo pulgar	thumb
diafragma	diaphragm
diente	tooth
diente de leche	milk-tooth
dientes	teeth
duodeno	duodenum
Empeine	instep
encía	gum
esófago	gullet
espalda	back
espinilla	shin
esqueleto	skeleton
esternón	sternum
estómago	stomach
extremidades	extremities
Falange	finger-bone
faringe	pharynx
frente	forehead, brow
Garganta	throat

glándula	gland
gusto	taste
Hiel	gall
hígado	liver
hombro	shoulder
hueso*	bone
Ingle	groin
intestino	intestine
intestino delgado	small intestine
intestino grueso	large intestine
intestinos	bowels
iris	iris
Labio	lip
lágrima	tear
laringe	larynx
lengua	tongue
lóbulo	lobe
lomo	loins
lunar	beauty-spot, mole
Mandíbula	jaw
mano	hand
palma de la mano	palm
médula	marrow
mejilla	check
miembro	limb
muela	tooth
muela del juicio	wisdom tooth
muelas	teeth
muñeca	wrist
músculo*	muscle
muslo	thigh
Nariz	nose
ventana de la nariz	nostril
nervio	nerve
nuca	nape
nudillo	knuckle
nuez	Adam's apple
Oído	hearing (sentido)
ojo	eye
cuenca del ojo	eye-socket
globo del ojo	eye-ball
olfato	smell
ombligo	navel
oreja	ear
órgano	organ

Paladar	palate
páncreas	pancreas
pantorrilla	calf
párpado	eye-lid
patillas	whiskers
pecho (tórax)	chest
pecho (seno)	breast
pelo	hair
pestaña	eyelash
pie	foot
piel	skin
pierna	leg
pies	feet
planta del pie	sole
pómulo	cheekbone
pulmón	lung
pulso	pulse
puño	fist
pupila	pupil
Retina	retina
riñón	kidney
rodilla	knee
Saliva	saliva
sangre	blood
sien	temple
sudor	sweat
Tacto	touch
talón	heel
tendón	sinew, tendon
tobillo	ankle
tórax	thorax
tráquea	windpipe
tronco	trunk
tubo digestivo	alimentary canal
Uña	nail
úvula	uvula
Vejiga	bladder
vejiga de la orina	urinary bladder
vena	vein
verruga	wart
vértebra	vertebra
vesícula biliar	gall bladder
vientre	belly
vista	eyesight
Yugular	jugular

30

CUARTO DE BAÑO, UN   A BATHROOM (11)

ESPAÑOL	ENGLISH
Afeitadora	razor
afeitadora eléctrica	electric razor
agua corriente	running water
alfombrilla	rug
armario de baño	bathroom cupboard
Bañera	bath, bathtub
brocha de afeitar	shaving-brush
Cañería	pipe
cañería de agua clara	clean-water pipe
cañería de desagüe	waste-water pipe
cepillo de dientes	tooth-brush
cepillo para el pelo	hair-brush
cisterna	water-tank
cortina	curtain
crema de afeitar	shaving-cream
Dentífrico	tooth-paste
desagüe del lavabo	plug-hole
ducha	shower
Espejo	mirror
esponja	sponge
estante	shelf
Frasco	bottle
Grifo	tap
grifo de agua caliente	hot-water tap
grifo de agua fría	cold-water tap
Hoja de afeitar	razor-blade
Jabón	soap
jabón de afeitar	shaving-soap
jabonera	soap-dish
Lavabo	wash-basin
loción para el afeitado	shaving-lotion
Maquinilla de afeitar	safety-razor

CUARTO DE BAÑO, UN	A BATHROOM
Papel higiénico	toilet-paper
peine	comb
polvos de talco	toilet-powder
Taburete	stool
tapa del «water»	toilet-cover
tapón del desagüe	plug
tarro	jar
taza del «water»	lavatory-pan
toalla	towel
toallero	towel rail
tubo	tube
«Water»	water-closet

31

DEPORTES Y JUEGOS	SPORTS AND GAMES (84)
ESPAÑOL	ENGLISH
Aficionado	amateur
ajedrez*	chess
alpinismo	mountaineering
atleta	athlete
Balón	ball, football
balón volea	volleyball
baloncesto	basketball
billar	billiards
bolos	bowling (juego), skittles (los elementos)
boxeador	boxer
boxeo	boxing
buceo	under-water swimming
Campeón	champion
campeonato	championship
campo de golf	golf link
canicas	marbles
carrera	race
carrera de caballos	horse-race
carrera de obstáculos	obstacle-race

carrera de vallas	hurdle-race
carreras de caballos	horse-racing
carreras de coches	motor-racing
carreras de galgos	greyhound racing
carreras de lanchas motoras	motor-boat racing
carreras de motos	motor-cycle racing
cartas*	cards
caza mayor	hunting
caza menor	shooting
ciclismo	cycling
corredor	runner
Damas	draughts
dardos	darts
dominó	dominoes
Encuentro	match
equitación	riding
escalada	climbing
esgrima	fencing
esquí	ski-ing
esquí acuático	water ski-ing
Fútbol*	football
Golf	golf
Hockey	hockey
hockey sobre hielo	ice-hockey
Juego del «bridge»	bridge
juego del «criquet»	cricket
juego del «croquet»	crocket
juego de naipes	card game
juegos al aire libre	outdoor games
juegos en pista cubierta	indoor games
juegos gimnásticos	gymnastics
juegos Olímpicos	Olympic games
Lanzamiento de disco	throwing the discus
lanzamiento de jabalina	throwing the javelin
lanzamiento de martillo	throwing the hammer
levantamiento de pesos	weight-lifting
lucha	wrestling
Manga	leg
motorismo	motor-cycling
Natación	swimming
navegación	boating
navegación a motor	motor-boating
navegación a vela	sailing
Olympiad	olimpiada

DEPORTES Y JUEGOS	SPORTS AND GAMES
Patinaje	skating
patinaje en pista	roller-skating
patinaje sobre hielo	ice-skating
pelota	ball
pelota base	baseball
pesca	fishing
pesca con caña	angling
«ping pong»	table tennis
pista	track
pista de tenis	tennis court
Remo	rowing
«rugby»	rugby
Salto	jumping, jump
salto de altura	high jump
salto de longitud	long jump
salto con pértiga	pole vault
Tenis	tennis
tiro con arco	archery

32

DOCTOR Y EL HOSPITAL, EL

THE DOCTOR AND THE HOSPITAL (26)

ESPAÑOL	ENGLISH
Ambulancia	ambulance
amígdalas	tonsils
ampolla	blister
análisis de sangre	blood test
anestesia	anaesthesia
anginas	sore throat
antibiótico	antibiotic
aparato respiratorio	respiratory organs
apendicitis	appendicitis
asfixia	asphyxia
aspirina	aspirin
ataque	fit
Bacilo	bacillus
bacterias	bacteria

bilis | bile
bisturí | bistoury, scalpel

Calambre | cramp
callo | corn
camilla | stretcher
camillero | stretcher-bearer
cardenal | bruise
cirugía | surgery
cirujano | surgeon
clínica | clinic, nursing home
cojera | lameness
coma | coma
contagio | contagion
contagioso | contagious
corriente sanguínea | blood stream
costra | scab
cura | cure
curar | to cure

Debilidad | weakness
dentista | dentist
desmayarse | to faint
desmayo | faint
diagnosticar | to diagnose
diagnóstico | diagnosis
dieta | diet
digestión | digestion
doctor | doctor
dolor | pain, ache
dolor de cabeza | headache
dolor de espalda | backache
dolor de estómago | stomachache
dolor de muelas | toothache
dolor de oídos | earache
dosis | dose

Electrocardiograma | electrocardiogram
enfermedad* | illness, disease
enfermedad crónica | chronic disease
enfermedad infecciosa | infectious disease
enfermera | nurse
enfermo | ill, sick (adj.); patient (sus.)
esguince | sprain
especialista | specialist
estetoscopio | stethoscope
estreptomicina | streptomycin
exploración por rayos X | X-ray examination

Fallo cardíaco | heart failure

DOCTOR, EL	THE DOCTOR
fiebre	fever, temperature
fractura	fracture
Ganglio	ganglion
germen	germ
glándula	gland
glóbulos	corpuscles
glóbulos blancos	white corpuscles
glóbulos rojos	red corpuscles
grupo sanguíneo	blood group
Hemorragia	hemorrhage
herida	injury, wound
herida infectada	infected wound
hipo	hiccough
hospital	hospital
hueso*	bone
Indigestión	indigestion
infección	infection
inflamación	inflammation
insolación	sunstroke
inyección	injection
irritación	irritation
Jarabe para la tos	cough mixture
jefe de enfermeras	matron
juanete	bunion
jugo gástrico	gastric juice
Laboratorio	laboratory
lesión	lesion
leucocito	leucocyte
LLaga	sore
Manicomio	mental hospital
medicina	medicine
médico de cabecera	family doctor
médico de medicina general	general practitioner
membrana	membrane
metabolismo	metabolism
muletas	crutches
músculo*	muscle
Nervios	nerves
Operación	operation
operar	to operate
organismo	organism
órgano	organ
orina	urine

DOCTOR, EL	THE DOCTOR
Paciente	patient
pastillas para la tos	cough lozenges
penicilina	penicillin
picor	itching
plasma	plasma
pleura	pleura
practicante	medical assistant
pulso	pulse
pus	pus
Quemadura	burn
quiste	cyst
quiste sebáceo	sebaceous cyst
Radiografía	radiograph
rayos X	X-rays
receta	prescription
respiración	respiration, breathing
Sala de hospital	ward
saliva	saliva
salud	healh
síntomas	symptoms
sistema nervioso	nervous system
sudor	perspiration
Tejido	tissue
tensión de la sangre	blood pressure
terapia	therapy
termómetro	thermometer
tortícolis	stiff neck
tos	cough
toser	to cough
transfusión de sangre	blood transfusion
tratamiento	treatment
Ungüento	ointment
Vacuna	vaccination
vacunar	to vaccinate
vaso sanguíneo	blood vessel
venda	bandage
vértigo	vertigo
virus	virus

33

EDAD, LA   AGE (1)

ESPAÑOL   ENGLISH

Adolescencia   adolescence
adolescente   adolescent
adulto   adult
anciana   old woman
anciano   old man

Bebé   baby

Centenario   centenarian
crecer   to grow up
cumpleaños   birthday

CHochear   to dote
chochez   dotage

Entrado en años   elderly
envejecer   to grow old

Hombre   man

Infancia   infancy
infante   infant

Joven   young (adj.), young man, young woman (sus.)

jovencito   youngster
juventud   youth

Longevidad   longevity

Madurez (de una mujer)   womanhood
madurez (de un hombre)   manhood
muchacha   girl, lass
muchacho   boy, lad
muerte   death
mujer   woman

Nacimiento   birth
niña   child
niñez   childhood
niño   child

| EDAD, LA | 315 | AGE |

niño de pecho	child in arms
niño que comienza a andar	todler
Senil	senile
señorita	young woman
señora	lady
sexagenario	sexagenarian
Uso de razón	age of discretion
Vejez	old age
vida	life
viejo	old
viejo chocho	dotard
EDIFICIO, UN	(Véase UNA CASA, 19)
EDIFICIO, CONSTRUCCION DE UN	(Véase CONSTRUCCION DE UN EDIFICIO, 25)

34

ELECTRICIDAD   ELECTRICITY (28)

ESPAÑOL	ENGLISH
Aislador	insulator
aislamiento	insulation
alambre para fusibles	fuse wire
alta tensión	high voltage
alumbrado	lighting
amperio	ampere
apagar	to switch off
arco	arc
Batería	battery
bombilla	bulb
Cable	wire
cable con corriente	live wire
cable de tierra	earth wire
cable neutro	neutral wire

ELECTRICIDAD — ELECTRICITY

caja de fusibles	fuse box
calambre	electric shock
campo magnético	magnetic field
central eléctrica	power-station
cinta aislante	insulating-tape
circuito	circuit
corto circuito	short-circuit
conductor	conductor
contador	meter
corriente	current
corriente alterna	alternating current
corriente continua	direct current
corriente eléctrica	electric current
Dinamo	dynamo
Electricista	electrician
eléctrico	electric(al)
electrificar	to electrify
electrodomésticos	electrical appliances
encender	to switch on
enchufe	plug (clavija), socket (receptáculo)
energía eléctrica	electric energy
Fase	phase
flexible	flex
fusible	fuse
Generador	generator
Hornillo eléctrico	electric fire
Instalación eléctrica	wiring
interruptor	switch
interruptor automático	circuit-breaker
interruptor general	main switch
Kilovatio	kilowatt
Lámpara	lamp
luz	light
luz eléctrica	electric light
Onda eléctrica	electric wave
Pila	battery
portalámparas	lampholder
Resistencia	resistor
Suministro de energía eléctrica	electric supply

Vatio	watt
voltaje	voltage
voltio	volt

35

ENFERMEDADES / ILLNESSES (50)

ESPAÑOL	ENGLISH
Acné	acne
alergia	allergy
almorranas	piles
amnesia	amnesia
anemia	anaemia
anginas	tonsillitis
antrax	anthrax
apendicitis	appendicitis
aplopejía	apoplexy
arterioesclerosis	arterio-sclerosis
artritis	arthritis
asma	asthma
Baile de San Vito	St. Vitus.' dance
bocio	goitre
bronquitis	bronchitis
Cálculo hepático	gall-stone
cáncer	cancer
catarata	cataract
catarro	catarrh
ceguera	blindness
cirrosis	cirrhosis
claustrofobia	claustrophobia
colapso	collapse
cólera	cholera
cólico	colic
colitis	colitis.
conjuntivitis	conjunctivitis
Daltonismo	colour blindness
dermatitis	dermatitis
diabetes	diabetes
difteria	diphtheria

| ENFERMEDADES | ILLNESSES |

disentería — dysentery
dispepsia — dyspepsia

Ezcema — eczema
enfermedad — sickness, disease, illness
enfermedad alérgica — allergic disease
enfermedad crónica — chronic disease
enfermedad del corazón — heart disease
enfermedad del riñón — kidney disease
enfermedad del sueño — sleeping sickness
enfermedad de la piel — skin disease
enfermedad de la sangre — blood disease
enfermedad de los nervios — nervous disease
enfermedad endémica — endemic disease
enfermedad mental — mental disease
enfermedad venérea — venereal disease
epilepsia — epilepsy
escarlatina — scarlet fever
esclerosis — sclerosis
esquizofrenia — schizophrenia
estrabismo — squint
estreñimiento — constipation

Faringitis — pharyngitis
fiebre — fever
fiebre amarilla — yellow fever
fiebre de Malta — Mediterranean fever
fiebre del heno — hay fever
fiebre intermitente — intermittent fever
fiebre paratífica — paratyphoid fever
fiebre perniciosa — malignant fever
fiebre reumática — rheumatic fever
fiebre tifoidea — typhoid fever
flatulencia — flatulence
flebitis — phlebitis

Gangrena — gangrene
gastritis — gastritis
gota — gout
gripe — infuenza, flu

Hepatitis — hepatitis
hernia — rupture
hidrofobia — hydrophobia
hipertensión — hypertension
hipocondria — hypochondria
hipotensión — hypotension
histeria — hysteria

Ictericia — jaundice

ENFERMEDADES	ILLNESSES
insomnio	insomnia
Laringitis	laryngitis
lepra	leprosy
leucemia	leukemia
locura	madness
lumbago	lumbago
Mal de garganta	sore throat
mal de oídos	sore ears
mal de ojos	sore eyes
malaria	malaria
meningitis	meningitis
miopía	myopia
mudez	dumbness
Neuralgia	neuralgia
neurosis	neurosis
Obesidad	obesity
Paludismo	malaria
paperas	mumps
parálisis	paralysis
parálisis infantil	infantile paralysis
pie plano	flat foot
pleuresía	pleurisy
polio	polio
poliomielitis	poliomyelitis
pulmonía	pneumonia
Rabia	rabies
raquitismo	rickets
resfriado	cold
reumatismo	rheumatism
rubéola	German measles
Sabañones	chilblains
sarampión	measles
sarna	scabies
septicemia	bloodpoisoning
sífilis	syphilis
sinusitis	sinusitis
sordera	deafness
sordomudez	deaf-mutism
Tartamudez	stuttering, stammering
tensión alta	high blood pressure
tensión baja	low blood pressure
tensión de la sangre	blood pressure

ENFERMEDADES — ILLNESSES

tétanos	tetanus
tifus	typhus
tiña	favus
tos ferina	whooping cough
trombosis	thrombosis
trombosis coronaria	coronary thrombosis
tuberculosis	tuberculosis, TB
tuberculosis galopante	galloping consumption
tumor	tumour
tumor benigno	benign tumour
tumor maligno	malignant tumour
Úlcera	ulcer
úlcera de estómago	stomach ulcer
úlcera duodenal	duodenal ulcer
úlcera gástrica	gastric ulcer
urticaria	hives
Varicela	chicken-pox
varices	varicose veins
vegetaciones	adenoids
viruela	smallpox

ESCUELA, LA (Véase LA VIDA EN LA ESCUELA, 99)

ESCULTURA (Véase PINTURA Y ESCULTURA, 81)

36

ESTACION DE FERROCARRIL, UNA — A RAILWAY STATION (75)

ESPAÑOL	ENGLISH
Andén	platform
asiento	seat
Bar	refreshment room
baúl	trunk
billete	ticket
billete de ida	single ticket

ESTACIÓN DE FERROCARRIL — A RAILWAY STATION

billete de ida y vuelta — return ticket

Cantina — refreshment room
carretilla de equipajes — luggage trolley
carril — rail
coche — coach, carriage
coche cama — sleeping-car
coche de viajeros — passenger coach
coche restaurante — dining-car
compartimento — compartment
consigna — left-luggage office

Departamento cama — sleeper
depósito de máquinas — engine shed

Entrada — entrance, way in
equipaje — baggage (USA), luggage (GB)
estación — station

Factor — guard
ferrocarril — railway
ferroviario — railwayman
fogonero — stoker
furgón — van

Guardaagujas — pointsman

Horario — time-table

Jefe de estación — station master

Litera — berth
locomotora — engine, locomotive
locomotora diesel — diesel locomotive
locomotora de vapor — electric locomotive
locomotora eléctrica — steam locomotive

LLegada — arrival

Maleta — suitcase, case
máquina de maniobras — shunting engine
maquinista — engine-driver
mozo — porter

Parada de taxis — taxi-rank
partida — departure
pasajero — passenger
paso subterráneo — subway
primera clase — first class

Quiosco de periódicos — bookstall

ESTACIÓN DE FERROCARRIL   322   A RAILWAY STATION

Raíles	rails
rejilla para el equipaje	rack
revisor	ticket collector
Sala de espera	waiting-room
salida	exit, way out
segunda clase	second class
semáforo	signals
Taquilla	ticket office, booking-office
tender	tender
tren	train
tren correo	mail-train
tren de mercancías	goods-train
tren de vapor	steam train
tren de viajeros	passenger train
tren eléctrico	electric train
tren expreso	express train
tren local	local train
tren rápido	fast train
Vagón	wagon
vagón abierto	open wagon
vagón cisterna	tank wagon
vagón de carga	truck
vagón de equipajes	luggage van
vagón de ferrocarril	railway coach
ventanilla	window
viajero	traveller
vías	lines, tracks

37

FAMILIA, LA   THE FAMILY (29)

ESPAÑOL	ENGLISH
Abuela	grandmother
abuelita	grandma
abuelito	grandpa
abuelo	grandfather
ahijada	god-daughter
ahijado	godson

Bebé	baby
Cuñada	sister-in-law
cuñado	bother-in-law
Esposa	wife
esposo	husband
Hermana	sister
hermanastra	step-sister
hermanastro	step-brother
hermano	brother
hija	daughter
hijastra	step-daughter
hijastro	step-son
hijo	son
huérfano	orphan
Madrastra	step-mother
madre	mother
madrina	godmother
marido	husband
Nieta	granddaughter
nieto	grandson
niña	child
niñas	children
niño	child
niños	children
novia	fiancée, bride (en la boda)
novio	fiancé, bridegroom (en la boda)
nuera	daughter-in-law
Padrastro	step-father
padre	father
padres	parents
padrino	godfather
pariente	relative
prima	cousin
primo	cousin
Sobrina	niece
sobrino	nephew
suegra	mother-in-law
suegro	father-in-law
Tía	aunt
tío	uncle
Viuda	widow
viudo	widower

FAMILIA, LA		THE FAMILY

Yerno — son-in-law

FERROCARRIL, ESTACION DE — (Véase UNA ESTACION DE FERROCARRIL, 36)

FESTIVIDADES — (Véase FIESTAS, 38)

38

FIESTAS Y FESTIVIDADES	**HOLIDAYS AND FESTIVITIES (45)**
ESPAÑOL	ENGLISH
Año Nuevo	New Year
Corpus Christi	Corpus Christi
Cuaresma	Lent
cumpleaños	birthday
Día de Año Nuevo	New Year's Day
Día de la Ascensión	Ascension Day
Día de la Asunción	Assumption Day
Día de la Raza	Columbus Day
Día de los Inocentes (28 de diciembre)	All-Fools'-Day (1st April)
Día del Santo (de una persona)	Saint's day
Día de Navidad	Christmas Day
Día de Todos los Santos	All-Saints'-Day, All-Hallows
Domingo de Pentecostés	Whitsunday
Domingo de Ramos	Palm Sunday
Fiesta del Espíritu Santo	Whitsuntide
Jueves Santo	Holy Thursday
Lunes de Pascua	Easter Monday
Lunes de Pentecostés	Whitmonday
Martes de Carnaval	Shrove Tuesday
Miércoles de Ceniza	Ash Wednesday
Navidad	Christmas
Nochebuena	Christmas Eve

FIESTAS		HOLIDAYS

Noche de Reyes	Twelfth Night
Nochevieja	New Year's Eve
Pascua	Easter
Semana Santa	Holy Week
Vacaciones de Navidad	Christmas holidays
vacaciones de verano	summer holidays
Viernes Santo	Good Friday

FLORES (Véase ARBOLES, PLANTAS Y FLORES 6)

39

FOTOGRAFIA, LA	PHOTOGRAPHY (72)
ESPAÑOL	ENGLISH
Ampliación	enlargement
ampliar	to enlarge
Cámara	camera (máquina), camera-man (persona)
color	colour
cuarto oscuro	dark-room
Desenfocado	out of focus
distancia	distance
Emulsión	emulsion
enfocado	in focus
enfocar	to focus
exposición	exposure
Filtro	filter
«flash»	flash
«flash» electrónico	electronic flash
foco	focus
foto	photo
fotogénico	photogenic
fotografía	photograph (retrato, imagen); photography (arte)

FOTOGRAFÍA, LA   **326**   PHOTOGRAPHY

hacer una fotografía	to take a photograph
fotografiar	to photograph
fotográfico	photographic
fotógrafo	photographer
fotómetro	photometer
Imagen	image
instantánea	snapshot
Lámpara «flash»	flashbulb
lente	lens
luz	light
Negativo	negative
Obturador	shutter
Película	film
positivo	print
primer plano	close-up (foto de cerca), fore-ground (en una foto)
Revelado	development
revelar	to develop
rollo de película	roll
Segundo plano	background (en una foto)
Tienda de artículos fotográficos	photo-dealer's
tomavistas	cine-camera
trípode	tripod
Velocidad	speed

40

FRUTA   FRUIT (35)

ESPAÑOL   ENGLISH

Albaricoque   apricot
Breva   fig

Cereza	cherry
ciruela	plum
ciruela pasa	prune
CHirimoya	custard-apple
Dátil	date
Frambuesa	raspberry
fresa	strawberry
Granada	pomegranate
grosella negra	blackcurrant
Higo	fig
higo chumbo	prickly pear
higo seco	dried fig
Lima	lime
limón	lemon
mandarina	tangerine
manzana	apple
melocotón	peach
melón	melon
mora	blackberry
Naranja	orange
Pera	pear
piña de América	pineapple
plátano	banana
pomelo	grapefruit
Sandía	water-melon
Uva espina	gooseberry
uvas	grapes
uvas pasas	raisins

41
FRUTOS, HORTALIZAS, LEGUMBRES Y CEREALES
FRUITS, VEGETABLES AND CEREALS (36)

ESPAÑOL	ENGLISH
Ajo	garlic
alcachofa	artichoke

almendra	almond
apio	celery
arroz	rice
avellana	hazel-nut
avena	oats
Batata	yam
berenjena	egg-plant, aubergine
berro	watercress
Cacahuete	peanut
calabacín	marrow
calabaza	pumpkin, gourd
castaña	chestnut
cebada	barley
cebolla	onion
cebolletas	chives
centeno	rye
coco	coconut
col	cabbage
coles de Bruselas	Brussels-sprouts
coliflor	cauliflower
CHampiñón	mushroom
chirivía	parsnip
Endibia	endive
espárragos	asparagus
espinacas	spinach
Garbanzo	chickpea
grelos	turnip tops
guisante	green pea
Haba	broad bean
Judía	bean
judía verde	French bean
Lechuga	lettuce
lenteja	lentil
Maíz	maize
mijo	millet
Nabo	turnip
nuez	walnut
Patata	potato
patatas	potatoes
pepinillo	gherkin
pepino	cucumber

FRUTOS, ETC.	FRUITS, ETC.
perejil	parsley
pimiento	pepper
piña (del pino)	pine-cone
piñón	pine-nut
puerro	leek
Rábano	radish
remolacha	beet
Seta	mushroom
Tomate	tomato
tomates	tomatoes
trigo	wheat
trufa	truffle
Zanahoria	carrot

42

FÚTBOL — FOOTBALL (33)

ESPAÑOL	ENGLISH
Árbitro	referee
Balón	ball, football
Defensa	back
defensa central	centre half back
defensa lateral derecho	right back
defensa lateral izquierdo	left back
delantero centro	centre forward
despeje	clearance
Encuentro	match
equipo	team
esquina	corner
extremo derecha	outside right
extremo izquierda	outside left
Interior derecha	inside right
interior izquierda	inside left
Juez de línea	linesman
Larguero	cross-bar
liga	league

FUTBOL	FOOTBALL
Marcar	to score
medio volante derecho	right half back
medio volante izquierdo	left half back
Portería	goal
portero	goal-keeper
Red	net
Sacar	to kick off
saque	kick-off
saque de esquina	corner-kick

43

GARAJE, EN EL	AT THE GARAGE (38)
ESPAÑOL	ENGLISH
Abolladura	dent
aceite	oil
cambiar el aceite	to change the oil
acelerar	to accelerate
admisión	induction
anticongelante	anti-freeze
árbol de levas	cam shaft
árbol de transmisión	transmission shaft
Ballesta	spring
bidón de gasolina	petrol can
bomba de gasolina	petrol pump
bujía	spark plug
Caballos de fuerza	horse power
caja de cambios	gear-box
cámara del neumático	inner-tube
camión	lorry (GB), truck (USA)
carburador	carburettor
carrera del émbolo	stroke
cilindro	cylinder
coche*	car, motor-car
compresión	compression
correa del ventilador	fanbelt
culata	cylinder head
Delco	distributor

tapa del delco	distributor-head
desembragar	to throw out of gear
diferencial	differential gear
dinamo	dynamo
Émbolo	piston
embragar	to thow into gear
embrague	clutch
embrague de disco	disk clutch
engranaje	gear
engrasar	to grease
engrase	greasing
escape	exhaust
Frenar	to brake
funcionar	to work
furgoneta	van
Gasolina	petrol
gato para levantar pesos	jack
Mecánico	mechanic
moto	motor-cycle
motor	engine, motor
motor de arranque	starter
motor de combustión interna	internal combustion engine
motor refrigerado por agua	water-cooled engine
motor refrigerado por aire	air-cooled engine
muelle	spring
Neumático	tyre
neumático pinchado	flat tyre
nivel	level
nivel del aceite	oil level
Pinchazo	puncture
polea	pulley
poner en marcha	to start
presión de los neumáticos	tyre pressure
Radiador	radiator
recambios	spare parts
reparar	to repair
rueda	wheel
rueda dentada	gear-wheel
Suspensión	suspension
Tornillo (para sujetar piezas)	vice
torno	lathe

transmisión transmission
Válvula valve

44

GEOGRAFÍA GEOGRAPHY (40)

ESPAÑOL ENGLISH

Acantilado — cliff
albufera — lagoon
archipiélago — archipelago
arroyo — stream

Bahia — bay
barranco — ravine
bosque — wood

Cabo — cape
caleta — cove
campo — field
canal — channel
catarata — cataract, waterfall
caverna — cave
cayo — key
cima — summit
colina — hill
continente — continent
cordillera — mountain range
costa — coast, seaside
cráter — crater
cuenca — basin
cueva — cave

Delta — delta
desembocadura — mouth
desfiladero — gorge
desierto — desert

Ensenada — bight
este — east
estrecho — strait

Falla — fault

GEOGRAFÍA	GEOGRAPHY
Glaciar	glacier
golfo	gulf
Isla	island, isle
istmo	isthmus
Jungla	jungle
Ladera	slope
lago	lake
litoral	coastline
loma	ridge
LLanura	plain
Mapa	map
mapa en relieve	relief map
mar	sea
meseta	table-land
montaña	mountain
cima de una montaña	top of a mountain
pie de una montaña	foot a mountain
puerto de montaña	mountain pass
Norte	north
Oasis	oasis
océano	ocean
oeste	west
Paisaje	landscape
península	peninsula
playa	beach
precipicio	precipice
Región	region
región montañosa	highland
riachuelo	rivulet
río	river
Sabana	savannah
selva	forest
sur	south
Tierra	earth, land
tierra baja	lowland
torrente	torrent
tundra	tundra
Valle	valley
vegetación	vegetation
volcán	volcano

45

GEOMETRÍA	GEOMETRY (41)
ESPAÑOL	ENGLISH

Altura	altitude
anchura	breadth
ángulo	angle
ángulo agudo	acute angle
ángulo obtuso	obtuse angle
ángulo recto	right angle
arco	arc
área	area
Base	base
Centro	centre
círculo	circle
circunferencia	circumference
cono	cone
cuadrado	square
cuadrángulo	quadrangle
cuadrilátero	quadrilateral
cuadro	square
cubo	cube
cuerda	chord
curva	curve
Desarrollo	revolution
diagonal	diagonal
diámetro	diameter
dimensión	dimension
Eje	axis
elipse	ellipse
equilátero	equilateral
escaleno	scalene
esfera	sphere
espacio	space
espiral	spiral
Figura geométrica	geometrical figure
Grosor	thickness
Hipérbola	hyperbola

GEOMETRÍA	GEOMETRY
hipotenusa	hypotenuse
horizontal	horizontal
Intersección	intersection
isósceles	isosceles
Lado	side
línea	line
línea curva	curved line
línea recta	straight line
líneas convergentes	convergent lines
líneas divergentes	divergent lines
líneas paralelas	parallel lines
longitud	length
Mediana	median
Parábola	parabola
paralelo	parallel
paralelogramo	parallelogram
perpendicular	perpendicular
plano	plane
polígono	polygon
prisma	prism
proyección	projection
punto	point
Radio	radius
rectangular	rectangular
rectángulo	rectangle
redondo	round
rombo	rhomb, rhombus
romboide	rhomboid
Secante	secant
sección	section
segmento	segment
semicírculo	semicircle
simetría	symmetry
superficie	surface
Tangente	tangent
trapecio	trapezium
trapezoide	trapezoid
triangular	triangular
triángulo	triangle
triángulo equilátero	equilateral triangle
Vertical	vertical
vértice	vertex

46

GRANJA, UNA	A FARM (30)
ESPAÑOL	ENGLISH

Abeja — bee
arado — plough
arar — to plough
árbol* — tree
asno — donkey
azada — hoe

Buey — ox
burro — donkey

Caballo — horse
cabra — goat
campo — field
carretilla — wheelbarrow
carro — cart
cerca — fence
cerdo — pig
cobertizo — shed
colmena — bee-hive
conejo — rabbit
corral — farmyard
cosecha — harvest
crecer — to grow
cuadra — stable
cubo — pail
cultivar — to grow

Espantapájaros — scarecrow
esquilar — to shear
esquileo — shearing
establo — stable
estación del año — season
estanque — pond

Gallina — hen
gallinero — hen-coop
gallo — cock
ganado — cattle
ganso — goose
gansos — geese
granero — barn

| GRANJA, UNA | A FARM |

granjero	farmer
grano	grain, corn
guadaña	scythe
Hierba	grass
hierbajo	weed
horquilla	pitchfork
hoz	sickle
huerta	kitchen garden
huerto	orchard
huevos	eggs
Invierno	winter
Jardín*	garden
Lana	wool
leche	milk
LLover	to rain
lluvia	rain
Manada	herd
miel	honey
molino	mill
mula	mule
Nevar	to snow
nieve	snow
Ordeñar	to milk
ovejas(s)	sheep
Paja	straw
paja de heno	hay
pala	shovel
pala para cavar	spade
paloma	dove, pigeon
parra	vine
patio	yard
pato	duck
peón de granja	farm-worker
perro	dog
perro pastor	sheep-dog
piara	herd
pichón	pigeon
pienso	feed
planta	plant
plantar	to plant
pollo	chicken
polluelo	chicken
pozo	well
primavera	spring
puerta de verja	gate

Español	English
Queso	cheese
Raíz	root
rastrillo	rake
rebaño	flock
redil	sheep-fold
regar	to water
Saco	sack
sembrar	to sow
simiente	seed
sol	sun
suelo	soil
Tiempo atmosférico	weather
tractor	tractor
trigo	wheat
Vaca	cow
valla	fence
verano	summer
Yegua	mare

47

GUERRA, LA   WARFARE (96)

ESPAÑOL	ENGLISH
Abanderado	flag bearer
alambrada	barbed-wire entanglement
alarma	alarm
alarma aérea	air-raid alarm
alférez	second lieutenant
aliado	ally
alistamiento	enlistment
almirantazgo	admiralty
almirante	admiral
aprovisionamiento	supply
arma*	weapon, arm
armamento	armament
artillería	artillery
artillería antiaérea	antiaircraft artillery
artillería de campaña	field artillery
artillería de largo alcance	long-range artillery

GUERRA, LA	WARFARE
artillería de montaña	mountain artillery
artillería ligera	light artillery
artillería pesada	heavy artillery
artillero	gunner
atacar	to attack
ataque	attack
ataque aéreo	air attack
ataque a la bayoneta	bayonet charge
avanzadilla	outpost
aviación	aviation
avión*	aircraft
avión de bombardeo	bombing aircraft
avión de caza	fighter aircraft
Bajas	casualties
bandera	flag
barco*	ship
barrera aérea	air barrage
barricada	barricade
base	base
base aérea	air base
base naval	naval base
batalla	battle
batalla aérea	air-battle
batalla naval	sea-battle
batallón	battalion
batallón de infantería	infantry battalion
batería	battery
batería de costa	coast battery
blindaje	armour
bombardeo	bombing, bombardment
bombardeo en picado	dive bombing
brigada	brigade
Caballería	cavalry
cabo	corporal
camillero	stretcher-bearer
campamento	camp
campaña	campaign
campo de batalla	battle-field
campo de concentración	concentration camp
campo de minas	mine field
camuflaje	camouflage
capitán	captain
carga (ataque)	charge
centro de instrucción	training centre
centro de reclutamiento	recruiting centre
columna	column
comandante	major (rango), commander (jefe con mando)

combate	combat
compañía	company
contraataque	counter-attack
contraofensiva	counter-offensive
corneta	bugle
banda de cornetas	bugle band
coronel	colonel
cuartel	barracks
cuartel general	headquarters
cuerpo de ejército	army-corps
Declaración de guerra	declaration of war
defensa	defence
destacamento	detachment
día D	D-day
división	division
división acorazada	armoured division
división aerotransportada	airborne division
división de infantería	infantry division
división mecanizada	mechanized division
división motorizada	motorized division
Ejército	army
emplazamiento	emplacement
emplazamiento artillero	artillery emplacement
enemigo	enemy
escuadra	squadron
escuadrilla	squadron
escuadrilla de aviones	aircraft squadron
escuadrón	squadron
estrategia	strategy
estratégico	strategic
Fila	rank
flanco	flank
flota de combate	battle fleet
frente	front
fuerzas	forces
General	general
grado	rank
guerra	war
guerrero	warrior
guerrillero	guerrilla fighter
Hospital de campaña	field hospital
hostilidades	hostilities
Individuo de tropa	enlisted man
infantería	infantry
instrucción	drill
instrucción militar	military training

Lucha		fight
luchar		to fight

Mando — command
  alto mando — high command
maniobras — manoeuvres
mariscal — marshal
munición — ammunition

Objetivo — objective
ofensiva — offensive
oficial — officer
oficial del ejército — army officer

Parada — parade
patrulla — patrol

Recluta — recruit
reconocimiento — reconnaissance
reconocimiento aéreo — air reconnaissance
refuerzos — reinforcements
regimiento — regiment
rendición — surrender
rendirse — to surrender
resistencia — resistance
retaguardia — rearguard
retirada — retreat, withdrawal
retirarse — to retreat, to withdraw

Saludo — salute
sargento — sergeant
servicio militar — military service
sitiar — to siege
sitio — siege
soldado — soldier
soldado licenciado — discharged soldier
soldado raso — private

Táctica — tactics
táctico — tactical
tambor — drum
teniente — lieutenant
teniente coronel — lieutenant colonel
tienda de campaña — tent
toque de queda — curfew
tratado de paz — peace treaty
trinchera — trench
trompeta (soldado) — trumpeter
tropas — troops
tropas aerotransportadas — airborne troops
tropas de montaña — mountain troops

GUERRA, LA	WARFARE
tropas paracaidistas	paratroops
Ultimatum	ultimatum
unidad	unit
uniforme	uniform
uniforme de campaña	battledress
Veterano	veteran
voluntario	volunteer

48

HERRAMIENTAS E INSTRUMENTOS	TOOLS AND INSTRUMENTS (89)
ESPAÑOL	ENGLISH
Aceitera	oil-can
alicates	pliers
azadón	hoe
Barrena	gimlet
berbiquí	brace
broca	bit
Calibrador	gauge
cepillo de carpintero	plane
cincel	chisel
compás	a pair of compasses
compás de punta seca	dividers
cortafrío	cold chisel
Destornillador	screwdriver
Escoplo	chisel
escuadra	square
Formón	chisel
fresa	milling-tool
Gato	jack
grúa	crane
guadaña	scythe
Hacha	axe
horquilla	pitchfork
hoz	sickle

HERRAMIENTAS, ETC.   TOOLS, ETC.

Lámpara de soldar	blowlamp
lezna	awl
lima	file
LLana	trowel
llave de tuercas	spanner
llave inglesa	wrench
llave para cañerías	pipe-wrench
Martillo	hammer
mazo	mallet
metro plegable	rule
Nivel	level
nivel de burbuja	spirit level
Pala de mango corto	scoop
pala de mango largo	shovel
pala para cavar	spade
paleta	trowel
pico	pick
pinzas	tweezers
pistola de engrase	grease gun
plomada	plumb line
prensa de tornillo	clamp, cramp
punzón	pick
Rastrillo	rake
Serrucho	hand saw
sierra	saw
sierra circular	band saw, circular saw
sierra de bastidor	frame saw
sierra de marquetería	fretsaw
sierra para metales	hacksaw
soldador	soldering-iron
Taladro	drill
taladro que se apoya en el hombro	breast drill
tenazas	tongs, pincers
tenazas de garfios	crampon
tijeras	scissors
tijeras de jardin	shears
tornillo	vice
torno	lathe
Yunque	anvil
Zapapico	pickaxe

49

HISTORIA   HISTORY (44)

ESPAÑOL	ENGLISH
Aliados	allies
anglo-sajones	Anglo-Saxons
árabes	Arabs
archiduque	archduke
armada	navy
Armada Invencible, la	the Armada
Barón	baron
batalla	battle
batalla naval	sea battle
Caballero	knight
Carta Magna	Magna Carta
cartagineses	Carthaginians
castillo	castle
católico	Catholic
cisma	schism
colonia	settlement
colonizadores	settlers, colonists
concilio	council
conquista	conquest
conquistador	conqueror
conquistar	to conquer
corona	crown
coronación	coronation
coronar	to crown
corte	court
Cruzadas, Las	the Crusades
cruzados	crusaders
Derrota	defeat
derrotar	to defeat
dinastía	dynasty
duque	duke
Edad de Piedra, la	the Stone Age
Edad del Bronce, la	the Bronze Age
Edad Media, la	the Middle Ages
edicto	edict

HISTORIA	HISTORY
ejecución	execution
ejecutar	to execute
ejército	army
emperador	emperor
emperatriz	empress
enemigo	enemy
esclavitud	slavery
esclavo	slave
estado	state
hombre de estado	statesman
Fenicios	Phoenicians
feudalismo	feudalism
flota	fleet
frontera	frontier
fundar	to found
General	general
gobernante	ruler
gobernar	to rule
gobierno	government, rule
golpe de estado	coup d'etat
Grecia	Greece
griego	Greek
guerra	war
guerra civil	civil war
guerra de la Independencia (española)	the Peninsular War
guerra de los Cien Años	the Hundred Years War
Hegemonía	hegemony
heráldica	heraldry
heraldo	herald
heredero	heir
hereje	heretic
herejía	heresy
héroe	hero
heroína	heroine
historia	history
historiador	historian
histórico	historic
Imperio	empire
Inquisición, la	the Inquisition
invadir	to invade
invasión	invasion
invasores	invaders
Jefe	leader

Liga   league
liza   lists
lucha   struggle

Medieval   mediaeval
ministro   minister
  primer ministro   prime minister
monarca   monarch
monarquía   monarchy
monasterio   monastery

Nación   nation

Papa, el   the Pope
parlamento   parliament
patriota   patriot
paz   peace
política   policy
posesiones   possessions
potencia   power
princesa   princess
príncipe   prince
protestante   Protestant

Rebelarse   to rebel
rebelde   rebel
rebelión   rebellion
reconquista   reconquest
Reforma, la   the Reformation
reina   queen
reinado   reign
reinar   to reign
reino   kingdom
Renacimiento, el   the Renaissance
rendición   surrender
rendirse   to surrender
república   republic
restauración   restoration
restaurar   to restore
revolución   revolution
rey   king
Roma   Rome
romanos   Romans

Santa Sede, la   the Holy See
saquear   to sack
sarracenos   Saracens
senado   senate
siglo   century
sitiar   to besiege

HISTORIA 347 HISTORY

sitio	siege
poner sitio	to besiege
soberano	sovereign
suceder	to succeed
sucesión	succession
supremacía	supremacy
Torneo	tournament
traición	treason
traidor	traitor
tratado	treaty
tribu	tribe
trono	throne
Unidad	unity
Victoria	victory

HOGAR, EL (Véase LA VIDA EN EL HOGAR, 11)

HORTALIZAS (Véase FRUTOS, 41)

HOSPITAL, EL (Véase EL DOCTOR Y EL HOSPITAL, 32)

50

HOTEL, UN   A HOTEL (46)

ESPAÑOL   ENGLISH

Agua corriente	running water
agua mineral	mineral water
almuerzo	lunch
ascensor	lift
Baño	bath
bar	bar

HOTEL, UN — A HOTEL

«barman» — barman
bono — voucher
botones — bellboy

Cama — bed
camarera — chamber-maid (de piso), waitress (en el restaurante)
camarero — waiter
cena — dinner
cocina — kitchen
cocinero — cook
comedor — dining-room
comida — meal
cuarto de baño — bathroom

Desayuno — breakfast
dormitorio — bedroom
ducha — shower

Equipaje — luggage (GB), baggage (USA)

Factura — bill

Gerente — manager

Habitación — room
habitación doble — double room
habitación individual — single room
hospedarse (en un hotel) — to stay (at a hotel)
hotel de cinco estrellas — five-star hotel
hotel de cuatro estrellas — four-star hotel
hotel de dos estrellas — two-star hotel
hotel de tres estrellas — three-star hotel
hotel de una estrella — one-star hotel

Jabón — soap

Lavandería — laundry

Llave — key

«**M**aitre» — headwaiter
maleta — suitcase

Número — number

Pasillo — corridor
pensión completa — board and lodging, full board
pinche — kitchen boy
portero — hall porter
propina — tip

Recepción — reception desk

HOTEL, UN	A HOTEL
recepcionista	receptionist
restaurante	restaurant
ropa blanca	linen
Sala de estar	lounge
Timbre	bell
toalla	towel
W.C.	lavatory

51

HUESOS Y MÚSCULOS	BONES AND MUSCLES (14)
ESPAÑOL	ENGLISH

Biceps	biceps
Carpo	carpal bone
clavícula	collarbone
columna vertebral	spinal column
coxis	coccyx
cúbito	ulna
Deltoides	deltoid
Esfenoides	sphenoid
esternón	breastbone
etmoides	ethmoid
Falange	finger-bone, phalanx
falange (de un dedo del pie)	toe-bone
falanges	phalanges
fémur	femur
fíbula	fibula
frontal	frontal bone
Hueso	bone
húmero	humerus
Mandíbula	jaw
maxilar	maxillary bone
metacarpo	metacarpal bone
metatarso	metatarsal bone
músculo	muscle

| HUESOS, ETC. | BONES, ETC. |

músculo estriado
músculo oblicuo
músculo plano

Occipital
omóplato

Parietal
pectoral
pelvis
pubis

Radio
rótula

Sacro

Tarso
temporal
tendón
tendón de Aquiles
tibia
triceps

striated muscle
oblique muscle
plain muscle

occipital bone
shoulder-blade

parietal bone
pectoral muscle
pelvis
pubis

radius
knee-cap

sacrum

tarsal bone
temporal bone
tendon
Achilles tendon
tibia
triceps

52

IMPRENTA, LA — PRINTING (74)

ESPAÑOL — ENGLISH

Caja alta
caja baja
cajista
corregir

Dibujo

Editor
editorial
encuadernador
encuadernar
errata
error
estereotipia

upper case
lower case
compositor, typesetter
to correct

picture

publisher
publishing firm
binder
to bind
misprint
mistake
stereotype

IMPRENTA, LA — PRINTING

Formato — format
fotograbado — photogravure

Galeradas — galley proofs
grabado — engraving, picture (ilustración)
grabado al agua — etching
grabar — to engrave

Hoja de papel — sheet

Ilustración — picture, illustration
imprenta — print shop
impresor — printer
imprimir — to print

Lector de pruebas — proof-reader
letra — letter
letra cursiva — italic type
letra mayúscula — capital letter
letra minúscula — small letter
letra negrita — bold-faced type
letra redonda — Roman type
libro — book
línea — line
linotipia — linotype
litografía — lithography

Mano de papel — quire
manuscrito — manuscript
máquina de imprimir — printing machine
margen — margin
matriz — matrix
minerva — Minerva machine
monotipia — monotype

Página — page
papel — paper
papel biblia — Indian paper
periódico — newspaper
prensa — press
prueba — proof
publicar — to publish
puntuación — punctuation

Resma — ream
revista — magazine
rotativa — printing press

Tinta — ink
tipo — type

IMPRENTA, LA		PRINTING

tipografía / typography
tipógrafo / typographer

Versales / capitals
versalitas / small capitals

53

INDUSTRIA DE LA MADERA WOOD INDUSTRY (99)

ESPAÑOL / ENGLISH

Árbol* / tree
aserrar / to saw

Barnizar / to varnish
bosque / wood, forest

Caoba / mahogany
carpintería / carpentry (oficio), carpenter's shop (taller)
  obra de carpintería / woodwork
carpintero / carpenter
cepillo de carpintero / plane
clavar / to nail
clavo / nail
cola / glue
corteza de árbol / bark

CHopo / poplar

Depósito de maderas / lumber-yard, woodyard
desmochar / to pollard

Ebanista / cabinetmaker
ebanistería / cabinetmaking
ébano / ebony

Fábrica de maderas / timber-yard
fábrica de pasta para papel / pulping-mill
formón / chisel

Hacha / axe

Leñador / wood-cutter

lija	sandpaper
lijar	to sandpaper
Madera	wood
madera aserrada	lumber
madera blanda	soft wood
madera dura	hard wood
madera para la construcción	timber
maderero	lumberman
marquetería	inlaid work
martillo	hammer
muebles*	furniture
Pino	pine
podar	to prune
pulpa de madera	wood-pulp
Repoblación forestal	afforestation
roble	oak
Savia	sap
serrería	sawmill
serrín	sawdust
serrucho	handsaw
sierra	saw
sierra circular	band saw
sierra de vaivén	jigsaw
Tabla	board
tablón	plank
talar	to fell
tenazas	tongs
tornillo	screw
torno	lathe
tronco	log,
tronco de árbol	trunk
Virutas	shavings

54

INSECTOS, ARÁCNIDOS Y ANÉLIDOS

INSECTS, ARACHNIDS AND ANNELIDS (51)

ESPAÑOL   ENGLISH

Abeja   bee
abeja obrera   working bee

INSECTOS, ETC.

abeja reina — queen bee
abejarrón — bumblebee
alacrán — scorpion
araña — spider
avispa — wasp

Ciempiés — centipede
cigarra — cicada
cucaracha — cockroach

CHinche — bug

Escarabajo — beetle
escorpión — scorpion

Grillo — cricket
gusano — worm
gusano de seda — silkworm

Hormiga — ant

Ladilla — crab louse
langosta — locust
libélula — dragonfly
lombriz — earthworm
luciérnaga — glow-worm, firefly

Mantis — mantis
mariposa — butterfly
mariquita — ladybird
mosca — fly
moscardón — bluebottle
mosquito — mosquito

Oruga — caterpillar

Piojo — louse
piojos — lice
polilla — moth
pulga — flea

Saltamontes — grasshoper
sanguijuela — leech
solitaria — tapeworm

Tarántula — tarantula
termita — termite

INSTRUMENTOS

(Véase HERRAMIENTAS E INSTRUMENTOS, 48)

55

INSTRUMENTOS MUSICALES / MUSICAL INSTRUMENTS (65)

ESPAÑOL	ENGLISH
Acordeón	accordion
armónica	mouth-organ
arpa	harp
arpicordio	harpsicord
Banjo	banjo
bombo	bass drum
boquilla	mouthpiece
Caja de música	musical box
castañuelas	castanets
clarinete	clarinet
clavicordio	clavichord
contrabajo	contrabass, double-bass
corneta	cornet
cornetín	bugle
Espinete	spinet
Fagot	bassoon
flauta	flute
Guitarra	guitar
guitarra eléctrica	steel guitar
Instrumento	instrument
instrumento de cuerda	stringed instrument
instrumento de metal	brass instrument
instrumento de percusión	percussion instrument
instrumento de viento	wind-instrument
instrumento de viento de madera	wood-wind instrument
instrumento musical	musical instrument
Mandolina	mandolin
Oboe	oboe, hautboy
órgano	organ
órgano eléctrico	electric organ
Pandereta	tambourine
pedal	pedal

INSTRUMENTOS MUSICALES	MUSICAL INSTRUMENTS
piano	piano
piano de cola	gran piano
piano vertical	upright piano
platillos	cymbals
Saxofón	saxophone
Tambor	drum
timbal	kettle drum
trombón	trombone
trompa	horn
trompeta	trumpet
tuba	tuba
Ukelele	ukelele
Viola	viola
violín	violin
primer violín	first violin
segundo violín	second violin
violón	bass viol
violoncelo	cello
Xilófono	xylophone

56

JARDIN, UN	A GARDEN (39)
ESPAÑOL	ENGLISH
Abono	manure
árbol*	tree
arbusto	bush
azadón	hoe
Banco	bench
baya	berry
boca de riego	faucet
brotar	to sprout
brote	sprout
bulbo	bulb
Capullo	bud

| JARDÍN, UN | A GARDEN |

capullo de rosa — rosebud
carretilla — wheel-barrow
cavar — to dig
cenador — summerhouse
césped — lawn
cortar el cesped — to mow
corola — corolla
corona — wreath
crecer — to grow
cultivar — to grow

Enredadera — creeper
enroscarse — to wreathe
espina — thorn
esqueje — cutting
estanque — pond

Fertilizante — fertiliser
flor* — flower
florecer — to flower
follaje — foliage
fruto* — fruit
fuente — fountain

Garabato — pothook
guirnalda — garland

Hierba — grass
hoja — leaf
hojas — leaves

Injertar — to graft
injerto — graft
insecticida — insecticide
invernadero — hothouse, green-house

Jardinería — gardening
jardinero — gardener
jarrón — vase

Macizo de florés — flower-bed
manguera — hose
manojo — bunch
mantillo — rotten manure
máquina para cortar el césped — lawn-mower

Pala para cavar — spade
paseo (avenida) — walk
perfume — scent
pétalo — petal
pistilo — pistil
planta* — plant

planta anual	annual plant
planta perenne	perennial plant
planta que se arrastra	trailing plant
planta siempre verde	evergreen plant
planta trepadora	climbing plant
plantar	to plant
poda	pruning
podar	to prune
cuchillo para podar	pruning-knife
tijeras para podar	pruning-shears
puerta de verja	gate
Raíz	root
rama	bough, branch
ramillete	posy
ramo	bouquet
rastrillo	rake
regadera	watering-can
regar	to water
rosaleda	rose garden
Savia	sap
sembrar	to sow
semilla	seed
seto	hedge
Tallo	stalk, stem
terreno	soil
tierra	earth
tiesto	flower-pot, pot
tronco	stock
Valla	fence
vástago	offshoot
vereda	path

57

JOYERIA   JEWELLERY (52)

ESPAÑOL	ENGLISH
Ágata	agate
aguamarina	aquamarine

JOYERÍA	JEWELLERY
amatista	amethyst
ámbar	amber
anillo	ring
anillo de boda	wedding-ring
Brillante	diamond
broche	brooch
Camafeo	cameo
colgante	pendant
collar	necklace
Diamante	diamond
Engastar	to set
esmaltado	enamelled
esmalte	enamel
esmeralda	emerald
Gema	gem
Jade	jade
joya	jewel
joyero	jeweller
Montura	mount
Ópalo	opal
orfebre	goldsmith
oro	gold
Pendiente	earring
perla	pearl
piedra	stone
piedra preciosa	precious stone
piedra preciosa tallada	brilliant
piedra semi-preciosa	semi-precious stone
plata	silver
platino	platinum
pulsera	bracelet
Quilate	carat
Rubí	ruby
Sello	signet-ring
solitario	solitaire
sortija	ring

JOYERÍA		JEWELLERY

sortija de brillantes — diamond ring
Topacio — topaz
turquesa — turquoise

Zafiro — sapphire

JUEGOS (Véase DEPORTES Y JUEGOS, 31)

LEGUMBRES (Véase FRUTOS, HORTALIZAS, LEGUMBRES Y CEREALES, 41)

58

LEY, LA	THE LAW (54)
ESPAÑOL	ENGLISH

Abogado	lawyer, barrister, attorney
abogado defensor	counsel for the defence
acusación	accusation
acusado, el	the accused
acusador	accuser
acusar	to accuse
agente de policia	police-officer
apoderado	attorney
arrestado	under arrest
arrestar	to arrest
arresto	arrest
asesor legal	legal adviser
atestiguar	to witness
Banquillo de los acusados	dock
Cárcel	gaol, jail
castigar	to punish
castigo	punishment
código	code
comisaría	police-station

LEY, LA	THE LAW
confesar	to confess
consejo de guerra	court martial
Daños y perjuicios	damages
deber	duty
defender	to defend
defensa	defence
delincuente	criminal
delito	crime
demandante	prosecutor
demandar	to sue
detenido	prisoner
derecho internacional	law of nations
derechos	rights
Estrado de los testigos	stand
estudiante de derecho	law student
Fiscal	public prosecutor
Guardia	constable, policeman
Homicida	murderer
homicidio	murder
Ilegal	unlawful, illegal
indemnización	indemnification
indemnizar	to indemnify
Juez	judge
juicio	trial
jurado	jury
jurista	jurist
Ladrón	burglar, thief
legal	lawful, legal
legislación	legislation
legislador	law-maker
legislar	to legislate
letrado	advocate
ley	law
ley natural	natural law
Magistrado	magistrate
multa	fine
multar	to fine
Notario	notary
Obligaciones	obligations
Palacio de justicia	courthouse

LEY, LA	THE LAW
pleito	law-suit
policía	policeman, police-officer
mujer policía	policewoman
policía, la	the police
prisión	prison
procesamiento	prosecution
procesar	to prosecute
procurador	attorney at law, solicitor
Robar	to steal, to rob
robo	robbery, theft, burglary
Sala de justicia	court of justice
sentencia	sentence
sentenciar	to sentence
Testificar	to testify
testigo	witness
testigo de cargo	witness for the prosecution
testigo de descargo	witness for the defence
transgresor de la ley	law-breaker
tribunal de justicia	court
Veredicto	verdict

59

LITERATURA — LITERATURE (57)

ESPAÑOL	ENGLISH
Agotado (un libro)	out of print
alegoría	allegory
anónimo	anonymous, anon
antología	anthology
autor	author
autora	authoress
Balada	ballad
biografía	biography
biógrafo	biographer
Canción	song
canto (en un poema)	canto

capítulo	chapter
carta	letter
clásico	classical
comedia	comedy
copla	couplet
crítico	critic
cuento	tale
Describir	to describe
descripción	description
dramaturgo	dramatist, playwright
Edición	edition
ejemplar	copy
elegía	elegy
epígrama	epigram
epístola	epistle
epopeya	epic
escribir	to write
escrito	written
escritor	writer
escritor satírico	satirist
escritos	writtings
escritos en prosa	prose writings
escuela	school
estilo	style
estrofa	couplet, stanza
estudio	study
Guión	script
Himno	hymn
historia	story
Imprimir	to print
incompleto	incomplete
influencia	influence
inspirar	to inspire
isabelino	Elizabethan
Latín	latin
lector	reader
leer	to read
lenguaje	language
letra de una canción	lyrics
libro	book
libro de gran éxito	best seller
lírico	lyrical
literario	literary
literatura	literature

Manuscrito	manuscript
metáfora	metaphor
metáfora poética	poetic metaphor
metro	metre
misticismo	mysticism
místico	mystic
musa	muse
Narrador	story teller
novela	novel
novelista	novelist
Obra	work
obra de teatro	play
obra maestra	masterpiece
obras	works
oda	ode
Párrafo	passage
período	period
pluma	pen
poema	poem
poema lírico	lyric
poesía	poetry
poesía épica	epic poetry
poesía lírica	lyrical poetry
poesía religiosa	religious poetry
poeta	poet
poeta lírico	lyrical poet
poeta metafísico	metaphysical poet
poeta místico	mystical poet
poeta romántico	Romantic poet
poético	poetic(al)
poetisa	poetess
premio literario	literary prize
prensa, en (un libro)	in print
prosa	prose
pseudónimo	pen-name
publicar	to publish
Recitar	to recite
recopilador	compiler
retórica	rhetoric
rima	rhyme
rimar	to rhyme
romance	romance
romanticismo	romanticism
romántico	romantic
Salmo	psalm

LITERATURA	LITERATURE
sátira	satire
satírico	satirical
sermón	sermon
soneto	sonnet
Teatro (género)	drama
tema	theme, subject
título	title
traducción	translation
traducir	to translate
tragedia	tragedy
Verso	verse
verso libre	blank verse
verso rimado	rhymed verse
volumen	volume

MADERA (Véase INDUSTRIA DE LA MADERA, 53)

60

MAMÍFEROS — MAMMALS (58)

ESPAÑOL	ENGLISH
ANIMALES DOMÉSTICOS	**DOMESTIC ANIMALS**
Buey	ox
burro	donkey
Caballito	pony
caballo	horse
caballo de carreras	race-horse
caballo de silla	saddle-horse
caballo de tiro	draught-horse
cabra	goat
cabrito	kid
caniche	poodle
carnero	ram
cerda	sow
cerdito	piglet
cerdo	pig
conejo	rabbit

corcel	steed
cordero	lamb
Galgo	greyhound
gatito	kitten
gato	cat
gato de Angora	Angora cat
gato siamés	Siamese cat
Gran Danés	Great Dane
Mastín	mastiff
mula	mule
mulo	mule
Oveja	sheep
oveja hembra	ewe
Perrito	puppy
perro	dog
perro de caza	hound
perro de presa	bulldog
perro de Terranova	Newfoundland dog
perro guardián	watch-dog
perro pastor	shepherd's dog
perro policía	police-dog
perro San Bernardo	St Bernard dog
potranca	filly
potro	colt
Rocín	hack
Semental	stallion
Ternera	calf
Vaca	cow
vaquilla	heifer
Yegua	mare

ANIMALES SALVAJES / WILD ANIMALS

Alce	elk
ante	chamois
ardilla	squirrel
armadillo	armadillo
Ballena	whale
bisonte	bison
búfalo	buffalo

MAMÍFEROS — MAMMALS

Cachalote — sperm whale
camello — camel
canguro — kangaroo
castor — beaver
cebra — zebra
cierva — hind
ciervo — deer

CHimpancé — chimpanzee

Delfín — dolphin
dromedario — dromedary

Elefante — elephant
erizo — hedgehog

Foca — seal

Gacela — gazelle
gamo — buck
   hembra del gamo — doe
gato montés — wildcat
gibón — gibbon

Hiena — hyena
hipopótamo — hippopotamus
hurón — ferret

Jabalí — boar, wildboar
jirafa — giraffe

León — lion
león marino — sea lion
leona — lioness
leopardo — leopard
liebre — hare
lince — lynx
lirón — dormouse
lobo — wolf

LLama — llama

Mandril — baboon
mapache — racoon
marmota — marmot
marsopa — porpoise
marta — marten
mofeta — polecat, skunk
mono — monkey, ape
morsa — walrus
muciélago — bat

| MAMÍFEROS | MAMMALS |

Nutria — otter
Ocelote — ocelot
orangután — orang-outang
ornitorrinco — duck-billed platypus
osezno — bear cub
oso — bear
oso hormiguero — ant-eater
oso pardo — brown bear
oso polar — polar bear

Pantera — panther
perezoso — sloth
puercoespín — porcupine
puma — puma

Rata — rat
ratón — mouse
ratones — mice
reno — reindeer
rinoceronte — rhinoceros

Tapir — tapir
tejón — badger
tigre — tiger
tigresa — tigress
topo — mole
toro — bull

Venado — stag, hart
visón — mink

Yak — yak

Zorro — fox

61

MAQUINA DE ESCRIBIR, UNA — **A TYPEWRITER (95)**

ESPAÑOL — ENGLISH

Carro — carriage
cinta — ribbon

MÁQUINA DE ESCRIBIR — A TYPEWRITER

colocador del margen — margin setter
copia — copy

Dispositivo para hacer que vuelva la cinta — ribbon reverse
dispositivo para variar los espacios — variable line spacer

Espaciador — space bar
espacio — space

Letra — letter
letra mayúscula — capital letter
letra minúscula — small letter

Máquina de escribir de oficina — office typewriter
máquina de escribir eléctrica — electric typewriter
máquina de escribir portátil — portable typewriter
margen — margin

Palanca — lever
palanca (con el tipo) — typebar
palanca para dejar libre el carro — carriage release lever
palanca para dejar libre el papel — paper release lever
palanca para espacios — line space lever

Rodillo — roller

Segmento — segment
sujetador de mayúsculas — shift lock

Tabulador — tabulador
tecla — key
tecla de mayúsculas — shift-key
tecla de retroceso — back space key
tecla para fijar el tabulador — tabulador set key
tecla para soltar el margen — margin release key
teclado — keyboard
tipo — type

MAR, UN PUERTO DE

(Véase UN PUERTO DE MAR, 84)

MATEMÁTICAS

(Véase ARITMETICA Y MATEMATICAS, 7)

62

MECÁNICA   MECHANICS (59)

ESPAÑOL	ENGLISH
Árbol	shaft
articulación	joint
Biela	connecting-rod
Cilindro	cylinder
cojinete de bolas	ball-bearing
cuña	wedge
Eje	axle
engranaje	gear
diente de engranaje	gear tooth
equilibrio	equilibrium
Fuerza	force
flucro	fulcrum
Manivela	crank
brazo de la manivela	crank arm
movimiento	motion
Palanca	lever
perno	bolt
peso	weight
polea	pulley
Rueda	wheel
rueda dentada	toothed wheel
juego de ruedas dentadas	gear wheels
rueda loca	free wheel
Tornillo	screw
tornillo sin fin	worm gear
trinquete	pawl
tuerca	nut
Vástago	rod
volante	flywheel

MEDIDAS

(Véase PESOS Y MEDIDAS, 80)

63

METALES, MINERALES Y ALEACIONES / METALS, MINERALS AND ALLOYS (61)

ESPAÑOL	ENGLISH
Acero	steel
aluminio	aluminium
antimonio	antimony
asbesto	arbestos
azurita	azurite
Barita	barytes
basalto	basalt
bauxita	bauxite
berilo	beryl
blenda	blende
bronce	bronze
Cadmio	cadmium
caolín	kaolin
carbón	coal
casiterita	cassiterite
cinabrio	cinnabar
cinc	zinc
cobre	copper
cromo	chromium
cuarzo	quartz
Duraluminio	duraluminium
Estaño	tin
Feldespato	feldspar
Galena	galena
grafito	graphite
granito	granite
Hierro	iron
Iridio	iridium
Latón	brass
lignito	lignite
Manganeso	manganese
mármol	marble

| METALES, ETC. | METALS, ETC. |

mercurio
mica

Níquel

Oro

Pedernal
pirita
plata
platino
plomo

Radio

Sal
siderita

Titanio

Uranio

mercury
mica

nickel

gold

flint
pyrites
silver
platinum
lead

radium

salt
siderite

titanium

uranium

64

METALURGIA

METALLURGY (60)

ESPAÑOL

ENGLISH

Alambre
aleación
alto horno

Barra

Calentamiento
calentar
crisol

CHatarra

Densidad
derretir(se)
ductilidad
dureza
duro

wire
alloy
blast-furnace

bar

heating
to heat
crucible

scrap iron

density
to melt
ductility
hardness
hard

METALURGIA	METALLURGY

Endurecer(se)	to harden
enfriamiento	cooling
enfriar	to cool
Flexibilidad	flexibility
flexible	flexible
forma	shape
dar forma	to shape
fragua	forge
fundición	foundry
fundición de hierro	iron foundry
fundir	to cast
fusibilidad	fusibility
Hierro	iron
hierro colado	cast iron
hierro en lingotes	pig iron
hierro forjado	wrought iron
horno	furnace
Lingote	ingot
lustre	lustre
Maleabilidad	malleability
maleable	malleable
metal	metal
metalúrgico	metallurgist (sus.), metallurgical (adj.)
mineral	mineral
Plancha (de metal)	sheet
Soldadura	soldering, welding
soldar	to solder, to weld
solidificarse	to solidify
Yunque	anvil

65

METEOROLOGÍA   METEOROLOGY (62)

ESPAÑOL	ENGLISH
Aguacero	rainfall
aire	air

METEOROLOGÍA — METEOROLOGY

alto-cúmulo — alto-cumulus
alto-estrato — alto-stratus
arco iris — rainbow

Barco meteorológico — weather-ship
barómetro — barometer
brisa — breeze
bruma — haze

Calma — calm
calor — heat
ciclón — cyclone
cielo — sky
cirro — cirrus
cirro-cúmulos — cirro-cumulus
cirro-estratos — cirro-stratus
clima — climate
condiciones atmosféricas — atmospheric-conditions
cúmulo — cumulus
cúmulo-nimbo — cumulus-nimbus

CHaparrón — shower

Despejado — cloudless

Escarcha — frost

Frío — cold

Granizar — to hail
granizo — hail

Helar — to freeze
hombre del tiempo — weather-man
huracán — hurricane

LLover — to rain
llovizna — drizzle
lloviznar — to drizzle
lluvia — rain
lluvioso — rainy

Mapa del tiempo — weather-map
mar gruesa — rough sea
mar rizada — smooth sea

Neblina — mist
nebuloso — misty
nevar — to snow
niebla — fog
   con niebla — foggy
nieve — snow
nimbo — nimbus

METEOROLOGÍA		METEOROLOGY

nube — cloud
nublado — cloudy

Ola — wave

Predicción del tiempo — weather forecast
presión atmosférica — atmospheric pressure
presión barométrica — barometric pressure

Rayo — thunderbolt
relámpago — lightning
remolino — whirlwind

Soleado — sunny

Temperatura — temperature
termómetro — thermometer
tiempo atmosférico — weather
tormenta — storm, thunder-storm
tronar — to thunder
trueno — thunder

Ventarrón — gale
viento — wind
vórtice — vortex

MINERALES   (Véase METALES, MINERALES Y ALEACIONES, 63)

66

MINERÍA / MINING (63)

ESPAÑOL / ENGLISH

Ascensor — hoist

Barreno — blasting-cartridge

Capa — layer
carbón — coal

MINERÍA	MINING
cavar	to dig
cinc	zinc
coque	coke
Derrumbamiento	falling-in
diamante	diamond
dinamita	dynamite
Entibado	pit props
estaño	tin
explotación subterránea	underground workings
explotación a cielo abierto	open-cast workings
extraer	to extract
Filón	lode
Galería	gallery
grisú	firedamp
Hierro	iron
Ingeniero de minas	mining-engineer
Lámpara de seguridad	safety-lamp, davy-lamp
Mercurio	mercury
metal	metal
mina	mine
mina de carbón	coalmine, coal-pit
mineral	mineral
mineral de hierro	iron-ore
minero	miner
minero de carbón	collier
Oro	gold
Pala	shovel
pepita	nugget
pepita de oro	gold nugget
perforadora	driller
perforar	to drill
pico	pick
plata	silver
plomo	lead
pozo	shaft
pozo de mina	pit
Túnel	surface
Superficie	tunnel
Vagoneta	mine-car, truck
veta	vein

veta de carbón	coal-seam
Yacimiento de carbón	coalfield

67

MOBILIARIO — FURNITURE (37)

ESPAÑOL	ENGLISH
Alfombra	carpet
aparador	sideboard, dresser
aparato de radio	radio set
aparato de televisión	television set
arcón	chest
archivador	filing-cabinet
armario	wardrobe, cupboard
armario de baño	bathrooom cupboard
armario de cocina	kitchen cupboard
Banco	bench
Cajón	drawer
cama	bed
cama con dosel	four-poster bed
cama de matrimonio	double bed
cama de un cuerpo	single bed
cama plegable	folding bed, foldaway bed
cama turca	divan bed
cocina	cooker
cocina de gas	gas-cooker
cocina eléctrica	electric-cooker
cómoda	chest-of-drawers
cómoda alta	tall-boy
consola	console-table
coqueta	dressing-table
cortina	curtain
cuadro	picture
Escritorio	desk
espejo	mirror
espejo de cuerpo entero	full-length mirror
estante	shelf
estantes	shelves
Lámpara	lamp

| MOBILIARIO | FURNITURE |

lámpara de brazos — chandelier
lámpara de mesa — table-lamp, reading-lamp
lámpara de pie — floor-lamp
lavadora — washing-machine
lavaplatos — dish-washer
librería — bookcase

Mesa — table
mesilla de noche — bedside table
mesita de centro — coffee-table
mueble — piece of furniture
mueble bar — cocktail cabinet

Piano — piano
piano de cola — grand piano
piano vertical — upright piano

Refrigerador — refrigerator, fridge
reloj — clock

Silla — chair
silla de mimbre — cane chair
silla plegable — folding chair
sillón — arm-chair
sillón tapizado — upholstered arm-chair
sofá — settee, sofa

Taburete — stool
tapiz — tapestry
tocador — dressing-table

Vitrina — cabinet

MODISTA, LA   (Véase EL SASTRE Y LA MODISTA, 90)

MOLUSCOS   (Véase PECES Y MOLUSCOS, 76)

MUEBLES   (Véase MOBILIARIO, 67)

68

MUNDO Y EL UNIVERSO, EL
THE WORLD AND THE UNIVERSE (100)

ESPAÑOL	ENGLISH
Aire	air
agua	water
alba	dawn
amanecer	daybreak
anillo (alrededor de un planeta)	ring
año luz	light-year
asteroide	asteroid
astro	heavenly body
atmósfera	atmosphere
aurora	dawn
Calor	heat
cenit	zenith
cielo	sky
clima	climate
constelación	constellation
cometa	comet
crepúsculo	dusk, twilight
cuarto creciente (de la luna)	first quarter
cuarto menguante (de la luna)	last quarter
Día	day
Eclipse	eclipse
ecuador	equator
elementos, los	the elements
esfera	sphere
este	east
estratosfera	stratosphere
estrella	star
estrella polar	pole-star
Fenómenos atmosféricos	atmospheric phenomena
fuego	fire
Galaxia	galaxy
Hemisferio	hemisphere

horizonte	horizon
Júpiter	Jupiter
Latitud	latitude
longitud	longitude
luna	moon
luna llena	full moon
luna nueva	new moon
luz	light
luz del día	daylight
luz del sol	sunlight
Mancha solar	sunspot
mar	sea
marea	tide
Marte	Mars
Mercurio	Mercury
meridiano	meridian
meteoro	meteor
Nebulosa	nebula
Neptuno	Neptune
noche	night
nordeste	north-east
noroeste	north-west
norte	north
nube	cloud
Observatorio	observatory
océano	ocean
oeste	west
Osa Mayor	Great Bear (GB), Big Dipper (USA)
Osa Menor	Little Bear (GB), Little Dipper (USA)
Paralelo	parallel
planeta	planet
Plutón	Pluto
Rayo	ray, beam (del sol, de luz), thunderbolt (en una tormenta)
relámpago	lightning
Saturno	saturn
sísmico	seismic
sol	sun
puesta del sol	sunset
salida del sol	sunrise
sudoeste	south-west

MÚSICA	MUSIC
sur	south
sudeste	south-east
Telescopio	telescope
terremoto	earthquake
tiempo atmosférico	weather
tierra	earth, land
tormenta	storm
troposfera	troposphere
trueno	thunder
Urano	Uranus
Venus	Venus
Vía Láctea	Milky Way
viento	wind
MÚSCULOS	(Véase HUESOS Y MUSCULOS, 51)

69

MÚSICA / MUSIC (64)

ESPAÑOL	ENGLISH
Afinar	to tune
amante de la música	music lover
armonía	harmony
atril	music-stand
Bajo	bass
banda	brass band
barítono	baritone
batuta	baton
Canción	song
canción folklórica	folksong
cantar	to sing
compositor	composer
concierto	concert (programa), concerto (pieza)
sala de conciertos	concert hall
contralto	contralto

MÚSICA / MUSIC

coro	choir, chorus
cuarteto	quartet
cuerda	string
Director de orquesta	conductor
do	C
Escala	scale
estribillo	refrain
Fa	F
Guitarrista	guitar player
Instrumento musical	musical instrument
Jazz	jazz
La	A
Marcha	marching tune
mayor	major
melodía	tune, melody
menor	minor
mi	E
música	music
música clásica	classical music
música de cámara	chamber music
músico	musician
Nota	note
nota musical	key-note
Obertura	overture
octava	octave
ópera	opera
orquesta	orchestra
Partitura	score
pentagrama	staff, stave
pianista	pianist
profesor de música	music teacher
Quinteto	quintet
Re	D
ritmo	rhythm
Si	B
sinfonía	symphony
sol	G
sonido	sound
soprano	soprano
Tecla	key
teclado	keyboard
tenor	tenor
tiple	treble

MÚSICA		MUSIC

tocar — to play
Vals — waltz
violinista — violinist
voz — voice

70

NAIPES	**CARDS (17)**
ESPAÑOL	ENGLISH

As	ace
Baraja	pack of cards
bastos	clubs
Carta	card
carta de abajo	bottom card
carta de arriba	top card
comodín	joker
compañero	partner
copas	hearts
corazones	hearts
cortar	to cut
Dar	to deal
Espadas	spades
Juego	game
jugador	player
Mano	hand
Oros	diamonds
Palo	suit
picos	spades
pinta	turn-up
Reina	queen
rey	king
rombos	diamonds
Sota	jack, knave
Tréboles	clubs
triunfo	trump

71

NEGOCIOS Y EL COMERCIO, LOS

BUSINESS AND TRADE (15)

ESPAÑOL	ENGLISH
Almacén	wharehouse
grandes almacenes	stores
anunciar	to advertise
anuncio	advertisement
Banco	bank
Carta comercial	business letter
comercio	trade
comercio al por mayor	wholesale trade
comercio al por menor	retail trade
comercio exterior	foreign trade
comercio interior	home trade
compañía	company
compra	purchase
comprador	buyer
comprar	to buy
consumidor	consumer
Dependiente	shop-assistant
descuento	discount
director	manager
Empleado	clerk
empresa	firm
existencias	stock
exportaciones	exports
exportar	to export
Fábrica	factory
fabricante	manufacturer
fabricar	to manufacture
factura	invoice
Ganga	bargain
Hombre de negocios	business-man
Importaciones	imports
importar	to import
intermediario	middleman

NEGOCIOS, LOS	BUSINESS

Lista de precios — price-list

Mayorista — wholesaler
mercado — market
mercancías — goods
minorista — retailer

Oficina* — office
oficina principal — head office

Precio — price
precio fijo — fixed price
producir — to produce
producto — product
productor — producer

Regatear — to bargain

Secretaria — secretary
sucursal — branch

Tendero — shop-keeper
tienda* — shop

Vendedor — salesman
vender — to sell
venta — sale

72

NOMBRES / NAMES (66)

ESPAÑOL — **ENGLISH**

NOMBRES MASCULINOS / MEN'S NAMES

Adán — Adam
Adrián — Adrian
Alberto — Albert
Alejandro — Alexander
Alfredo — Alfred
Ambrosio — Ambrose
Andrés — Andrew
Antonio — Anthony

NOMBRES	NAMES
Archibaldo	Archibald
Arturo	Arthur
Augusto	Augustus
Bartolomé	Bartholomew
Basilio	Basil
Benjamín	Benjamín
Bernardo	Bernard
Carlos	Charles
Cecilio	Cecil
Cirilo	Cyril
Claudio	Claude
Conrado	Conrad
Cristóbal	Christopher
Daniel	Daniel
David	David
Dionisio	Dennis
Edmundo	Edmund
Eduardo	Edward
Enrique	Henry
Ernesto	Ernest
Esteban	Stephen
Federico	Frederic(k)
Felipe	Philip
Fernando	Ferdinand
Francisco	Francis
Gaspar	Jasper
Gerardo	Gerard
Gilberto	Gilbert
Gregorio	Gregory
Guillermo	William
Hilario	Hillary
Horacio	Horace
Hugo	Hugh
Humberto	Humbert
Jaime	James
Jerónimo	Jerome
Jorge	George
José	Joseph
Juan	John
Juanito	Johnny
Julián	Julian
León	Leo
Leonardo	Leonard

NOMBRES	NAMES
Lorenzo	Lawrence
Lucas	Luke
Luis	Lewis
Marcos	Mark
Martín	Martin
Mateo	Matthew
Mauricio	Maurice
Miguel	Michael
Nicolás	Nicholas
Oliverio	Oliver
Pablo	Paul
Patricio	Patrick
Pedrito	Pete
Pedro	Peter
Pepe	Joe
Pepito	Joey
Ramón	Raymond
Ricardo	Richard
Roberto	Robert
Rodolfo	Ralph
Rogelio	Roger
Samuel	Samuel
Timoteo	Timothy
Tomás	Thomas
Vicente	Vincent

NOMBRES FEMENINOS   WOMEN'S NAMES

Adelaida	Adelaide
Adelina	Adeline
Agueda	Agatha
Alejandra	Alexandra
Alicia	Alice, Elsa
Amelia	Amelia
Ana	Anne, Ann
Angela	Angela
Anita	Nancy
Bárbara	Barbara
Beatriz	Beatrice
Berta	Bertha
Brígida	Bridget
Carlota	Charlotte

NOMBRES	NAMES
Carolina	Caroline, Carol
Catalina	Catherine
Cecilia	Cecily
Cristina	Christine
Diana	Diana
Dorotea	Dorothy
Elena	Helen
Eloísa	Alison
Ema	Emma
Emilia	Emily
Engracia	Grace
Enriqueta	Harriet
Ester	Esther
Eva	Eve
Evelina	Evelyn
Francisca	Frances
Florencia	Florence
Genoveva	Genevieve, Gwendolen
Gerarda	Geraldine
Gertrudis	Gertrude
Inés	Agnes
Isabel	Elizabeth
Isabelita	Betty
Josefina	Josephine
Juana	Jane, Joan, Janet
Juanita	Jean
Laura	Laura
Leonor	Eleanor
Lucía	Lucy
Luisa	Louise
Magdalena	Magdalen
Margarita	Margaret
María	Mary
Mariana	Marian, Marion
Marta	Martha
Mónica	Monica
Nora	Nora
Pamela	Pamela
Patricia	Patricia
Paulina	Pauline
Raquel	Rachel
Rebeca	Rebecca

NOMBRES		NAMES

Rita
Rose

Sara
Sofía
Susana

Teresa

Victoria

Rita
Rose

Sarah
Sophia
Susan

Theresa

Victoria

73

OBJETOS PERSONALES	PERSONAL BELONGINGS (71)
ESPAÑOL	ENGLISH

Agenda — diary
alfiler — pin
alfiler de sombrero — hatpin
anillo — ring

Barra de jabón de afeitar — stick of shaving-soap
bastón — walking-stick
billete (entrada) — ticket
billete de autobús — bus-ticket
billete de banco — bank-note
bolígrafo — ball-pen, ball-point pen
bolso — bag, handbag
boquilla — cigarette-holder
borla de polvos — powder-puff
botón — button
brocha de afeitar — shaving-brush

Caja de cerillas — box of matches
cartera (billetera) — wallet
cartera de mano — bag
cepillo — brush
cepillo de dientes — tooth-brush
cepillo para el pelo — hair-brush
cinturón — belt
colonia — toilet water
collar — necklace
cortauñas — nail clipper

OBJETOS PERSONALES	PERSONAL BELONGINGS
Espejo	mirror
estilográfica	fountain pen
Gafas	glasses
gafas de sol	sun-glasses
gemelos	cuff-links
Hoja de afeitar	razor blade
horquilla	hairpin
horquilla invisible	hairpin
horquilla pasador	bobby pin
imperdible	safety-pin
Lápiz	pencil
lápiz de labios	lipstick
lima de uñas	nail file
LLavero	key-ring, key-holder
llaves	keys
Máquina de afeitar	razor
máquina de afeitar eléctrica	electric-razor
maquinilla de afeitar	safety-razor
mechero	lighter
Navaja	penknife
«neceser»	dressing-case
Pañuelo	handkerchief
paquete de cigarrillos	packet of cigarettes
paraguas	umbrella
pasador de la camisa	collar-stud
pasaporte	passport
pasta de dientes	tooth-paste
pastilla de jabón	cake of soap, bar of soap
peine	comb
pendientes	ear-rings
perfume	perfume
petaca	tobacco pouch
pipa	pipe
pitillera	cigarette-case
pluma	pen
polvera	powder-box
portamonedas	purse
pulsera	bracelet
Reloj de pulsera o bolsillo	watch
rizapestañas	eye-lash curlers
Sortija	ring

| OBJETOS PERSONALES | 391 | PERSONAL BELONGINGS |

Tarjeta de indentidad
toalla
tónico para el pelo

identity card
towel
hair-tonic

74

OFICINA, UNA — AN OFFICE (68)

| ESPAÑOL | ENGLISH |

Archivar
archivo

to file
filing-cabinet (mueble), records (documentos archivados)

Bolígrafo

ball-pen

Calculadora
carta
carta comercial
centralita del teléfono
cesto de los papeles
cinta para la máquina de escribir
circular
copia
correspondencia

calculating-machine
letter
business letter
switch-board
waste-paper basket
ribbon
circular letter
copy
correspondence

CHincheta

drawing-pin

Departamento
dictar
dirección

department
to dictate
adddress

Escribir a máquina

to type

Ficha
fotocopiadora

filing-card, index card
photo-copying machine

Goma de borrar
grapadora
grapas

rubber
stapler
staples

Hoja de papel

sheet of paper

OFICINA, UNA	AN OFFICE
Informe	report
Jefe de oficina	office-manager
Lacre	sealing-wax
lápiz	pencil
lápiz mecánico	propelling-pencil
Máquina de escribir	typewriter
mecanógrafo, a	typist
mesa escritorio	desk
multicopista	copying-machine
Oficio	official letter
Papel	paper
papel carbón	carbon paper
papel para cartas	writing paper
pisapapeles	paper-weight
pluma	pen
Sacapuntas	pencil-sharpener
secretaria	secretary
sello	stamp
sobre	envelope
sumadora	adding-machine
Taquigrafía	shorthand
taquimecanógrafo, a	shorthand typist
teléfono	telephone
tinta	ink

75

PÁJAROS / BIRDS (13)

ESPAÑOL	ENGLISH
Agachadiza	snipe
águila	eagle
albatros	albatross
alondra	lark
ave	bird
ave de paso	bird of passage

ave de rapiña	bird of prey
ave del paraíso	bird of paradise
ave zancuda	wading bird
avestruz	ostrich
avetoro	bittern
Búho	owl
buitre	vulture
Cacatúa	cockatoo
canario	canary
cernícalo	kestrel
cigüeña	stork
cisne	swan
codorniz	quail
colibrí	humming-bird
cormorán	cormorant
corneja	crow
cuclillo	cuckoo
cuervo	raven
Chorlito	plover
Estornino	starling
Faisán	pheasant
flamenco	flamingo
Gallina	hen
gallo	cock
ganso	goose
gansos	geese
garza	heron
gavilán	hawk
gaviota	gull
golondrina	swallow
gorrión	sparrow
grajo	rook
grulla	crane
guacamayo	macaw
guaco	grouse
Halcón	falcon
Jilguero	goldfinch
Lechuza	owl
loro	parrot
Martín pescador	kingfisher
mirlo	blackbird
mochuelo	little owl

PÁJAROS		BIRDS

Pájaro	bird
pájaro cantor	songbird
pájaro carpintero	woodpecker
paloma	dove
pardillo	bullfinch
pato	duck
pato macho	drake
pato silvestre	mallard
pavo	turkey
pavo real	peacock
pelícano	pelican
perdiz	partridge
periquito	parakeet
petirrojo	robin, robin redbreast
pichón	pigeon
pingüino	penguin
pinzón	chaffinch
pollo	chicken
Rascón	rail
ruiseñor	nightingale
Tordo	thrush
tucán	toucan
Urraca	magpie

76

PECES Y MOLUSCOS FISH AND MOLLUSCS (31)

ESPAÑOL	ENGLISH
Almeja	clam
anchoa	anchovy
anguila	eel
arenque	herring
atún	tuna, tunny
Bacalao	cod, codfish
ballena	whale
barbo	barbel, catfish
barracuda	barracuda
besugo	sea-bream

PECES Y MOLUSCOS — FISH AND MOLLUSCS

bonito	striped tunny
boquerón	fresh anchovy
Caballa	mackerel
caballito de mar	sea horse
cachalote	sperm whale
calamar	squid
cangrejo	crab
cangrejo de río	crayfish, crawfish
caracol	snail
caracola	shell
carpa	carp
centollo	large crab
concha	shell
congrio	conger eel, conger
Delfín	dolphin
Estrella de mar	starfish
esturión	sturgeon
Gallo	dory
gamba	shrimp
Lamprea	lamprey
langosta	lobster
langostino	prawn
lenguado	sole, flounder
lobina	striped bass
lucio	pike,
Marisco	shellfish
mejillón	mussel
merluza	hake
Ostra	oyster
Pechina	shell
perca	perch, bass
perca negra	black bass
percebe	barnacle
pescadilla	whiting
pez	fish
pez espada	swordfish
pez volador	flying fish
platija	plaice
pulpo	octopus
Raya	skate, ray
róbalo	haddock
rodaballo	turbot
Salmón	salmón
salmonete	red mullet, mullet

PECES Y MOLUSCOS	FISH AND MOLLUSCS
sardina	sardine
sepia	cuttlefish
Tenca	tench
tiburón	shark
trucha	trout

77

PELUQUERIA DE SEÑORAS, EN LA	AT THE LADIES' HAIRDRESSER'S (42)
ESPAÑOL	ENGLISH
Bucle	curl
Cabello	hair
cepillo para el pelo	hair-brush
CHampú	shampoo
Depilatorio	depilatory
Horquilla	hairpin
Laca para el pelo	hair-lacquer
laca para las uñas	nail-varnish
lavado de cabeza	wash
lavar	to wash
lima para uñas	nail-file
Manicura	manicurist (persona), manicure (servicio)
moño	bun
Onda	wave
Peinado	hair-style, hair-do
peinador	cape
peinar	to comb
peine	comb
pelo	hair
pelo canoso	grey hair
pelo castaño	brown hair

PELUQUERIA DE SEÑORAS	LADIES HAIRDRESSER'S
pelo graso	greasy hair
pelo liso	straight hair
pelo moreno	dark hair
pelo ondulado	wavy hair
pelo rizado	curly hair
pelo rubio	fair hair
pelo seco	dry hair
permanente	permanent wave, perm
puntas	ends
Quitaesmalte	nail-varnish remover
Raya	parting
redecilla	hair-net
rizo	curl
rulos	hair-curlers
Secador	hair-dryer
Tenacillas	curling tongs
tenazas	irons
teñir	to dye
tijeras para las uñas	nail-scissors
tinte para el cabello	hair-dye

78

PERSONA, UNA — A PERSON (70)

ESPAÑOL	ENGLISH
Ágil	nimble
alegre	gay
alto	tall
Bajo	short
bien parecido	good-looking
bien vestido	well-dressed
blanco	white
buenos modales, de	well-mannered
Calvo	bald
ciego	blind
cojo	lame, one-legged
corpulento	stout, portly

cortés	polite
cuello corto, de	short-necked
cuello largo, de	long-necked
cuerdo	sane
culto	well-educated
CHato	flat-nosed
chiflado	crazy
Delgado	slim, thin
muy delgado	skinny
descalzo	bare-footed
descortés	impolite
distraído	absent-minded
Elegante	elegant
enfermo	ill, sick
esbelto	slender
espaldas anchas, de	broad-shouldered
Feo	ugly
fuerte	strong, sturdy
Grande	big
grosero	rude
grueso	fat
guapa	pretty
Hermosa	beautiful
Inteligente	intelligent
Joven	young
Listo	clever
loco	mad
Mal educado	badly-mannered
mal vestido	badly-dressed
manco	one-armed, one-handed
moreno	dark
mudo	dumb
mutilado	crippled
Negro	black
nervioso	nervous
Ojos azules, de	blue-eyed
ojos verdes, de	green-eyed
Pálido	pale
pelo castaño, de	brown-haired
pelo moreno, de	dark-aired
pelo rubio, de	fair-haired

| PERSONA, UNA | A PERSON |

pequeño	small
picado de viruelas	pock-marked
piernas cortas, de	short-legged
piernas largas, de	long-legged

Regordete — chubby
robusto — robust
rollizo — plump
rubio — fair

Sano — healthy
sensato — sensible
sensible — sensitive
sordo — deaf

Terco — stubborn
tonto — foolish, silly
tosco — rude
triste — sad
tuerto — one-eyed

Viejo — old

79

| PESCA, LA | FISHING (32) |

| ESPAÑOL | ENGLISH |

Agua poco profunda — shallow water
agua profunda — deep water
aguas jurisdiccionales — territorial waters
anzuelo — fish-hook
arpón — harpoon
avíos de pesca — fishing-tackle

Banco de peces — shoal
barco de pesca — fishing-boat

Captura — catch
caña de pescar — fishing-rod
cebo — bait
costa — coast

PESCA, LA	FISHING
Flota pesquera	fishing-fleet
Industria pesquera	fishing industry
Lago	lake
Mar	sea
marea	tide
marea alta	high tide
marea baja	low tide
mercado del pescado	fish market
Pesca a la rastra	trawling
pesca con caña	fishing by line
pesca con red	fishing by net
pescadería	fishmonger's shop
pescadero	fishmonger
pescado	fish
pescador	fisherman
pescar	to fish
pez	fish
playa	beach
puerto	port, harbour
Red	net
red para pescar	fishing-net
río	river
Sedal	fishing-line
Vivero	fish-pond
vivero de ostras	oyster bed

80

PESOS Y MEDIDAS	WEIGHTS AND MEASURES (98)
ESPAÑOL	ENGLISH
Acre	acre
altitud	altitude
altura	height
amperio	ampere
anchura	width, breadth

| PESOS, ETC. | WEIGHTS, ETC. |

Balanza, una — a pair of scales
barómetro — barometer
báscula — weighing machine
braza — fathom

Caballo de vapor — horse-power
caloría — calorie
centígrado — centigrade
centígramo — centigramme
centímetro — centimetre
cero — zero
   bajo cero — below zero
   sobre cero — above zero
cinta métrica — tape measure

Compás, un — a pair of compasses
contador — meter
cuarto — quarter

Decibelio — decibel
decígramo — decigramme
decílitro — decilitre
decímetro — decimetre
dracma — dram

Espesor — thickness

Fahrenheit — Fahrenheit

Galón (cuatro cuartos) — gallon
grado — degree
gramo — gramme

Hectárea — hectare
hectólitro — hectolitre
hectómetro — hectometre

Kilogramo — kilogramme
kilómetro — kilometre
kilómetro cuadrado — square kilometre

Legua — league
libra — pound
litro — litre
longitud — length

Mano de papel — quire
medida — measure
   instrumento de medida — measuring instrument
medidas cúbicas — cubic measures
medidas de líquidos — liquid measures
medidas de longitud — linear measures

medidas de superficie	square measures
medidor	meter
medir	to measure
metro	metre
metro cuadrado	square metre
metro cúbico	cubic metre
metro plegable	folding rule
milímetro	millimetre
milla	mile
milla cuadrada	square mile
milla náutica	nautical mile
mitad	half
Nudo	knot
Ohmio	ohm
onza	ounce
Pesar	to weigh
peso	weight
pie	foot
pie cuadrado	square foot
pie cúbico	cubic foot
pies	feet
pinta	pint
profundidad	depth
pulgada	inch
pulgada cuadrada	square inch
pulgada cúbica	cubic inch
punto de congelación	freezing point
punto de ebullición	boiling point
Quintal	hundredweight
Regla	ruler
resma de papel	ream
Sistema métrico	metric system
superficie	area
Tamaño	size
temperatura	temperature
termómetro	thermometer
tonelada	ton
Voltio	volt
volumen	volume
Watio	watt
Yarda	yard
yarda cuadrada	square yard

81

PINTURA Y ESCULTURA

PAINTING AND SCULPTURE (69)

ESPAÑOL	ENGLISH

Abstracto — abstract
acuarela — water-colour
alabastro — alabaster
arcilla — clay
arte — art
artista — artist

Bajo relieve — bas-relief
bodegón — still life
bronce — bronze
busto — bust

Caballete — easel
caja de colores — paint box
cincel — chisel
color — colour
cuadro — painting
cuadro al óleo — oil painting
cubismo — cubism

Escuela — school
esculpir — to carve
escultor — sculptor
estatua — statue
estatua ecuestre — equestrian statue
estatuilla — statuette
estilo — style

Fondo — background
fundir — to cast

Impresionismo — impressionism

Lienzo — canvas

Marina — sea-piece
mármol — marble
modelar — to model
modelo — model

Oleo — oil-colour

| PINTURA, ETC. | PAINTING, ETC. |

Paisaje — landscape
paleta — palette
perspectiva — perspective
piedra — stone
pincel — brush
pintar — to paint
pintor — painter
pintura — paint (para pintar)
    picture (cuadro)

pintura al óleo — oil painting

Realismo — realism
retrato — portrait

Sombra — shadow
surrealismo — surrealism

Talla — carving

PLANTAS (Véase ARBOLES, PLANTAS Y FLORES, 6)

PLAYA, EN LA (Véase EN LA COSTA, 28)

82

PRENDAS DE CABEZA — HEAD-DRESS (43)

ESPAÑOL	ENGLISH
Boina	Beret
Capucha	hood
casco	helmet
CHistera	topper
Fez	fez
Gorra	cap
gorra de visera	peaked cap
gorro	cap

PRENDAS DE CABEZA	HEAD-DRESS (43)
gorro de dormir	nightcap
Morrión	bearskin cap
Pamela	broad straw hat
pañuelo de cabeza	headscarf
Quepis	kepi
Salacot	sun-helmet
sombrero	hat
ala de sombrero	brim
sombrero de copa	top hat
sombrero de fieltro	felt hat
sombrero de paja	straw hat
sombrero de tres picos	three-cornered hat
sombrero hongo	bowler-hat
sombrero tejano	sombrero
Turbante	turban
Visera	peak

83

PROFESIONES   OCCUPATIONS (67)

ESPAÑOL	ENGLISH
Abogado	lawyer
actor	actor
actriz	actress
administrador de correos	postmaster
agente de la propiedad	estate agent
albañil	bricklayer
ama de casa	housewife
arquitecto	architect
artista	artist
ascensorista	liftman
asistenta	charwoman
autor	author
azafata	air-hostess
Bailarín	dancer

PROFESIONES — OCCUPATIONS

bailarina — dancer
barbero — barber
barman — barman
botones — bellboy

Cajero — cashier, teller (banco)
cajista — compositor
camarera — waitress
camarero — waiter
camarero de un buque — steward
camarero jefe — head-waiter
camionero — lorry-driver
cantante — singer
cantero — mason
capataz — foreman
carnicero — butcher
carpintero — carpenter
cartero — postman
cirujano — surgeon
cobrador de autobús — conductor
cocinero — cook
comerciante — shopkeeper, shopman, merchant
comerciante de vinos — wine-merchant
compositor — composer
concertista de guitarra — guitar-player
conductor — driver
conductor de autobús — bus-driver
conductor de tren — train engineer
constructor — builder
contable — accountant
corrector de pruebas — proof-reader
criada — maid-servant, maid
criado — man-servant

CHico de tienda — shop-boy
chófer — chauffeur

Dependiente — shop-asistant
deshollinador — chimney-sweep
director — director
director de orquesta — conductor
doctor — doctor
domador de leones — lion-tamer
dueño de una papelería — stationer

Editor — publisher
electricista — electrician
empapelador — paperhanger
empleado — clerck
empleado de banca — bank clerk

PROFESIONES	OCCUPATIONS
encuadernador	bookbinder
enfermera	nurse
escritor	writer
escultor	sculptor
estanquero	tobacconist
Fabricante	manufacturer
farmacéutico	chemist
florista	florist
fontanero	plumber
fotógrafo	photographer
frutero	fruiterer
Gerente	manager
granjero	farmer
guardia	policeman
Herrero	blacksmith
Impresor	printer
ingeniero	engineer
intérprete	interpreter
Jardinero	gardener
jefe de estación	station master
joyero	jeweller
juez	judge
Labrador	ploughman
lechero	milkman
leñador	wood-cutter
librero	bookseller
limpiabotas	boot-black
locutor	announcer
locutor de radio	radio announcer
locutor de televisión	television announcer
Manicura	manicurist
marinero	sailor
mayordomo	butler
mecánico	mechanic
mecánico de coches	motor repairman
mecanógrafa	typist
mercero	haberdasher
minero	miner
modista	dressmaker
molinero	miller
músico	musician
Oficial del ejército	army officer
orfebre	goldsmith
Panadero	baker

PROFESIONES	OCCUPATIONS
pastelero	confectioner
pastor	shepherd
peluquero	hairdresser
peón	labourer
periodista	journalist
pescador	fisherman
pianista	pianist
piloto	pilot
pintor	painter
platero	silversmith
poeta	poet
portero	porter
profesor	teacher
Químico	chemist
Recepcionista	recepcionist
relojero	watchmaker
reportero	reporter
revisor	ticket-collector
Salchichero	porkbutcher
sastre	tailor
secretario, a	secretary
soldado	soldier
sombrerero	hatter (de caballeros), milliner (de señoras)
Taquimecanógrafo, a	shorthand typist
taxista	taxi-driver
técnico	technician
técnico electricista	electrical technician
tendero	grocer
tenedor de libros	bookkeeper
traductor	translator
Vendedor	sales-man
vendedor ambulante	pedlar, hawker
vendedor de periódicos	news-boy
vendedor de periódicos y revistas	news-agent
vendedora	sales-woman
verdulero	greengrocer
vigilante	watchman
violinista	violinist
Zapatero	shoemaker

84

PUERTO DE MAR, UN **A SEA-PORT (79)**

ENGLISH	ESPAÑOL
Amarra	mooring
amarrar	to moor
Base naval	naval base
buque*	ship
buque de carga	cargo ship
Cargar	to load
Defensa (para evitar golpes)	fender
derechos de dique	dockage
descargar	to unload
desembarcadero	quay
desembarcar	to disembark
dique	dock
dique seco	dry dock
Embarcar	to embark
escollera	pier
estibador	docker
Gaviotas	seagulls
grúa	crane
Instalaciones petrolíferas	oil installations
Malecón	jetty
muelle	quay, dock
muelle de carga y descarga	wharf
Noray	bollard
Paseo marítimo	promenade
petrolero	tanker
práctico de puerto	harbour pilot
puerto	port, harbour
puerto exterior	outer habour
puerto franco	free port
puerto interior	inner harbour
Remolcador	tug

PUERTO DE MAR, UN		A SEA-PORT

remolcar to tow
rompeolas breakwater

Tinglado wharf
transatlántico liner

85

QUÍMICA — CHEMISTRY (18)

ESPAÑOL	ENGLISH
Acetato	acetate
acetona	acetone
ácido	acid
ácido bórico	boric acid
ácido carbónico	carbonic acid
ácido cítrico	citric acid
ácido nítrico	nitric acid
ácido sulfúrico	sulphuric acid
aluminio	aluminium
arsénico	arsenic
atmósfera	atmosphere
atómico	atomic
átomo	atom
azufre	sulphur
Bario	barium
boro	boron
bromo	bromine
bromuro	bromide
Cadmio	cadmium
calcio	calcium
carbono	carbon
cloro	chlorine
cobre	copper
cromo	chromium
Dióxido	dioxide
Elemento	element
estaño	tin

QUÍMICA	CHEMISTRY
estroncio	strontium
Flúor	fluorine
fósforo	phosphorus
frasco de laboratorio	flask
Gas	gas
gaseoso	gaseous
Helio	helium
hidrógeno	hydrogen
hierro	iron
Iones	ions
iridio	iridium
Laboratorio	laboratory
líquido	liquid
Magnesio	magnesium
materia	matter
mercurio	mercury
mezcla	mixture
mezclar	to mix
molécula	molecule
Nitrato	nitrate
nitrógeno	nitrogen
Óxido	oxide
oxígeno	oxygen
Partícula	particle
plata	silver
plomo	lead
potasio	potassium
probeta	test-tube
Química inorgánica	inorganic chemistry
química orgánica	organic chemistry
químico	chemist (sus), chemical (adj.)
Radio	radium
reacción química	chemical reaction
Sal	salt
silicio	silicon
sodio	sodium
sólido	solid
sustancia	substance
Titanio	titanium
tungsteno	tungsten
Valencia	valency

QUÍMICA		CHEMISTRY

Yodo — iodine
yoduro — iodide

Zinc — zinc

RADIO (Véase TELEVISION Y RADIO, 91)

86

RELIGIÓN — RELIGION (76)

ESPAÑOL — ENGLISH

Abel — Abel
Adán — Adam
adoración — worship
adorar — to worship
alma — soul
ángel — angel
Antiguo Testamento, El — The Old Testament
apóstol — apostle
ateísmo — atheism
ateo — atheist

Bautismo — baptism
bautizar — to baptize
bendecir — to bless
bendito — blessed
Biblia, La — The Bible
bien — good (sus.)
Buda — Buddha
budismo — Buddism

Caín — Cain
castigar — to punish
castigo — punishment
catedral — cathedral
catolicismo — catholicism
católico — Catholic

cielo	heaven
clérigo	clergyman
clero	clergy
convento	convent
creación	creation
credo	creed
creencia	belief
cristianismo	christanism
cristiano	Christian
Cristo	Christ
cruz	cross
Demonio	demon
diablo	devil
Día del Juicio Final	Doomsday
Diez Mandamientos, Los	The Ten Commandments
Dios	God
divinidad	deity
dogma	dogma
Escrituras	Scriptures
Espíritu Santo	Holy Ghost
Eva	Eve
Fe	faith
Hereje	heretic
herejía	heresy
hermanos	brethren
Hijo	Son
himno	hymn
hinduísmo	Hinduism
Iglesia	church
Iglesia Católica, Apostólica y Romana	Roman Catholic Church
Infierno	Hell
Jesucristo	Jesus Christ
Jesús	Jesus
Judaísmo	Judaism
Mahoma	Mahomet
mal	evil (sus.)
milagro	miracle
misionero	missionary
Moisés	Moses
monja	nun
monje	monk
Nuevo Testamento, El	The New Testament

RELIGIÓN	RELIGION
Oración	prayer
Padre	Father
paganismo	paganism
pagano	pagan
Papa, el	The Pope
parábola	parable
pecado	sin
pecador	sinner
pecar	to sin
procesión	procession
profeta	prophet
protestante	Protestant
Recompensa	reward
recompensar	to reward
Redención	Redemption
Redentor	Redeemer
retablo	altar-piece
rezar	to pray
rito	rite
Sacerdote	priest
Sagrada Escritura	Holy Writ
sagrado	sacred
santo	saint (sus.), holy (adj.)
Satán	Satan
Semana Santa	Holy-Week
Señor, El	The Lord
Tierra Santa	Holy Land
Última Cena, la	the Last Supper
Virgen	Virgin

87

RELOJES	CLOCKS AND WATCHES (21)
ESPAÑOL	ENGLISH
Adelantado	fast
atrasado	slow

RELOJES	CLOCKS

Caja del reloj — watch case
carrillón — chimes
cronómetro — stop-watch

Dar cuerda — to wind
dar las horas — to strike the hours
despertador — alarm clock

Esfera — clock-dial, clock-face

Manilla — hand
manilla de las horas — hour-hand
manilla de los minutos — minute-hand
manilla de los segundos — second-hand
mecanismo de relojería — clockwork, watchwork
movimiento contrario a las agujas del reloj — anticlockwise
movimiento de las agujas del reloj — clockwise

Pesa — clock weight
péndulo — pendulum

Reloj — watch (de pulsera o bolsillo), clock (no de pulsera o bolsillo)

reloj automático — keyless watch
reloj de arena — sand-glass
reloj de bolsillo — pocket-watch
reloj de carrillón — chiming clock
reloj de cuco — cuckoo clock
reloj de cuerda — key-watch
reloj de fábrica u oficina — time clock
reloj de pared — wall clock
reloj de petaca — travelling-clock
reloj de pie — grandfather clock, long-case clock
reloj de pulsera — wrist-watch
reloj de sobremesa — mantel clock
reloj de sol — sun-dial
reloj de torre — tower clock
reloj despertador — alarm clock
relojero — clockmaker, watchmaker

Sonería — striking-mechanism

88

REPTILES Y ANFIBIOS   REPTILES AND AMPHIBIANS (77)

ESPAÑOL	ENGLISH
Boa	boa
Caimán	alligator
camaleón	chameleon
cobra	cobra
cocodrilo	crocodile
culebra	snake
Iguana	iguana
Lagartija	small lizard
lagarto	lizard
Pitón	python
Rana	frog
Salamandra	salamander
sapo	toad
serpiente	snake
serpiente coralillo	coral snake
serpiente de cascabel	rattlesnake
Tortuga	tortoise
tortuga de mar	turtle
tritón	newt
Víbora	viper, adder

89

RESTAURANTE, EN EL   AT THE RESTAURANT (78)

ESPAÑOL	ENGLISH
Aceite	oil
aceitunas	olives

| RESTAURANTE, EN EL | AT THE RESTAURANT |

aceitunas rellenas	stuffed olives
agua	water
agua mineral	mineral water
albóndigas	meat balls
almendras saladas	salted almonds
almuerzo	lunch
anguila ahumada	smoked eel
apetito	appetite
arroz	rice
aves de corral	poultry
azúcar	sugar
azucarero	sugar-bowl
Bandeja	tray
bebida*	drink
bistec	beefsteak
bocadillo	sandwich
bocadillo de jamón	ham sandwich
bocadillo de queso	cheese sandwich
Cabrito asado	roast-kid
café	coffee
café con leche	white coffee
café instantáneo	instant coffee
café solo	black coffee
camarera	waitress
camarero	waiter
carne	meat
carne asada	roast meat
caza	game
cebolletas en vinagre	pickled onions
cena	supper, dinner
cliente	customer
cocinero	cook
cochinillo asado	roast suckling-pig
colador para el té	tea-strainer
comida	meal
comida caliente	hot meal
comida fría	cold meal
compota	stewed fruit
consomé	clear soup
copa	wine-glass
cordero	lamb, mutton
cordero lechal asado	roast-lamb
cubierto	set lunch
cuchara	spoon
cucharilla	teaspoon
cuchillo	knife
cuenta	bill

RESTAURANTE, EN EL — AT THE RESTAURANT

CHuleta — chop, cutlet
chuleta de cerdo — pork chop
chuleta de cordero — lamb cutlet, mutton chop
chuleta de cordero lechal — lamb chop
chuleta de ternera — veal cutlet

Desayuno — breakfast
dieta — diet

Encargar — to order
ensalada — salad
ensalada de lechuga — lettuce salad
ensalada variada — green salad
ensaladilla rusa — Russian salad
entremeses — hors d'oeuvres
estofado — stew

Fiambre — cold meat
fideos — vermicelli noodles
filete — steak
flan — caramel custard
fruta* — fruit
fruta en conserva — tinned fruit

Galletas — biscuits
guarnición — garnish
guisar — to cook

Helado — ice-cream
hielo — ice
hígado — liver
huevo — egg
huevo duro — hard-boiled egg
huevo frito — fried egg
huevo pasado por agua — boiled egg
huevos con bacón — bacon and eggs
huevos escalfados — scrambled eggs
huevos revueltos — poached eggs

Jamón — ham
jarra — jug
jarra de agua — water jug

Legumbres — vegetables

Mantel — table-cloth
mantequilla — butter
manzana asada — baked apple
marisco — shell-fish
mayonesa — mayonnaise

membrillo	quince jelly
menú	menu
mermelada	jam
mermelada de cereza	cherry jam
mermelada de frambuesa	gooseberry jam
mermelada de fresa	strawberry jam
mermelada de naranja	marmalade
mesa	table
reservar una mesa	to book a table
mondadientes	toothpick
mostaza	mustard
Natillas	custard
nota	bill
Pan	bread
pan con mantequilla	bread and butter
panecillo	loaf, roll
parrillada de carne	mixed grill
pastel	cake
pastelería (pasteles)	pastry
patatas	potatoes
patatas asadas	roast potatoes, baked potatoes
patatas fritas	chips, fried potatoes, chipped potatoes
patatas fritas a la inglesa	crisps
pescado	fish
pimienta	pepper
platillo (de taza)	saucer
plato	plate (pieza de vajilla), dish (condimentado)
plato (en la lista)	course
plato de carne	meat dish
plato frío	cold dish
plato vegetariano	vegetarian dish
pollo	chicken
postre	dessert, sweet
propina	tip
puré	thick soup
puré de lentejas	lentil soup
puré de patatas	mashed potatoes
Queso	cheese
Ración	portion
restaurante	restaurant
restaurante de autoservicio	self-service restaurant
riñones	kidneys
«rosbif»	roast-beef

Sal	salt
salchicha	sausage
salero	saltcellar
salmón ahumado	smoked salmon
salsa	sauce
salsa (jugo)	gravy
salsa de tomate	tomato sauce
salsa verde	green sauce
salsa vinagreta	vinegar sauce
servilleta	napkin
servir	to serve
solomillo	sirloin
sopa	soup
sopa de avena	porridge
sopa de cebolla	onion soup
sopa de pescado	fish-soup
sopa de rabo de buey	oxtail-soup
sopa de tomate	tomato soup
Tarta	cake, pie
tarta de manzana	apple pie
tenedor	fork
ternera	veal
tortilla	omelette
tortilla a la española	Spanish omelette
tortilla a la francesa	plain omelette
tostada	toast
tostada con mantequilla	buttered toast
Vajilla*	tableware
vaso	glass
verduras	vegetables, greens
vinagre	vinegar
vino	wine
lista de vinos	wine-list

ROPA (Véase VESTIMENTA, 98)

SASTRE Y LA MODISTA, EL   90   THE TAILOR AND THE DRESSMAKER (86)

ESPAÑOL	ENGLISH
Abrigo	overcoat
acerico	pincushion
acortar (una prenda)	to shorten

aguja	needle
ajustado (una prenda)	tight, close-fitting
muy ajustado	skin tight
alargar (una prenda)	to lengthen
alfiler	pin
americana	coat
ante	suede
arruga	crease
automático (botón)	snap fastener
Bobina (de hilo)	bobbin
bocamanga	wristband
bolsillo	pocket
bolsillo de costado	side pocket
bolsillo de pecho	breast pocket
bolsillo interior	inside pocket
bordado (sus.)	embroidery
bordar	to embroider
botón	button
Canesú	yoke
capa	cloak
carrete (de hilo)	reel
cinta	ribbon
cinta de algodón	tape
cinta métrica	tape measure
cintura	waist
cinturón	belt
cola (de un vestido)	train
confección, de (prenda)	ready-made
cortar	to cut
corte	cut
coser	to sew
cosido	sewn
cosido a mano	hand-sewn
cosido a máquina	machine-sewn
costura	seam
costurero	work-basket
cretona	cretonne
cuadros, a (una tela)	checked
cuello (de una prenda)	collar
cuero	leather
cuerpo de un vestido	bodice
CHaqueta	jacket
chaqueta de dos filas	double-breasked jacket
chaquea de «sport»	sports jacket
chaqueta de una fila	single-breasted jacket
cheviot	cheviot
Dedal	thimble

Encaje	lace
entretela	buckram
escote bajo	low neck
escote puntiagudo	V-shaped neck
espejo	mirror
estambre	worsted
Falda	skirt
felpa	plush
fieltro	felt
forro	lining
franela	flannel
frunce	tuck
Hebilla	buckle
hilo	thread
hilo de algodón	cotton
Imperdible	safety-pin
Jaboncillo	chalk
Lana	wool
Manga	sleeve
manga corta	short sleeve
manga larga	long sleeve
maniquí de sastre o modista	mannequin bust
máquina de coser	sewing-machine
medida	measure, measurement
a la medida (una prenda)	made to measure
medir	to measure
meter (una prenda)	to take in
modista	dressmaker
Nylón	nylon
Ojal	buttonhole
Pana	plush
pantalón	trousers
pernera del pantalón	trouserleg
paño	cloth
patrón	pattern
percal	calico
plancha	iron
planchar	to iron, to press
pliegue	pleat
plisado	pleating
ponerse (una prenda)	to put on
prenda	garment

llevar una prenda	to wear
probador	fitting-room
probarse (una prenda)	to try on
prueba	fitting
puntilla	lace
puño (de una prenda)	cuff
Quitarse (una prenda)	to take off
Raya (del pantalón)	crease
rayas, a (una tela)	striped
retor	calico
Sacar (una prenda)	to let out
sastra	seamstress
sastre	tailor
satín	satin
seda	silk
seda artificial	artificial silk
seda natural	natural silk
sentar bien (una prenda)	to fit
solapa	lapel
suelto (una prenda)	loose
tejido	fabric
tela	cloth
pieza de tela	roll of cloth
tela de hilo	linen
tela de «tweed»	tweed
terciopelo	velvet
tijeras	scissors
traje	suit
tul	tulle
Vainica	hemstitch
vestido	dress
Zurcido (sus.)	darn
zurcir	to darn

SOMBREROS   (Véase PRENDAS DE CABEZA, 82)

TEATRO, EL   (Véase EL CINE Y EL TEATRO, 20)

91

TELEVISION Y RADIO

TELEVISION AND RADIO (87)

ESPAÑOL	ENGLISH
Alfabeto Morse	Morse Code
altavoz	**loudspeaker**
amplificador	amplifier
amplificar	to amplify
antena	aerial
Batería	battery
Cámara	camera
circuito	circuit
Electrón	electron
estación de radio	radio station
estación transmisora	transmitting station
Frecuencia	frequency
Imagen	image, picture
impulsos eléctricos	electrical impulses
Kilociclos	kilocycles
Mando (de un aparato)	knob
megaciclos	megacycles
Onda	wave
onda corta	short wave
onda de sonido	sound-wave
onda larga	long wave
onda media	medium wave
ondas electromagnéticas	electro-magnetic waves
ondas de radio	airwaves
Pantalla	screen
película	film, picture, movie
película muda	silent film
película sonora	sound-film, talking picture
Radio	radio
aparato de radio	radio set, wireless set
receptor	receiver
receptor de radio	radio receiver
recibir	to receive

TELEVISIÓN, ETC.	TELEVISION, ETC.

Señal
señales acústicas
sincronizar
sonido
  efectos de sonido
  pista de sonido

Televisión
  aparato de televisión
transformador
transistor
transmisión
transmisor
transmisor de radio
transmitir
tubo de rayos catódicos

U.H.F.

Válvula
V.H.F.
voltaje
volumen
  control del volumen

signal
acoustic signals
to synchronize
sound
sound effects
sound-track

television
television set
transformer
transistor
transmission
transmitter
radio transmitter
to transmit, to broadcast
cathode-ray tube

Ultra High Frequency

valve
Very High Frequency
voltage
volume
volume control

92

TIEMPO, EL   TIME (88)

ESPAÑOL	ENGLISH

Abril
agosto
almanaque
anoche
anteayer
año
año bisiesto
ayer

Calendario
calendario de taco
cronometrar

April
August
almanac
last night
the day before yesterday
year
leap-year
yesterday

calendar
block calendar
to time

TIEMPO, EL — TIME

Década — decade
día — day
  medio día — midday
diciembre — December
domingo — Sunday

Edad* — age
enero — January
época — epoch
era — era
estación — season
eternidad — eternity

Febrero — February
fecha — date
futuro — future

Hora — hour
  un cuarto de hora — a quarter of an hour
  media hora — half an hour
horario — time-table
hoy — today

Instante — instant
invierno — winter

Jueves — Thursday
julio — July
junio — June

Lunes — Monday

Mañana — tomorrow (adv.), morning (sus.)
  pasado mañana — the day after tomorrow
martes — Tuesday
marzo — March
mayo — May
mes — month
miércoles — Wednesday
minuto — minute
momento — moment

Noche — night
  esta noche — tonight
  media noche — midnight
noviembre — November

Octubre — October
otoño — autumn

TIEMPO, EL	427	TIME

Pasado
período
presente
primavera

Quincena

Reloj*

Sábado
segundo
semana
   fin de semana
septiembre
siglo

Tarde

temporada
temprano
trimestre

Verano
viernes

past
period
present
spring

fortnight

watch (de pulsera o bolsillo), clock (no de pulsera o bolsillo)

Saturday
second
week
week-end
September
century

late (adv.), afternoon (sus.), evening (sus.)

season
early
term

summer
Friday

93

TIENDAS	SHOPS (83)
ESPAÑOL	ENGLISH

Almacenes

Barbería

Cafetería
camisería
carnicería
cliente
confitería

department store

barber's

café
outfitter's
butcher's
customer
confectioner's

TIENDAS	SHOPS

Dependiente
droguería

shop-assistant
drug store

Escaparate
estanco

shop window
tobacconist's

Farmacia
ferretería
floristería
frutería

chemist's
hardware shop
florist's
fruiterer's

Joyería
juguetería

jeweller's
toy-shop

Lavandería
lechería
librería

laundry
dairy
bookshop, bookseller's

Mercería
mostrador

haberdasher's
counter

Óptico

optician

Pajarería
panadería
papelería
pastelería

pet-shop
baker's
stationer's
cake-shop
   pastry-cook's, confectimer's

peluquería
perfumería
pescadería
puesto de periódicos

hairdresser's
drug store
fishmonger's
newsagent's

Quiosco de libros y periódicos

bookstall

Relojería

watchmaker's

Sastrería
supermercado

tailor's
supermarket

Tendero
tienda
tienda de antigüedades
tienda de aparatos de radio
tienda de comestibles
tienda de objetos de cerámica
tienda de tejidos
tintorería

shopkeeper
shop
antique shop
radio-shop
grocer's
ceramics shop
draper's
cleaner's

Verdulería

greengrocer's

Zapatería

shoe-shop

94

TRÁFICO / TRAFFIC (92)

ESPAÑOL	ENGLISH

Accidente — accident
alto — stop
aparcamiento — car park
arrancar — to start
atasco de tráfico — traffic-jam
automovilista — motorist
autopista — motorway

Barreras — gates

Calzada irregular — uneven surface
calzada resbaladiza — slippery surface
calle — street
calle cortada — no thoroughfare
calle de doble dirección — two-way street
calle de una dirección — one-way street
camionero — lorry-driver
carretera en reparación — road works
ciclista — cyclist
Código de la Circulación — Highway Code
conducir — to drive
conductor — driver
congestión de tráfico — traffic congestion
cruce — crossing, cross-roads
cruce de carretera principal — main road ahead
cruce de carreteras — road junction
cruce de cebra — zebra crossing
cruce de niños — children crossing
cruce de peatones — pedestrian crossing
curva — bend

CHocar — to crash

Derecha — right
   manténgase a la derecha — keep right
desviación — diversion
doble curva — double bend

Estacionar — to park
estrechamiento de calzada — road narrows

| TRÁFICO | | TRAFIC |

Giro en el centro de la glorieta — roundabout
guardia urbano — traffic policeman

Izquierda — left
   manténgase a la izquierda — keep left

Límite de velocidad — speed limit

Motorista — motor-cyclist

Parar — to stop
paso a nivel — level-crossing
paso a nivel con barrera — guarded level-crossing
paso a nivel sin barrera — unguarded level-crossing
permiso de conducir — driving licence
prohibido aparcar — no parking
prohibido el giro a la derecha — no right turn
prohibido el giro a la izquierda — no left turn
prohibido estacionarse — no waiting

Regulación del tráfico — traffic control

Semáforo — traffic lights
señal — sign
señales de tráfico — road signs, traffic signs

Tráfico — traffic
policia de tráfico — traffic police

Vía pública — thoroughfare

95

TRANSPORTE, EL   TRANSPORTATION (93)

ESPAÑOL   ENGLISH

Aeronave — aircraft
ambulancia — ambulance
autobús — bus
avión* — plane
avión de pasajeros — air-liner
avión de reacción — jet

Barco* — ship, boat
barco de vela — sailing-boat

TRANSPORTE, EL	TRANSPORTATION
bicicleta	bicycle
burro	donkey
Caballo	horse
calesín	chaise
camello	camel
camión	lorry (GB), truck (USA)
carretilla	wheelbarrow
carro	cart
carro romano	chariot
carroza	state coach
coche*	car, motor-car
coche de línea	coach
Diligencia	stage coach
Ferrocarril	railway
furgoneta	van
Helicóptero	helicopter
Jeep	jeep
Metro	underground
moto	motor-cycle
moto «escuter»	motor-scooter
mula	mule
Nave espacial	space-ship
Silla de manos	sedan-chair
silla de posta	post-chair
submarino	submarine
Taxi	taxi
transatlántico	liner
tranvía	tram, tramcar
tren	train
trineo	sleigh
trolebús	trolley-bus
Vapor	steamer

TURISMO Y VIAJES — TOURISM AND TRAVELLING (90)

96

ESPAÑOL	ENGLISH
Aduana	Customs
derechos de Aduana	Customs duty

edificio de la Aduana	Customs House
oficial de Aduanas	Customs-officer
aeropuerto*	airport
agencia de viajes	travel agency
agente de viajes	travel agent
andén	platform
asiento	seat
autobús	bus
avión*	plane
azafata	airhostess, stewardess
Barco*	ship, boat
baúl	trunk
billete	ticket
medio billete	half fare
billete de avión	air-ticket
billete de ida	single ticket
billete de ida y vuelta	return ticket
buque de vapor	steamer
Camarote	cabin
camino	way
«camping»	camping-site
cantina	refreshment room
carretera	road
cinturón de seguridad	safety-belt
clase	class
primera clase	first class
segunda clase	second class
tercera clase	third class
clase de lujo	luxury class
clase turista	tourist class
coche*	car, motor-car
coche cama	sleeper
coche de línea	coach
coche restaurante	dining-car, restaurant car
compañía de aviación	airline
compañía de navegación	steamship company
compartimento	compartment
conducir	to drive
consigna	left-luggage office
Departamento para fumadores	smoker
departamento para no fumadores	non-smoker
desembarcar	to disembark
Embarcar	to embark
equipaje	luggage (GB), baggage (USA)
rejilla del equipaje	luggage-rack

TURISMO	TOURISM
estación	station
estación de ferrocarril*	railway-station
estación terminal	terminus
estancia	stay
Ferrocarril	railway
fonda	inn
frontera	frontier
Guía	guide (empleado), guide-book (libro)
guía de ferrocarriles	railway-guide
Horario	time-table
hotel*	hotel
Itinerario	itinerary
Litera	berth, bunk
LLegada	arrival
Maleta	suitcase, case
mapa	map
mareo (en avión)	air-sickness
mareo (en barco)	sea-sickness
monumentos	monuments
mozo	porter
muelle (desembarcadero)	quay
Navegar	to sail
«neceser»	toilet case
Oficina de información	inquiry office
Parada	stop
partida	departure
pasajero	passenger
pasaporte	passport
pensión	boarding-house
precio del viaje	fare
puerto*	port
Reservar	to book
restaurante*	restaurant
revisor	ticket collector
ruta	route
Sala de espera	waiting-room
servicio	service
servicio regular	regular service

TURISMO — TOURISM

Talón de facturación de
  equipajes — registration slip
taquilla — booking-office, ticket-office
taxi — taxi
transatlántico — liner
transbordo — connection
transporte* — transportation
travesía — passage, crossing
tren — train
tren directo — through train
tren expreso — express train
tren omnibus — slow train
tren rápido — fast train
tripulación — crew
turista — tourist

Vacaciones — holidays
  lugar de vacaciones — holiday-resort
vagón — carriage
velocidad — speed
viajar — to travel
viajar en avión — to travel by air
viajar en coche — to travel by car
viajar en tren — to travel by rail
viajar por mar — to travel by sea
viaje — trip, journey, voyage (por mar)
viajero — traveller
visado — visa
visado de entrada — entry visa
visado de salida — exit visa
visita a una ciudad — sight-seeing
volar — to fly
vuelo — flight

Zarpar — to sail

UNIVERSO, EL — (Véase EL MUNDO Y EL UNIVERSO, 68)

97

VAJILLA — **TABLEWARE (85)**

ESPAÑOL — ENGLISH

Azucarero — sugar-bowl

VAJILLA	TABLEWARE
Cafetera	coffee-pot
cazo	ladle
copa	wine-glass
cristalería	glassware
cubertería	cutlery
cuchara	spoon
cuchara grande	table spoon
cuchara sopera	soup-spoon
cucharilla	tea-spoon
cucharilla de postre	dessert-spoon
cuchillo	knife
cuchillos	knives
Ensaladera	salad-bowl
Fuente	dish
Jarra	jug
jarra con pitorro	beaker
jarra sin pitorro	mug
Loza	crockery
Platillo para taza	saucer
plato	plate
plato de postre	dessert-plate, sweet-plate
plato llano	dinner-plate
plato sopero	soup-plate
Sopera	soup-tureen
Taza	cup
taza para café	coffee-cup
taza para té	tea-cup
tazón	bowl
tenacillas para el azúcar	sugar-tongs
tenedor	fork
tetera	teapot
Vajilla	tableware
vaso	glass

98

VESTIMENTA	CLOTHING (22)
ESPAÑOL	ENGLISH
Abrigo	overcoat
abrigo de piel	fur-coat

VESTIMENTA — CLOTHING

abrigo de piel de leopardo — leopard-skin coat
albornoz — bath-robe
americana — coat, jacket
americana escolar — blazer

Babero — bib
bata — dressing-gown, gown
blusa — blouse
blusa marinera — sailor blouse
botines — spats
braga bikini — bikini brief
bragas — panties

Calcetín — sock
   un par de calcetines — a pair of socks
calzado* — footwear
calzoncillos — underpants (USA), pants (GB)
calzones — breeches
camisa — shirt
camisa de deporte — polo shirt
camiseta — undershirt (USA), vest (GB)
camisón — night-dress, nightie
capa — cloak, cape
capote — great-coat
cinturón — belt
corbata — necktie, tie
   nudo de corbata — knot
corsé — corset
cuello — collar
cuello blando — soft collar
cuello de pajarita — bow tie
cuello duro — stiff collar

CHaleco — waistcoat (GB), vest.(USA)
chaleco de punto — pullover
chaqué — morning-coat
chaqueta — jacket, coat
chaqueta de «sport» — sports jacket

Delantal — apron
delantal de niño — pinafore

Enagua — underskirt (USA), petticoat, slip (GB)

Faja (banda) — sash
falda — skirt
falda al bies — gored skirt
falda escocesa — kilt
falda plisada — pleated skirt
frac — tail-coat, dress-coat

| VESTIMENTA | **437** | CLOTHING |

Gabardina — raincoat
guante — glove
  un par de guantes — a pair of gloves
guantes de cabritilla — kid gloves
guantes de gamuza — chamois gloves
guerrera — tunic

Jersey ajustado — sweater
jersey con mangas — jersey
jersey suelto — jumper

Kimono — kimono

Lazo de pajarita — bow
leotardos — tights
liga — garter
ligas de caballero — sock-suspenders
liguero — suspenders (GB)

Manguito — muff
media — stocking
  un par de medias — a pair of stockings
mitones — mittens
mono de trabajo — overalls

Pantalón corto — shorts
pantalones — trousers, pants (USA), slacks
  un par de pantalones — a pair of trousers
pantalones de montar — riding-breeches
pañuelo para el cuello — scarf
pechera — shirt-front
«picardías» — shortie nightie
pijama — pyjamas, pyjama suit
prenda — garment
prenda ajustada — close-fitting garment
prenda de cabeza* — head-dress
prenda interior — inner garment, undergarment
prenda suelta — loose garment

Rebeca — cardigan
ropa — clothes
ropa blanca — linen
ropa de confección — ready-made clothes
ropa de invierno — warm clothes
ropa de luto — mourning-clothes
ropa de verano — cool clothes
ropa interior — underwear, underclothing, underclothes

«Slip» de caballero — brief(s)

[handwritten annotations: "impermeable", "playera"]

VESTIMENTA	CLOTHING
«smoking»	dinner-jacket, tuxedo (USA)
sombrero*	hat
sostén	brassière, bra
Tirantes	braces (GB), suspenders (USA)
toga	gown
traje	costume, suit of clothes, suit
traje a la medida	suit made to measure
traje azul marino	navy blue suit
traje de baño	bathing-costume, bathing-suit
traje de buzo	diving-suit
traje de confección	ready-made suit
traje de etiqueta	evening-dress
traje de gala	full dress
traje de noche	evening-dress
traje de Príncipe de Gales	Prince of Wales check suit
traje regional	regional costume
traje sastre de señora	tailored suit
túnica	tunic
Uniforme	uniform
uniforme de campaña	battledress
uniforme de gala	full-dress uniform
Velo	veil
vestido	frock, dress
vestido de noche	evening-gown
vestido estampado	print dress
Zapatos*	shoes
un par de zapatos	a pair of shoes
VIAJES	(Véase TURISMO Y VIAJES, 96)

99

VIDA EN LA ESCUELA, LA   LIFE AT SCHOOL (56)

ESPAÑOL	ENGLISH
Álgebra	álgebra
alumno interno	boarder
alumno mediopensionista	day-boarder

VIDA EN LA ESCUELA, LA   **439**   LIFE AT SCHOOL

aprobado   passed
aprobar   to pass
aprobar un examen   to pass an examination
aritmética*   arithmetic
asignatura   subject
aula   classroom

Banco   bench
biblioteca   library
biblioteca de préstamo   lending-library
blibliotecario   librarian
bolígrafo   ball-pen

Cartera de colegial   satchel
catedrático   lecturer
ciencia   science
ciencias exactas   exact sciences
ciencias naturales   natural sciences
clase   class
   dar una clase   to give a class
   tomar una clase to take a class
colegial   schoolboy
colegiala   schoolgirl
colegio   school
colegio universitario   college
compás, un   a pair of compasses
condiscípulo   school-fellow
conferencia   lecture
conferenciante   lecturer
copiar (de otro alumno)   to crib
corregir   to correct
cuaderno   note-book, copy-book,
                        exercise-book
cultura general   general knowledge
curso   course

«**CH**uleta»   crib

Deberes para casa   homework
dibujar   to draw
dibujo   drawing
diccionario   dictionary
dictado   dictation
director   headmaster
directora   headmistress
doctorado   doctor's degree

Educación física   physical-training
ejercicio   exercise
   hacer un ejercicio to do an exercise
encerado   blackboard

VIDA EN LA ESCUELA, LA   **440**   LIFE AT SCHOOL

enseñanza	teaching
enseñar	to teach
escritura	writing
escuela	school
escuela de niñas	girls' school
escuela de niños	boys' school
escuela diurna	day-school
escuela maternal	kindergarten
escuela mixta	mixed school
escuela nocturna	night-school
escuela primaria	primary school
escuela profesional	technical school
escuela secundaria	high school, secondary school
estrado	platform
estudiante	student
estudiante de derecho	law-student
estudiante de medicina	medical-student
estudiante externo	day-student
estudiante universitario	undergraduate
estudiar	to study
estudio	study
examen	examination, exam
presentarse a examen	to sit for an examination
examen de admisión	entrance examination
examen escrito	written examination
examen oral	oral examination
examinando	examinee
examinador	examiner
examinar	to examine
examinarse	to take an examination
Falta de ortografía	spelling mistake
física	physics
Gamuza para limpiar el encerado	duster
geografía*	geography
geometría*	geometry
goma de borrar	rubber
gramática	grammar
Historia*	history
historia natural	natural history
Internado	boarding-school
internado privado	public school (GB)
Lápiz	pencil
lección	lesson
lectura	reading
letras	letters

libro	book
libro de consulta	reference book
libro de lectura	reading-book
libro de texto	test-book
licenciado	graduate
licenciatura	bachelor's degree
literatura*	literature
Maestra de escuela	school-mistress
maestro de escuela	school-master
mapa	map
matemáticas*	mathematics
Nota(s)	mark(s)
sacar buena nota	to get a good mark
sacar mala nota	to get a bad mark
novillos, hacer	to play truant
Ortografía	spelling
Pluma	pen
profesor	teacher, man-teacher
profesor de arte	art teacher
profesor de idiomas	language teacher
profesor de música	music teacher
profesor de universidad	professor
profesor particular	private teacher
profesora	teacher, woman-teacher
programa de estudios	syllabus
pupitre	desk
Química*	chemistry
Redacción	essay
regla	ruler
Sala de conferencias	lecture-room
sala de lectura	reading-room
«soplar» (un alumno a otro)	to prompt
supuesto de examen	exam-paper
suspender	to fail
suspender un examen	to fail an examination
suspenso	failed
Terreno de juego	play-ground
tesis	thesis
test	test
título universitario	degree
tiza	chalk
tribunal examinador	board of examiners
Vacaciones	vacation, holidays

100

VIDA EN EL HOGAR, LA   LIFE AT HOME (55)

ESPAÑOL   ENGLISH

Alfombra — carpet
almohada — pillow
   funda de almohada — pillow-case
almuerzo — lunch
ama de casa — housewife
ama de llaves — house-keeper
aparato de radio — radio-set
aparato de televisión — television-set
asistenta — char-woman
aspiradora — vacuum cleaner

Bandeja — tray
batería de cocina — kitchenware
barrer — to sweep
bebé — baby
bolsa de la compra — shopping-bag
bolso — bag
bombilla — bulb
botón — button

Calefacción — heating
calefacción central — central heating
cazuela — pan
cena — dinner, supper
cenicero — ash-tray
cepillo — brush
cepillo de cabeza — hair-brush
cepillo de ropa — clothes-brush
cesto — basket
cesto de la colada — clothes-basket
cesto de la compra — shopping-basket
cocina* — kitchen (habitación), stove (mueble)

cocina de gas — gas stove
cocinera — cook
cochecito de niño — pram, baby-carriage
cogedor — dustpan
cojín — cushion
colcha — bedspread
colchón — mattress

VIDA EN EL HOGAR, LA   **443**   LIFE AT HOME

comida	meal
contador de la luz	electric meter
contador del gas	gas meter
cortina	curtain
coser	to sew
costurero	work-box
criada	maid
cubo	bucket
cubo de basura	rubbish bin, dustbin
cuerda para tender la ropa	clothes-line
cuna	cot
Desayuno	breakfast
despensa	pantry
Enchufe	plug
escoba	broom
escobón	mop
espejo	mirror
estera	mat
estufa de gas	gas fire
Florero	vase
fregar	to wash up (la vajilla), to scrub (el suelo)
fregasuelos	mop
Gamuza	duster
gas	gas
guisar	to cook
Hornillo de gas	gas ring
Jabón	soap
Lámpara	lamp
lavadora	washing-machine
lavaplatos	wash-disher
lavar	to wash
limpiar	to clean
limpiar el polvo	to dust
lumbre	fire
LLave	key
Manta	blanket
mantel	table-cloth
máquina de coser	sewing-machine
muebles*	furniture
Niñera	nurse
niños	children

Parque (para un niño) — play-pen
percha — hook
plancha — iron
planchar — to iron
plata (objetos) — silverware
plumero — duster

Renta — rent
ropa — clothes
ropa blanca — linen
ropa de cama — bed-clothes

Sábana — bed sheet, sheet
sala — parlour

Tapete — runner
tapiz — tapestry
teléfono — telephone
tenedor — fork
timbre de la puerta — door-bell
toalla — towel
tocadiscos — record-player
trabajo de la casa — housework

Vajilla* — tableware
vecino — neighbour
visillo — window shade, window curtain

ZAPATOS (Véase CALZADO, 18)

OTROS DICCIONARIOS PUBLICADOS POR PARANINFO S.A.

DICCIONARIOS FILOLOGICOS

Diccionario de dudas. Inglés-Español
Merino. 332 páginas.

Permite analizar y resolver las dudas con que suelen encontrarse los estudiantes del inglés. Incluye vocablos de referencia, con relación completa de todas las palabras españolas, para que, partiendo del castellano, sea fácil su localización.

Sinónimos, palabras de fácil confusión entre ambos idiomas, reglas prácticas y concisas sobre el uso de vocablos que ofrecen dificultad, componen el cuerpo principal de este diccionario.

Diccionario de gentilicios y topónimos
Santano. 488 páginas.

De indudable utilidad práctica para estudiantes, profesores y profesionales de Ciencias de la Información, redactores de periódicos, revistas y agencias de prensa.

Estructurado en dos extensas partes: la primera, dedicada a los gentilicios, y la segunda a los topónimos, con su correspondiente gentilicio.

Diccionario de incorrecciones, particularidades y curiosidades del lenguaje
Santamaría, Cuartas, Mangada y Martínez de Sousa. 472 páginas.

15.000 vocablos y locuciones incorrectas que debemos conocer y palabras de uso indebido que debemos eliminar.

Diccionario imprescindible para periodistas, escritores, profesores y alumnos universitarios, de bachillerato y de formación profesional. Numerosos apéndices sobre curiosidades, dudas ortográficas, etc.

Diccionario de métrica española
Domínguez Caparrós. 200 páginas.

Exhaustivo trabajo que permite resolver cualquier duda sobre el sentido en que se emplea un término referido a la métrica castellana.

Especialmente recomendado para estudiosos de Literatura, Filología y Lingüística. Todas las reglas de la métrica clásica incidiendo en el significado específico de su aplicación al verso castellano.

Diccionario múltiple
Onieva. 540 páginas.

Abarca nueve diccionarios en un solo volumen. Incluye sinónimos y antónimos, palabras homófonas, isónomas, parónimas, rimas poco comunes, refranes, dichos y sentencias y otras muchas curiosidades que hacen del diccionario una obra poco común.

De evidente interés en múltiples actividades. De gran ayuda para adaptaciones literarias y traducciones.

Diccionario de sinónimos e ideas afines y de la rima
Horna. 364 páginas.

Más de 80.000 vocablos en ordenación sinónima. De gran sentido orientativo para quienes intentan componer escritos con ambición literaria o deban redactar textos comerciales con las palabras justas y precisas.

Incluye asimismo nombres propios, principalmente de divinidades y personajes mitológicos, aspecto de suma utilidad para poetas.

OTROS DICCIONARIOS

Diccionario de Arquitectura, Construcción y Obras Públicas. Inglés-Español. Español-Inglés
Putman y Carlson. 536 páginas.

Completo diccionario bilingüe para estudiantes de arquitectura y profesionales. Incluye numerosos términos legales, tablas de medida y materiales de construcción.

Explicación muy extensa de cada término y su traducción inglesa. Glosario inglés-español de todos los vocablos del diccionario.

Diccionario del Basic
Hart. 152 páginas.

Recopila todas las sentencias y comandos Basic existentes. Permite traducir programas de unas versiones Basic a otras. Recomendable especialmente para cuantos se inician en el empleo de ordenadores o utilización de diversos programas de Informática.

Diccionario de la Comunicación. Dos tomos
De la Mota. Tomo I: 376 páginas. Tomo II: 368 páginas.

Más de 20.000 vocablos explicados de una forma sencilla y clara. Aparte de las palabras usuales en los Medios de Comunicación, integra numerosos términos de otros campos: música, pintura, decoración, interpretación, caracterización, gramática, etc.

Diccionario de Economía y Comercio. Francés-español. Español-francés
Garnot. 286 páginas.

Agrupa la mayoría de los términos introducidos en Economía y Comercio en lengua francesa y española. Unifica este tipo de lenguaje en una forma de expresión cada día más estrechamente relacionada. Resuelve fácilmente la redacción de textos comerciales, correspondencia, etc.

Diccionario de la gestión financiera. Inglés-español. Español-inglés
Conso, Lavaud, Colasse y Fousse.

Excelente obra de consulta, incluye más de 800 términos del dominio financiero y de la empresa. Cada término es definido ampliamente.

Especialmente recomendado para todos aquellos que se mueven en el campo de las finanzas y estudiantes de Ciencias Empresariales.

Diccionario de la Información, Comunicación y Periodismo
Martínez de Sousa. 596 páginas.

De gran interés para profesionales del periodismo, agencias de prensa, artes gráficas, publicidad y emisoras de Radio y TV. Imprescindible para estudiantes de Ciencias de la Información.

De gran rigor científico, contiene más de 6.000 entradas, 10.000 definiciones, 50 cuadros sinópticos y referencias bibliográficas.

Diccionario marítimo. Inglés-español. Español-inglés.
Rodríguez Barrientos. 232 páginas.

Repertorio de frases y voces inglesas más usuales relativas al manejo de los buques, diálogos entre marinos, modos de comunicarse, y expresiones generales relacionadas con el lenguaje marítimo.

Diccionario técnico. Fránces-español.
Malgorn. 544 páginas.

Exhaustiva exposición de términos científicos y técnicos. Comprende todas las acepciones que pueden tener en su utilización. Muy útil para especialistas profesionales y traductores.

Diccionario técnico. Inglés-español
Malgorn. 608 páginas.
Diccionario técnico. Español-inglés
Malgorn. 608 páginas.
(Tomos independientes)

Exposición exhaustiva de terminología técnica y científica. Equivalencia de cada vocablo en español o inglés con todas las acepciones en que puede ser aplicado o utilizado. Terminología referida a numerosas ramas técnicas.